VIRTUAL F

# VIRTUAL PUBLICS

## Policy and Community in an Electronic Age

EDITED BY BETH E. KOLKO

Columbia University Press, New York

References to Internet Web Sites (URLs) were accurate at the time of writing. Neither the volume editor, the contributors, nor Columbia University Press is responsible for Web sites that may have expired or changed since the articles were prepared.

Chapter 5 was originally published in 81 *Boston University Law Review* 635 (June 2001)

Columbia University Press
*Publishers Since 1893*
New York, Chichester, West Sussex


Library of Congress Cataloging-in-Publication Data

Virtual publics : policy and community in an electronic age ;
edited by Beth E. Kolko.
p. cm.
Includes bibliographical references and index.
ISBN 0–231–11826–0 (cloth : alk. paper)
ISBN 0–231–11827–9 (paper)
1. Internet—Social aspects 2. Information technology—
Social aspects. 3. Information society.
I. Kolko, Beth E.

HM851.V576 2003
303.48'33—dc21 2002041525

Columbia University Press books are printed
on permanent and durable acid-free paper

Printed in the United States of America

c 10 9 8 7 6 5 4 3 2 1
p 10 9 8 7 6 5 4 3 2 1

## CONTENTS

*List of Contributors* *vii*

*Acknowledgments* *xiii*

Introduction. The Reality of Virtuality
BETH E. KOLKO 1

**Part 1. Users and the Structure of Technology**

1. The Net Effect: The Public's Fear and the Public Sphere
GILBERT B. RODMAN 9

2. The Internet, Community Definition, and the Social Meaning of Legal Jurisdiction
PAUL SCHIFF BERMAN 49

3. Architectural Design for Online Environments
ANNA CICOGNANI 83

4. Community, Affect, and the Virtual: The Politics of Cyberspace
J. MACGREGOR WISE 112

5. Securing Trust Online: Wisdom or Oxymoron?
HELEN NISSENBAUM 134

## Part 2. Technology and the Structure of Communities

6. TV Predicts Its Future: On Convergence and Cybertelevision
TARA MCPHERSON 173

7. Women Making Multimedia: Possibilities for Feminist Activism
MARY E. HOCKS AND ANNE BALSAMO 192

8. Is It Art, in Fact?
MITCH GELLER 215

9. Making the Virtual Real: University-Community Partnerships
ALISON REGAN AND JOHN ZUERN 239

10. Where Do You Want to Learn Tomorrow? The Paradox of the Virtual University
COLLIN GIFFORD BROOKE 265

11. Community-Based Software, Participatory Theater: Models for Inviting Participation in Learning and Artistic Production
SUSAN CLAIRE WARSHAUER 286

12. Communication, Community, Consumption: An Ethnographic Exploration of an Online City
DAVID SILVER 327

13. Can Technology Transform? Experimenting with Wired Communities
MARK A. JONES 354

*Index* 385

# CONTRIBUTORS

**ANNE BALSAMO** is a founding partner of Onomy Labs, a Silicon Valley technology design company. She has faculty affiliations with the Stanford University Center for design Research and the Feminist Studies program. Until 2001, she was a principal scientist and a member of RED (Research in Experimental Documents) at Xerox Corporation, Palo Alto Research Center (PARC), where she served as project manager and new media designer for the development of RED's recent museum exhibit, "XFR: Experiments in the Future of Reading." Prior to 1999, Balsamo was an associate professor in the School of Literature, Communication, and Culture at the Georgia Institute of Technology, where she taught courses in communication and culture, as well as in science, technology, and gender. Her first book, *Technologies of the Gendered Body: Reading Cyborg Women* (Duke, 1996) investigated the social and cultural implications of emergent biotechnologies. She is currently working on a new book titled *Designing Culture: A Work of the Technological Imagination*, which examines the relationship between cultural theory and the design of new media.

**PAUL SCHIFF BERMAN** is a professor at the University of Connecticut School of Law, where he has taught courses in legal and cultural issues in cyberspace, cyberspace and the state action doctrine, and copyright law, as well as conflict of laws, civil procedure, and law, culture, and community. He has served as law clerk to then Chief Judge Harry T. Edwards, of the United States Court of Appeals for the District of Columbia Circuit, and to Associate Justice Ruth Bader Ginsburg, of the United States Supreme Court. His scholarship focuses on the intersection of cyberspace law, international law, and the cultural role of law in society.

**COLLIN GIFFORD BROOKE** is an assistant professor of rhetoric and writing at Syracuse University. His scholarship focuses on the intersections among rhetoric, critical theory, and information technologies. His work appears in a number of journals and edited collections, and he is currently working on his first book-length project, *Lingua Fracta: Rhetorical Ecologies in the Late Age of Print*.

**ANNA CICOGNANI** is a researcher with an interest in a range of topics associated with electronic environments, philosophy of technology, and ontological models of cyberspace. She has a Ph.D. in design science and linguistics from the University of Sydney, and she has published extensively on topics related to virtual communities and online education. Currently, she works in a senior mangement role in Australia's largest telecommunication company. She is also affiliated with various organizations that are influential in the shaping of electronic policy.

**MITCH GELLER** spent ten years as a professor of video and multimedia, combining backgrounds in art, psychology, and media technologies. He currently divides his time between making experimental video and interactive media and running a full-service multimedia development company, Nu-Design (www.nu-design.com). His work has appeared at numerous festivals in the United States and abroad.

**MARY HOCKS** is an assistant professor at Georgia State University, where she teaches courses in writing and digital rhetoric and directs the Writing Across the Curriculum Program. Her research focuses on intersections between writing practices, cultural discourses, and changing notions of literacy within digital writing environments. She has published articles on hypertext writing, gender and technology, and multimedia design. Her collection, *Eloquent Images: Writing Visually in New Media*, coedited with Michelle Kendrick, was published by MIT Press in 2003.

**MARK A. JONES** currently works at IDEO, a technology-related design firm. His background is in design research methods and human-centered design. His focus is understanding how users adopt new computing and communications technologies. He attended the Institute of Design at the Illinois Institute of Technology (M.Des., 1995) and

Amherst College (1981). Before attending IIT, Mark spent ten years as a clothing and jewelry designer in New York City.

**BETH E. KOLKO** is an associate professor of technical communication at the University of Washington. She is the coeditor of *Race in Cyberspace* (Routledge, 2000) and a coauthor of *Writing in an Electronic World* (Addison-Wesley, 2001). Her research has appeared in *Information Society*, *Computers and Composition*, and *Cybersociety 2.0*. In 2000 she was a Fulbright scholar in Uzbekistan, where she currently researches cross-cultural patterns of information and communication technology adoption.

**TARA MCPHERSON** is an associate professor of gender studies and critical studies in the University of Southern California School of Cinema-TV, where she teaches courses in television, new media, and contemporary popular culture. Her writing has appeared in numerous journals and edited anthologies. She is a coeditor, along with Henry Jenkins and Jane Shattuc, of *Hop on Pop: The Politics and Pleasures of Popular Culture* and the author of *Reconstructing Dixie: Race, Place, and Femininity in the Deep South*, both forthcoming from Duke. She is also currently coediting two anthologies on new technology, was co-organizer of the 1999 conference Interactive Frictions, and is a founder and co-organizer of the Race in Digital Space conference and exhibit series.

**HELEN NISSENBAUM** is an associate professor in the Department of Culture and Communication and a senior fellow of the Information Law Institute, New York University. She specializes in social, ethical, and political dimensions of information technology. Her published works on privacy, property rights, electronic publication, accountability, the use of computers in education, and values embodied in computer systems have appeared in scholarly journals of philosophy, applied ethics, law, and computer science. She is the author of *Emotion and Focus* (University of Chicago Press), a coeditor (with D. J. Johnson) of *Computers, Ethics, and Social Values* (Prentice Hall), and a founding coeditor of the journal *Ethics and Information Technology* (Kluwer Academic Press).

**ALISON REGAN** is head of the Technology Assisted Curriculum Center at the University of Utah Marriott Library. Previously, she was an assistant professor of English at the University of Hawaii and the University of Utah. She is a coauthor of *Writing in an Electronic World* (Addison-Wesley, 2001), and her work has appeared in a variety of journals.

**GILBERT B. RODMAN** is an associate professor of communication at the University of South Florida. His research and teaching interests include cultural studies, media criticism, and the study of popular culture. He is the author of *Elvis After Elvis: The Posthumous Career of a Living Legend* (Routledge, 1996), a coeditor of *Race in Cyberspace* (Routledge, 2000), and the founder/manager of the CULTSTUD-L listserv.

**DAVID SILVER** is an assistant professor in the Department of Communication at the University of Washington and the founder/director of the Resource Center for Cyberculture Studies. His research interests focus generally around the intersections between computers, the Internet, and contemporary American cultures, and more specifically on the social and cultural construction of cyberspace. He is currently working on a cultural history of dot-coms.

**SUSAN CLAIRE WARSHAUER** is an adjunct professor in the Communication, Culture and Technology Program at Georgetown University. She directed the Technology Across the Curriculum Program at George Mason University in Fairfax, Virginia, where she was a visiting assistant professor from 2000–2002. From 1996 to 2000, she directed the Center for Literary Computing and was an assistant professor at West Virginia University. She has written theater and performance art works that have been produced in Wilmington, North Carolina, and San Francisco, California. Her articles have been published in *Literary and Linguistic Computing, Computers and Composition* and other journals. She currently consults with organizations and individuals on designing online environments and holding real-time online events.

**J. MACGREGOR WISE** is an associate professor of communication studies at Arizona State University West. His work in cultural studies and technology draws on the philosophy and sociology of technology and on communication and media studies. He is the author of *Exploring Technology and Social Space* (Sage, 1997) and coauthor with Jennifer Daryl Slack of the forthcoming book *Culture and Technology: A Primer* (Peter Lang).

**JOHN ZUERN** is an associate professor in the Department of English at the University of Hawaii at Mānoa, where he teaches courses in computer-mediated communication, rhetoric, and literary theory. He has coordinated a number of technology-based community service projects, and he currently serves as a mentor in the Pacific New Media Web Development Certificate Program. His work on information technology and education has appeared in such journals as *Computers and Writing*, *Literary and Linguistic Computing*, and *Text Technology*.

## A BRIEF ACKNOWLEDGMENT

*Many thanks to the contributors for their committment to this project.*

## Introduction: The Reality of Virtuality

BETH E. KOLKO

This book grew out of a panel originally presented at the American Studies Association conference in 1997. The goal of that panel was the same as the goal of this volume—namely, to argue that the Internet is a complex and often incompletely understood influence on public discourse and public life, that while offline interaction affects online activity, what happens online also shapes what happens in face-to-face environments. The distinction of this volume, however, rests not only in the recursiveness of the overall argument in examining how the virtual feeds back into offline environments, but also in the interdisciplinary nature of the contributions.

Whether it is called cyberculture or the more broadly defined technology and culture, research on how technology intersects with lived experience is an interdisciplinary endeavor. This book is designed to be an inquiry into how technology affects culture, but it refuses to subscribe to one disciplinary or methodological approach. Having researched technology and its effects on interaction and communication from the perspective of rhetoric, I have found that while most fields share a general research concern regarding technology and culture, the debate over disciplinary approaches tends to occlude useful conversation. This volume, then, attempts to bring together a range of scholars who are looking at the same overall question, but from varying perspectives. It is my hope that no one discipline represented in this collection becomes prioritized over the others. Indeed, I would argue that useful analyses are most likely to emerge when various approaches are simultaneously applied to the same question. The essays are presented in order to introduce researchers to the range of possible analyses necessary for developing a comprehensive understanding of how technology affects community and how culture affects the way technology is implemented and used.

One of the debates raging most intensely across disciplines that consider the Internet is how technology affects patterns of interaction. Technology is not value-neutral; it is embedded in the social contexts in which it is created, and such connections necessarily affect how technology is used. What is less clear is the extent of such effects. This book does not seek to provide an answer to that particular question. Rather, it proposes an alternate series of questions. The thirteen essays here come from a range of disciplines: law, philosophy, architecture, media studies, communication, theater, American studies, rhetoric, art. Each individual essay demonstrates how the use of technology raises a series of questions about the effect it has on our lives. The essays in the first part of the book approach these questions in more general terms, theoretically situating their queries and turning to technology studies in general. The essays in the second part of the volume approach the topic with specific instances of technology use in mind, examining community network initiatives, specific software programs and Web sites, and educational technology initiatives. As a whole, though, both approaches demonstrate that technology affects patterns of interaction, community formation, and self-definition in more ways than are commonly addressed. Each of these essays provides a set of questions that overlaps with some of the issues raised in the other essays but also presents a new perspective on how in fact networked technologies challenge traditional conceptions of social interaction.

The breadth of the material included here allows a provocative glimpse into the possibilities of interdisciplinary inquiry. This volume provides a new vocabulary for researching the Internet, as well as a survey of useful methodologies. For example, the theater critic argues that performance and narrative provide key heuristics for understanding the Internet, the legal scholar asserts the importance of jurisdiction, the philosopher urges us to consider the notion of trust, and the television critic points us to the history of broadcast media to help us understand the patterns of development of the Internet. They all provide a model for conversation in this emerging field of research.

Perhaps one of the strongest elements binding together these scholars from such disparate disciplines is their collective history with the Internet. Nearly all of the contributors have been online for several years, and nearly all have extensive histories of online media from the days before Netscape and a graphical World Wide Web. This continuity is key, because it means that their analyses are grounded in a thorough understanding of the cultural shifts that the Internet has produced—and has been affected by. Because these authors were online before CNN was, they have an appreciation for the potential of the medium as well as for its current manifestations.

The first section, "Users and the Structure of Technology," presents five essays that interrogate broad questions raised in the wake of significant technological change, carefully differentiating faddish cyber-hype from substantive cultural shifts. Taken together, these pieces provide an insightful overview of the varied ways in which the shift to virtual technologies demands a concurrent reconfiguration of how we conceptualize social structures and policies.

The second part, "Technology and the Structure of Communities," includes eight interdisciplinary essays that present detailed studies of particular applications of technology being used in communities. The authors present wide-ranging analyses of how users push the boundaries of the configurations imposed by technology. The essays in this section, reporting on topics from 3-D learning environments to an electronic neighborhood, focus on lived experience, presenting a series of what can be called virtual publics that negotiate the demands of electronic interactions in a changing technological landscape.

In the first essay in part 1, "The Net Effect: The Public's Fear and the Public Sphere," Gilbert B. Rodman complicates the general understanding of the Internet and its effects on society. Looking at both assumptions and generalizations, he dissects public discourse about the Internet, from simplistic hysteria to uncritical utopianism. His essay is a key opening salvo, and he lays bare many claims that have been gone unchallenged for far too long. In part, his goal foreshadows the aim of the entire volume—to complicate our understanding of how technology affects lived experience.

Chapter 2, "The Internet, Community Definition, and the Social Meaning of Legal Jurisdiction," by Paul Schiff Berman, is a compelling and well-crafted exploration of the historical roots of jurisdiction.

Demonstrating how bodies are implicated in the legal concept, Berman takes a longitudinal view of jurisdiction as an issue of both social and geographical space, and as a sidebar to commercial concerns. He provides an essential intervention into the conversation regarding legislating interaction that occurs via the Internet.

Chapter 3, "Architectural Design for Online Environments," by Anna Cicognani, considers the correlation between space and experience. Cicognani, an architect, asks how we can better develop organizational schemas for online spaces--from virtual worlds to information sites—in order to facilitate interaction. Looking at cyberspace as an environment for community building, Cicognani emphasizes the need to view the Internet as, ultimately, a space within which people (rather than just data) interact.

In chapter 4, "Community, Affect, and the Virtual: The Politics of Cyberspace," J. Macgregor Wise tackles the thorny issue of community and politics as theoretical constructs. He examines a variety of definitions for community, including moral, normative, proximate, and foraging-society communities, in part to provide an in-depth exploration of how online organizations come to affect participants. His argument strives to map out the varying ideological stances that inform our constructions of cyberspace, addressing our difficulties in responding to the social changes wrought by technological developments.

Chapter 5, "Securing Trust Online: Wisdom or Oxymoron?" by Helen Nissenbaum, is an investigation of privacy and security issues from a philosophical perspective. Nissenbaum discusses the limitations of current debates regarding trust and security online, and she approaches e-commerce from a unique standpoint, arguing for a new set of practices that might more ably help users negotiate the online world. Her argument is informative for both users and system designers; with the provocative assertion that increased security and increased trust do not necessarily go hand in hand, she seeks to change the direction of current policies about online security.

Part 2 opens with chapter 6, Tara McPherson's "TV Predicts Its Future: On Convergence and Cybertelevision," a consideration of media transformation, the lack thereof, and how changes in media outlets affect the information-gathering habits of viewers. Examining the early hybrid of NBC and Microsoft—MSNBC—McPherson argues that current patterns of media evolution threaten to circumscribe the possibilities of new media, reinscribing linearity and models of passive consumption.

In chapter 7, "Women Making Multimedia: Possibilities for Feminist Activism," Mary E. Hocks and Anne Balsamo discuss the results of a CD-ROM that they authored during the 1995 United Nations Fourth World Conference on Women; they attended the Non-Governmental Organization forum as multimedia producers with their in-progress project Women of the World Talk Back. Their argument centers on the need for women to make use of new media technologies in order to accomplish significant political work—and on their ability to do so. Hocks and Balsamo discuss processes of both production and consumption in the context of an international feminist community.

Chapter 8, "Is It Art, in Fact?" is by Mitch Geller, a video and new media artist whose work explores the intersection of technology and manufactured truth. Geller has worked in video and multimedia for more than a decade, and here he explores the background of his interest in how technology can be used to blur the lines of documentary and fiction, discussing film, television, video, and, finally, 3-D new media experiments with truth-blurring. He discusses his project *R.U.OUT.THERE,* an interactive CD-ROM that incorporates 3-D, Web-based, and video technology in a true and fictional exploration of UFO phenomena. His essay behaves much like an installation, wending its way through the larger questions of representation and truth while providing excerpts of his manufactured artifacts. He challenges us as a community of media users and as viewers, throwing into question the newness of what we call the virtual.

In chapter 9, "Making the Virtual Real: University-Community Partnerships," Alison Regan and John Zuern explore service learning in the context of wired communities, discussing an initiative at the University of Hawaii that brings students into the local community for technology-based work. They explore the wiring of local public housing projects and student involvement in teaching residents about the Internet, arguing that such work involves a complex intersection of the real and the virtual, challenging notions of community and demanding a sophisticated understanding of policy and of political and cultural issues.

Chapter 10, "Where Do You Want to Learn Tomorrow? The Paradox of the Virtual University," by Collin Gifford Brooke, continues the educational theme by exploring the implications of distance education on communities of learners. Brooke argues that contemporary understandings of what constitutes a university education are often oversimplified, and he presents a timely critique of both the function of the university and the role of distance education on a changing cultural and educational landscape.

Chapter 11, "Community-Based Software, Participatory Theater: Models for Inviting Participation in Learning and Artistic Production," by Susan Claire Warshauer, adds a drama perspective to the educational conversation. Writing with a background in theater as well as interactive technologies, Warshauer analyzes the links between community-based software developers and theater artists. She traces the roots of political theater, including Happenings and Theater of the Oppressed, and shows how interactive multiuser educational worlds can more effectively provide possibilities for transformative user participation. She investigates the worlds of ExploreNet, tracing use patterns and speculating on the boundaries of the technology, demonstrating that just as interactive political theater sought to create a virtual world that could change the real world, online virtual worlds share a similar potential.

In chapter 12, "Communication, Community, Consumption: An Ethnographic Exploration of an Online City," David Silver looks at the Blacksburg Electronic Village (BEV), arguing, like Warshauer, that interactive networks have potential that remains unexploited. Silver's critique demonstrates that the emphasis on consumption has destroyed much of the political potential of the BEV, and his essay resonates with that of McPherson in its exploration of public discourse about new media.

Chapter 13, "Can Technology Transform? Experimenting with Wired Communities," by Mark A. Jones, is both a rejoinder to Silver and an optimistic note on which the volume ends. Jones spent a year doing ethnographic work with online communities in various locations, including Blacksburg, Helsinki, and Barcelona. Here he lays out some guidelines for successful and diverse community networks, extracting from his research models for building such electronic neighborhoods. Jones's essay focuses on the link between the virtual and the real, highlighting the need for offline policy development that understands the complexity of online communities.

Distilled down, each essay in the book asserts that the Internet is complicated, at times contradictory in its potential and implementation, but still replete with possibility. Each essay demonstrates a commitment to thinking critically about the role that technology plays in our lives and, concurrently, the role that each of us can play in affecting the shape of technology as it continues to evolve.

Ultimately, the virtual publics of this volume are very real. In the years since the now infamous MCI commercial that asserted "there are no bodies" online (nor genders, nor ages), scholarship on cyberculture has repeatedly emphasized that our offline selves determine how we are able to use technology, that real life affects what we do online. This volume is an attempt to demonstrate that the way we live online—work, shop, socialize, teach, and learn—affects our lives offline as well. A virtual public is not an unreal one; it requires the same acuity of vision and astuteness of analysis that we apply to traditional communities. As we broaden our activities online in an electronic age, it will become increasingly important that we bring with us a recognition that technology structures social experience in powerful ways. Consequently, it is imperative that we continually strive to assess the complex ways that virtuality and reality recursively shape each other.

# Part 1

# USERS AND THE STRUCTURE OF TECHNOLOGY

1

## The Net Effect: The Public's Fear and the Public Sphere[1]

GILBERT B. RODMAN

Our world is about to be transformed beyond all recognition, and nothing will ever be the same. All because of the Internet.

Such, at least, is the impression one gets from much of what's been said and written about the Net over the past few years. The Net, we are told, will dramatically change how we work, play, shop, learn, live, and even love—if, in fact, it hasn't done so already. On this point, few critics seem to disagree. Where the real debates begin is over the question of whether those changes are ones we should embrace or resist.

This essay will not bring those debates to any final resolution, if for no other reason than that the Internet is still far too new for us to make claims about its long-term social and cultural impact with any real certainty.[2] For that matter, given the speed with which computer hardware, software, and protocols continue to move in and out of the picture, even short-term predictions about the future of cyberspace need to be taken with large grains of salt. Today, for example, people often talk about the World Wide Web as if it's all there is to the Net.[3] As recently as 1994, however, the Web barely existed,[4] Netscape was just another start-up venture with an uncertain future,[5] Microsoft was only beginning to realize that cyberspace might be worth looking into,[6] and serious Net users needed to be well versed in what are now largely forgotten cybertools (e.g., Gopher, Veronica, Archie, WAIS). Even observers sharp enough to predict back then that the Web would be "the next big thing" would have been hard-pressed to envision a future right around the corner when the Web would commonly be equated (however inaccurately) with the entirety of the Net.

Keeping the ever-shifting nature of cyberspace in mind, I'm not going to make any rash predictions about where the Net will take us tomorrow. Instead, my goal for this essay is to provide a modest, yet productive, intervention in the ongoing debates over "the Net effect." In particular, I want to examine some of the more problematic assumptions made by parties on all sides of those debates about the nature of both "the Internet" and "the public"—assumptions that flatten out the multifaceted complexities of both of these phenomena and, in turn, serve to steer the public conversation about cyberspace away from crucial questions of access, democracy, and the public sphere.

Perhaps the biggest problem with the existing public discourse about the Net is that it is dominated by extreme positions. On the one hand, there are feverish cyber-utopians who see the Net as the best thing to happen to the human race "since the capture of fire" (John Perry Barlow, in Barlow et al., 36). On the other hand, there are apocalyptic doomsayers who are convinced that the Net is a monstrous threat to our future that we need to resist and contain, if not eliminate entirely. Sven Birkerts, for instance, sees the Net as a dangerous distraction from pressing real-world concerns and rebuts Barlow's sound bite about the expanding cyberculture with one of his own: "refuse it" (Barlow et al., 37). To be sure, at each end of this spectrum one can find a mosaic of distinct—and even mutually incompatible—positions. For example, however much they may agree that the Net is a Good Thing™, the digital entrepreneurs who embrace cyberspace as a bottomless gold mine for commerce and investment don't necessarily hold the same political or cultural values as the wired communitarians who see the Net as the quintessential democratic global village. Similarly, the moral conservatives who rail against the online traffic in sex and violence don't necessarily share much (if any) philosophical common ground with the neo-Luddites who see computers as soulless boxes that take us away from our already disintegrating families and communities. Whatever the specific differences between (and within) these camps may be, however, they all share a problematic overinvestment in monolithic visions of the Net's impact, with commentators from both ends of the spectrum apparently unwilling to make more than token gestures in the direction of "the other side."[7]

One of the major reasons for the prevalence of such extreme positions is that many commentators discuss the Internet as if it were a single, relatively uncomplicated medium—a gross misrepresentation that, in turn, makes it easier to speak of the Net in overgeneralized terms. What makes this especially ironic is that a large part of the Net's impact can be traced to its multifaceted flexibility and diversity. The Net can be as private as a personal e-mail note between lovers or as public as a Usenet post available to millions of readers in dozens of countries. It can be as ephemeral as a "real-time" conversation in a chat room or as permanent as a Web-based database or archive. It can be as serious as a listserv-based support group for survivors of incest or as lighthearted as an evening of checkers in an online game room. And it can function in ways that are analogous to an incredibly broad range of offline modes of communication, including face-to-face conversation, public lectures, university seminars, telephone calls, radio, television, film, video games, family photo albums, diaries, letter writing, bulletin boards, newsletters, newspapers, magazines, scholarly journals, and books. All of which makes it more accurate to think of the Net as *multiple media* rather than as a single medium.

As obvious as this observation may seem, it's a point that bears special emphasis here, given the common tendency for both cyber-utopians and cyber-skeptics of cyberspace to focus only on the facets of the Net that bolster their larger claims. It's easy, for instance, to portray the Net as a wonderful new space for nurturing community and human interaction if one concentrates on interactive, dialogue-driven cyber-environments such as the WELL (Rheingold) and glosses over more static and/or corporatized forms of CMC (computer-mediated communication, e.g., Web sites that imitate more traditional forms of commercial publishing).[8] And it's just as easy to portray the Net as an impersonal, alienating technology if one focuses on the ways that multinational conglomerates use computer networks to create atomized, post-Fordist workplaces (Breslow) and minimizes the ways that individual people use the Net to establish and maintain interpersonal relationships and social groups.[9] Ultimately, the main problem with such analyses is not that they can't provide valuable insights about certain aspects of cyberspace, but that they fail to recognize the Net for the messy—and often self-contradictory—multiplicity that it really is. Put simply, while the Net may consist of binary code (e.g., digital strings of 0's and 1's), its social, cultural, and political impact can't safely be reduced to similar either/or dichotomies.

With this last point in mind, what I want to do in the remainder of this essay is to offer a critical analysis of some specific examples of both cyberphobia and cybermania. Admittedly, to frame my argument this way is to run the risk of reproducing the very same sort of binary opposition I'm critiquing. To paraphrase Deleuze and Guattari (20), however, I'm invoking one dualism (i.e., cyberphobia versus cybermania) not to champion one over the other or to craft some sort of rapprochement between them, but to challenge the notion that reducing the public discourse on cyberspace to simple dualisms (e.g., is the Net good or bad for us? heaven or hell? the cause of or the solution to all our problems?) will provide us with the best answers to the question of the Net's effects.

## THE PUBLIC'S FEAR

It may seem odd to talk about the public's fear of cyberspace when the number of people who use the Net continues to grow (though not quite as impressively as some observers predicted it would), the tech-dominated NASDAQ continues to be a prominent benchmark for the health of the U.S. economy (even after the dramatic stock market downturn of 2000–2001, much of which was attributed to the bursting of the hyper-inflated dot-com bubble), and even noncomputer businesses seem to feel that establishing a Web presence is now a necessity (even if only so they *look* like they're "cutting edge"). Looking at the ways in which millions of people and companies have embraced the Net (and how millions more seem eager to climb on the bandwagon), one could easily believe that whatever fear the Net once generated among the general public is now a thing of the past.

Once again, however, we need to resist the temptation to explain the Net by using simple binary oppositions. Not only is it possible for the Net's exceptional popularity to coincide with a broad level of Net-related anxiety, but, I would argue, the Net's success actually *heightens* that anxiety. After all, if the Net were floundering (e.g., if it were clearly headed the way of computer punch cards, eight-track tapes, Betamax, or DIVX), no one would be worried about the changes it might bring to their lives. But the Net isn't floundering. On the contrary, it's rapidly acquiring a pervasiveness in U.S. culture that makes it difficult to ignore, even for people without the ability or desire to go online themselves. And it's precisely this aura of inevitability that makes some people uncomfortable. As Birkerts puts it:

> If we're merely talking about this phenomenon as an interesting, valuable supplement for those who seek it, I have no problem with it. What I'm concerned by is this becoming a potentially all-transforming event that's going to change not only how I live but how my children live. I don't believe it's going to be merely auxiliary. I think it's going to be absolutely central. (Barlow et al., 45)

As much as Birkerts is concerned with the specific effects the Net will have on people who actually use it (e.g., his fears that Net users will lose interest in reading books or talking with their neighbors), his major fear seems to be that the Net's success will have devastating ripple effects on life in the *un*wired world—that neither the already fragile print culture nor the waning sense of physical community in the United States will be able to survive the relentless spread of cyberspace.

Nor is Birkerts alone in this fear. As positive as much of the mainstream media commentary on the growing cyberculture is, there is also more than enough doomsaying and fear-mongering to constitute at least a low-grade *moral panic* around the subject. Sociologist Stan Cohen explains the concept of a moral panic this way:

> A condition, episode, person or group of persons emerges to become defined as a threat to societal values and interests; its nature is presented in a stylized and stereo-typical fashion by the mass media; the moral barricades are manned [*sic*] by editors, bishops, politicians, and other right-thinking people; socially accredited experts pronounce their diagnoses and solutions; ways of coping are evolved or (more often) resorted to; the condition then disappears, submerges or deteriorates and becomes more visible. Sometimes the object of the panic is quite novel and at other times it is something which has been in existence long enough, but suddenly appears in the limelight. Sometimes the panic is passed over and is forgotten, except in folklore and col-

> lective memory; at other times it has more serious and long-lasting repercussions and might produce such changes as those in legal and social policy or even in the way society conceives itself.
>
> (Quoted in Hall et al., 16–17)

To be sure, the Net has been embraced widely enough (at least in the United States) to offset the most extreme instances of cyberspace-related panic in significant ways and, compared to the events that led Stuart Hall and company to invoke Cohen (i.e., media-stoked fears about the rise of "mugging" in 1970s Britain), most of the public expressions of anxiety over the Net are relatively tame. As Cohen's definition suggests, however, moral panics come in a wide variety of shapes and sizes, and one doesn't have to look very hard to find "stylized and stereo-typical" media representations of the Net being invoked in demonizing ways.

Probably the most prominent example here is the wave of moral outrage over online pornography from U.S. politicians, pundits, and concerned citizens' groups: a stream of discourse that began in mid-1995 and ultimately led Congress to add the Communications Decency Act (CDA)—which severely restricted the circulation of "adult" material online—to the Telecommunications Act of 1996.[10] While the U.S. Supreme Court eventually ruled the CDA to be unconstitutional (*Reno v. ACLU*), the extensive public debate over "cybersmut" helped to propagate and reinforce a public image of the Net as an insidious threat to both home and family—and thus, by extension, to the moral fabric of society as a whole.[11] Moreover, the public spectacle over the CDA served one of the crucial functions of any "good" moral panic: i.e., it exaggerated the Net's threat to the status quo in ways that (1) mobilized public support for what would otherwise have been seen as overtly repressive measures (i.e., the criminalization of a broad segment of online expression that retained First Amendment protection in offline contexts) and (2) directed public attention away from controversial policy decisions that might otherwise have received closer scrutiny. In the case of the CDA, Congress's primary agenda was arguably to ensure that the rest of the Telecommunications Act—which effectively transferred permanent ownership of the broadcast spectrum from the general public to the telecommunications industry—was implemented without being subjected to public discussion about its broader ramifications. As Robert McChesney notes:

> The overarching purpose of the . . . Act is to deregulate all communications industries and to permit the market, not public policy, to determine the course of the information highway and the communications systems. . . . Some of the law was actually written by the lobbyists for the communication firms it affects. The only "debate" was whether broadcasters, long-distance companies, local telephone providers, or cable companies would get the inside track in the deregulatory race. . . . "I have never seen anything like the Telecommunications Bill," one career lobbyist observed. "The silence of public debate is deafening. A bill with such astonishing impact on all of us is not even being discussed." (42–43)

In the end, the only portion of the bill that received extended public scrutiny prior to its ultimate passage was the CDA. And even though the Supreme Court held in *Reno* that the public sphere should be free from unwarranted governmental control, the fact that the rest of the Telecommunications Act permitted the government to auction off huge portions of the public sphere means that the ultimate impact of the CDA on the general public amounted to a net loss.

This victory for "the media monopoly" (Bagdikian) notwithstanding, the continued growth of the Net presented a serious challenge to more traditional media outlets—especially the national broadcast television networks. From a market perspective, the Net provided an alternate source of news and entertainment to a highly profitable demographic group (i.e., the segment of the population with both the income and the inclination to purchase high-end personal electronics) at a moment when the broadcast networks were already struggling to minimize losses in market share and profits margins in the face of competition from cable and satellite TV. Network responses to this threat varied considerably. All of the major networks established some sort of Web presence for themselves, but only NBC went so far as to establish a "TV presence" for the Net (i.e., MSNBC, a joint cable/Net venture with Microsoft; see McPherson in this volume). ABC's parent company (Disney) adopted an "if you can't beat 'em, join 'em" philosophy by creating the "Go" network: an expansion and reconfiguration of its previously unconnected online offerings into a collection of cross-linked family, news, sports, and entertainment Web sites.[12]

On occasion, however, the broadcast networks have dealt with the threat of the Net by going on the offensive. For instance, in March 1997, in the wake of the first wave of cyberspace-driven rumors about the Clinton/Lewinsky scandal, CBS aired an episode of *60 Minutes* in which Lesley Stahl took a close look at the Net—and was appalled to learn that ordinary people could "publish" virtually anything online without the benefit of formal gatekeeping procedures to screen out slander and falsehoods. In particular, Stahl's story decried Web publishers' irresponsible dissemination of scandalous news items that relied on unsubstantiated information from unidentified sources.

Insofar as anonymity and pseudonymity are commonplace features of the Net, such concerns are not without merit: cyberspace contains its fair share of lies and misinformation, and users should be cautious about automatically accepting information they find online as true. These very same concerns, however, also apply to more traditional media outlets: after all, it's not uncommon for traditional print and broadcast news reports to rely on never-identified sources (e.g., "friends of the Clintons," "lawyers familiar with the investigation," "sources inside the White House"). To hear *60 Minutes* describe it, however, such practices are all but unheard of offline and practically inescapable online. And while it's easy to interpret Stahl's report as a case of CBS trying to protect its corner of the news-reporting turf from an upstart newcomer, the overall tone of the story recast this expression of self-interest in terms that exaggerated and misrepresented the threat posed by the Net: i.e., CBS apparently felt that the unfiltered quality of online information did grave and potentially irreparable harm to the integrity of the public sphere, and thus Stahl's report was framed as an example of the network looking out for the public's interest, rather than its own.

The spring and summer of 1999 also saw the Net come under public fire for its alleged role in three otherwise unrelated 1999 tragedies: Eric Harris and Dylan Klebold's deadly assault on Columbine High School in Littleton, Colorado, in April, Benjamin Smith's murderous three-day rampage through Illinois and Indiana in early July, and Mark Barton's fatal shooting spree in Atlanta in late July. Of the three, the Internet connection in the Smith case is probably the most indirect.

The general consensus across major media news reports and editorial commentaries on Smith's crimes[13] was that they were primarily the by-product of his white supremacist beliefs: in marked contrast to the Columbine case, these were not shootings that most commentators seemed willing to blame directly on violent media fare.

At the same time, however, the initial flurry of newswire reports on the Smith shootings invoked computer games in ways that suggested at least an implicit connection between the shootings and Smith's involvement in cyberculture. As one article claimed, Smith "was known to be an aficionado of Dungeons and Dragons, the Gothic computer game of violence, something that his mother, Beverly Smith, confided to others on their street was worrisome to her" ("Out of Hatred"). While this seemingly innocuous sentence doesn't actually blame the game for either Smith's racism or his crimes, it does suggest that playing D&D is a vital fact about Smith's background that helps to explain where his hateful views and/or violent actions came from. Moreover, the references to the focal points of other moral panics serve to amplify the apparent significance of this "clue" from Smith's past. D&D, for instance, has spent the past twenty-five years on the receiving end of sporadic public outcries over role-playing teens losing touch with reality and overinvesting in the fantasy worlds inspired by the game. Ultraviolent computer games (e.g., Mortal Kombat or Street Fighter) have spent much of the past decade as one of the recurring targets of moral outrage over the rising tide of gore in popular culture. And over the past several years, the Goth subculture has been repeatedly demonized as a haven for maladjusted—and potentially disturbed—social misfits. Put together into one compact phrase, these three otherwise distinct moral panics add up to an imposing object of extreme terror.

The problem here, however, is that D&D is not necessarily (or even usually) a computer game. Or Gothic. Or even violent. While there are CD-ROM versions of the game's user manuals and adventure modules, D&D is not a game designed primarily for computer play. While there is some overlap between elements of Goth fashion and some brands of D&D fantasy, it's doubtful that most Goths play the game or that most players are Goths. And while the "sword and sorcery" aspects of D&D often involve role-played combat, the bulk of the "violence" involved in staging those battles consists of the forceful clatter of plastic dice on tabletops. In short, if D&D is really "the Gothic computer game of violence," then chess—with its historical roots in ancient Persia, hundreds of different computerized versions, and its underlying metaphor of warring kingdoms—could just as reasonably be called "the Iranian computer game of combat."

I'm unpacking this particular quote at some length because it helps to demonstrate an important aspect of how moral panics function—i.e., the way that they articulate a seemingly natural and logical connection between an allegedly dangerous phenomenon and others that are already known (or at least assumed) to be genuine threats. In the example at hand, those articulations work in several different directions at once, with each of the various objects of moral approbation being used to confirm the legitimacy of the threat posed by the others: i.e., to label Smith as *only* a D&D aficionado (or a Goth, or a computer game player) would not be enough to complete the portrait being painted of him as a dangerous individual who had been obsessed with violence for many years. In the end, however, it's the heinousness of Smith's actual crimes that most powerfully reinforces the notions that D&D, Goths, and computers are potentially deadly threats to the social order. We don't need to be told that Smith played D&D, for instance, to be horrified at the cold-blooded hatred of his violent trek through the Midwest, but outside the context of the shootings, it is not clear that Smith's history of fantasy role-playing or computer use would be enough to brand him a threat to society in most people's eyes. What such news reports accomplish, then, is the public construction of a "logical" and seemingly natural connection between heavy computer use and deadly violence.

Tellingly, a fact *not* included in the early reports about Smith's crimes was that "he had been forced to withdraw from the University of Illinois after beating up a girlfriend in the dorm" (Pollitt, 10). And while this detail from Smith's past may have surfaced only in the weeks between the initial coverage of the event and the time that Pollitt wrote the column quoted here, it's nonetheless significant that reporters who were actively working to trace Smith's history of violence and racism could overlook an instance of actual violence from Smith's recent past—one serious enough to merit expulsion from a major university—while his D&D-playing ways were deemed important enough to report right away. Smith's story could just as easily have been written as that of a man who had a troubled history of "solving" problems with physical violence, rather than that of someone whose involvement with computers and role-playing games may have contributed to his violent ways.

A similar pattern of panicky reporting can be seen in at least some of the initial press coverage of the Atlanta massacre, which emphasized Mark Barton's career as a day trader (a person who uses the Internet to play the stock market in risky but potentially lucrative ways) to the point that it appeared to be at least as relevant to his crimes as the fact that he was the primary suspect in the brutal 1993 murder of his first wife and her mother. The day after the shootings, for instance, the *St. Petersburg Times* banner headline read DAY TRADER CUTS A DEADLY SWATH, and the stories clustered inside the front section under the heading ATLANTA SHOOTINGS included an eleven-paragraph article on the economic riskiness of day trading ("Few Day Traders") that, except for a gratuitous half-sentence reference to the shootings buried deep in paragraph nine, could just as easily have been an ordinary article in the paper's Business section. Meanwhile, the article that ostensibly profiles the 1993 murders ("An Ordinary Man") dismisses Barton's suspected role in those deaths as an "exception" (albeit a glaring one) to his "mostly unremarkable life" and devotes most of its space to the tale of how he met his second wife. Even more astonishingly, the fact that Barton apparently killed his two children and his second wife earlier in the week is barely mentioned at all. To be sure, day trading *is* financially risky, Barton *was* a day trader, and the two offices he shot up *are* involved in day trading . . . but even if the dip in the stock market on the Thursday of the shootings really did cost Barton a lot of money, it's not clear how that would have compelled him to kill his second wife on Tuesday, his children on Wednesday, or (assuming the police's suspicions are accurate) his first wife and her mother six years before that.

I should note that my argument here is based primarily on the initial flurry of news reports on the Atlanta massacre; subsequent events and revelations have changed our collective understanding of what actually happened. Because of the notes he left behind, for instance, we now know (rather than merely suspect or assume) that Barton murdered his second wife and two children. And, roughly twenty-four hours after the shootings (i.e., too late for the following day's morning papers to reflect this), it was revealed that Barton's last trading day was Tuesday, not Thursday, which makes it more plausible that stock market losses might have played a role in Barton's murder of his family. The subsequent discovery of these facts, however, doesn't do anything to fix the logical gaps in Friday's news coverage or to explain away the speed and eagerness with which the media were willing to blame day trading for Barton's murders. In much the same way that the first news reports on the 1995 Oklahoma City bombing were too quick to blame Arab terrorists for the event, early press coverage of Barton's crimes was too eager to pin the blame for them on his "dangerous" uses of the Net. Like Smith, Barton appears to have had a history of using violence to solve his problems and, as was the case with Smith, the press seemed less interested (at least at first) in discussing Barton's history of actual violence than they were in exploring his involvement with the Internet.

Not all invocations of virtual culture as a source of real violence, however, are as subtle as those found in the media coverage of the Smith and Barton shootings. In the wake of the Littleton tragedy,[14] a flood of public commentary wrestled with the question of locating the causes of Harris and Klebold's deadly assault. Suggested answers to the "who's to blame?" question ran the gamut from the plausible (e.g., ready access to firearms, inadequate numbers of school counselors) to the dubious (e.g., Marilyn Manson's music—which Harris and Klebold apparently hated [Manson, 77]), the Goth subculture (which isn't inherently violent and which the pair wasn't a part of anyway) to the absurd (e.g., the U.S. House of Representatives responded by passing a bill that, had it become law, would have allowed public schools to display the Ten Commandments on school property—as if Harris and Klebold would have been deterred from their shooting spree had the magic words "Thou Shalt Not Kill" been painted on the walls).

While clearly not all commentators were willing to point fingers at the mass media, the claim that violent entertainment directly led to the Littleton shootings was a recurring theme in the discourse. Writing in *Harper's*, Thomas de Zengotita presented a particularly blunt version of this argument:

> We come closest to addressing the situation as a whole when asking how violence in the media influences behavior. Cultural conservatives focus on permissive standards related to content, and surely that content goes way beyond anything imaginable thirty years ago. People who commit these acts always show evidence of

> its influence. The Littleton shooters spent a lot of time with *Natural Born Killers* and goth CDs and hate Web sites, but libertarians point out that Charlie Starkweather was inspired by comics and rock and roll, and argue that agency must be attributed to the person, not the muse. So the debate resolves itself into this question: Is the influence of today's media qualitatively different from yesterday's? The answer is obviously yes. (55)

De Zengotita's comments rely on many of the same rhetorical tactics found in the media coverage of the Smith shootings: guilt by association (do Goth CDs really belong in the same category as hate Web sites?), factual errors (would *libertarians* blame Starkweather's crimes on mass media texts?), and the substitution of unsupported assertion for actual argument ("we come closest," "surely," "obviously," and so on). Beyond this, however, de Zengotita's larger argument reframes the problem in language that invokes the Net as the primary culprit; even when he is specifically referring to TV talk shows or Hollywood films, his operative metaphors—"virtuality," "virtual reality," "new technologies"—come from cyberspace rather than from older media. By implication, at least, what leads de Zengotita to see contemporary forms of more traditional media as "qualitatively different" in their ability to cause harm is the new, hyper-corrupting influence of the Net.

Significantly, one of the most commonly cited scapegoats in the Littleton shootings was *The Matrix*: a film that (1) makes extensive use of stylized violence in a visually striking computer-generated virtual reality and (2) was the nation's leading box office success at the time. Given the film's overall look and feel, it's not difficult to understand why some commentators saw it as a contributing factor to what happened at Columbine. If nothing else, one of the movie's most adrenaline-filled, tightly choreographed scenes depicts the two principal heroes, ultra-cool and ultra-stylish in their black trenchcoats, using high-powered assault rifles to annihilate a squad of security guards and lay waste to the lobby of a high-rise office building: a virtual reality sequence with enough similarities to Harris and Klebold's real-life shoot-out to be seen as an inspiration for their murderous rampage.

However plausible such an interpretation of the film's relationship to the Columbine massacre might seem, however, I think that it ultimately falls short of the mark—and not simply because Harris and Klebold needed actual weapons (rather than just media-enhanced revenge fantasies) to carry out their attack. On the surface, *The Matrix* seems to glorify the slickness of virtual reality and the physically impossible feats of violence that it enables: only in VR, after all, could someone turn one-handed cartwheels while firing multiple rounds from an assault rifle with pinpoint accuracy, while the film's gravity-defying hand-to-hand combat sequences resemble nothing so much as "live" action versions of recent martial arts computer games. Where such a reading of the film begins to fall apart, however, is in its treatment of the film's surface as all-important and its willingness to overlook substantive details from the film's story line. The real world of the film, after all, is one in which sentient machines have enslaved the majority of the human race and plugged them into "the Matrix"—a computer simulation of late 1990s human civilization so vivid as to be indistinguishable from reality—and the quest that drives the film's plot forward is about the destruction of that virtual reality. "As long as the Matrix exists," we're told at one point, "the human race will never be free." Given that the alternative to life in the Matrix is a grungy, lower-tech bombed-out shell of a world—one where hydraulic pistons and rotary-dial phones are "cutting edge" and where the primary food is a protein-laden slop that's comparable to "runny eggs" or "a bowl of snot"—I think it's hard to argue that the film simply glorifies or embraces cyber-technology in a straightforward fashion. If anything, *The Matrix* could plausibly be said to take Birkerts's "refuse it" philosophy to a level that even he might resist, one where the "better," computer-free world that people fight and die for is a post-apocalyptic ecological nightmare.

To his credit, de Zengotita actually recognizes that *The Matrix* has a more complicated relationship to computers and virtual reality than its special-effects-laden surface would seem to indicate (58). At the same time, there is an inherent contradiction in his ability to recognize the nuances and depths to be found in contemporary media texts while simultaneously arguing that the (harmful) effects of those texts are "obviously" visible on their surfaces. For instance, how does de Zengotita manage to see through *The Matrix*'s slickly packaged hyper-violence to its "real" anti-technology message while simultaneously citing *Natural Born Killers* as an "obvious" and "influential" glorification of gunplay? Both films, after all, can plausibly be said to revel in their graphic visual display of brutal shoot-outs, and both can plausibly be said to offer pointed critiques of contemporary media culture. The problem with de Zengotita's claims for these films is not so much that he gets one (or both) of them wrong but that he fails to recognize that, like most (if not all) mass media fare, both are complicated, multifaceted texts that are subject to multiple, and perhaps even contradictory, interpretations.

And it's this polysemic quality that ultimately makes it difficult to predict the specific "effects" of particular texts—from "hate websites" to Horace Walpole—with any accuracy, regardless of whether one is skimming their surfaces or plumbing their depths. To be sure, one can point to recurring patterns of media taste and usage (for example, Doom and Myst are more likely to be played by teens and twentysomethings than by senior citizens) and there are always limits to the plausible interpretations of a text (it strains credibility to read *The Matrix* as a romantic comedy or a nature documentary), but the predictions one can safely make based on those patterns and limits are a far cry from the sort of direct cause-and-effect claims ("Hollywood made them do it") that are the primary rhetorical product of moral panics around "violent" media. When one gets down to cases, real audience responses to specific texts vary too much to be able to say with absolute certainty that *this* film inspires gunplay or *that* medium fosters alienation. Media scholar Henry Jenkins reframes the question this way:

> The key issue here isn't what the media are doing to our children but rather what our children are doing with the media. Eric Harris and Dylan Klebold weren't victims of video games. They had a complex relationship to many forms of popular culture. All of us move nomadically across the media landscape, cobbling together a personal mythology of symbols and stories, and investing those appropriated materials with various personal and subcultural meanings. Harris and Klebold happened to be drawn toward dark and brutal images, which they invested with their personal demons, their antisocial impulses, their maladjustment, their desires to hurt those who had hurt them. (23)

Jenkins goes on to tell the tale of a sixteen-year-old girl who created a Web site consisting of pop-culture-based writings by teens from across the country:

> She had reached into contemporary youth culture, including many of the same media products that had been cited in the Littleton case, and found images that emphasized the power of friendship, the importance of community, the wonder of first romance. The mass media didn't make Harris and Klebold violent and destructive and they didn't make this girl creative and sociable, but they provided them both with the raw materials necessary to construct their fantasies. Of course, we should be concerned about the content of our culture. But popular culture is only one influence on our children's imagination. Real life trumps media images every time. (23)

Jenkins's efforts to the contrary notwithstanding, however, scapegoating "violent media" regularly trumps more nuanced responses to real-life violence. Jenkins's full essay describes his frustrations at testifying before Congress in the immediate aftermath of the Littleton shootings and being the only expert witness present who refused to blame "violent media" for Harris and Klebold's crimes—which, in turn, made him the only witness the mainstream news media didn't pursue for post-hearing interviews. And while Jenkins's commentary did appear in a "quality" national magazine, significantly, it did so in the same issue of *Harper's* as de Zengotita's essay. Moreover, given that the latter was billed on the cover as the issue's number two article, while the former was relegated to the magazine's monthly collection of assorted "readings," it would appear that even in a "quality" magazine like *Harper's*, "Violent media cause real-life violence" is a cover story, but "It's more complicated than that" isn't.

Nevertheless, the Net's effect *is* more complicated than that. The main problem with the public's various cyberspace-related fears isn't so much that there's nothing about the Net that merits serious concern but that such concerns are rarely as novel—or as unique to cyberspace—as they're often made out to be: one can find strikingly similar fears expressed in response to the rise of virtually any communication medium or technology one chooses, from the telegraph and telephone (Marvin) to the present day. To be sure, cyberspace is not a completely safe and trouble-free environment, and if you venture online, it's wise to be cautious about what you believe, who you trust, how much you reveal about yourself, and (if you have them) where your children are.

At the same time, such precautions don't exactly reflect dangers that are unique to the Net: they're pretty good advice for offline life as well.

Part of what makes cyberspace seem to be radically different from "real life"—and thus part of what makes it the subject of hyperbolic fears—is that, to many people, it appears to be an environment that is both out of control and uncontrollable in ways that "real" space isn't. *New York Times* columnist Thomas L. Friedman expresses this particular fear quite plainly, claiming that the Net

> is different from radio, television and newspapers in that it is a totally open, interactive technology—but with no built-in editor, publisher, censor or even filters. With one mouse click, you can wander into a Nazi beer hall or a pornographer's library, hack the NASA computers or roam the Sorbonne library, and no one is there to stop or direct you. You interact with the network naked. . . . When you take such a totally open network and you combine it with parents' being able to spend less time building their kids' internal codes and filters, then you add the fact that the Internet is going to become the nervous system of our commerce and society, you have a potentially dangerous cocktail. (12)

Some of the fear over this lack of control is probably attributable to the lingering novelty of the Net—especially for those people just now beginning to find their way online. After all, this is a technology that most current users had barely heard of (much less experienced firsthand) before 1996 that has a relatively steep learning curve, and that seems to undergo a dramatic makeover (in terms of "essential" new protocols and browser plug-ins) every few months. And while "newbies" may very well feel "naked" in their initial forays online, more experienced users know that it takes more than "one mouse click" to hack anyone's computers (much less NASA's) or to find oneself in any of the online "trouble spots" that Friedman mentions. Thus it's quite possible that some of these fears may disappear as the Net becomes a regular and familiar part of more people's daily lives.

Nevertheless, much of this lack of control is (literally) hardwired into the structure of the Net. While Friedman is simply wrong about the ease with which one can unwittingly stumble onto virtual Nazis and cyberporn,[15] he's right to point out that the Net has no central processing office to manage traffic, no government bureau to regulate it, and no professional guild to control content quality. Nor is it likely that such institutions will come into existence in the foreseeable future (if ever).[16] The Internet, after all, was deliberately constructed as a *de*centralized network in order to protect its basic communicative functions from damage to any specific piece of it: a technical fact that also makes it difficult (and probably impossible) to *control* the Net from any single point. And, in the end, this is one of the most significant obstacles to creating any meaningful rapprochement between cyber-refuseniks like Birkerts and cyber-utopians like Barlow, as the very facet of the Net that most terrifies the former camp is precisely what most exhilarates the latter.

## THE PUBLIC SPHERE

For many of cyberspace's more vocal champions, the Net's built-in resistance to centralized control makes it inherently more egalitarian and democratic than other forms of mass media. At a moment when an overwhelming (and ever-expanding) percentage of the world's media is controlled by an ever-shrinking number of multinational conglomerates (Bagdikian; McChesney; Schiller), one of the primary appeals of the Net for many observers is that it bypasses the media monopoly altogether. Not only does the Net give relatively ordinary people access to a seemingly endless wealth of information from a diverse range of sources, but it also provides them with the unprecedented ability to package and distribute their own ideas to a global audience. And if, as many media critics (Carey; McChesney; Williams) argue, a crucial facet of a healthy democracy is the ability of ordinary people to participate actively in the public sphere as both "speakers" and "listeners," then the Net may be the only form of mass media that has the potential to be genuinely democratic.

The key word in that last sentence, however, is "potential," as a sizable—and perhaps even unbridgeable—gap still exists between the reality of the Net and that democratic ideal. To be sure, in the absence of governmental or corporate gatekeepers, the average Netizen *can* express him- or herself to a global audience in ways that are simply impossible via other forms of mass communication. Listservs, Usenet groups, and personal Web pages (to name only the most obvious examples) make Net-mediated communication much more interactive and multivocal than that provided via, say, the *New York Times*, CNN, or Universal Studios. At the same time, however, there are at least three sizable barriers to making a truly democratic Net a reality: the hierarchies of power inherent in network architecture, the lack of meaningful access to the Net for huge portions of the global public, and the subtle (yet formidable) gatekeepers of education and literacy.

The first of these barriers—the nature of network architecture—is perhaps the one that is the most difficult to overcome. In theory, at least, access to the Net can be expanded to include a larger and more representative portion of the population, while educational policies and practices can be improved to help make expanded access truly meaningful (though, as I argue below, neither of these issues is likely to be resolved as easily or as quickly as many cyber-utopians would like to believe). The hierarchies inherent in the architecture of computer networks and the servers that run them, however, don't appear to be quite so subject to change.

In a nutshell, most contemporary software and hardware design places the ultimate power to configure, maintain, and control any given server or network in the hands of a single person: the systems administrator (SysAdmin).[17] To be sure, a SysAdmin's job is to manage computer resources so that others have access to them, and this duty inevitably requires SysAdmins to share portions of that power with other users. If you have an Internet account, for instance, your SysAdmin has given you a measure of power over his or her server(s)—for example, you have permission to read and write to certain directories on a particular hard drive and to make use of the system's link to the Net—that is unparalleled in other media. A comparable form of power sharing by a newspaper publisher, for instance, would require the publisher to print and distribute stories written by any and all of the paper's subscribers on a regular basis. Nevertheless, this power appears more revolutionary than it actually is precisely because of the ways that other media have taken over (and eviscerated) the public sphere: in a society where the average citizen rarely has access to a public forum where he or she can *share* (and not just consume) opinions and ideas, the ability to "publish" one's thoughts where potentially millions of people might read them is a dramatic deviation from the status quo. At the same time, the extent to which this power actually makes the Net a democratic space is questionable, and we need to be cautious about conflating the power that individual users have to "speak" online with actual power over the networks that comprise the Net.

To illustrate this point, I want to look at a specific example of an "open" online forum: a cultural studies listserv called CULTSTUD-L.[18] In terms of its normal day-to-day operations, the list appears to be very democratic and egalitarian: anyone with a working e-mail account can subscribe to the list, any subscriber can contribute to the discussions, and (with the exception of some rudimentary spam/security filters) there are no technological restrictions on what subscribers can say in their posts. Even nonsubscribers can read the list's archives as long as they have access to the Web. To be sure, CULTSTUD-L is not a virtual soapbox where any and all forms of public expression are acceptable. If nothing else, the list's focus on cultural studies places implicit filters on the conversation and, as is the case with any community (virtual or otherwise), prevailing social norms and pressures create de facto limits on who feels free to speak, what subjects people are willing to discuss, and what sort of on-list behavior is deemed appropriate. Nonetheless, in the absence of formal restraints on who can join the list and what can be said there, on-list conversation tends to be free, open, and spontaneous.

Still, for all of the openness of the list, CULTSTUD-L isn't a real democracy—nor can it readily be made into one. In a genuinely democratic organization, after all, the people who make up the group have a significant measure of control over the structure and governance of the organization: if they disapprove of their leaders, they have the ability and the authority to replace them peacefully; if they want to change the basic rules by which the organization operates, they have mechanisms at their disposal to implement such changes. Such conditions, however, simply don't—and can't—exist in a networked environment like CULTSTUD-L.

As is the case with most listservs, most of the power to control the actual shape and governance of CULTSTUD-L remains in the hands of one person—me. While I usually refer to myself as a "list manager," the more common title (largely because of its prevalence in the support documentation for most listserv software) is the proprietary one of "list owner"—and even that is something of a euphemism. Because essentially I'm a dictator: a benevolent one, I hope, but a dictator nonetheless. In the final analysis, the list's subscribers—individually and/or collectively—have no power to regulate the list: that is, they don't have access to the server in ways that would allow them to (re)configure the list's basic settings for who can subscribe, who can post, who can read the archives, whether the list is open or moderated, what content is available on the list's Web site, and so on. These are powers reserved for me as the list's "owner," and I can invoke them without seeking permission from—or even giving notice to—the list's membership. Moreover, my status as list manager isn't—and can't be—determined by democratic ballot. Should list members be unhappy with my governance of the list, they have no way to overrule my policy decisions or to vote me out of "office."[19] To a large extent, this is because the *ultimate* authority over the list rests not with me but with the SysAdmins who run the server that CULTSTUD-L calls home and who have given me *just* enough authority to run the list. In much the same way that I can unilaterally restructure the list's shape and policies, the university's computing staff can, at any time they see fit, reconfigure the list's server—e.g., shutting it down (temporarily or permanently), changing the software used to support and maintain listservs (and thus potentially changing the possible ways the list itself operates), refusing to host listservs altogether, deleting users' accounts, and so on—without having to inform (much less get consent from) anyone who has an account on the server.

The example of CULTSTUD-L is not a unique or isolated one. The Net is almost entirely composed of hierarchical networks and virtual environments such as this: environments where access to (and thus control of) the heart of the system is severely restricted. And, if for no other reasons than those connected to issues of network security and viability, such conditions are not likely to change anytime soon. A truly open-ended network—one where anyone who logged in has access to the core operating system, the network software, the accounts and passwords for other users, etc.—runs the high risk of degenerating quickly into chaos and anarchy.[20] The main gap between cyber-democracy and "real" democracy, then, is that even in online communities where "the public" is deliberately given a voice in how systems are configured and governed, such "democracies" still depend on the willingness of the relevant SysAdmin to follow through on publicly expressed mandates.[21] So while I believe that it's possible to create places online where *democratic participation* can take place, the hierarchies of access that are built into the hardware and software of networked environments make it far more difficult (if not impossible) to actually make the Net a space for *participatory democracies*.

The second major barrier to online democracy that I want to address here is the question of access. While I would maintain that the Net provides ordinary users with something closer to an ideal public sphere than other media do, it's debatable whether most Net users qualify as "ordinary" members of the broader population, as the actual "public" who can be found online remains a relatively small and privileged one. And while statistics on how many people actually use the Net need to be taken with a grain of salt,[22] those that exist suggest that, as of late 2000, more than 40 percent of the United States—and more than 95 percent of the world—are not online in *any* capacity at all (Nua Internet Surveys).

The fact that the Internet is a relative newcomer to the realm of public communication undoubtedly accounts for some of those sizable numbers, and I think that it's reasonable to expect the online population to continue to grow for several years to come. It is not clear, however, that the Net is expanding anywhere near as rapidly as people predicted it would; for instance, in 1995, Nicholas Negroponte forecast one billion Net users worldwide by 2000 (182), but the *highest* estimates for global users as 2000 drew to a close placed the actual total at less than half of that. In spite of its continued growth, then, it's highly unlikely that the Net will achieve the sort of (near-)universal penetration that currently exists (at least in the United States) for telephones, radio, and television in the foreseeable future.

Of course, not everyone agrees with such pessimistic predictions. For instance, David Boaz, "vice president of the libertarian Cato Institute," told the *Washington Post*:

> We've got a new technology spreading more rapidly than any new technology has spread in history. . . . And of course it doesn't spread absolutely evenly. Richer people always adopt new technology first—and that's not news. There's no such thing as information haves and information have-nots. . . . There are have-nows and have-laters. The families that don't have computers now are going to have them in a few years. (Quoted in Schwartz, A-1)

Even if such claims are true for the United States (which, for reasons I discuss below, I seriously doubt), they're certainly not applicable to most of the rest of the globe. Given that 65 percent of the world's households still don't have basic telephone service ("Wired World Atlas," 162) and that major telecommunications firms aren't exactly racing to change that (Wresch), it's hard to imagine that "in a few years" more than a tiny fraction of the 5.9 billion so-called "have-laters" around the globe will even have the theoretical potential to go online (much less actually be there).

Ironically, one of the best examples of the global gap between information haves and have-nots comes from a 1998 issue of *Wired* magazine, which included a map designed to show the relative "wiredness" of different nations: a map where the size and color of the boxes used to represent individual countries were determined by each nation's relative penetration of telephone lines and television sets ("Wired World Atlas"). Thus, a wealthy, media-saturated nation like the United States was represented by a large yellow rectangle, while a poorer, largely unwired country like the Democratic Republic of Congo was represented by a tiny purple square. As a visual display of the global distribution of phone lines—and thus the *potential* for global distribution of computer networks and online capabilities—the disparities between nations (and, more significantly, entire segments of the globe) are stunning. For instance, Monaco, the world's second-smallest nation but one of the wealthiest and *the* most heavily wired, is represented by a huge yellow box that's almost bigger than the entire continent of Africa. Moreover, Africa is apparently so unwired that *twenty-two* nations don't even rate a name tag on the map (they're simply minuscule, unmarked squares squeezed into the center of the continent)—an ignominious fate that befalls no other countries anywhere on the globe. However wide the Web may actually be, the *Wired* map demonstrates that it's still a long way from living up to the "World" portion of its full name.[23]

In the United States, the magnitude of the information have/have-not gap isn't as great as it is globally, but it remains significant—and largely for the same reason that it does in the unwired portions of the world: economics. Going (and staying) online, after all, still requires a sizable expenditure of money for hardware, software, and Internet service. And with economic surveys indicating that the gap between the economic haves and have-nots in the United States continues to widen (Schor), it is not surprising that media-use surveys continue to show that low- and moderate-income households are still less likely to be Net users than high-income ones.

Part of the reason for this is that PCs remain expensive to buy and use. To be sure, when measured according to "bang for your buck" (as *PC Magazine* likes to describe it), computer prices have plummeted steadily for at least a decade now (if not more): the same money you would have spent ten years ago on a dual floppy drive system with no hard drive would buy a multimedia Pentium 4 system with all the silicon bells and whistles you could hope for today. Nevertheless, until very recently, the average price of a low-end home computer remained fairly stable—you still couldn't buy a new computer system for much less than $1,000—because the *trailing*-edge technology simply drops off the market completely before it actually becomes cheap enough for lower-income households to buy it.

Moreover, recent shifts in the hardware market toward affordable computing—in particular, the boom in sub-$1,000 PCs[24]—haven't changed the real costs of owning and operating a computer as significantly as industry cheerleaders suggest they have. The range of ways that hardware manufacturers and retailers have brought the (apparent) price of computers down varies wildly, and I won't pretend to account for all of them here. Most, however, revolve around cutting prices by skimping on important features and/or hiding the real costs of purchasing a system in the fine print of potentially seductive advertisements. For instance, a number of retailers and national Internet service providers (ISPs) have formed partnerships that claim to offer rock-bottom prices—as low as $99—on "full" systems. If these offers were even half as good as they appear to be on the surface, then maybe Boaz's claims about have-nows and have-laters would hold water. But a closer look at the details and obligations associated with buying those "cheap" systems reveals that the bottom line for consumers remains a pricey one. For starters, that "$99" computer is as bare-boned as they come in terms of basic features (e.g., RAM, hard disk size, processor speed), and if you want a printer or a monitor, the price goes up, as those "peripherals" are sold separately.[25] Moreover, the bulk of that deep "discount" comes in the form of a mail-in rebate that also requires you to purchase a multi-year service contract with the ISP half of the partnership. All of which means that before you can walk out of the store with that "$99" computer, you have to pay the full list price of the system, plus the cost of a monitor (and probably a printer, too), and at least $700–$800 for the service contract.[26] And then you get to wait eight to ten weeks for a $400 rebate check. At best, then, your net cost for this *low-end* system still comes to (surprise!) about $1,000.

Beyond the deceptiveness of such promotions, it's also worth noting that three years (the typical length of these service contracts) is an eternity in computer time. The laptop I used to complete this essay, for instance, is the fifth different computer I've owned in the past decade. Each of those machines was near (though never quite at) the leading edge of the available technology when I acquired it, but each of the four that I've retired (as well as my current laptop) took less than two years (and as little as six months) to fall behind the *trailing* edge of the market: i.e., the point where no major manufacturer still offered a comparably equipped machine as part of its standard product line. Not only does this render a computer purchase tied to a three-year service contract a less-than-stellar bargain—that service contract may very well outlast your PC—but it helps to underscore the extensive investment required to stay online over time, as hardware and software become obsolete far more quickly than other comparably priced items.

Of course, for many people, some of the "need" to buy a new computer every two or three years is nothing more than the consumption-crazed desire to have the hippest, newest cybertoys on the block. But there are also a range of practical pressures behind the drive to replace or upgrade with some regularity. For starters, older computers typically have a harder time handling newer software and/or peripheral hardware, assuming they can handle it at all: a limitation that can be frustrating (if not debilitating) when it comes to sharing files with other people, even if you never use your computer to go online. Second, when older systems need repairs, it's usually more difficult to find affordable parts for them, and they often lack the ability to handle upgrades that might bring them up to speed with newer machines.[27] Finally, older machines are typically more limited in terms of where they can take you online, as content providers are often more intent on crafting Web sites and coding virtual environments that require multimedia capabilities that older computers simply can't handle.

By way of comparison, major shifts in other technologies rarely (if ever) render older machines fully obsolete. A ten-year-old car in good working order will still get you around town, even if it doesn't have four-wheel-drive-on-demand or ergonomic seating; a fifteen-year-old TV in good working order will still show your favorite programs, even if it's not cable-ready or equipped with "picture-in-picture" capability; a twenty-year-old refrigerator in good working order will still keep your milk cold, even if it lacks a fancy icemaker or a door that beeps when you leave it open too long. But a computer as little as five years old, no matter how well its various pieces work, may simply be incapable of running the software necessary to access large portions of the Net. As Clifford Stoll notes:

> Despite having few moving parts and little to wear out, these devices have short life spans. They're discarded before they break. . . . An original IBM PC, now over ten years old, is fully obsolete. Likely, it will still work perfectly and do everything it was built for; after all, the silicon and copper haven't deteriorated. But you can't get software for it any longer. Who could run a computer without a hard disk? What word processor can squeeze into 64 Kbytes? Within two years, the value of a computer drops in half. Within five years, it's pretty much been superseded. And within a decade, you find them at Goodwill. (69–70)

In short, buying a new computer—even if you're willing to take the steeper economic plunge of a high-end, no-gimmick system—makes it likely that in three to five years (if not sooner), you'll either be buying another computer or you'll have a very expensive doorstop.

Finally, and perhaps even more important than the question of the economics of buying and using a computer, however, are the surprisingly underdiscussed questions of education and literacy. Without denying that there's an important learning process associated with any communication technology—no one, after all, is born with an intuitive understanding of how to use a telephone or with a full working knowledge of the cultural codes necessary to make sense of the average evening of prime time TV—the fact remains that using the Internet effectively requires that one know how to read, to write, to type, and to be at least minimally competent with a computer. And in the end, these skills—or, more accurately, the lack thereof—may matter even more than economic barriers when it comes to limiting the online population to a relatively small and exclusive club. Even if a magical financial windfall allowed us to put a modem-equipped computer in every classroom and household in the country (or, as long as we're pipe-dreaming, to build telecommunication networks that would fully wire the world), such economic changes would still not amount to very much in terms of broadening the online population in any meaningful way without simultaneous shifts in priorities and funding toward bolstering basic educational skills. And, unfortunately, the current public discourse around closing the gap between the information haves and have-nots seems to be largely unconcerned with the relatively basic question of giving people the knowledge and skills necessary to use the hardware and software necessary to use the Net.[28]

One would think that some of the strongest advocates for such educational reforms would come from the ranks of professional educators. Sadly, however, academics writing about cyberspace have all too often been silent on this question. A somewhat dated, but still glaringly problematic, example of this oversight is a 1995 anthology, *Public Access to the Internet* (Kahin and Keller), a collection of papers presented at a 1993 conference on the topic. The book includes seventeen essays, all of which are ostensibly concerned with the problems of bringing more of the general public online . . . and only one of these (Civille) deals with economically disadvantaged users (or would-be users) at any length. And it addresses the question of literacy and education for only about two pages; the bulk of the paper is devoted to laying out statistical evidence proving that (surprise!) poor people are not heavy users of the Internet.[29]

Worse than being silent, however, academic commentators on the Net have too frequently been complicit in excluding large portions of the population from "the public" whose world the Net is transforming. Too often it seems that we discuss cyberculture—whether we praise it or condemn it—as if our experiences online were universal (or at least universalizable). Granted, the body of scholarly literature on cyberspace is growing almost as fast as the Net itself, and I won't pretend to have gone through every scholarly book, article, and journal on the subject with a fine-tooth comb, but to date I've encountered relatively few scholars writing about their experiences online who have also been self-reflexive enough to note that those experiences are rooted in (1) higher than average levels of literacy (computer and otherwise) and (2) heavily (if not wholly) subsidized access to the hardware, software, and networks that are necessary to use the Net in the first place.[30]

## CONCLUSION(?)

Given that I began this essay by refusing to offer predictions about where the Net would take us tomorrow (much less next year or in the coming decades), I'm loathe to end with anything that feels like a pat conclusion. But I do want to offer a few closing thoughts.

I think it's important to recognize that, as a relatively new technology, the Internet has yet to fully come into its own. We're still very much in a moment where both our uses of and our expectations for the Net are often rooted in our visions of older forms of communication. Cyber-skeptics, for instance, often seem to be working from the assumption that the Net is—and should be—nothing more than a new conduit for already existing modes of address. So they look, for instance, at face-to-face conversation (or some idealized notion of it, anyway), see how difficult it is to duplicate online what they value most about that form of communication (e.g., the warmth of a smile, the tangibility of physical presence), and declare the Net to be a failure.[31] Cyber-utopians, on the other hand, tend to reverse this focus in equally problematic ways: i.e., they look at the inherent drawbacks of face-to-face communication (such as judging people by their appearances rather than their words or deeds), see ways in which these can be circumvented or eliminated online, and declare the Net to be a success.[32] In either case, however, what makes such assumptions troubling are the ways that they lead us to assess the value and impact of new technology according to inappropriate standards.[33]

In many respects, such problematic assumptions aren't all that surprising. After all, the formative years of almost any new communication technology are often devoted to awkward attempts to use that technology as little more than a new means of delivering some older form of communication. The early years of cinema, for example, frequently saw filmmakers place static cameras in front of traditional theatrical performances. It took years for such uniquely cinematic devices as close-ups, pans, dolly shots, zooms, and montages to develop into the norms of a new and different medium for storytelling. Similarly, even though magnetic recording tape was available as early as the 1940s, it took at least until the late 1950s (or perhaps even the late 1960s, depending on which version of popular music history one believes) before the music industry regularly began using the recording studio as more than a place to try and capture an artist's "live" sound on tape: splicing, overdubbing, multitracking, and similar studio techniques that are now taken for granted (at least in the industrialized West) were not instant developments of the new technology.

In the current context, what these historical examples should teach us is that, even while the Net is already changing our world in visible and significant ways, we can't begin to predict what its real impact is going to be until it takes a turn toward a mode (or, more likely, several modes) of expression that are *unique* to cyberspace. There are, of course, already places you can go and things you can do online that can't readily be duplicated either by other media or in "real" life. More often than not, however, such uses of the Net are overshadowed and outnumbered by more mundane ones: for every Web site that experiments in creative, groundbreaking approaches to design, there are probably a dozen (if not more) that are merely online versions of offline texts; for every MUD or MOO that stretches our notion of what sort of worlds we can build in cyberspace, there are probably twenty chat rooms that do their best to duplicate existing offline environments like bars and coffeehouses. And until those proportions start to shift in the other direction, the Net's ultimate effects remain impossible to predict with any precision.

In the meantime, I think we need to resist the temptation to assess the Net's effect in broad terms: after all, depending on where and when you're looking at it, the Net is simultaneously good *and* bad, empowering *and* alienating, educational *and* misleading, populist *and* elitist. Which means that the questions we most need to be asking are not the broad ones that have simple binary answers but the messy and complicated ones that require us to make nuanced distinctions between the different ways that specific people use the Net in particular contexts. For in the end, the only simple claim that we can safely make about the Net's social and cultural effects is that those effects are (and will continue to be) incredibly complicated. If we truly want to understand the Net's impact, we need to avoid simply retreating to one of the camps at either end of the cybermania/cyberphobia spectrum. Instead, we need to be able to see the Net in all its complexity and to wrestle with the question(s) of its impact in correspondingly complicated ways. Of course, such an approach to studying cyberspace is a difficult one. But if our main goal is not simply to produce easy answers about the Net's effects, but to try and recognize the best ones, then that difficult task is one that we need to embrace more fully.

## NOTES

I would like to thank Alice Crawford, John Hardin, Barbara Jago, Lisa Nakamura, and Greg Wise for providing helpful comments and insights. Extra-special thanks due to Beth Kolko for her careful and thoughtful editorial work.

1. Much as I would like to take credit for coming up with this subtitle on my own, the pun in question comes from a student reporter at Kansas State University in 1995. Conducting a telephone interview with one of the organizers of a conference sponsored by the KSU English Department, the reporter wrote up the story with the conference's title—"Western Humanities, Pedagogy, and the Public Sphere"—spelled out the way she heard it: " . . . the Public's Fear." I can't even take credit for being the first person to invoke this gaffe in the context of a scholarly article on cyberspace; that honor belongs to Joseph Tabbi (233).

2. As a technological reality, the Internet could reasonably be said to date back to the development of ARPANET by the U.S. Department of Defense in the 1960s and 1970s. As a prominent *cultural formation* (see Grossberg, 69–70; Rodman, 158–161, 165–169), however, the Net is a much more recent phenomenon than that.

3. Perhaps the most commonplace example of this is the default label—"The Internet"—that Microsoft gives to the desktop icon for its Web browser. One can also find this slippage, however, in settings where the stakes are much higher. For instance, the U.S. Department of Justice's failed attempt to defend the constitutionality of the 1996 Communications Decency Act focused almost entirely on ways to keep minors from accessing Web-based "adult" materials: e.g., the use of credit cards as de facto adult verification devices for logging into age-restricted Web sites, filtering software for Web browsers, and the implementation of special age-rating HTML tags, etc. The fact that the CDA would also have applied to e-mail, Usenet groups, MOOs/MUDs, IRC, and other non-Web-based forms of CMC—and that none of their proposed

safeguards would have worked in such environments—appears to have slipped completely by the Department of Justice (*Reno v. ACLU*).

4. The Web was so new in 1994 that it received the barest of mentions in two highly regarded "how to" books on the Internet published that year. Adam Gaffin's *Everybody's Guide to the Internet*—a book sponsored by the Electronic Frontier Foundation—devotes all of two pages (out of 188) to the Web. Kevin Savetz's *Your Internet Consultant: The FAQs of Life Online* fares slightly better, mentioning the Web on a whopping eight pages out of 414.

5. The second edition of *Hoover's Guide to Computer Companies* (1996) doesn't include Netscape in its list of 108 "industry leaders," though it does show up in its supplemental list of 148 "selected industry players" (336) and tops the list of "the 200 fastest-growing companies" in terms of one-year sales growth (14). While Netscape's future certainly looked bright in 1995 (the last fiscal year covered by this edition of the guide), it is worth remembering that in an industry where major players can (and do) go belly-up almost overnight (like Atari and Commodore), a future that *looks* bright is not necessarily a guarantee of success.

6. In 1994, after all, Windows 95—which included Microsoft's first serious attempts to provide Internet-related software of any sort—was still a year away from public release . . . though even that wasn't exactly a certainty. The operating system's name notwithstanding, a host of development problems had many industry observers predicting that Windows 95 wouldn't ship until at least 1996.

7. For example, Nicholas Negroponte's 1995 best-seller *Being Digital* devotes more than 230 pages to extolling the blissful virtues of digital culture, while relegating discussion of the potential downsides of the changing socio-technological landscape (for example, questions of access, censorship, privacy, regulation) to a breezy eight-page afterword tacked onto the end of the book's paperback edition. Not surprisingly, given the brevity of this section, Negroponte doesn't offer much in the way of solutions to these problems besides a few sound bites: e.g., proclaiming that "cyberspace . . . should be private" (236), "national law has no place in cyberlaw" (237), and would-be cyberspace regulators should "lighten up" (235). Clifford Stoll's more pessimistic best-seller, *Silicon Snake Oil*, is slightly more balanced than Negroponte's, at least insofar as he doesn't limit the positive things he has to say about cyberspace to the margins of his text. At the same time, virtually all the benefits he sees to the Net are either limited to a *very* small fraction of the population (scientists engaged in large-scale, multinational research projects) or buried so thoroughly under the weight of his more scathing criticisms that they hardly seem like good things at all.

8. The specific contrast here isn't entirely fair to Rheingold, whose celebration of the WELL predates the rise of the Web by several years. At the same time, the moment in cyberculture reflected in Rheingold's book wasn't

necessarily any more dominated by WELL-like environments than today's cyberspace is. "Gopherspace," for example, consisted of millions of sites that were often nothing more than online databases: there's nothing particularly community-like, after all, about an archive of the National Oceanographic Administration Agency (NOAA) weather data or an electronic storehouse of government press releases.

9. Breslow's position on the Net may be somewhat less extreme than my summary here allows, as he briefly acknowledges that many people use the Net to create "friendships and systems of alliance" that would otherwise not be possible (255). At the same time, he also shrugs off such possibilities as trivial in the face of multinational capitalism's ability to use the Net to eliminate the opportunity for worker solidarity to come about.

10. Pinpointing the starting date of a moral panic isn't an exact science, by any means, but a plausible candidate here is the cover story for the 3 July 1995 issue of *Time* magazine, which showed a wide-eyed child gazing at a computer screen with a headline that read, ON A SCREEN NEAR YOU: CYBERPORN. Jonathan Wallace and Mark Mangan provide a useful discussion of the dubious study on which the *Time* story was based (125–152) and how it came to be an important piece of "evidence" in the congressional push to regulate cyberspace (173–191).

11. The basic argument here was that the unprecedented danger of the Net lay in its ability to serve as a gateway through which the most vile examples of pornography and obscenity imaginable could enter—and violate—the pristine sanctity of private domestic space.

12. A partial list of various pieces of the Go network includes sites for ABC, ABC News, ABC Sports, Disney, ESPN, five major sports leagues/associations (NASCAR, NBA, NFL, NHL, and WNBA), MrShowbiz, and Family.com.

13. In seven separate incidents across two states from 2 July to 4 July 1999, Smith shot at more than a dozen people, killing two and injuring nine, before killing himself.

14. On 20 April 1999, Eric Harris and Dylan Klebold—part of a group of outcast students known to their peers as the Trenchcoat Mafia—went on a shooting spree inside Columbine High School in Littleton, Colorado, killing twelve students and one teacher before taking their own lives.

15. Annette Markham provides an eloquent explanation of the flaws in the sort of "one click" assumption that Friedman makes here. Describing her own attempts to go online for the purpose of interviewing "heavy" Net users, she writes: "Going online took a long time and involved far more than turning on the computer, tapping out words on the keyboard, and pressing the send/enter button. It was more like entering a strange new world where the very metaphysics defied my comprehension of how worlds should work. To even begin to understand what was happening online, or to communicate with other

users, I had to learn how to move, see, and talk. Until I learned these basic rules, I was paralyzed in the dark, isolated from that world as much as I would be if I were a mind without a body on the planet Earth (or so I believe)" (23). The steep learning curve that Markham describes is all the more significant in light of the fact that she was *trying* to get online to accomplish specific tasks, yet found both the technology and the social norms of cyberculture to be intimidating and (initially) difficult to master—which makes it all the more implausible for Friedman's hypothetical child Web surfer to be a single click away from unspeakable cyber-horrors.

16. A minor caveat is necessary here, insofar as there are countries (e.g., China) that attempt to monitor, regulate, and control the flow of information on the Internet within their borders. Such efforts, however, depend on all Net traffic being routed through a government server before being made "publicly" available: an immense undertaking that (1) is only possible in countries where most telecommunications facilities are already under tight government control and (2) has little (if any) effect on Net traffic in the rest of the world.

17. In some organizations and institutions, circumstances can result in root access being shared by a small handful of people, which affords a humane solution to the problem of always having to drag the same person out of bed when the server crashes at three o'clock in the morning.

18. For more information on the listserv itself, see http://www.cas.usf.edu/communication/rodman/cultstud.

19. Having outed myself as a cyber-dictator, I feel compelled to explain that I *want* the list to remain as open and democratic as is possible (given the limitations of the environment) and that I do my best to "rule" with a light hand . . . though this is not always as easy as it sounds. In a twist of fate that would seem highly implausible had it been used in a Hollywood movie script, while I was sitting at my computer writing an earlier draft of this essay, a brief—but ugly—flame war broke out on the list that led me to invoke (for the first and hopefully last time in the list's history) the ultimate penalty for an individual subscriber: banishment from the list. If nothing else, the incident underscores the inherently undemocratic nature of most networked environments. Ordinary list members had no power to control the situation except to (a) plead with me to "do something" about it or (b) fight flames with more flames (Almost by definition, the obvious third option—to try to persuade the person to behave—is ineffective in a flame war. If reasonable discussion was likely to settle the matter, there would probably have been no matter in need of settling), and no authority to enforce a disciplinary decision of any sort.

20. See Allucquère Rosanne Stone (99–121) for an informative discussion of an early BBS system called CommuniTree and how its demise at the hands of "hackerkid" interlopers (who took advantage of the system's open access

architecture in a "nearly continual assault that the system operators were powerless to prevent") helped to make hierarchical mechanisms for "surveillance and social control" a standard aspect of network architecture.

21. One well-known example of an online "democracy" that has struggled with this gap is LambdaMOO, which has experimented with a democratic system of ballots about MOO policy for several years now—and where, on a handful of occasions, the MOO's "wizards" (the SysAdmins) have refused to implement "the will of the people." Short of gathering together offline and storming the building where the MOO's server is housed, however, "the people" of Lambda have no actual power to enforce or implement their will, nor can (or should) the wizards simply give them that power.

22. For example, the decentralized nature of the Net makes census taking difficult, the Net's rapid and continuing growth renders any data one collects on its overall size instantly outdated, and what actually counts as "using the Net" varies dramatically from survey to survey.

23. Space does not permit me to discuss this point in full detail, but it is worth noting that the use of ASCII as the standard character set for most online communications and the default status of English as cyberspace's lingua franca combine to place sharp restrictions on which global populations can (and can't) readily assimilate themselves into the current cyberculture.

24. According to one news report, the sub-$1,000 segment of the market "has exploded, growing from about 13 percent of the market in January 1997 to about 46 percent in June [1998]," and at least some industry figures were anticipating that that figure would rise to 67 percent within six months (Gussow, 13).

25. Insofar as one can potentially use a computer without ever wanting or needing to print anything out (though I confess that I've never met anyone who used a computer in this way), I can understand how a printer might safely be seen as a "peripheral." Monitors, on the other hand, aren't exactly an optional piece of a completed system—any more than a steering wheel is an optional piece of a functioning car.

26. This figure may actually be deceptively low, given that most of these contracts are based on the lowest tier of the ISP's service: that is, you're paying for a limited number of hours per month or access to that ISP's basic offerings. If you want to be online more than, say, twenty hours per month, or if you have any interest in your ISP's "premium" content, the actual costs for your Net use will rise accordingly. It's also worth noting that the penalties for early termination of your service contract are substantial enough to guarantee that, one way or another, you will pay your ISP several hundred dollars.

27. Two of my four upgrades came about because parts were no longer readily available to repair my "obsolete" machine. After combining inflated prices for scarce parts with high bench-labor rates, it was actually cheaper for me to

buy a new computer than to repair the old one. In one case, I was told that I could try to upgrade pieces of the system—by adding more RAM, replacing the CPU, and so on—but that my system's BIOS was so old that it might not be able to handle the newer chips anyway.

28. "Though it should be blandly obvious to readers that access to a computer and the skills to make use of it are prior conditions for a person or a group of people to go online, surprisingly little Internet research follows through on this basic premise" (Sterne, 192).

29. A notable, and important, exception to this trend is William Wresch's *Disconnected: Haves and Have Nots in the Information Age*.

30. Even scholars whose research and politics would suggest that they would know better have been known to fall prey to utopian reveries about the democratizing effects of cyberspace, as is evident in this quote from an essay on critical pedagogy and the Internet: "For example, assuming access to a modem, and the wish to do so(!), it is not at all difficult to envisage a peasant-born woman of color from a remote village conversing on equal terms with a white male professor located in one of the world's most prestigious universities" (Lankshear, Peters, and Knobel, 164).

31. For example, Clifford Stoll complains that online pedagogy eliminates the possibilities for informal face-to-face interaction between teachers and students ("The computer is a barrier to close teaching relationships. When students receive assignments through e-mail and send in homework over the network, they miss out on chances to discuss things with their prof. They don't visit her office and catch the latest news. They're learning at arm's length" [118]), while overlooking the (sad) fact that the sort of "close teaching relationships" he envisions are hardly the rule in offline pedagogical environments. Ingrid Banks offers a similar critique of the virtual classroom, in which she brushes aside reports from colleagues who assert "that certain students are willing to say things on line [*sic*] that they would not mention in the classroom" because she doesn't "like the idea of students' hiding behind a computer monitor" (B-6). Mind you, this isn't a bad reason for an individual teacher to resist taking his or her own courses online, but it's a bit of a logical leap to move from a desire for face-to-face interactions with one's students to the broader claim that "reliance on technology threatens the essence of teaching."

32. Perhaps the most oft-cited example of this phenomenon is an MCI television ad from 1997 that proclaimed the Net to be a space where "there is no race. There are no genders. There is no age. There are no infirmities. There are only minds." For a more extended critique of this ad, see Nakamura.

33. Christopher Anderson makes a similar argument with respect to traditional aesthetic critiques of television: "We refuse to admit that what appears to be the impoverishment of television programming may, in fact, arise from our

misrecognition of the medium, from our attempts to identify it in accordance with previous cultural forms and to define it with critical methods developed for those forms. (If a misinformed taxonomist tosses a frog from a cliff and it crashes to the ground, must we blame the frog for failing to fly?)" (114–115).

## REFERENCES

"Amazon.com Targets New Markets." *St. Petersburg Times*, 14 July 1999, Tampa edition.

Anderson, Christopher. "Reflections on *Magnum, P.I.*" In Horace Newcomb, ed., *Television: The Critical View*, 112–125. 4th ed. New York: Oxford University Press, 1987.

Bagdikian, Ben H. *The Media Monopoly*. 6th ed. Boston: Beacon, 2000.

Banks, Ingrid. "Reliance on Technology Threatens the Essence of Teaching." *Chronicle of Higher Education*, 16 October 1998.

Barlow, John Perry, Sven Birkerts, Kevin Kelly, and Mark Slouka. "What Are We Doing On-line?" *Harper's*, August 1995, 35–46.

Breslow, Harris. "Civil Society, Political Economy, and the Internet." In Steven G. Jones, ed., *Virtual Culture: Identity and Communication in Cybersociety*, 236–257. Thousand Oaks, Calif.: Sage, 1997.

Carey, James W. "'A Republic, If You Can Keep It': Liberty and Public Life in the Age of Glasnost." 1991. Reprinted in Eve Stryker Munson and Catherine A. Warren, eds., *James Carey: A Critical Reader*, 270–291. Minneapolis: University of Minnesota Press, 1997.

"Church of Creator's Web Site Closes." *St. Petersburg Times*, 6 July 1999, Tampa edition.

Civille, Richard. "The Internet and the Poor." In Brian Kahin and James Keller, eds., *Public Access to the Internet*, 175–207. Cambridge, Mass.: MIT Press, 1995.

"Day Trader Cuts a Deadly Swath." *St. Petersburg Times*, 29 July 1999, Tampa edition.

Deleuze, Gilles, and Félix Guattari. *A Thousand Plateaus: Capitalism and Schizophrenia*. Trans. Brian Massumi. Minneapolis: University of Minnesota Press, 1987.

de Zengotita, Thomas. "The Gunfire Dialogues: Notes on the Reality of Virtuality." *Harper's*, July 1999, 55–58.

"Few Day Traders Live Up to Profitable Image." *St. Petersburg Times*, 29 July 1999, Tampa edition.

"A Free PC?: Sign an Internet Deal and It's Yours." *St. Petersburg Times*, 2 July 1999, Tampa edition.

Friedman, Thomas L. "Parents Need to Be Internet Ready." *St. Petersburg Times*, 2 June 1999, Tampa edition.

Gaffin, Adam. *Everybody's Guide to the Internet*. Cambridge, Mass.: MIT Press, 1994.

Grossberg, Lawrence. *We Gotta Get Out of This Place: Popular Conservatism and Postmodern Culture*. New York: Routledge, 1992.

Gussow, Dave. "Cheap PCs." *St. Petersburg Times*, 14 September 1998, Tampa edition, Tech Times section.

Hall, Stuart, Chas Crichter, Tony Jefferson, John Clarke, and Brian Roberts. *Policing the Crisis: Mugging, the State, and Law and Order*. New York: Holmes and Meier, 1978.

*Hoover's Guide to Computer Companies*. 2d ed. Austin: Hoover's Business Press, 1996.

Jenkins, Henry. "Professor Jenkins Goes to Washington." *Harper's*, July 1999, 19–23.

Kahin, Brian, and James Keller, eds. *Public Access to the Internet*. Cambridge, Mass.: MIT Press, 1995.

Lankshear, Colin, Michael Peters, and Michele Knobel. "Critical Pedagogy and Cyberspace." In Henry A. Giroux, Colin Lankshear, Peter McLaren, and Michael Peters, *Counternarratives: Cultural Studies and Critical Pedagogies in Postmodern Spaces*, 149–188. New York: Routledge, 1996.

Manson, Marilyn. "Columbine: Whose Fault Is It?" *Rolling Stone*, 24 June 1999, 23.

Markham, Annette N. *Life Online: Researching Real Experience in Virtual Space*. Walnut Creek, Calif.: AltaMira, 1998.

Marvin, Carolyn. *When Old Technologies Were New: Thinking About Electric Communication in the Late Nineteenth Century*. New York: Oxford University Press, 1988.

McChesney, Robert W. *Corporate Media and the Threat to Democracy*. New York: Seven Stories Press, 1997.

Nakamura, Lisa. "'Where Do You Want to Go Today?': Cybernetic Tourism, the Internet, and Transnationality." In Beth E. Kolko, Lisa Nakamura, and Gilbert B. Rodman, eds., *Race in Cyberspace*, 15–20. New York: Routledge, 2000.

Negroponte, Nicholas. *Being Digital*. New York: Vintage, 1995.

Nua Internet Surveys. "How Many Online." http://www.nua.ie/surveys/how_many_online/[15 July 2001].

"An Ordinary Man with a Dark Past." *St. Petersburg Times*, 29 July 1999, Tampa edition.

"Out of Hatred, a Killer Emerges." *St. Petersburg Times*, 6 July 1999, Tampa edition.

"PCs Join Cell Phones as Tool for Marketing." *St. Petersburg Times*, 10 May 1999, Tampa edition, Tech Times section.
Pollitt, Katha. "Natural Born Killers," *Nation*, 26 July/2 August 1999.
*Reno v. ACLU.* 1997. U.S. Supreme Court decision No. 96–511. http://caselaw.findlaw.com/scripts/getcase.pl?court=US&vol=000&invol=96–511 (1 August 1999).
Rheingold, Howard. *The Virtual Community: Homesteading on the Electronic Frontier*. New York: HarperPerennial, 1993.
Rodman, Gilbert B. *Elvis After Elvis: The Posthumous Career of a Living Legend*. New York: Routledge, 1996.
Savetz, Kevin M. *Your Internet Consultant: The FAQs of Life Online*. Indianapolis: SAMS Publishing, 1994.
Schiller, Herbert I. *Culture, Inc.: The Corporate Takeover of Public Expression*. New York: Oxford University Press, 1989.
Schor, Juliet B. *The Overspent American: Why We Want What We Don't Need*. New York: HarperPerennial, 1998.
Schwartz, John. "U.S. Cites Race Gap in Use of Internet." *Washington Post*, 9 July 1999. http://www.washingtonpost.com/wp=srv/national/daily/july99/divide9.htm (11 July 1999).
Srivastava, Vinita. "Info Ban: Tangles in Bombay's Net." *Village Voice*, 18 June 1996.
Sterne, Jonathan. "The Computer Race Goes to Class: How Computers in Schools Helped Shape the Racial Topography of the Internet." In Beth E. Kolko, Lisa Nakamura, and Gilbert B. Rodman, eds., *Race in Cyberspace*, 191–212. New York: Routledge, 2000.
Stoll, Clifford. *Silicon Snake Oil: Second Thoughts on the Information Highway*. New York: Anchor Books, 1995.
Stone, Allucquère Rosanne. *The War of Desire and Technology at the Close of the Mechanical Age*. Cambridge, Mass.: MIT Press, 1995.
Tabbi, Joseph. "Reading, Writing, Hypertext: Democratic Politics in the Virtual Classroom." In David Porter, ed., *Internet Culture*, 233–252. New York: Routledge, 1997.
Wallace, Jonathan, and Mark Mangan. *Sex, Laws, and Cyberspace: Freedom and Censorship on the Frontiers of the Electronic Revolution*. New York: Henry Holt, 1996.
Williams, Raymond. "Communications and Community." 1961. Reprinted in Raymond Williams, *Resources of Hope: Culture, Democracy, Socialism*, 19–31. New York: Verso, 1989.
"The Wired World Atlas." *Wired*, November 1998, 162–167.
Wresch, William. *Disconnected: Haves and Have Nots in the Information Age*. New Brunswick, N.J.: Rutgers University Press, 1996.

## 2

# The Internet, Community Definition, and the Social Meaning of Legal Jurisdiction

PAUL SCHIFF BERMAN

Consider the following scenario. A British physicist, participating in an online discussion group, denigrates people of Canadian descent. In response, a Canadian graduate student at an American university posts a message to the group, using the university's computer system. This message falsely implies that the physicist is a pedophile. The physicist, enraged, wishes to bring a suit against both the student and the university for defamation. Leaving aside the physicist's likelihood of success on the merits of his claim, the first question to be answered is, Where can the suit be brought? In Great Britain, where the professor resides? In Canada, where the student is a citizen? Or in the United States, where the university is located?[1]

Interestingly enough, the problem is not much easier if we transplant this dispute so that it occurs entirely within the United States. Indeed, if our physicist were from California, our student from Maine, and our university located in New York, we still would be hard-pressed to determine in which *state* the suit could be brought. In legal terms, this question concerns *jurisdiction*, a doctrine used to decide whether a court has legitimate adjudicatory authority over the parties to a conflict. Historically, jurisdiction has been determined primarily by reference to the territorially based power of a sovereign. Because a person physically present in New York State literally could be seized by state law enforcement officials, New York courts could legitimately subject that person to jurisdiction. Under this doctrine, the student and the university in my example could be sued only in places where they were physically present.

In the twentieth century, territorially based jurisdictional rules were loosened considerably. The United States Supreme Court's primary jurisdictional test now requires only that the defendant in a lawsuit have sufficient contacts with the relevant state to satisfy "traditional notions of fair play and substantial justice."[2] While this test clearly lacks the definitiveness of the historical rules, its flexibility has been thought necessary to accommodate an increasingly mobile culture. Nevertheless, this rule, like its predecessor, is based on the extent of contact with a specific geographically based sovereign.

In the 1990s the emergence of a global network of interconnected computers forced legal scholars and courts to wrestle with the issue of jurisdiction over online activities. Originally heralded as a free-floating community unconstrained by territorially based legal rules, the online world is now a frequent target of government regulation. And disputes based on Internet[3] activities are increasingly being brought into courts. Indeed, my hypothetical defamation scenario is based on an actual case.[4]

Thus far, the jurisdictional dilemma with regard to cyberspace has been framed primarily as a question of how to apply notions of territorial sovereignty to this seemingly borderless environment. Academics have proposed a number of possible approaches to the issue of Internet jurisdiction, with some arguing that older, geographically based conceptions of jurisdiction cannot survive and others disagreeing. Meanwhile, U.S. courts have offered makeshift analogies to the physical world in an attempt to apply the Supreme Court's geographically based jurisdictional tests.

Given this uncertainty, it seems appropriate to take a slightly different approach and revisit the idea of jurisdiction itself. Debates about jurisdictional rules usually rest on various political theories about when a sovereign's exercise of authority is legitimate. There is more to the assertion of jurisdiction, however, than simply the wielding of governmental power. Thus we must ask what it is we are saying in cultural and symbolic, as well as legal, terms when we decide that some person or corporation is subject to our community's jurisdiction. And how does the idea of jurisdiction relate to conceptions of geographic space, community membership, and self-definition? Although largely ignored in the debates over Internet jurisdiction, these foundational issues must be considered seriously if we are to develop a coherent theory of what borders actually mean in our increasingly interconnected world.

Just as important, the resolution of such questions should not be left solely in the legal arena, where the discussion is often limited to debates about historical precedent, political philosophy, or economic efficiency. Instead, jurisdiction is an issue that should engage theorists from a variety of disciplines, who might help forge a more complex account of our jurisdictional rules and point to ways we might think about jurisdiction in the era of online communication.

This essay therefore has two primary aims. First, I attempt to summarize the development of Supreme Court case law on jurisdiction as well as the recent attempts by courts and commentators to apply that case law to the Internet. Second, I suggest three possible ways of analyzing the social meaning of jurisdiction so as to encourage further study by scholars across disciplines. Only by first understanding the various cultural roles played by our choice of jurisdictional rules will we be prepared to discuss how best to define such rules in the new online century.

## THE BACKGROUND LAW OF LEGAL JURISDICTION

I begin by surveying principles of jurisdiction that are not specific to the Internet, but are instead relevant in any legal suit. These principles have been the subject of numerous court decisions and scholarly analyses, and I do not here attempt a detailed discussion of the intricacies of jurisdictional doctrine. Instead, I offer an overview of a few of the most important trends in American jurisdictional law[5] along with brief summaries of some of the key judicial decisions on the subject. I do so because, although lawyers are generally introduced to the question of jurisdiction in the first year of law school, my sense is that most people outside of the legal profession have not given much thought to this issue. Accordingly, it seems useful to touch on some basics at least.

Once a plaintiff has decided to initiate a civil action, one of the first questions to be asked is, Where to sue? To which courthouse should the plaintiff proceed? In order to answer this question, the plaintiff must determine which court has jurisdiction (and therefore the proper adjudicatory authority) over the claim. This jurisdictional inquiry breaks down into two categories: subject matter jurisdiction and personal jurisdiction.

The subject matter jurisdiction analysis asks, Which *type* of court has the authority over the subject matter of the claim? For example, should the claim be brought in a state court or a federal court? It turns out that, under the United States Constitution, the subject matter jurisdiction of a federal court is ordinarily limited to controversies between parties from different states or disputes that arise under federal statutes or the Constitution itself. Even within the state system, many courts also possess only limited subject matter jurisdiction. For example, a small claims court, true to its name, usually will have jurisdiction only over claims up to a predetermined amount of money. Likewise, a housing court would probably not have subject matter jurisdiction over a defamation claim like the one in my example. But all states have established at least one set of courts with more general subject matter jurisdiction.

The jurisdictional question on which this essay focuses, however, concerns the second issue—personal jurisdiction. With personal jurisdiction, the inquiry is this: Assuming the plaintiff has found the right *type* of court, where, *geographically*, can the lawsuit be brought? Which one of the many courts of that type has the authority to make decisions that will be binding on the parties to the suit? As to the *plaintiff*, this is a relatively easy question. The plaintiff, after all, has chosen to file the suit with a particular court. By bringing the lawsuit and thereby invoking the authority of that court, the plaintiff seems clearly to have consented to be bound by its ultimate rulings. But the *defendant* has not invoked the court's authority or consented to its power. What gives a court the authority to issue binding orders with respect to that defendant?

The resolution of this issue is not merely a matter of theoretical interest. Indeed, the choice of location for a lawsuit may be extraordinarily important to the litigants. For example, in my hypothetical scenario, the English libel law may be substantially different from the law in Canada or in the United States. Although a court in one jurisdiction sometimes will apply the law of another jurisdiction (and there is an entire body of legal doctrine on the subject), it is more often the case that a court will use the law of the jurisdiction in which it sits. Even apart from this choice-of-law issue, litigants may fear that a "hometown" jury or judge will favor the party who resides in the country or state where the court is located. And, of course, it is far more convenient and less costly to litigate closer to home. Finally, there is the issue of whether a court's ruling will later be recognized as valid by other courts.[6] Accordingly, the question of where a suit can be brought carries tremendous significance.[7]

The answer to this question, at least in the United States, was originally grounded in the territorial power of the sovereign. Each sovereign was deemed to have jurisdiction, exclusive of all other sovereigns, to bind persons and things present within its territorial boundaries. This conception of jurisdiction implicitly adopted an idea of "community" as a local territorial unit ruled by a single power. Over the past two hundred years, changes in commerce, transportation, and communications technology have repeatedly challenged both this idea of community and its accompanying jurisdictional rules.

In the nineteenth century, the United States Supreme Court determined that a territorially based conception of jurisdiction was an inherent part of constitutional due process itself. In *Pennoyer v. Neff*, the Court ruled that "[t]he authority of every tribunal is necessarily restricted by the territorial limits of the State in which it is established. Any attempt to exercise authority beyond those limits would be deemed in every other forum . . . an illegitimate assumption of power, and be resisted as mere abuse."[8] According to the Court, although "every State possesses exclusive jurisdiction and sovereignty over persons and property within its territory. . . . No State can exercise direct jurisdiction and authority over persons and property without its territory."[9] The *Pennoyer* decision reflected a conception of jurisdiction based on territorial borders and pure power. The underlying message was, if a state can "tag" you, it can have power over you; if it can "tag" your property, it can have power over your property. Under this formulation, the limits of judicial power were rigidly defined by the boundaries of each state.

By the early twentieth century, growth of interstate commerce and transportation put pressure on the idea that a state's judicial power extended only to its territorial boundary. In particular, the invention of the automobile and the development of the modern corporation meant that faraway entities could inflict harm within a state without actually being present there at the time of a lawsuit. In response, a number of states enacted statutes based on a theory of "consent" to jurisdiction, a theory that the *Pennoyer* Court had recognized as valid.

For example, a Massachusetts statute decreed that an out-of-state motorist using the state's highways would be deemed to have consented to Massachusetts jurisdiction in actions arising from accidents on those highways. The United States Supreme Court ultimately upheld this rather strained notion of consent in 1927.[10] Similarly, most states enacted statutes essentially requiring out-of-state corporations to agree to jurisdiction within the state as a condition of conducting business there. Moreover, even if the corporation did not explicitly agree, it was often viewed as having implicitly consented to state jurisdiction simply by transacting business in the state.[11] Alternatively, courts sometimes ruled that corporations were physically "present" in any state in which that corporation was "doing business," making the corporations subject to jurisdiction regardless of their consent.[12] While allowing more flexibility in the jurisdictional calculus, the concepts of "consent" and "presence" were analytically unsatisfying, in large part because corporations have neither individual wills nor physical reality. Speaking of "consent" to jurisdiction and "presence" in a state was no more than a legal fiction invented to cope with changing economic times (Kurland, 585–586).

Perhaps in response to these societal changes, the Supreme Court, in the 1945 case of *International Shoe Co. v. Washington*, adopted a new test for analyzing jurisdiction. The Court replaced the strict territorial rules of *Pennoyer* with a more flexible due process inquiry based on whether the defendant had sufficient contact with the relevant state such that jurisdiction would be consistent with "traditional notions of fair play and substantial justice."[13] This "minimum contacts" test would be satisfied as long as the "quality and nature of the activity" of the defendant within the state was sufficient "in relation to the fair and orderly administration of the laws which it was the purpose of the due process clause to insure."[14]

Since the decision in *International Shoe*, the minimum contacts test has provided the framework for determining the outer limits of personal jurisdiction under the United States Constitution.[15] Although the test's flexibility is its greatest strength, such flexibility means that the minimum contacts analysis does not provide a clearly defined rule, relying instead on a highly particularized, fact-specific inquiry. Accordingly, it is difficult to be certain in advance how many and what sort of contacts will be enough for a state to exercise jurisdiction under the federal Constitution. The Supreme Court has variously looked to whether defendants have "purposely availed" themselves of the state,[16] whether they could "reasonably anticipate"[17] that they would be sued there, or whether the interests of the plaintiff and the forum state[18] in adjudicating a dispute outweighed the defendant's concerns about increased cost, inconvenience, or potential bias.[19] As transportation and interstate commerce have continued to grow in the decades since 1945, the Supreme Court has many times been called upon to determine how far to expand the reach of personal jurisdiction.[20] I will briefly discuss just two of those cases in order to provide a sense of how difficult the application of the minimum contacts test has been.

In *World-Wide Volkswagen Corporation v. Woodson*, decided in 1980, the defendant, a car dealership, sold a car in New York to a New York resident. Later, the purchaser was injured in an accident while driving the car in Oklahoma. The purchaser filed suit in Oklahoma, naming as defendants the New York dealership and regional distributor, among others. The United States Supreme Court ruled that neither the dealership nor the regional distributor could be sued in Oklahoma because neither of them had any contacts with the state and because it was not reasonably foreseeable that they would be hauled into court there. In so doing, the Court rejected the argument that, because an automobile is mobile by its very design and purpose, it was therefore foreseeable that the car could cause injury beyond the boundaries of the state where it was sold. Instead, the Court held that "the mere unilateral activity of those who claim some relationship with a nonresident defendant cannot satisfy the requirement of contact with the forum State."[21] Nevertheless, the Court permitted Oklahoma to assert jurisdiction over Audi, the manufacturer of the car. The Court distinguished the New York dealership and distributor from the manufacturer because, although the dealership limited its sales to the New York area, Audi itself was attempting to serve a national market. According to the Court, a state may assert "personal jurisdiction over a corporation that delivers its products into the stream of commerce with the expectation that they will be purchased by consumers in the forum State."[22]

Despite the Court's apparent approval of a "stream of commerce" test to establish purposeful contacts with a state, it remains unclear how far this logic extends. Seven years after *World-Wide Volkswagen*, in a different case, four justices indicated that simply placing a product in the stream of commerce would *not* be sufficient to establish jurisdiction wherever that product happened to end up. Instead, these justices would require some sort of "additional conduct" by the defendant that would demonstrate that the defendant had the specific "intent or purpose" to serve the market in the state exercising jurisdiction. Four other justices disagreed, however, arguing that simply placing a product in the stream of commerce was sufficient. The ninth justice found that, based on the facts of the case, jurisdiction was proper under either test and therefore declined to choose between them. As a result, neither rationale achieved a majority.[23]

Because of the Court's fractured opinion, the stream of commerce question was never resolved, and it remains unclear precisely how much contact one may have with a particular jurisdiction before subjecting oneself to the possibility of being sued there. While the strict territorial rule of *Pennoyer* ultimately may have been unsuited to the realities of modern economic life, the *International Shoe* minimum contacts test, with its flexible yet indeterminate approach to territoriality, provides little conceptual grounding for jurisdictional decisions beyond a general appeal to fairness.

## EMERGING CASE LAW ON JURISDICTION AND THE INTERNET

Even this brief survey of Supreme Court doctrine on personal jurisdiction should make it clear how difficult the issue can be. Not surprisingly, the growth of the Internet has added new wrinkles to the minimum contacts test. After all, when I post information on a Web site, it is immediately accessible throughout the world. Have I then "purposely availed" myself of any jurisdiction where someone views that Web site? Can I "reasonably anticipate" that the information posted will be viewed elsewhere? And how should the "stream of commerce" rationale, assuming it is viable at all, be applied to commercial transactions online?

By 1995 such questions were beginning to arise in courts around the country. At first, it appeared that at least some courts would find that the exercise of personal jurisdiction was proper even over defendants whose only contact with the relevant state was an online advertisement available to anyone with Internet access. For example, in *Inset Systems, Inc. v. Instruction Set, Inc.*, a federal district court in Connecticut ruled that it had proper jurisdiction over the defendant, Instruction Set, a Massachusetts-based provider of computer technology, even though Instruction Set maintained no offices in Connecticut and did not conduct regular business there. The court ruled that the defendant's promotional Web site, because it was *accessible* in Connecticut, supported the exercise of jurisdiction in the state. According to the court, the Web site advertisements were directed to all states within the United States. Therefore, Instruction Set had "purposefully availed itself of the privilege of doing business within Connecticut."[24] Similarly, other courts have at times indicated that the posting of a Web site accessible within a state, without any additional contact with that state, might be sufficient to justify jurisdiction.[25]

Although the United States Supreme Court has yet to address the issue of personal jurisdiction based on Internet contacts, some lower courts, perhaps concerned over the broad implications of cases like *Inset*, have attempted to craft a more moderate rule. The most influential case thus far has been *Zippo Manufacturing Co. v. Zippo Dot Com, Inc.* There, the district court applied a "sliding scale" to Internet contacts in order to determine the "nature and quality of commercial activity that an entity conducts over the Internet." On one end of the court's spectrum was a "passive" Web site, where a defendant has simply posted information on the Internet "available to those who are interested." According to the court, such a site, absent additional contact with the forum state or its citizens, would not be enough to support jurisdiction. At the other end of the spectrum, the court placed "active" Web sites where the defendant "enters into contracts with residents of a foreign jurisdiction that involve the knowing and repeated transmission of computer files over the Internet." The existence of an active site would be sufficient to establish jurisdiction anywhere the site is accessed. In between, the court identified a middle ground "occupied by interactive Web sites where a user can exchange information with the host computer. In these cases, the exercise of jurisdiction is determined by examining the level of interactivity and commercial nature of the exchange of information that occurs on the Web site."[26]

Although other courts quickly latched on to the *Zippo* framework,[27] this sliding-scale analysis has proved to be unstable and difficult to apply. First, drawing the distinction between an active and a passive site is often problematic. For example, if my Web site includes only a list of articles I have written, that site appears to be passive under the *Zippo* decision. If I then include a sentence at the bottom of the site inviting readers to e-mail their comments about my articles or providing links to other sites where the full text of the articles can be found, is the addition of that extra material enough to transform my passive site into an active one? And while the active/passive distinction was difficult to draw in 1997, when *Zippo* was decided, the line between active and passive sites is even more blurry now and is likely to become increasingly so in the future, as Web sites grow ever more complex and sophisticated.[28] Ultimately, most sites probably will fall into the middle ground, and "examining the level of interactivity and commercial nature of the exchange of information" is unlikely to yield predictable or consistent results. Moreover, some sites that seem passive may sell advertising based on the number of "hits" the sites receive or collect and market data about the user (Kang, 1226–1229), both of which may seem to render the sites more active.

Perhaps most important, few large organizations or corporations will spend the money necessary (Legard) to create a sophisticated Web site without including some mechanism to earn money back from the site. But if all such sites are deemed interactive under the *Zippo* framework, then they will all subject the site owner to universal jurisdiction, returning us to a solution like the one reached in *Inset*.

Perhaps because of these difficulties, courts already appear to be shifting away from the *Zippo* approach toward a test based on the effect of the activity within the jurisdiction.[29] This test derives from the U.S. Supreme Court's 1984 decision in *Calder v. Jones*,[30] a suit in which a Florida publisher allegedly defamed a California entertainer. In *Calder*, the Court reasoned that, because the plaintiff lived and worked in California and would suffer emotional and perhaps professional harm there, the publisher had deliberately caused harmful effects in California and California could legitimately assert jurisdiction over the case. Thus, under *Calder*'s "effects test," personal jurisdiction may be based on "(1) intentional actions (2) expressly aimed at the forum state (3) causing harm, the brunt of which is suffered—and which the defendant knows is likely to be suffered—in the forum state."[31]

Courts have applied the effects test not only to Internet libel cases,[32] but to a broad range of other Internet-related cases as well. For example, in a domain name trademark suit brought by an Illinois-based retailer of housewares and furniture against an Irish retailer, the court found that the defendant had established minimum contacts with Illinois under the effects doctrine. The court determined that any injury from the infringement of the Illinois retailer's trademark would be felt mainly in Illinois, thereby rendering jurisdiction appropriate there.[33]

In another case opting for the effects test over the *Zippo* framework, a Michigan plaintiff sued a Texas defendant in Michigan, alleging copyright infringement in the design of craft patterns. According to the plaintiff, the Michigan court could properly exercise jurisdiction because the defendant both maintained an interactive Web site accessible to Michigan residents and had sold patterns to Michigan residents on two occasions. The court, however, ruled that jurisdiction was not proper in Michigan. Eschewing the *Zippo* test, the court refused to accept the idea "that the mere act of maintaining a Web site that includes interactive features ipso facto establishes personal jurisdiction over the sponsor of that Web site anywhere in the United States."[34] Further, the court deemed the two Michigan sales an insufficient basis for jurisdiction because they were sold in an eBay auction and therefore the defendant had no say as to where the products would end up.

The discussion of the sales on eBay may signal yet another shift in the case law. Instead of focusing either on the interactivity of the Web site or on the ultimate effect a defendant's activities may cause in a jurisdiction, courts may base jurisdictional decisions on whether a defendant deliberately targets individuals in any particular state. One commentator, advocating such a targeting inquiry, has argued:

> Unlike the *Zippo* approach, a targeting analysis would seek to identify the intentions of the parties and to assess the steps taken to either enter or avoid a particular jurisdiction. Targeting would also lessen the reliance on effects-based analysis, the source of considerable uncertainty since Internet-based activity can ordinarily be said to create some effects in most jurisdictions. (Geist, 598)

At least one federal Court of Appeals has embraced a targeting analysis, ruling that jurisdiction is proper "when the defendant is alleged to have engaged in wrongful conduct targeted at a plaintiff whom the defendant knows to be a resident of the forum state."[35]

Nevertheless, targeting too may ultimately prove to be an unstable test because even if courts embrace this approach they will need to identify criteria to be used in assessing whether a Web site has actually targeted a particular jurisdiction. This will not be an easy task. For example, the American Bar Association Internet Jurisdiction Project, a global study on Internet jurisdiction released in 2000, referred to the language of the site as a potentially significant way of determining whether a site operator has targeted a particular jurisdiction (American Bar Ass'n, 1.4). Thus, for example, a site in French is likely targeting French users. With the development of new language translation capabilities, however, Web site owners may soon be able to create their site in any language they wish, knowing that users will automatically be able to view the site in the user's chosen language. As one commentator notes, "Without universally applicable standards for targeting assessment in the online environment, a targeting-based test is likely to leave further uncertainty in its wake" (Geist, 601).

In sum, although courts have begun to address jurisdictional issues in cyberspace, the efforts are still tentative and not completely satisfying. The problem, of course, is that sovereignty has generally been defined with respect to some physical location. Cyberspace, however, weakens the significance of physical location in a number of different ways.[36] For example, events in cyberspace do not merely cross geographical boundaries, they ignore the existence of the boundaries altogether. Messages can be sent from place to place without any of the physical cues or barriers that customarily keep geographically remote places and people separate from one another. Moreover, many online events and transactions "have no recognizable tie at all to physical places but take place only on the network itself, which, by its very nature, is not a localizable phenomenon" (Post, 160). Indeed, certain online services consist of continuously changing collections of messages that are routed from one network to another across the global network, with no centralized location at all.[37] In addition, the architecture of cyberspace means that many transactions occur between people who do not and cannot know the physical location of the other party, creating a kind of geographical anonymity. Although domain name addresses often include references to countries, those names need not correspond to the location of the server on which the Web site is located. Thus, while it is certainly possible to apply territorially based rules to the online world (as the cases discussed in this section demonstrate), the fit is imperfect at best.

## POSSIBLE RESPONSES TO THE QUESTION OF INTERNET JURISDICTION

Faced with the conceptual uncertainties involved in applying territorially based jurisdictional rules to online interaction, theorists and policymakers have advanced at least three possible responses. First is what might be called the internationalist view. If one of the problems of online interaction is the existence of conflicting state and national laws, then a potential solution is to try to create more-harmonious laws at the national or international level and establish supragovernmental institutions to administer them, thereby decreasing the significance of jurisdiction. In this vein, the World Intellectual Property Organization has attempted to draft uniform rules with regard to intellectual property protection online,[38] the United States and the European Union have recently agreed on a set of principles intended to harmonize their views about the privacy of online transactions,[39] and an international quasi-governmental body has been formed to administer the online domain name system.[40] This approach is similar to trends within international trade more broadly, with the General Agreement on Trade and Tariffs and the World Trade Organization playing an increasing role in the resolution of cross-border disputes.

A second perspective is to see the Internet not as a governance problem requiring international legal bodies but as a radically decentralized environment demanding grassroots, *nongovernmental* lawmaking.[41] Like the internationalist view, this decentralist approach starts from the belief that territorial borders and national (or state) laws have little relevance in cyberspace. Rather than seek international norms imposed by governmental bodies, however, decentralists would defy the ability of governments, even working together, to control from the top down the vast, spontaneously regenerating network of cyberspace. Instead, they would see government regulation itself as inherently foreign to the networked environment.[42] The decentralist vision asks us to think of cyberspace not merely as a network that *crosses* sovereign boundaries, but as a distinct *place* (or set of places) in and of itself, where the rules are generated by each Web site or each service provider, rather than by geographical sovereigns.

Finally, we could take the position that the Internet does not destabilize territorially based lawmaking at all.[43] Instead, we could view the Internet as merely another communications device that may create some difficult problems, but none that requires rethinking traditional jurisdictional rules. Indeed, the existence of cross-border transactions is not a new phenomenon, and arguably our jurisdictional rules and choice-of-law principles are sufficiently flexible to adapt to advances in industry, transportation, and communication. Accordingly, one might conclude that no new paradigm is necessary.

All these positions, which have been debated extensively in the legal literature, are attractive in different ways, and in this essay I do not necessarily wish to support any one over the others or to provide a detailed discussion of the arguments. Instead, I note only that the debate usually has been pitched, either implicitly or explicitly, as a question of political philosophy: When does a sovereign have legitimate power? As a result, the discussion tends to pit social contract arguments regarding the consent of the governed against theories supporting the state's pure power to exercise control over acts or effects within its territory.

These are important issues, but I think the uncertainty and possible incoherence of jurisdictional rules with regard to the Internet offer us a good opportunity to think about what jurisdiction is and what it means as a broader cultural matter, and not just as an issue of political philosophy. How are our ideas about jurisdiction shaped by our changing sense of geographical space? And why might it be important psychologically or symbolically for a community to assert jurisdiction over an actor? These are the questions to which I will now turn.

## SOCIAL MEANINGS EMBEDDED IN THE CONCEPT OF JURISDICTION

In this final section, I wish to make three tentative observations about the idea of jurisdiction, all of which are intended to encourage scholars (both in law and in other disciplines) to consider the *social* meaning of jurisdiction, and not just its legal or philosophical rationales. First, our choice of jurisdictional rules not only reflects our ideas about political sovereignty but also articulates and reinforces our cultural intuitions about physical location, distance, and geography. Thus it may be fruitful to study more closely the relationship between jurisdiction and the social construction of space. Second, the exercise of jurisdiction may have a symbolic function in helping a community to assert its dominion and therefore its social order over an external threat to that order. And third, the very act of asserting jurisdiction may also serve symbolically to extend community membership to whoever is brought within the society's reach. These observations suggest that the exercise of jurisdiction has important cultural and psychological ramifications that have not been explored adequately in our legal discussions of jurisdictional rules. Moreover, serious study of the social meaning of jurisdiction and its relation to conceptions of geographical space, community membership, and boundaries is especially important given the broad cultural changes brought about by the rise of online interaction.

### Jurisdiction and the Social Meaning of Physical Space

Jurisdictional rules do not simply emerge from a utilitarian calculus about the most efficient forum for adjudicating a dispute. Rather, the exercise of jurisdiction is also part of the way in which a society demarcates space, delineates communities, and draws both physical and symbolic boundaries. Such boundaries do not exist as an intrinsic part of the physical world; they are a social construction. As a result, our choice of jurisdictional rules reflects the attitudes and perceptions that members of a community hold toward their geography and the physical spaces in which they live.

Although it has become commonplace for cultural critics and others to identify the ways in which social structures shape and constrain our conduct, the link between social structure and physical space has received less attention.[44] Nevertheless, "the production of space and place is both the medium and the outcome of human agency and social relations" (Pred, 10). This cultural construction of space includes the decisions we make about land use and zoning, the appropriation and transformation of "nature" as both a concept and a physical description, the use of specialized locations for the conduct of economic, cultural, and social practices, the creation of patterns of movement within a community, and "the formation of symbolically laden, meaning-filled, ideology-projecting sites and areas" (Pred, 10).

In addition, we must understand the differences between *topological* space, which consists of the formal boundary lines we have chosen, and *social* space, which includes the meanings given to space (both local and nonlocal), to the distances between delineated spaces, and to the time necessary to traverse those distances (Kogan, 634). For example, in the United States a hundred-mile automobile trip may seem like a greater journey to residents of the Northeast, who are accustomed to relatively short distances between destinations, than to residents of the West, where cities and towns are more dispersed. Similarly, a thousand-mile trip carries a very different social meaning today, in the age of relatively inexpensive air travel, than it did a hundred years ago, even if the topological space remains the same. And of course America's well-documented postwar demographic shift from city to suburb is not merely a change of topography but a politically and symbolically significant cultural transformation.

The social meaning of geographical space also includes the way in which an individual or community perceives those who are *outside* the community's topological or social boundaries. While people tend to develop attitudes of familiarity toward the spaces in which they reside and conduct their daily activities, they may come to view unfamiliar people and locations as alien, forbidding, or foreign. Or, alternatively, the outside "other" can be seen as inviting, friendly, and hospitable, or as mysterious, exotic, and romantic. These are just a few examples of the infinite variety of possible attitudes one may hold toward unfamiliar social spaces. "These attitudes will be influenced by a host of factors, including the political governance of that 'other' location, the socio-economic involvement that the individual has on a daily basis with that other location, and the extent of contact that a person has . . . with that other location" (Kogan, 637).

Jurisdictional rules cannot fully be understood without studying the relationship of such rules to conceptions of social space. For example, the territorially based jurisdictional principle articulated in the nineteenth century by the Supreme Court in *Pennoyer v. Neff* does not merely reflect a preference for such a rule as a matter of political philosophy. Rather, *Pennoyer*'s emphasis on state boundaries derives in part from the reality of social space in the United States at the time.

Historian Robert Wiebe has observed that

> America during the nineteenth century was a society of island communities. Weak communication severely restricted the interaction among these islands and dispersed the power to form opinion and enact public policy. . . . The heart of American democracy was local autonomy. A century after France had developed a reasonably efficient, centralized public administration, Americans could not even conceive of a managerial government. Almost all of a community's affairs were still arranged informally. (Wiebe, xiii)

According to Wiebe, geographical loyalties tended to inhibit connections with a whole society. "Partisanship . . . grew out of lives narrowly circumscribed by a community or neighborhood. For those who considered the next town or the next city block alien territory, such refined, deeply felt loyalties served both as a defense against outsiders and as a means of identification within" (Wiebe, 27).

As the nineteenth century progressed, massive socioeconomic changes brought an onslaught of seemingly "alien" presences into these island communities. Immigrants were the most obvious group of outsiders, but perhaps just as frightening was the emergence of powerful distant forces such as insurance companies, major manufacturers, railroads, and the national government itself. Significantly, these threats appear to have been conceived largely in spatial terms. According to Wiebe, Americans responded by reaffirming community self-determination and preserving old ways and values from "outside" invasion (Wiebe, 52–58).

Given such a social context, it is not surprising that the jurisdictional rules of the period emphasized state territorial boundaries. Indeed, as even this brief (and obviously incomplete) discussion indicates, the burdens of litigating in another state far exceeded simply the time and expense of travel, substantial as those burdens were. Just as important was the *psychic* burden of being forced to defend oneself in a foreign state, which may have felt little different from the idea of defending oneself in a foreign country. An 1874 Pennsylvania state court decision issued shortly before *Pennoyer* illustrates the extent of this psychic burden. In the case, a resident of New York had contested jurisdiction in Pennsylvania. The court acknowledged that the Pennsylvania courthouse was only "a few hours' travel by railroad" from New York, but nevertheless ruled that the defendant could not be sued personally, in part because "nothing can be more unjust than to drag a man thousands of miles, perhaps from a distant state, and in effect compel him to appear."[45] The court disregarded the relatively slight literal burden in the case at hand, and instead focused on the specter of being "dragged" to a "distant state" located "thousands of miles" away. The decision even equated other states with foreign countries, referring to a "defendant living in a remote state or foreign country . . . [who] becomes subject to the jurisdiction of this, to him, foreign tribunal."[46] These passages indicate that the psychic significance of defending oneself in another state was an important factor in the court's analysis.

Both the literal and psychic burdens associated with out-of-state litigation changed as a result of the urban industrial revolution at the turn of the twentieth century, a revolution that profoundly altered American social space. Increasingly, most economic and governmental activities were administered from afar by impersonal managers at centralized locations. In such a world, another state was likely to be viewed less as a foreign country and more as yet another distant power center, just one of many "anonymous, bureaucratic, regulatory bodies in an increasingly complex society" (Kogan, 651).

In addition, advances in transportation and communications helped to weaken territoriality as the central category through which Americans understood their space. "As long as daily lives were focused to a large extent on the local, a state boundary symbolized the edge of the world, and everything outside that boundary was alien and foreign" (Kogan, 652). With increased mobility, however, Americans regularly crossed state boundaries by train, by car, and in the air, which inevitably diminished the sense that other places were alien. The rise of radio and television meant that events in other states could become a regular part of one's daily consciousness. And the functional interdependence that has characterized the United States in this century has meant that almost all of us are regularly affected by people, institutions, and events located far away.

In this altered social space, the call to defend a lawsuit in the courts of another state remains an imposition, but the burdens are no longer perceived in simple territorial terms. In other words, though many economic and practical burdens remain, the psychic burden is no longer as strong. Thus, it is not surprising that *International Shoe* substituted a flexible "fairness" test for the more rigidly territorial scheme of *Pennoyer*.

So now we must ask whether, with the rise of global capitalism and the Internet, our sense of social space has shifted once again. As many commentators on globalization have observed, peoples around the world now share economic space to a greater degree than ever before, in large part because of the increase in online interaction. Modern electronic communications, record-keeping, and trading capacities have allowed the world financial markets to become so powerful that the actions of individual territorial governments often appear to be ineffectual by comparison. Essential services, such as computer programming, can easily be "shipped" across national boundaries and can even be produced multinationally. The international production and distribution of merchandise means that communities around the country (and even around the world) increasingly purchase the same name-brand goods and shop at the same stores. Our online communities (to the extent that we are willing to call them communities) ignore territoriality altogether and instead are organized around shared interests. We fly more than ever, carry telephones and laptop computers with us as we travel, and keep in touch by e-mail. All these changes radically reshape our relationship with our geography. If that is so, then do territorially based courts make sense any longer, even with the looser jurisdictional rules established in *International Shoe*?

I do not presume to have a definitive answer to this question, but I do suggest that whatever the answers might be, they must respond not only to questions of efficiency or political theory but also to the changing social meaning of physical space. For example, it is possible that the psychic burden of foreign jurisdiction is less significant today because of our increased contact with foreign places. On the other hand, we may feel the need to cling even more tenaciously to localism in the face of the encroaching global economic system. Thus we must study more closely the psychological and symbolic meanings that may be embedded within the idea of jurisdiction. The following two sections offer an example of the shape such study might take.

### Jurisdiction and the Assertion of Community Dominion

When a transgressor behaves in some way contrary to society's moral code, the community can come to view the transgressor in one of two ways. First, the community can close ranks by defining itself in opposition to the transgressor and by treating the transgression purely as an *external* threat. Or, second, the community can claim dominion over the transgression by conceptualizing the transgressor as a member of the community who has committed what might be considered an *internal* offense.

The definition of a threat as internal or external is, in part, a question of jurisdiction. When a community exercises legal jurisdiction, it is symbolically asserting its dominion over an actor. This jurisdictional reach can serve to transform what otherwise might have been considered an external threat into an internal adjudication. Accordingly, the assertion of jurisdiction can be seen as one way that communities domesticate chaos.

I have written previously about the surprisingly widespread and elaborate practice in medieval Europe and ancient Greece of putting on trial animals and inanimate objects that caused harm to human beings (Berman 2000; Berman 1994). Although such trials may seem far removed from any discussion of contemporary jurisdictional rules, I believe they illuminate the symbolic content of such rules. In deciding how to respond to acts of violence or depredation caused by animals, communities were faced with a choice of whether to view the acts as internal or external threats. Random acts of violence caused by insensate agents undoubtedly brought a deep feeling of lawlessness—not so much the fear of laws being broken but the far worse fear that the world might not be a lawful place at all (Humphrey, xxv). To combat such a fear, it may have been essential to view the animals not as uncontrollable natural forces belonging to the outside world, but as members of the community who could actually break the community's laws. By asserting dominion over the animals, members of communities could assure themselves that even if the social order had been violated, at least there was *some* order, and not simply undifferentiated chaos.

The scrupulous concern for according due process to animal transgressors can be seen as a necessary part of restoring this sense of social order. After all, simply lashing out to destroy the animal would continue to imply that the animal was an uncontrollable "other," a part of the "natural" world that could not be reasoned with or domesticated. Such "unlawful" punishment might even mean that the community had symbolically succumbed to the disorder of the natural world and that it was now propelled into an ongoing war with forces of darkness it could not control. Just as retaliatory acts of a lynch mob are unlikely to restore a sense of order to a community, so too punishment of animals without legal procedures could well have increased a sense of impending chaos.

Instead, the trials implicitly adopted a narrative asserting that animals, along with human beings, were *part of* a community and *subject to* universal norms of justice. Paradoxically, even though the trials often resulted in the execution of the individual animal, the proceedings, by their very nature, first ensured that the animal was conceptualized as a member of the community. Just as the animal trials implicitly communicated a symbolic message that nonhuman transgressors were nevertheless subject to human control, so too our contemporary notions of jurisdiction continue to be linked to how we define the limits of the community and who should be within its dominion.[47] This exercise of jurisdiction, in and of itself, can be part of the process of healing after the breach of a social norm. For example, a person injured by a defective product may feel powerless to affect the behavior of a distant, seemingly uncontrollable corporation. Indeed, while animals may have been viewed as an uncontrollable "other" in medieval Europe, the products of global capitalism today likewise may seem to be external forces of destruction that obey only their own law. By bringing the corporation within local jurisdiction, the individual and the community may feel they have regained some control over their world.

Finally, the need to assert community dominion may also be a significant part of our desire to use legal and quasi-legal proceedings to respond to atrocities such as war crimes or crimes against humanity. For example, the trial of accused Nazi war criminal Klaus Barbie, held in France several years ago, arguably was concerned less with punishing the individual (who, after all, was extremely old and in failing health at the time of the trial) than with asserting the community's authority and sense of control after a horrific and chaotic human tragedy.

The rise of online communication may create increased pressure to assert community dominion over the activities of outsiders. A foreign

Web site can easily breach community boundaries and threaten community order. For example, material that a community might wish to ban nevertheless may be readily accessible from Web sites outside the bounds of that community. Likewise, a community that adopts strict consumer protection laws to regulate corporate activity may feel threatened when outside businesses can ignore the local laws through Internet sales.[48] These "external" threats appear to flout local norms.

It is against this backdrop that we may understand the seemingly extreme position of the district court in *Inset*. There the court ruled that, if an individual's Web site is accessible in a community, then the community can claim dominion over that individual. Similarly, a French court recently asserted jurisdiction over the American company Yahoo because Yahoo's American servers, accessible in France, permitted French citizens to access Nazi memorabilia, in violation of French law.[49]

Although we may ultimately decide that such an approach is impractical or unsatisfying for other reasons, we must understand that the impulse to assert jurisdiction over an outsider who "invades" a community via the Internet is tied to the need to assert dominion in order to domesticate external chaos. On the other hand, we will tend to view the jurisdictional puzzle quite differently if we think of the online interaction not as a foreign Web site "sending" information into a community but rather as members of a community choosing to "travel" to a foreign Web site to obtain information. Thus the metaphors we use to conceptualize online interaction may help determine our responses to jurisdictional questions.

## Jurisdiction and the Extension of Community Membership

The previous section discussed how the exercise of jurisdiction functions in part as a symbolic assertion of community *dominion*. A corollary to this observation is that the exercise of jurisdiction also symbolically extends a form of community *membership*. As discussed above, a true outsider is either fought as an external threat or ignored entirely. By exercising jurisdiction, a community constructs a narrative whereby the outsider is not truly an outsider but is in some way a member of that community.

A rather extreme example of this phenomenon is the death sentence issued in the Islamic world against author Salman Rushdie.

Chances are that if I had written the same novel as Rushdie, I would not have been treated in the same way. Instead, it is likely that I would have been dismissed as a total outsider or targeted in an ad hoc fashion as a purely external threat. The death sentence therefore reflects the fact that Rushdie was considered a *member* of the Islamic community. Even this violent exercise of jurisdiction acted in part to extend community membership.

Similarly, by prosecuting war criminals we are insisting that the defendants are members of the world community. The assertion of jurisdiction therefore can be seen as an educative tool and not simply an exercise of coercive power. The community, in effect, tells the defendants that they share a membership bond with the rest of the world and therefore cannot simply impose their will with impunity. Meanwhile, the assertion of jurisdiction also implicitly delivers a message to the public at large that the defendants are neither subhuman nor the product of chaotic fate but are instead members of the world community, to be considered in their full humanity and punished according to human law.

This idea of jurisdiction as the assertion of community membership may also have relevance in evaluating the usefulness of alternative legal procedures aimed at restorative justice, such as the growing use of truth commissions as a mechanism for societal reconciliation. For example, the Truth and Reconciliation Commission (TRC) proceedings in South Africa have attempted to restore psychic membership in the South African community to both victims and perpetrators. Instead of a criminal prosecution against a nonparticipative "other," as at the trial of Adolf Eichmann after World War II,[50] the TRC required that those perpetrators seeking amnesty first acknowledge the community's jurisdiction by appearing before the commission, and then describe their misdeeds to the entire nation. Likewise, victims who for years were not recognized as full-fledged members of the South African community were given a forum to speak about their pain and enter into the community's legal system instead of remaining outside of it. The TRC proceedings, therefore, implicitly expressed the hope that victims, perpetrators, and spectators could all be integrated into the new South African community.

Even in more commonplace legal proceedings, the idea of jurisdiction as a way of asserting community membership may be important.

For example, while a community may need to assert its dominion over the products of a distant corporation in order to feel some control over seemingly random misfortune, it may also be that, because of the potential exercise of local jurisdiction, a multinational corporation comes to conceive of itself as a corporate citizen of many different localities. Accordingly, the exercise of jurisdiction may encourage corporations to rethink their sense of responsibility to communities far beyond the boundaries of their corporate headquarters.

In addition, the ability to assert the jurisdiction of a court may give people some sense of *their own* membership in the community. A prison inmate bringing a civil rights action against an abusive guard, for example, may feel vindicated simply by the fact that he or she is able to invoke the jurisdiction of a court. Regardless of outcome, the fact that the inmate's grievance is aired and considered, however briefly, may give a marginal member of society more of a sense of community affiliation.[51] As a result, the assertion of community dominion may be therapeutic both for the community, which can assert its control over otherwise uncontrollable behavior, and for the individual, who achieves a form of community membership through the legal process. Even a criminal defendant is implicitly deemed to be a member of the community who has gone astray (and therefore retains certain rights), rather than a purely external pariah (who has none).

The assertion of community membership is relevant to discussions of Internet jurisdiction as well. As discussed previously, the growth of electronic communications is closely linked to our increasing global economic and psychological interdependence. Indeed, it is probably no coincidence that the terms "globalization" and "cyberspace" have become clichés almost simultaneously. Online interaction contributes to our awareness of outsiders and our sense of connection with them. People develop friendships and business relationships regardless of physical proximity; they may even fall in love online. Many of the psychic bonds that in a previous era were shared only within the confines of one's local community now stretch far beyond any single geographical location. Given this change in economic and psychological interdependence, it would not be surprising to see the definition of community membership change as well. And, if jurisdiction is one of the ways we express our intuitions about community membership, then jurisdictional rules, in turn, must evolve. Otherwise, we will risk being trapped in a legal doctrine that no longer represents the reality of modern life, just as we were during the first half of the twentieth century, when courts struggled to expand the strict territorial rule of *Pennoyer*.

Those who have been reading this essay hoping to discover a definitive answer to the jurisdictional puzzle posed by my hypothetical defamation case may be disappointed (but perhaps not surprised) to learn that the result is not at all clear under current law. Perhaps the fact that the Canadian student made false statements about a British citizen is enough to say that the student "targeted" Great Britain with his e-mail message, which might make British jurisdiction appropriate. The same logic could also render the university amenable to suit in Great Britain, but the university's indirect and noneconomic role would be a strong argument against subjecting the university to British jurisdiction. Intriguingly, the student and the university likely would be required to advance their jurisdictional arguments in a British court, at least initially. And of course Great Britain has its own jurisdictional rules and traditions, which are beyond the scope of this essay. Nevertheless, even if the physicist wins his suit in Great Britain, unless the defendants have assets there he will probably be required to convince a United States or Canadian court that it should enforce the judgment. How such courts would treat the British judgment in these circumstances is also uncertain. Thus, we can see that our jurisdictional rules can be quite unilluminating with respect to claims arising from online interactions.

As this essay has attempted to demonstrate, however, the probable outcome of this case under current jurisdictional rules is not the only relevant question to ask. Indeed, in the long run, such a question may not even be the most important one. Therefore, rather than attempt to decide which country might exercise jurisdiction over the online defamation, we could ask instead what the concept of a territorial sovereign even means in the context of an online dispute such as this. Or we could ask whether British jurisdiction would properly reflect our intuitions about distance, foreignness, and the relationship between topological and social boundaries. Or we could consider whether the exercise of jurisdiction might fulfill the local community's need to assert dominion over the acts of the defendants and whether there might be some benefit to the defendants from being made symbolic members of the local British community (however that community might be defined). Or we could go still farther and question not only the conception of community implicit in jurisdictional rules but also the continued viability of maintaining the idea of a single, legally cognizable "Self." Perhaps we may ultimately perceive multiple legal entities within one persona, including both a traceable geographic identity and other legal identities tied to an e-mail address or a Web site or an online chat room. Likewise, we might ask whether territorially defined nation-states are any longer the relevant entities to consider when asking about community membership. And, of course, there are dozens of other questions we might ask about the social and symbolic significance of the assertion of jurisdiction.

My aim here is not to propose a new jurisdictional test or to make normative judgments about when jurisdiction might be proper. Indeed, recognizing the symbolic or psychological significance embedded in the assertion of jurisdiction is unlikely to result in a clearly defined rule for jurisdiction on the Internet or anywhere else. Nevertheless, such an understanding does yield an added framework for discussion of jurisdictional issues.

Accordingly, I argue only that jurisdictional rules necessarily must evolve alongside changes in our conceptions of distance, community definition, and boundaries. Moreover, it is not enough simply to assert, without serious consideration, that the *International Shoe* minimum contacts test is flexible enough to be adapted to the online environment. Obviously a test based on generalized conceptions of fairness *can* be applied to cyberspace. The real question is whether such an adaptation will truly capture the reality of our lives in the twenty-first century. And in order to answer *that* question, we must first take seriously the social meaning of jurisdictional rules. Thus, legal theorists attempting to study or formulate such rules must account for changes in the social meaning of jurisdiction and not simply argue about jurisdiction as a matter of political philosophy, logistical efficiency, or historical precedent.

Scholars in fields other than law could also profitably focus their attention on the legal doctrine surrounding jurisdictional rules. As we have seen, such rules historically have been one of the fault lines in the transition from one set of ideas about our topological and social environment to the next. As a result, the law of jurisdiction provides a useful case study for trying to understand how our ideas about physical space and community develop over time. Those who wish to analyze our social, political, and psychological intuitions about the online world, therefore, would do well to study the various ways in which courts are wrestling with the problem of jurisdiction.

In short, scholars from many different disciplinary backgrounds have much to offer each other with regard to the idea of legal jurisdiction. By seeking a more complex understanding of jurisdiction, we can help not only to develop appropriate legal rules for a changing cultural context but also to articulate the social and symbolic significance of those rules.

## NOTES

An earlier version of this essay was presented at a faculty workshop sponsored by the Department of Translation Studies, State University of New York at Binghamton. My thanks to the participants in the workshop for their many insightful questions and comments. In addition, I thank Laura A. Dickinson, Lisa Kloppenberg, and David G. Post for their invaluable criticism of earlier drafts, and Bryan A. Carey, Dorothy Puzio, and Allison Rohrer for diligent research assistance. A greatly expanded elaboration of the central argument presented here can be found at: Paul Schiff Berman, "The Globalization of Jurisdiction" U. Penn L. Rev. 151 (2002): 311–529.

1. There might also be questions regarding whether British, Canadian, or American law should be applied to the controversy, but this essay is confined to the jurisdictional inquiry.

2. *International Shoe Co. v. Washington*, 326 U.S. 310, 316 (1945) (internal quotation marks omitted).

3. Although the term "Internet" is not technically accurate here, I use it generically to refer to the entire global network of linked computers.

4. For a discussion of the case, see Tokasz.

5. It is beyond the scope of this essay to discuss the variety of jurisdictional rules that exist around the world. In Europe, the Brussels Convention on Jurisdiction and the Enforcement of Judgments in Civil and Commercial Matters has attempted to create some uniform limitations on assertions of jurisdiction within the European Union, but only with regard to defendants domiciled in a member state. For example, although a country such as France faces limitations in its ability to exercise jurisdiction over a British national, the Brussels Convention provides no such limitations with regard to the exercise of French jurisdiction over an American domiciliary (Clermont, 100–106; Morse). The

United States, through the Hague Conference on Private International Law, has initiated an effort to adopt a worldwide treaty on jurisdiction and judgments, but there is no telling whether such a treaty will be approved or what its precise provisions will be (Clermont, 103–105).

6. For example, the British House of Lords was recently forced to decide whether to permit the extradition of former Argentine head of state Augusto Pinochet to Spain to stand trial before a Spanish court. Although the Lords' decision to permit extradition was in the context of a criminal (rather than a civil) case, one of the key disputed questions was whether the Spanish court possessed proper jurisdiction over Pinochet under international law. For a discussion of the decision, see Reid; see generally *Regina v. Bow Street Metropolitan Stipendiary Magistrate et al. (ex parte Pinochet)*, 2 All. E.R. 97 (1999).

7. Some commentators argue that the significance of the location of a lawsuit has been overstated. They contend that, especially given the relative ease of modern transportation and communication, it is no longer true that a party will have significant difficulty litigating in a distant court. According to one author, the obsessive concern of courts regarding personal jurisdiction is just as silly as a belief "that an accused is more concerned with where he will be hanged than whether" (Silberman, 88).

Recent empirical work by Clermont and Eisenberg, however, indicates that, of three million cases terminated in the U.S. federal district courts in recent years, the plaintiffs' rate of winning drops from 58 percent of judgments to only 29 percent when the case has been transferred by the court to a new venue. Thus it appears that plaintiffs win more often when they get to choose the location. Although there may be other reasons for transferred cases' resulting in lower win rates for plaintiffs, the large difference probably indicates that choice of location continues to play a significant role in the outcome of the case (to say nothing of the potential difference in the expense of litigation).

Moreover, there can be little doubt that, with respect to *international* litigation, the choice of location remains crucial. As compared to the relatively minor variations of law within the United States, there may be extremely large differences in both the substantive and the procedural law to be applied from country to country, and the traditional concerns about local bias and increased expense are likely to have at least some continued significance.

8. 95 U.S. 714, 720 (1877).

9. Id. at 722.

10. *Hess v. Pawloski*, 274 U.S. 352 (1927).

11. See, e.g., *Smolik v. Philadelphia & Reading Co.*, 222 F. 148 (SDNY 1915).

12. See, e.g., *Philadelphia & Reading Ry. Co. v. McKibbin*, 243 U.S. 264, 265 (1917) ("A foreign corporation is amenable to process to enforce a personal liability, in the absence of consent, only if it is doing business within the State in

such a manner and to such extent as to warrant the inference that it is present there").

13. *International Shoe*, 326 U.S. at 316 (internal quotation marks omitted).

14. Id. at 319.

15. The minimum contacts test establishes only the outer limit for the exercise of personal jurisdiction. Although no state can assert jurisdiction *beyond* that which the federal Constitution allows, a state may choose to exercise *less* than the full authority granted by the Constitution. Some states have crafted their own statutes that voluntarily restrict their jurisdiction over out-of-state defendants further than the federal Constitution requires. In those states, courts may exercise personal jurisdiction only if the case falls within the limits of the state statute *and* jurisdiction is permitted under the federal Constitution.

16. See *Hanson v. Denckla*, 357 U.S. 235, 253 (1958).

17. See *World-Wide Volkswagen Corp. v. Woodson*, 444 U.S. 286, 297 (1980).

18. The "forum state" is the jurisdiction where the lawsuit is being heard.

19. See *Burger King v. Rudzewicz*, 471 U.S. 462, 476–477 (1985).

20. Indeed, the Supreme Court issued at least twelve major personal jurisdiction decisions between 1976 and 1990 alone. See *Burnham v. Superior Court*, 495 U.S. 604 (1990); *Omni Capital Intl., Ltd. v. Rudolf Wolff & Co.*, 484 U.S. 97 (1987); *Asahi Metal Indus. Co. v. Superior Court*, 480 U.S. 102 (1987); *Phillips Petroleum Co. v. Shutts*, 472 U.S. 797 (1985); *Burger King Corp. v. Rudzewicz*, 471 U.S. 462 (1985); *Helicopteros Nacionales de Colombia, S. A. v. Hall*, 466 U.S. 408 (1984); *Keeton v. Hustler Magazine, Inc.*, 465 U.S. 770 (1984); *Calder v. Jones*, 465 U.S. 783 (1984); *Insurance Corp. Of Ireland v. Compagnie des Bauxites de Guinee*, 456 U.S. 694 (1982); *World-Wide Volkswagen Corp. v. Woodson*, 444 U.S. 286 (1980); *Kulko v. Superior Court*, 436 U.S. 84 (1978); *Shaffer v. Heitner*, 433 U.S. 186 (1977).

21. *World-Wide Volkswagen*, 444 U.S. 286, 298 (1980) (internal quotation marks omitted).

22. Id.

23. See generally *Asahi Metal Indus. Co. v. Superior Court*, 480 U.S. 102 (1987).

24. *Inset Systems*, 937 F. Supp. 161, 165 (D. Conn. 1996).

25. For example, in *Maritz Inc. v. CyberGold, Inc.*, 947 F. Supp. 1328 (E.D. Mo. 1996), the court found jurisdiction in Missouri over a California corporation. Although the defendant's Web server was located in California, the court noted that the disputed Web site was "continually accessible to every internet-connected computer in Missouri" (id. at 1330). According to the court, "CyberGold has consciously decided to transmit advertising information to all internet users, knowing that such information will be transmitted globally. Thus, CyberGold's contacts are of such a quality and nature, albeit a very new quality and nature for personal jurisdiction jurisprudence, that they favor the

exercise of personal jurisdiction over defendant" (id. at 1333). Similarly, in *Humphrey v. Granite Gate Resorts, Inc.*, 568 N.W.2d 715 (Minn. 1997), the Minnesota Supreme Court ruled that the state attorney general's office could sue an online gambling service in Minnesota even though the service was based outside of the state. Relying on *Inset* and *Maritz*, the court determined that the defendants had "purposefully availed themselves of the privilege of doing business in Minnesota" (id. at 721), based on a finding that "computers located throughout the United States, including Minnesota, accessed appellants' websites" (id. at 718). See also, e.g., *Telco Communications v. An Apple a Day*, 977 F. Supp. 404, 407 (E.D. Va. 1997) (a Web site available twenty-four hours a day in the forum state constituted "a persistent course of conduct" in the state); *Heroes, Inc. v. Heroes Found.*, 958 F. Supp. 1, 5 (D.D.C. 1996) (suggesting that the existence of a Web site might be deemed a sustained contact with the forum because "it has been possible for a . . . resident [of the forum] to gain access to it at any time since it was first posted").

26. *Zippo Manufacturing*, 952 F. Supp. 1119, 1124 (W.D. Pa. 1997).

27. See, e.g., *Resnick v. Manfredy*, 52 F. Supp. 2d 462, 467–468 (E.D. Pa. 1999) (holding that a Web site with downloadable order forms was not interactive because the forms had to be submitted by mail); *Fix My PC, L.L.C. v. N.F.N. Assocs., Inc.*, 48 F. Supp. 2d 640, 643 (N.D. Tx. 1999) (holding that the defendant's Web site contained only passive advertising regarding his PC repair business).

28. As one commentator has observed:

> When the text was developed in 1997, an active Web site might have featured little more than an email link and some basic correspondence functionality. Today, sites with that level of interactivity would likely be viewed as passive, since the entire spectrum of passive versus active has shifted upward together with improved technology. In fact, it can be credibly argued that sites must constantly re-evaluate their position on the passive versus active spectrum as Web technology changes. (Geist, 597)

29. See, e.g., *American Info. Corp. v. American Infometrics, Inc.*, 139 F. Supp. 2d 696, 702–02 (D. Md. 2001); *Nissan Motor Co. Ltd. v. Nissan Computer Corp.*, 89 F. Supp. 2d 1154, 1160 (C.D. Cal. 2000).

30. 465 U.S. 783 (1984).

31. *Core-Vent Corp. v. Nobel Indus. AB*, 11 F.3d 1482, 1486 (9th Cir. 1993) (applying *Calder*).

32. See, e.g., *Blakey v. Continental Airlines, Inc.*, 164 N.J. 38, 70 (2000) (ruling that New Jersey can exercise jurisdiction over nonresident defendants who posted allegedly defamatory messages on electronic bulletin board of their New Jersey–based employer).

33. See *Euromark Designs, Inc. v. Crate & Barrel, Ltd.*, 96 F. Supp. 2d 824, 835–36 (N.D. Ill. 2000).

34. *Winfield Collection, Ltd. v. McCauley*, 105 F. Supp. 2d 746, 751 (E.D. Mich., 2000).

35. *Bancroft & Masters Inc. v. Augusta National Inc.*, 223 F.3d 1082, 1087 (9th Cir. 2000); see also, e.g., *American Info Corp. v. American Infometrics, Inc.*, 139 F. Supp. 2d 696, 700 (D. Md. 2001) (ruling that "[a] company's sales activities focusing generally on customers located throughout the United States and Canada without focusing on and targeting the forum state do not yield personal jurisdiction.") (internal quotation marks omitted).

36. My discussion of these three conceptual difficulties is based on arguments made by David Post (Post, 159–163).

37. Distributed message databases such as USENET newsgroups are perhaps the most prominent examples of such decentralized services, though "peer-to-peer" sites that link users' computers without a centralized server are also gaining in popularity.

38. According to a statement by President Clinton, the WIPO Copyright Treaty and the Performances and Phonograms Treaty, both negotiated in 1996, "grant writers, artists, and other creators of copyrighted material global protection from piracy in the digital age." William J. Clinton, Statement on Signing the Digital Millennium Copyright Act, 34 Weekly Comp. Pres. Doc. 2168 (Nov. 2, 1998). Some, though not all, of the treaty's provisions were enacted into United States law in 1998 as part of the Digital Millennium Copyright Act, Pub. L. No. 105–304, 112 Stat. 2860 (1998).

39. See U.S. Int'l Trade Comm'n, "Joint Report on Data Protection Dialogue to the EU/US Summit, 21 June 1999." 1 July 1999 http://www.ita.doc.gov/ecom/jointreport2617.htm. These principles were enacted in the United States as administrative agency rules. See Safe Harbor Principles, 65 Fed. Reg. 45, 666 (July 24, 2000).

40. See "Memorandum of Understanding between the U.S. Department of Commerce and the Internet Corporation for Assigned Names and Numbers." http://www.ntia.doc.gov/ntiahome/domainname/icann-memorandum.htm.

41. See, e.g., Johnson and Post.

42. John Perry Barlow's now famous "Declaration of the Independence of Cyberspace" forcefully expresses this sentiment: "Governments of the Industrial World, you weary giants of flesh and steel, I come from Cyberspace, the new home of Mind. On behalf of the future, I ask you of the past to leave us alone. . . . I declare the global social space we are building to be naturally independent of the tyrannies you seek to impose on us. You have no moral right to rule us nor do you possess any methods of enforcement we have true reason to fear. . . . Your legal concepts of property, expression, identity, move-

ment, and context do not apply to us. They are based on matter, There is no matter here."

43. See, e.g., Goldsmith, Stein.

44. One notable exception within legal scholarship is an article by Terry S. Kogan that describes the academic discipline of critical human geography and then attempts to link the observations of that discipline to America's jurisdictional rules. Although the article was published in 1991 and therefore does not discuss the Internet, my discussion in this section owes a great debt to Kogan's illuminating work.

45. *Coleman's Appeal*, 75 Pa. 441, 457 (1874).

46. Id.

47. For a related perspective on jurisdiction, see generally Cover.

48. Indeed, such e-commerce issues have caused the European Union to change course several times in recent years regarding jurisdiction over Internet sales. In early summer 2000, an EU Directive enshrined the "country of origin" principle for such sales. Under the directive, the law of the country of the merchant or service provider applies in the event of a dispute. See Council Directive 2000/31, 2000 O.J. (L 178). Several months later, however, the European Commission indicated that it might adopt the so-called Rome II Regulation, which would reverse the directive and make the laws of the consumer's country apply in cross-border e-commerce disputes, absent contractual provisions to the contrary. See Communications from the Commission on the law of non-contractual obligations, COM (2001) 66 final (7 February 2001). In the summer of 2001, under heavy pressure from the business community, the EU indicated it may revisit the question yet again (Meller). These flip-flops demonstrate how contentious the question of jurisdiction over e-commerce activities has become.

49. See TGI Paris, Ordonnance de référé du 20 nov. 2000, http://www.juriscom.net/txt/jurisfr/cti/tgiparis20001120.htm. Interestingly, a year earlier an Australian court reached the opposite conclusion in a similar type of case. The court refused to enjoin material posted on the Internet by a person in the United States that was defamatory under Australian law. According to the court, "Once published on the Internet material can be received anywhere, and it does not lie within the competence of the publisher to restrict the reach of publication." *Mcquarie Bank Ltd. v. Berg*, [1999] NSWSC 625, at 12. (New South Wales Supreme Ct., June 2, 1999). The court went on to explain:

> The difficulties are obvious. An injunction to restrain defamation in NSW [New South Wales] is designed to ensure compliance with the laws of NSW, and to protect the rights of plaintiffs, as those rights are

defined by the law of NSW. Such an injunction is not designed to superimpose the law of NSW relating to defamation on every other state, territory and country of the world. Yet that would be the effect of an order restraining publication on the Internet. It is not to be assumed that the law of defamation in other countries is coextensive with that of NSW, and indeed, one knows that it is not. It may very well be that, according to the law of the Bahamas, Tashakistan, or Mongolia, the defendant has an unfettered right to publish the material. To make an order interfering with such a right would exceed the proper limits of the use of the injunctive power of this court. (Id. at 14)

50. See generally Arendt.
51. See generally Acevedo.

## REFERENCES


Acevedo, Roland. "Thoughts of an Ex-Jailhouse Lawyer." N.Y. Law J. 5 August 1998: 2.

American Bar Association. "Achieving Legal and Business Order in Cyberspace: A Report on Global Jurisdiction Issues Created by the Internet." *Business Lawyer* 55 (2000): 1801–1946.

Arendt, Hannah. *Eichmann in Jerusalem: A Report on the Banality of Evil.* New York: Viking, 1963.

Barlow, John Perry. A Declaration of the Independence of Cyberspace, February 1996. http://www.eff.org/pub/Publications/John_Perry_Barlow/barlow_0296.declaration.

Berman, Paul Schiff. "An Observation and a Strange But True 'Tale': What Might the Historical Trials of Animals Tell Us about the Transformative Potential of Law in American Culture?" Hastings L.J. 52 (2000): 123–180.

——. "Rats, Pigs, and Statues on Trial: The Creation of Cultural Narratives in the Prosecution of Animals and Inanimate Objects." N.Y.U. L. Rev. 69 (1994): 288–326.

Clermont, Kevin M. *Civil Procedure: Territorial Jurisdiction and Venue.* New York: Foundation Press, 1999.

Clermont, Kevin M., and Theodore Eisenberg. "Exorcising the Evil of Forum-Shopping." Cornell L. Rev. 80 (1995): 1507–1535.

Clinton, William J. Statement on Signing the Digital Millennium Copyright Act. 34 Weekly Comp. Pres. Doc. 2168. 2 November 1998.

Cover, Robert. "The Folktales of Justice: Tales of Jurisdiction." In Martha Minow, Michael Ryan, and Austin Sarat, eds., *Narrative, Violence, and the*

*Law: The Essays of Robert Cover*, 173–201. Ann Arbor: University of Michigan Press, 1993.

Geist, Michael. "Is There a There There: Toward Greater Certainty for Internet Jurisdiction." Practicing L. Inst. 61 (2001): 561–624 (2001), also available at http://aix1.uottawa.ca~geist/geistjurisdiction-us.pdf.

Goldsmith, Jack L. "The Internet and the Abiding Significance of Territorial Sovereignty." Ind. J. Global Legal Stud. 5 (1998): 475–491.

Humphrey, Nicholas. Introduction to *The Criminal Prosecution and Capital Punishment of Animals*, by E. P. Evans. Paperback ed., xiii–xxix. London: Farber and Farber, 1987.

Johnson, David R., and David Post. "Law and Borders: The Rise of Law in Cyberspace." Stan. L. Rev. 48 (1996): 1367–1402.

Kang, Jerry. "Information Privacy in Cyberspace Transactions." Stan. L. Rev. 50 (1998): 1193–1294.

Kogan, Terry S. "Geography and Due Process: The Social Meaning of Adjudicative Jurisdiction." Rutgers L.J. 22 (1991): 627–657.

Kurland, Philip B. "The Supreme Court, the Due Process Clause and the In Personam Jurisdiction of State Courts—From *Pennoyer* to *Denckla*: A Review." U. Chi. L. Rev. 25 (1958): 569–624.

Legard, David. "Average Cost to Build E-commerce Site: $1 Million." *Industry Standard*, 31 May 1998. http://www.thestandard.com/article/article/0,1902,4731,00.html.

Meller, Paul. "Europe Panel Is Rethinking How It Views E-Commerce." *New York Times*, 27 June 2001.

Morse, C. G. J. "*International Shoe v. Brussels and Lugano*: Principles and Pitfalls in the Law of Personal Jurisdiction." U.C. Davis L. Rev. 28 (1995): 999–1025.

Post, David. "Governing Cyberspace," Wayne L. Rev. 43 (1996): 155–171.

Pred, Allan. *Making Histories and Constructing Human Geographies*. Boulder, Col.: Westview Press, 1990.

Reid, T. R. "Pinochet's Arrest Upheld, Most Charges Thrown Out." *Washington Post*, 25 March 1999.

Silberman, Linda J. "*Shaffer v. Heitner*: The End of an Era." N.Y.U. L. Rev. 53 (1978): 33–101.

Stein, Allan R. "The Unexceptional Problem of Jurisdiction in Cyberspace." *Int'l Lawyer* 32 (1998): 1167–1191.

Tokasz, Jay. "University Sued Over Student's Internet Posting." *Ithaca Journal*, 13 June 1998.

Wiebe, Robert H. *The Search for Order, 1877–1920*. New York: Hill and Wang, 1967.

3

# Architectural Design for Online Environments

ANNA CICOGNANI

## 1. INTRODUCTION

This essay is about how architecture can be of help in the design of *online environments*. These environments, which are also indicated here as *online worlds* or *places*, are born and mainly growing within the Internet. The relative absence of spatial organization in these environments often is an obstacle to the healthy establishment and growth of online communities: as a consequence, many of these communities dissolve after short periods, or require a substantial effort to reorganize the hosting "virtual" place. Commercially speaking, because of the costs involved in starting up and "refurbishing" such places, this is not a fortunate circumstance. For the community itself, it is discouraging, if not alienating, to see the space modified and reorganized too often. Hence, architects can help in the design of virtual environments, making them more comfortable and usable.

Here, I use the word "virtual"—often used synonymously with "online"—as little as possible, and only when it makes it easier to differentiate the physical from the nonphysical. I believe that the adjective "virtual" commonly bears a meaning of "not existing," which I think is inappropriate when referring to a place.[1] A place can be inhabited and filled with "things" that are suitable for it: physical things for physical places; nonphysical things for online worlds. The nature of the place—

physical or nonphysical—is a condition for the kinds of performance that can be attained. What can be done in a physical place usually cannot be done in a nonphysical one, and vice versa. The two kinds of space are not substitutes one for the other.

Architecture, commonly conceived as a discipline that deals with physical things, can, and should be, rethought as an instrument to understand the nonphysical world, now more than ever, since the introduction of networks is forcing us to re-elaborate on what space is. In this essay, I will show how architectural design can help in the definition of online environments, assuming that:

- architectural design and building activities are not (only) about physical matter;
- online environments express a legitimate form of space (e.g., we *go to* or *visit* a Web page);
- it is possible to design online environments;
- when an online environment is well organized, it is more usable and effective.

I also assert, and somehow assume, that architects are the most skilled professionals who understand space and how to manipulate it, and they should be given the responsibility to design online spaces. To help architects in this job, I indicate some parameters that can be used in designing online environments. These parameters have been formulated after research on the design of online environments, and they have subsequently been applied to the design of one of these environments (see Cicognani 1998a, 1998b ). I also indicate specific parameters for the design of flexible learning environments, used mostly by educational institutions to take advantage of networking technologies.

## 2. ARCHITECTURE FOR ONLINE ENVIRONMENTS

Examining a specific online environment,[2] I have observed a vernacular approach to organizing and distributing space, in relation to the activities required by that environment. I use the word "vernacular" to indicate a spontaneous and often unorganized approach to problem solving, a trial-and-error condition in which users, without specific intention, provide solutions on a case-by-case basis.

Although the individually provided solutions might seem optimal for specific cases, especially when users "own" the portion of online space hosting their products (e.g., the disk space on a Web server), on a global scale the environment suffers from long-term difficulties in its organization and accessibility. For example, given that a student of an online university needs a place for organizing his activities (such as assignments, private meetings, research), he will look at building a personal place—an office, a studio, a Web home page—privately located within the environment. If appropriate areas are assigned according to functionalities, users find it easier to navigate and to find the information they need.

Generally, users can build new zones by respecting hierarchies set by that world's designers. Users are then guided in selecting appropriate content, and a standard design is applied to the level of access of that zone.[3] Only by crossing a common area is it possible to access specific parts of the environment. For example, users' home pages may be accessible after passing through a "portal" site, or private "offices" by passing through an office area.

Figure 3.1 shows a sample organization of a Web site for a university. From the portal Web page, to reach student pages, a visitor must pass through four levels of progressively more specific areas. Aside from this organization, if the user knows the exact address (URL) he or she can access the student page directly, by typing the address in the browser. Each part of the above hierarchy can be reached independently only when the specific URL is known.

A URL represents in words the hierarchy of a particular Web site. For example, http://www.arch.usyd.edu.au/kcdc/people/index.html tells us that the portal (www.arch.usyd.edu.au) leads to a particular "place" (the KCDC), leading further to a list of its people (/people/index.html), and so on.[4]

The construction of hierarchies is seldom seen as an architectural problem. However, the success of online environments depends as much on their design as on their content. This is similar to what happens for real-life buildings. A good example to recall for the sake of

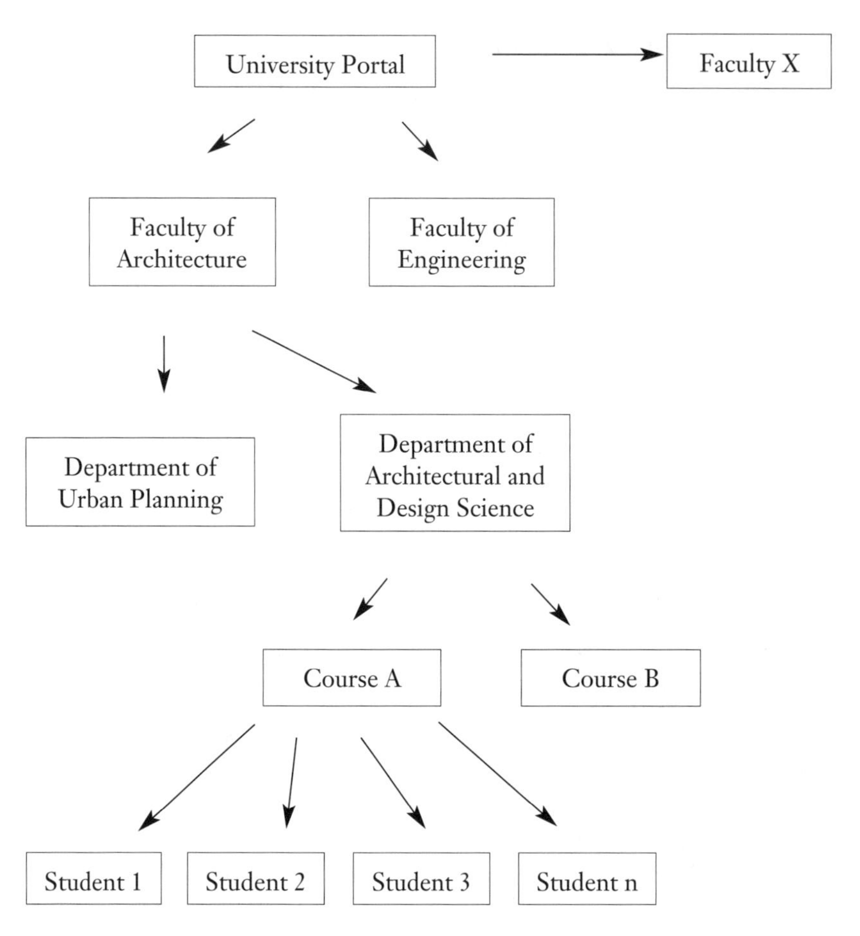


FIGURE 3.1. A typical hierarchy for a university Web site.

this argument is the Vitra Design Museum in Weil Am Rhein, Germany (fig. 3.2).[5]

The museum is another masterpiece from Frank Gehry, who managed to integrate the Vitra philosophy—devoted to innovation in design—with the display necessities of the museum. Content and space are related one to another, to enhance an experience of close contact with high-level design of the Vitra production. In this architecture, as the interior takes shape and hosts objects, the exterior grows to become a building and sit in the physical environment. We could think of a

© Yetsuh Frank / GreatBuildings com

FIGURE 3.2. The Vitra Design Museum, Weil Am Rhein, Germany (1989).

building as being the interface between the content and the space: as software interfaces organize the electronic space to host content (for example, tools for word processing, Web pages, and so on), so buildings contain and organize space, and make their content accessible and usable.

Rarely do the administrators of online worlds develop space-planning skills similar to those of physical-space planners. The organizational process of a physical place has to go through a series of approval procedures before it has any chance of being implemented. Moreover, changes to physical space are slow and difficult to revert. A project such as building a new town hall involves a long negotiation process, with several parties involved, and with an important impact on the layout of a town. The volatility of the electronic space, instead, allows rapid and easily reversible changes that affect only limited parties. For example, reorganizing the hierarchy of a Web site could be merely a question of renaming and/or relocating a few directories and files, and modifying a few HTML tags. On the other hand, moving a physical building is rarely possible at all.

Hypothetically, the flow of decisions and information in a classic design process for physical entities can be seen as follows:

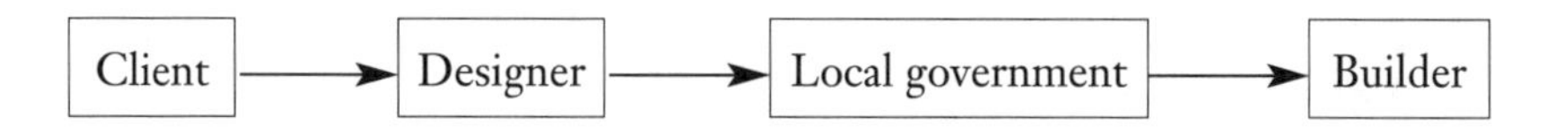


In an online environment, client, designer, and builder are often coincident, and the coordinators (often called system managers or administrators) of the online environment are substituted for the local government:

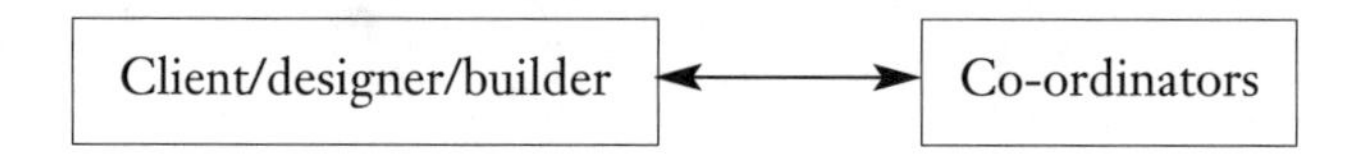


Table 3.1 compares some characteristics of building in the physical and electronic space. This table is indicative of the main issues involved in the design and execution process of entities in online environments, compared to physical entities:

Further factors involved in the design and execution processes will then complete the basic ones noted above, according to specific design briefs.

Although electronic entities seem to be much easier (and less expensive) to build and handle, I am not suggesting that they can in any way substitute for some of the fundamental structures used in the physical space (e.g., roads or houses). It would, however, be worth analyzing when and how an online structure can ease and decongest physical world situations, or create new solutions to common architectural problems. It is also worth mentioning that for businesses that establish an online presence, the construction of online environments modifies the ways in which (physical) real estate is handled. For example, banks that also operate online have already taken a step toward the reconsid-

TABLE 3.1. Some Elements of Comparison Between Physical and Online Space Design

| | PHYSICAL SPACE | ONLINE SPACE |
|---|---|---|
| *Portability of entities* | Rarely possible (for buildings) | Possible |
| *Modification of entities* | Slow, expensive | Fast, cheap |
| *Reversibility to original state* | Rarely possible, very slow | Possible, fast |
| *Distribution of elements (geographical organization)* | Continuous | Discrete |
| *Parties involved in the design and building process* | Multiple, often in conflict, often difficult to access | Reduced, easily accessible |
| *Length of negotiation process* | Long | Short |
| *Design responsibility* | Shared with local governments | Shared between designers (coordinators) and users |

eration of their real estate, sensibly cutting costs by closing physical branches and powering the online transactions (including ATM machines and phone banking).[6]

### 2.1. A New Role for Architects

Classically, architects have dealt with problems concerning physical structures and entities. By designing, architects have been able to improve our ways of populating space. Dwellings and workplaces benefit from the organization of space: order and hierarchies applied to space organization seem to provide a stable orientation for people, and a place well organized provides comfort and consistency over time. Specific tools to examine patterns of integration between "content" and "structure" in towns show interesting conclusions on shape analysis and city development (Hillier and Hanson; Stonor).

Until recently, a clear distinction has been made between "real world" and "virtual world" designers, the latter being almost always computer programmers. The expression “computer architecture” is meaningful when building operating systems, software, and even hardware. However, architects, in the classical sense of the word, are rarely involved in such building processes. Unfortunately, in the architectural culture designers have yet to see their expertise or roles as relevant to online environments.

I believe that architects can have an active and important role in the construction of online environments, for several reasons:

- they are familiar with space organization;
- they are aware of the relationships between space organization and performance;
- they have a good understanding of the design process and its negotiating and executive phases;
- they are used to transforming basic materials into functional elements (such as wood into a chair, bricks into a wall).

Moreover, architects have skills that allow them to solve spatial problems better than other kinds of practitioners. In the online venue, they will apply these skills to design a fully functional space. For instance, in an e-commerce environment, the owner might want to reflect the functionalities of a physical shop where items are exposed on shelves; where customers make selections on the basis of quality, appearance, price, and/or brand name; and finally, where customers pay at a cashier station and bring the items home. Different parts of the physical shop will have to be organized in order to meet each functionality. When designing the physical version of this shop, an architect will make decisions according to the kind of real estate he is dealing with: building structure, geometry (volumes, dimensions, height), colors, materials, furniture, and other physical properties of the place.

In the electronic environment, where physical properties do not need to be considered when designing to meet functionalities, other elements become relevant and can be reviewed with an architectural perspective in mind. Consequently, not only are architects an excellent resource for understanding these elements and their relevance, but they can also provide solutions that consider the connections between space and performance.

### 2.2. Elements of Online Design

So far, when discussing design of online environments, authors have concentrated more on the hierarchical organization of resources and their accessibility[7] than on an architectural analysis of the designed space. I propose a series of elements, formulated using an architectural perspective, that become important to easing and enhancing the online facility. Table 3.2 shows these elements, their architectural counterparts, and how they can be realized/built in an online environment.

These elements can be used when designing online environments such as corporate Web sites, community-based environments, flexible learning environments, services and goods providers (e.g., libraries, shops, banks), and, in general, all the places that involve a user-to-service relationship.[8] Users are actively involved in the design of certain areas of the environment, or, more precisely, they have some choices about the content of those areas. We could say, then, that users become also designers and builders, although they can design and build only by following prefabricated patterns, placed in a predetermined structure. Instead of pointing out the design opportunities created,[9] I prefer to note that users have the same level of choice in an online environment as they do in their physical dwellings (choosing the color of the walls, hanging family pictures, selecting furnishings, and so on). A user's home page is as personal as a house: it can be made private or public, the user can decide who will be able to access it and what kind of information will be available. The degree of personalization is very high even when templates are used; users become designers of their own online places. These forms of design are generally much less regulated than are real-life forms.

I will now simulate two different briefs and their realization, in order to provide a direct interpretation of the design elements of Table 3.2. The solutions are given in the form of a specification list.

***Brief One: The Virtual Classroom.*** This is a place where students and teachers enact an exchange of information in order to fulfill the requirements for a unit of study. Students expect to find all the information needed to pass the course; teachers must provide this necessary information and organize it so that the learning experience is successful. The geographical distribution of students and teachers is one of the

TABLE 3.2. Online Elements and Architectural Counterparts

| ONLINE ELEMENTS | ARCHITECTURAL COUNTERPARTS | REALISATION |
|---|---|---|
| *Quantitative relationship between information and layers of access* | How many "rooms" (links, pages) must be crossed before reaching the wanted one | Reducing the number of passages (e.g., "clicks" ) to reach wanted information |
| *Organization in areas of similar functionalities* | Classical function-based organization: day/night, public/private | Indexing of information |
| *Possibility to contact or isolate oneself from others* | Division of the inside from the outside | Enable privacy (e.g., with encryption), build forums-like environments (both synchronous and asynchronous) |
| *Level of user engagement in the place design* | Personalization of space | Let users decide what to put in their personal places |
| *User's ownership* | Ownership of the place, personal effects | Give users total access and control over their "real estate" |
| *Comfort in inhabiting the place (moving around, participating in activities, and similar)* | Elements of comfort, such as materials, furniture, textures, colors | Provide a series of items that can be used when designing a place (e.g., schemes, color graphic design elements) |
| *Possibility of transforming and evolving for collective purposes* | Community feedback on planning decisions | Provide forums to discuss changes related to a site design |

factors that make the virtual classroom different from the physical one: while there is no need that all parties be in the same place, there is still the need that they be able to reach that place. The virtual classroom centralizes all the learning material and must be reachable by everyone, at any given time. The virtual classroom does not distribute information, in the sense of sending it away: instead, it creates a "central deposit" that must be totally accessible and reliable.

Time limits on access to the classroom—in the form of time of day and time of permanence—should not be imposed. Every document should be accessible at all times, even in concurrence with others. For example, two students should be able to access the same document at the same time. Teachers should be in total control of learning material and its release, consistent with the course schedule and the educational program.

Layers of information: organize sections for course site, learning elements (tutorials, lectures, calendar, assignments, databases), private areas for each student and tutor.

Similar functionalities: separate learning materials (lectures, documents) from due materials (assignments, calendar of due dates); separate student areas from course coordinator areas.

Privacy: limit access to personal spaces, allow controlled synchronous contact (instant messaging), define public areas for both synchronous and asynchronous contact (chat rooms, forums).

User engagement in place design: designate a personal area for each student/tutor, where all information about the course is stored, including assignments, research documents, and similar items.

Ownership: structure the site so that users have total ownership and access control over personal areas and documents.

Comfort: allow students to choose features to add to personal area, provide an extended database of features.

Place transformation and feedback: establish a discussion group about the classroom design, invite students to design new features that might enhance the learning experience, encourage feedback.

***Brief Two: The Online Bank.*** From the customer's point of view, a bank is a place where money is handled. Online banking, in particular, is a place where the customer's personal money is handled, so the main thing to consider in the design of this place is that the customer must feel that he or she has full control over any operation on his or her property. Each operation should be fully transparent, showing where the money comes from and where it finishes. Tools that provide financial advice—for example, selecting a type of loan—should be used only as a means of providing information, never as a way of requiring decisions by the customer. The customer should always feel free to select a transaction and its terms (such as how much money and when), and the online bank should be proposed as an exact and consistent environment where the customer's personal property is handled carefully.

Time and date stamps and receipt numbers will ensure the validity of each transaction. Each additional cost should be made clear to the customer, and in some cases, a filter on the amount of money exchanged—for example, in the purchase of stocks—could be set in order to avoid irreversible and unwanted circumstances.

Layers of information: organize sections for the portal, departments (loans, accounts, investments), personal access with options (access to accounts, banking operations, financial and brokerage facilities); provide extended help on each page for each item presented.

Similar functionalities: group all the facilities related to similar operations (such as transferring money, paying bills); provide information consistent with the type of transaction performed (such as complete details on an investment package or full disclosure about interest rates and account procedures).

Privacy: protect users' identity and personal details; protect/encrypt all transactions and account details.

User engagement in place design: provide a private area for each customer, where personal information (account numbers, documents, research done on investments) can be stored, and special tools in the form of shortcuts (such as the ability to transfer money from one account to another with only one operation, without entering details).

Ownership: structure the site so that users control who can access accounts, whether further information on special deals is provided to them (that is, users should be able to choose whether they want to hear/see such information), and deny access to unwanted visitors. Users must feel that they have total control and privacy over their details.

Comfort: design a user-friendly interface, enable a "memory"[10] to check and respect the customer's preferences, provide a series of ad hoc shortcuts for each customer.

Place transformation and feedback: provide a system for efficient responses to customers (e.g., when a customer raises a question, be sure that it is answered efficiently and quickly), invite and encourage customers' comments.

These elements, and sample briefs, should be considered as a starting point for defining a design strategy. In each case, of course, the designer's expertise will be brought to bear in order to address individual needs.

## 3. WHAT IS DIFFERENT ABOUT DESIGN FOR ONLINE ENVIRONMENTS

Using the same word—"design"—to indicate the process that leads to the planning of space in both online and physical environments suggests that the process is, indeed, the same. In many respects, the same design process can be used for both: definition of a brief, analysis of the requirements, selection of resources, identification of solutions, development and realization. There are, however, notable differences between designing an online place (like an online bank) and a physical one (like the building for a bank).

During an extended research inquiry on virtual environments (Cicognani 1998a), I identified four criteria that can be used to differentiate the design of physical elements from that of online ones and that can be helpful when considered in the early stages of the design process. I re-propose here those elements, demonstrating their relevance for my larger argument.

### 3.1. Matter

The matter of the physical world is the physical material that we deal with (wood, concrete, bricks). Design operations resolve relationships between a number of elements, among them functional, constructive, social, cultural, political. This is true in both physical and online environments. While the physical world must respect the laws of physics (so that a building does not collapse), online environments must respect the rules of their underlying data-like structure as well: for example, syntax and relationships of words (commands), navigation tools, coherence with context, and access to parts of the system. In design, the fundamental rule for dealing with *matter* is the same for both physical and online environments: respect the nature of the material. For example, if we are building an arch with bricks, we must respect a certain construction methodology, different from that applied to building an arch with steel. Similarly, building an item in an online environment supported by, for example, a certain programming language (Java, Perl, HTML), implies that we use that language appropriately, respecting its syntax and the conditions of usability of its elements (class hierarchy, macro routines, permissions). The underlying structure of the environment is called *protocol*, and it sets certain standards, which become its own limits.

Whenever a discrepancy exists between physical and nonphysical functionalities, it is necessary to clarify what is expected from manipulation of matter in a specific environment. For example, in the physical world, we need to consider and include gravity force in structural design decisions, or the final product "will not make sense" in that world. In online environments, gravity force does not exist, and it does not need to be included as a possibility when making design decisions. On the other hand, nonphysical entities need to respond semantically to the environment's metaphor of reference (as the bank). It is through this metaphor that needs and expectations of matter manipulation can be defined. For example, even if the idea of "floor" does not represent a structural constraint in an online world, the metaphor of "standing on the floor" is important for users' understanding of their spatial position and their relationship to the rest of the world.

### 3.2. Coherence

The metaphorical coherence of an online environment is fundamental for its utility and flexibility. Designers need to consider how suitable the parts of the environment are in relation to the whole environment. This same issue operates in the physical world. For example, we would expect to find a cookstove in a kitchen rather than in a classroom, where it would appear "out of place." Similarly, in an online bank, we expect to find something that *functions like* a teller: something through which we can perform operations on our money; we would not expect to find there a menu for ordering takeout food.

If the use of an element does not correspond to the metaphor it represents, it becomes inconsistent, difficult to organize and to use. A virtual slide projector should show slides to an audience, but should not allow the audience to scribble on them. In online environments the functionalities can be easily adapted: in an online gambling service, for example, we should find facilities for withdrawing money (so we can have direct access to our bank account to gamble). But if we have to gamble each time we want to execute a transaction on our bank account, the metaphor (of the "virtual" account) ceases to be useful.

While in the physical world it is unlikely that people walk on ceilings rather than floors, in online worlds anything is possible, except that a continuous displacement (and replacement) of referent affects the understanding and, thus, the usability of the environment.

The concept of coherence allows designers of online environments to take the first steps toward understanding the principles applicable to these worlds. In architectural design of the physical world, *displacement* and *ambiguity* have been used as parameters in the analysis of contemporary urban aggregates (Venturi, Izenour, and Brown). In online worlds similar processes seem to occur from the opposite direction: from the displacement and ambiguity of the initial design, where there is no territory or any other trace of existence to relate to, these worlds tend to organize themselves so that an integral and coherent understanding emerges of the purposes of that environment. In the physical world, inconsistency is rarely found among physical properties—for example, on earth all objects fall toward the ground, but on an orbiting spaceship they do not—in online worlds, the absence of physical constraints is a starting point for displacement. What designers do is *replace* activities in order to reconstruct a certain familiarity between user and environment.

This "inverted" process of *replacement* will eventually disappear when the majority of activities and entities in online environments have stable responses—the "$" icon always brings us to our linked bank accounts—and when participation in these worlds becomes more diffuse. For the time being, it is still quite difficult to establish a set of parameters that are commonly accepted across different online environments; displacement and ambiguity are, in fact, what is *normal* in these places.

In the physical world, the architectural and urban design processes are very well known and regulated. Since the very beginning of the practice, policies and rules of design and construction have been developed,[11] put in place in order to protect the client and the designer and to ensure that the rest of the built environment is not adversely affected by new construction. The development of a deontology for design practitioners took into account two factors: the responsibilities of the designer toward the client and the impact of design decisions on the existing environment. These two concerns define the code of practice: designers have a responsibility toward the user/client, and toward what is already there, in the built environment.

The Internet as we know it, and in particular the World Wide Web, has become a regular "place" to go for many people. Meeting others, finding information, conducting transactions, and organizing communities are activities that used to happen only in real life, in physical space. Although it may not be readily apparent to the common Internet user that the online space is designed, it is clear how "bad" design affects the usability of a site.

First, users must be able to access, understand, and use each and every relevant part of the interface. Web designers often seem to forget this point, for they do not seem to cluster information in such a way that users are screened from unwanted information. For example, in a banking environment, if a user does not have a home loan with a particular bank, the section about home loans should not be included in that user's interface.

Second, considerable effort is required to acquire some familiarity in a community, physical or virtual, and bad design makes it even more difficult to achieve the goal, thus inhibiting the natural growth of confidence within the group.

Finally, designers have a social responsibility to make sure that the built environment—even in its electronic form—employs basic principles of usability and comfort. As design ecologies are being gradually integrated in design processes,[12] electronic space designers are beginning to recognize social issues of sustainability. Even if moral and social judgments are generally temporary, often depending on government policies and market trends, designers have a duty to plan a better environment in the present and for the future. Environmental sustainability must be associated, especially in the case of new technologies, with social sustainability,[13] which is concerned with individual behaviors that may adversely affect the environment (e.g., littering, talking on the phone while driving, producing genetically modified foods). How to design sustainable online places is an interesting challenge for designers to explore.

### 3.3. Speed

The capacity to modify an online environment is related to the capacity to use interface tools and to environmental responsiveness in the deployment of such tools. The execution of a command is almost immediate, related to the speed of the machine; thus, its output is immediately "visible" to a user.

The speed with which decisions are implemented is an important aspect of design: in online worlds, designers can see the effects of their actions in a relatively short period of time; in the physical world, however, results may not be observable for a much longer period of time.[14] Designing a (physical) building and constructing it are two completely separate processes, which engage completely different skills. In online worlds the design and construction processes very often overlap: while defining how an element must look, a designer simultaneously checks its final realization.

The planning part—the series of decisions that must be made in order to initiate the construction—can be incorporated in the interface, by suggesting a series of alternatives or making sure that some basic elements are considered during the design process. While the planning phase in physical world design does not incorporate the immediate realization of an object, in the online environment plans can be immediately transformed into an object, available for checking.[15]

The capability to check the results of a design decision almost instantly, without having to wait for the construction phase, leads to more *control* over these decisions and allows modification of the object until the desired results are achieved.

### 3.4. Control

One of the designer's goals is to have *control* over what is designed, in terms of usability, effects on the environment, functionality, appearance, and costs. Physical architecture designers know that controlling the design process has a great influence upon the final result. It is therefore important that the design and construction processes are monitored and corrected, and that attention is paid to marginal effects.[16]

In many respects the online environment allows the designer to exercise such control more effectively than the physical world does.

First, designers are able to check quickly and accurately to see if their design choices yield the results that they expect. For example, if we design a door in an online classroom that closes itself when a lecture starts, it is possible to simulate the specific situation and control that the door effectively shuts.

Second, designers can set the response of an online environment to specific actions so that it is always the same (e.g., typing a command always achieves the same result, clicking on a hyperlink always takes the user to the same Web page), and thus ambiguity is substantially reduced. Everything will appear exactly as the designer has set it.

Finally, control in online environments is exercised by ownership and access. Each item has an owner, and only that owner, or a system administrator, can modify or destroy it. The *digital ownership* of entities is much easier to organize and control in the online world than in the physical world.

The designer's control is a powerful instrument that can govern the access to the use of the environment to designated classes of users. Even the political and social organization of the online environment, which is directly related to access, becomes a function of the design.

## 4. LEARNING ONLINE

As architecture professor William Mitchell put it, architects need to find a way of integrating our new cyborg bodies into the renewed architecture of the "cities of bits." Many different activities that normally are part of the physical world need to be rethought and reorganized when they are "translated" into the online world.

One of these activities, *learning*, is being increasingly studied and experienced as research opens new directions. Online learning, run in online environments, is being used as a trial ground for the newest theories about education and self-driven teaching techniques.[17]

A person or group of persons willing to learn require:

- something to learn (a subject);
- a series of problems connected with the subject, which activate the learning process;

- an anthology of the existing knowledge, which provides the background for solving some of the problems;
- a learning party, willing to approach the knowledge and the problems related to the subject;
- a series of tools that allow access to the knowledge, and its extension as new findings are added;
- a feedback mechanism, which allows learners to check whether they have acquired the information and the methodologies expected;
- a publishing instrument, which allows dissemination of new findings.

New communication technologies have provided consistent ways of organizing self-driven learning and allowing access to tools and events from geographically distant locations, thus increasing the flexibility of this activity.[18] The adjective "flexible," when used to describe learning environments, indicates that:

- the environment can be accessed whenever a *student*—the person who is willing to learn—decides;
- usually, information is accessible independently from the location, as happens in a digital library;
- information is available in different formats, preferably digital (Web pages, word processing documents, audio);
- the methodology used to present information related to the subject being studied allows self-driven activities such as individual choice of what to read and when, how much time a course will take, how often a test can be repeated in order to master the answers.

The main issues to be considered when designing flexible learning environments are related to *time*, *format*, and organization of the resources, or *mapping*.

### 4.1. Time

Traditionally, most of the information flowing between a student and a teacher[19] was exchanged synchronously, in the form of lectures: at the same time, in the same place, over a period of time, the two parties convened to enact the exchange. If one of the parties could not make it (to the place at the agreed-upon time), the exchange would not happen. Physical architecture is not so tied to time issues as virtual places are. Physical architecture is permanent and occupies a limited space (for example, a building on a university campus). In contrast, online places offer a flexible use of space, and they can be kept out of the network when they are empty. Temporality in physical buildings is not explicitly represented: time becomes more a social issue of scheduling and meeting.

In online flexible learning environments, the exchange can be made independent from when and where the two parties meet: a lecture can be recorded at a certain time and then retrieved whenever it is needed. This possibility, which is related to the asynchronous nature of the medium (data), eases the process of learning, since, for example, a lecture can be repeated multiple times, until its contents are clear to the learner. Accessing information freely also has the advantage of relieving a learner of the commitment related to the time/space dyad: either she is there at that time or she will miss out on that lecture. I am not considering here social and personal issues that might interfere with the normal flow of learning dynamics: for example, the fact that a student does not need to be there at a given time might become an excuse not to access the lecture contents at all. Although a designer should consider this class of issues when planning a learning environment, I intend to identify here general principles related to online design, assuming that sociological and psychological studies will heuristically join in the planning.

Time, in online worlds, can be treated as a minor issue in terms of activity planning for synchronous events. Moreover, it can be favorably used as a means to anticipate and present to the learner the whole body of a certain subject, releasing and updating information periodically and thus maintaining a high value in the knowledge transmitted.

### 4.2. Format

A discussion of *format* addresses how information is available, distributed, and consequently accessed. This issue is not present in architectural design processes, as there is no control over the information delivered in the physical building in terms of a priori design. The format of information sets the terms for its accessibility and availability. For example, an essay used in a course can be made available as a document printed on paper, as a Web page, or as a file exchanged and shared among learners. Some format must be chosen in order to distribute any single item among learners. Although some of these items have a particular medium to respect (e.g., audio), they can be delivered using different carriers. For example, an audio piece can be sent as an analog tape, a file on a floppy disk, or a Web page, in the form of a Real Audio file. Online flexible learning environments will prefer formats that can be transported by the TCP/IP carrier,[20] including digital formats, which use proprietary protocols.[21]

Designers of online educational environments will have to consider carefully the format that they choose for transmitting information. Converting between formats, especially from a "physical" format, like paper, to digital, can be extremely time-consuming and expensive.

Other important considerations with regard to the concept of format include the following:

- the user interface must facilitate and enhance the learning experience, allowing learners easy access to and retrieval of information;
- the skills needed to handle different formats often require an additional investment of time for the learner, if he or she is to use resources in the best possible way;
- although redundancy of information does not seem to facilitate the learning experience,[22] it should be noted that technology might fail continuity—for example, when someone cannot access the network, or the local host seems to be down, or the batteries of the laptop are low. Some form of backup is needed for fundamental parts of information, when a phase of the learning activities cannot be allowed to fail. Physical items provide an invaluable backup when technology is stretched to its limits.

Computer networks and their protocols represent a good layer for implementing "electronic" places. They have demonstrated stability and the capacity to support high numbers of users while performing complex tasks. When a standard for protocols is established, communication and collaboration among participants become easier. Although not necessary, it is an advantage when designers know the technical details of protocols (e.g., what kind of data can be transported, how it is accessed); this kind of knowledge among designers can also help to avoid delays in the preliminary design of a new online place since it would allow initial implementation of the system to meet baseline requirements and take advantage of system abilities.

### 4.3. Mapping

Mapping means understanding how information is accessed, usually in a remote fashion for computer networks, creating a treelike structure that represents the passages from one piece of information to another. Information is distributed over a series of threads, connected one to another, in what forms the map. A well-designed information map, as a well-designed place, makes the space more comfortable, easy to access and navigate, and thus better for users and those who maintain (update) information.

Good mapping should include:

- an ordered treelike structure of information, which may be visible (e.g., with an index) or invisible to users;
- an intuitive way of navigating through the map, perhaps with a set of navigational instruments (like a toolbar on a Web site; active links from objects on a 3-D world; directional arrows);
- the possibility of retracing the path covered, going back to any previously visited point;
- the opportunity to add comments and links in order to further information;
- enough flexibility in the structure, so that if a piece of information is moved, it is easy and fast to update whatever is linked to it;
- control over whatever parts of the map should not be accessed by certain categories of users. For example, an online magazine might allow free access to some content but require the payment of a fee to access other content;
- the possibility of skipping steps if users know where the information they need is stored.

Mapping should be thought of in concurrence with interface design, in order to achieve the best results. An interface should always be integrated with the information and activities that it mediates. Designers can considerably improve the quality of an online world by making sure that users are able to access and retrieve the information they need in a simple and reliable way. Consistency of performance is also highly recommended—for example, to open a document, a user follows the same procedure each time, whatever document, wherever the user might be. The cause/effect principle—something happens in the same way each time—helps users to create and maintain familiarity with the interface, and therefore with the environment.

One way of mapping information could be implemented by gathering information of the same kind in the same area, as seen in the above architectural components,[23] as, for example, it is done in a library. Another way could use an indexing model (alphabet, numeric progression, or date of last access) to organize information. Whatever model, mapping works better if the model is kept consistent throughout the online environment.

## 5. DIRECTIONS

In online environments, designers and, selectively, architects, should rethink the concepts of place and space. On the one hand, the concept of space can be re-elaborated to include various instances, among them the issues that arise with electronic space; on the other, elaborating on the concept of place should lead to new strategies that can be adopted when designing online environments. Meyrowitz initiated these elaborations[24] when the Internet was not yet popularly widespread,[25] when it was still used mainly as an experimental ground for communication and file transfer.

Since then, electronic space has been the subject of various speculations,[26] but none of them succeeded in defining an architectural perspective that leads to design implementations. Most of these speculations consider possible representations of the electronic space, meaning 2-D or 3-D graphical visualizations. Some efforts by architects and researchers[27] have tried to define the role of architects in the construction of *virtual* places and the nature of this new instance of space that was unknown until a few years ago. Yet confusion seems to reign in the organization and use of nonphysical spaces. This is marginally surprising, as space had already been the subject of elaborations that went beyond physical consistency.[28] It is possibly the case that, although some of these elaborations have used design concepts extensively, not least architectural design, they see the nature of electronic space and architecture as being in conflict.

Some issues need to be clarified in order to conceive a discipline that deals with the design of online places:

- the definition of what can be designed;
- the identification of a set of methodologies that help the design process in a nonphysical space;
- the implementation of design tools specifically for online environments (software or interface design);
- the acknowledgment that physical structures must be reinterpreted metaphorically in online environments and still "sustain" the environment.

On the last issue, note that just as in the physical world, structure sustains the built environment, responding to physical constraints of matter, in the online world structure needs to equally respond to constraints that are not physical, but still must be recognized metaphorically. In the design of an online world, the absence of physical constraints seems to leave designers more free to transcend the boundaries normally set by the physical world. This is certainly possible, although some principles must be established in order to maintain a certain coherence in the whole environment.[29] While designers in the physical world have to face negotiation processes regarding the environment and the impact of their buildings on it, so-called online designers do not need to go through similar processes. I believe, however, that it is only a matter of time and maturity, of the medium and the users, before issues of sustainability and "green" design will be fundamental for all those involved with Internet-based design procedures.

Designers can also analyze and plan online environments as:

- *social environments*, in which the space is functional for the formation and the communication of the community. Thus, the environment needs to be designed to support and improve the capacity of users to interact among themselves, and to personalize their private space. A series of solutions that allows information sharing and communicative tasks is then researched, plus instruments like demographic and community formation analyses that help the designer to identify the key issues of a specific community;

- *familiar and user-friendly environments*, with various tools that guarantee a thorough integration between users and environment. This leads to considering, and designing, the use and accessibility of the online world in terms of the *interface*. What stands between the user and the software becomes functional for the use and accessibility of the online world. Solutions in this area look at how software interfaces can respond to the user's needs. The organization of the space enhances and reflects the possibilities of collaboration, sharing, and the needs of special-interest groups. The definition of standards and protocols for shared architectures facilitates collaboration tasks, especially on a larger network scale, where users access the network from different hardware platforms or software operating systems. Having a common set of standards that supports communication, video, audio, and the permanent construction of a shared environment enhances not only the interactions among users, but also the achievements and efficiency of the online environment;
- *environments that are graphically represented.* The designer's task is to find a way to visually reproduce the online world, in order for the users to inhabit it. Representational techniques, such as VRML,[30] are used for this purpose. Moreover, interactions among users, and between users and environment, are represented, for example, with the employment of "avatars," or virtual personæ, which visually identify users in the virtual space.

These perspectives look at the same problem—design in and of online worlds—from different angles. Underlying them all is the shared belief that these environments need to be designed in order to make them easier to relate to and thus easier to use.

As architects we have the responsibility to propose alternatives to the usual ways of designing online worlds. Moreover, we can advance a set of prototypes that can be diffused among all designers. Some principles that derive from architectural design can also be modified in order to suit the electronic media. Working with metaphors, architects extract (and abstract) meanings from needs and functionalities; the same meanings can then be hypostatized into physical and digital entities. The challenge for architects and architectural sciences is to renew and reconstruct these meanings in the online world, and thus face the design needs of environments powered by new media technology.

## NOTES

This essay is part of a research on design principles for online environments, conducted under a U2000 postdoctoral fellowship at the Faculty of Architecture, University of Sydney. Frank Lowe, Justin Milne, and Thomas Kvan helped with useful comments to the early drafts. Beth Kolko nicely commented and suggested changes to further drafts.

1. On this topic, see also Woolley.

2. A text-based virtual world is a specific environment that can be used for several purposes. See, for example, LambdaMOO, lambda.moo.mud.org:8888. For a thorough examination of text-based virtual worlds from an architectural perspective, see Cicognani 1998a:47–52.

3. Not only can users create personal home pages hosted by large-scale Web-based data banks (see http://www.geocities.com/), but they can also personalize how they access specific Web sites. See examples like My Netscape (http://my.netscape.com/) or My Yahoo (http://my.yahoo.com/).

4. This is also the nature of hyperlinks: creating connections between information chunks stored in separate documents.

5. See http://www.vitra.com/default.asp.

6. Another good example of how cutting the costs of real estate changes the nature of the business is Amazon.com (http://www.amazon.com). Many other online businesses are also worth considering in an analysis of real estate value against profit margins.

7. See Eisenstadt and Vincent.

8. One where a user accesses an online environment to obtain a service.

9. A clear commercial nuance to attract more users to an online environment.

10. For example, under the form of "cookies," information stored in the customer's client.

11. In Hammurabi's Code (King of Babylon, 1780 B.C.): Law 229—If a builder build a house for some one, and does not construct it properly, and the house which he built fall in and kill its owner, then that builder shall be put to death. See also Laws 230–233 (Hammurabi).

12. See the pages of EcoDesign Foundation (http://www.edf.edu.au/) and Thompson and Steiner.

13. The World Bank is taking strong positions toward making development equally environmentally and socially responsible. See http://wwwesd.worldbank.org/envmat/vol2f96/sustain.htm.

14. As a matter of fact, almost anywhere in the online world we can immediately see the effects of our decisions, like making a transaction on our bank account, or buying stock.

15. Consider how some Web editors simplify the design process so much that there is no difference between the planning and the realization processes.

16. The issue of control in design processes can also be intended as "control over the users" exercised via architectural design. However, this is not what I intend here. For literature regarding architecture as control, see Bentham and related critics.

17. See O'Malley, Eisenstadt and Vincent, and Sumner and Taylor for further references. Also Raikes, and other proceedings from the same conference (Third International Conference on Asynchronous Learning Networks).

18. See also Maher, Simoff, and Cicognani.

19. I use these words loosely to indicate the two parties involved in the learning dynamics, where one is willing to increase and the other is willing to transmit knowledge. I acknowledge that there is a mutual exchange in this dynamic, although one of the parties can be seen as a principal repository of information. The learning party has to demonstrate a certain flexibility in accepting that someone else might have more information related to a certain subject.

20. The suite of protocols on which Internet is based.

21. See for example WebCT, http://www.webct.com/webct.

22. See Sumner and Taylor.

23. Section 2.2.

24. Elaborations that then continued by both Benedikt and Mitchell, although not in strict contact with Meyrowitz's "sense of place."

25. In October 1984 the number of Internet hosts was just above 1,000.

26. See Coyne and Kollock.

27. Like the Transarchitectures Symposium held at the Getty Foundation on 5–6 June 1998. See http://home.LACN.org/LACN/trans/.

28. See Lefebvre and the essays in Bloom et al.
29. See section 3.2 of this essay.
30. VRML stands for Virtual Reality Markup Language.

## REFERENCES

Benedikt, Michael, ed. *Cyberspace: First Steps*. Cambridge, Mass.: MIT University Press, 1991.

Bentham, Jeremy. *The Panopticon Writings*. London and New York: Verso, 1995.

Bloom, Paul, Mary A. Peterson, Lynn Nadel, and Merrill F. Garrett, eds. *Language and Space*. Cambridge, Mass.: MIT Press, 1996.

Cicognani, Anna. *Design Speech Acts. "How to do things with words" in a VC. A Model for the Application of Speech Acts in a MOO*. Los Angeles: ACM, 1997.

——. "A Linguistic Characterisation of Design in Text-Based Virtual Worlds." Ph.D. diss., University of Sydney, 1998a.

——. "On the Linguistic Nature of Cyberspace and Virtual Communities." *Virtual Reality: Research, Development, and Application* 3, no. 1 (1998b): 25–33.

Coyne, Richard. *Designing Information Technology in the Postmodern Age*. Cambridge, Mass.: MIT Press, 1995.

Eisenstadt, Marc, and Tom Vincent, eds. *The Knowledge Web: Learning and Collaborating on the Web*. London: Kogan Page, 1998.

Hammurabi. Hammurabi's Code of Laws. http://www.wwlia.org/hamm1.htm.

Hillier, Bill, and Julienne Hanson. *The Social Logic of Space*. Cambridge, Eng.: Cambridge University Press, 1984.

Kollock, Peter. *Design Principles for Online Communities*. Cambridge: O'Reilly and Associates, 1997.

Lefebvre, Henri. *The Construction of Space*. Oxford, Eng.: Blackwell, 1991.

Maher, Mary Lou, Simeon J. Simoff, and Anna Cicognani. *Understanding Virtual Design Studios*. London: Springer-Verlag, 1999.

Meyrowitz, Joshua. *No Sense of Place: The Impact of Electronic Media on Social Behavior*. New York: Oxford University Press, 1985.

Mitchell, William J. *City of Bits*. Cambridge, Mass.: MIT Press, 1995.

O'Malley, Claire, ed. *Computer Supported Collaborative Learning*. Berlin, N.Y.: Springer-Verlag, 1995.

Raikes, Jeff. *Campus of the Twenty-first Century: A New Paradigm for Online Learning*. New York, 1997.

Stonor, Tim. "Space Syntax: Interdisciplinary Design." http://www.bartlett.ucl.ac.uk/spacesyntax/publications/topos/topos.htm.

Sumner, Tamara, and Josie Taylor. *New Media, New Practices: Experiences in Open Learning Course Design*. Los Angeles, 1998.

Thompson, George F., and Frederick R. Steiner, eds. *Ecological Design and Planning*. New York: Wiley, 1997.

Venturi, Robert, Steven Izenour, and Denise Scott Brown. *Learning from Las Vegas: The Forgotten Symbolism of Architectural Form*. Cambridge, Mass.: MIT Press, 1977.

Woolley, Benjamin. *Virtual Worlds*. Oxford, Eng.: Blackwell, 1992.

4

# Community, Affect, and the Virtual: The Politics of Cyberspace

J. MACGREGOR WISE

## COMMUNITY

The debate over the authenticity of online community is a debate over affect, whether one can match the intensity of real-life experience in a virtual realm. The term "community" has become a key word for research and debates around cyberspace. The usual argument, overgeneralized here, goes something like this: the modern world has lost some sense of community and commitment to others and has become alienated and fragmented. Perhaps it is the end of the modern and we are now living in some free-form postmodern society. In any case, social cohesion—not to say democracy—is in crisis and we as a society need to refocus on community. And technology, as it has so many times in the past, comes to our rescue. The Internet, a noncentralized, nonhierarchical, anarchic network of computer networks, would allow us to reconnect with one another, to open a forum for public discourse, to allow each and every one of us a voice in the grand debate that is society. The arguments are made to seem new and fresh, but have echoes of a deep past. Ever since Ferdinand Tönnies and Emile Durkheim, social scientists have been discussing the loss of community in the urbanization of the Western world. And ever since the printing press, communication technologies have been brought to the fore as, at last, the answer to all our problems (especially those of democracy).

The problem is, as Richard Sclove has pointed out, that despite revolution after revolution in communication technologies over the last 150 years, each of which has been touted as at last bringing us together and fostering democratic participation, democratic participation has significantly decreased in the United States (evidenced by meager voter turnout at presidential elections and even less in local forums). Perhaps, he argues, these technologies might not be democratic technologies after all, at least in the form and organization in which they are deployed. Sclove is an advocate for what he calls (following Benjamin Barber) "strong democracy," which is the basic belief "that people should be able to help shape the basic social circumstances of their lives" (91). Among those "basic social circumstances" is technology:

> If citizens ought to be empowered to participate in determining their society's basic structure, and technologies are an important species of social structure, it follows that technological design and practice should be democratized. (91)

Participatory design has been the hallmark of the most successful cybercommunities, especially the MUDs and MOOs (originally text-based but now often graphically oriented multiple-user environments) whose software is continually redeveloped and expanded by the community of users themselves. But such communities are fewer and rarer than ever on the commercialized landscape of the World Wide Web, which seems to have superseded and subsumed the rest of the Internet in the popular imaginary. Indeed, the Web's success may now ride on what Andrew Shapiro terms "personalization . . . the ability to shape one's experience more precisely" (11). But as we custom configure our interfaces with the world (as Nicholas Negroponte would have us do), and the media continue to narrowcast to more specific demographic niches, and intelligent agent software on commercial sites begins to limit our options by deciding based on demographics and purchase patterns what its programmers think we want, social cohesion is damaged in that society lacks any shared experience (Shapiro, 12).

All of which makes us wonder what's up with these promises about the Internet, the Web, and community. Especially, what is underlying these promises of new community and the articulation of the idea of community to democracy, egalitarianism, and freedom if these last are not fulfilled? One problem in such debates is that the term "community" is presented as a given, as if we all know what it means and we all share the same meaning and ideals. And so we have arguments stating that online communities are real communities (supportive structures in times of crisis, forums for public debate) and arguments stating that online communities are fake communities (shallow and inconsequential, they could even embody and enhance social fragmentation), and arguments stating that they are both. In addition to this, as Lee Komito has argued, these debates ignore decades of social science research on the idea of community and tend to conflate several different types of community. Such research is hampered not only by holding culture-specific ideals of rural, agrarian communities, but also by not realizing that such ideals are culture-specific (and, indeed, may never have existed).

Raymond Williams writes in his discussion of "community" in *Keywords* that the term historically has been used to describe both actual groups of people and "a particular quality of relationship" (75), which are not necessarily the same thing. In addition, "community" is usually given a more immediate and personal sense than, say, "society." "Community" is a very persuasive term, he argues, because of this immediacy and also because "it seems never to be used unfavourably, and never to be given any positive opposing or distinguishing term" (76). It is therefore not surprising that the term should be used so prominently to persuade a society to accept a new array of technologies (computer- and telecommunication-based Internet and service technologies), and with them a new industrial, economic, and social organization (moving from industrial mass production to postmodern, flexible production).[1] Indeed, adding a "community component" is said to be the latest way to draw (and hold) customers to commercial Web sites,[2] though Andrew Shapiro has argued that such attempts have not yet been very successful.

To clarify some of the debates, Komito outlines four types of community and how they figure in debates about cyberspace.

The first is what he terms *moral communities*, in which "individuals share a common ethical system that constrains interactions among members, emphasizing mutual benefit above self-interest or personal goals. This is community as communal solidarity" (98). Key to this version of community is the idea of affect, seen through the importance of commitment to the community and trust. Howard Rheingold's book

*The Virtual Community* seems exemplary of this type of community, especially since he opens with a discussion of "this emotional attachment to an apparently bloodless technological ritual" (1) and later states that "community is a matter of emotions as well as a thing of reason and data" (15). This version of community is also evident in his definition of virtual communities as "social aggregations that emerge from the Net when enough people carry on those public discussions long enough, *with sufficient human feeling*, to form webs of personal relationships in cyberspace" (5, emphasis mine). For example, Faith McClellan carefully describes a long-term discussion list on the WELL (the Whole Earth 'Lectronic Link, an early and prominent online community) regarding a young boy's continuing battle with leukemia. Though concerned primarily with the unique narrative strategies at work in the electronic medium, McClellan's account is notable for relaying the emotional power of the postings themselves and the creation of a supportive community. Most critiques of cybercommunities as being ersatz, as missing something, arise when this affective dimension is lacking. And when people lament the loss of community, it is the dimension of affect and identification that they are most likely referring to, not congregations of people (Howard Newby, quoted in Thompson, 24). A question that Komito raises with this version of community is whether electronic communication (i.e., words on a computer screen) alone is sufficient to create and maintain it.

A second version of community, according to Komito, is the *normative community*, "evidenced by the existence of agreed-upon rules of appropriate behavior" (99). This is community based upon shared values and perhaps shared experience, but not necessarily upon actual interaction (or even commitment to each other or the community). It is a cognitive community (e.g., the community of communication researchers or the community of dog groomers), not an affective or moral one. Komito suggests that such groups do form cultures, but not necessarily communities.

The third version of community is the *proximate community*, "in which people interact with each other not in terms of roles or stereotypes, but as individuals" (100), a notion of community that is based on the idea of the community as a particular space (e.g., a village) where involuntary interactions can occur, where one has complex and overlapping relations with the others in the community, and which it is not easy to leave (i.e., log out). The electronic communities that come closest to this version are those that seek to create a forum that acts much like a public space: MUDs and MOOs. Also, we must consider the rise in the number of community-based Web sites, electronic villages, community networks, and virtual cities that promise this sort of community.[3] It is this sort of story on cyberspace that seems to garner the most press, the stories on space-based versions of community. Such virtual communities are also at times referred to as virtual cities, which are often regarded as enhancements of actual cities and as a way of reintroducing community to the alienation of city life.

Urban geographers Stephen Graham and Alessandro Aurigi have argued that two basic types of virtual cities or "electronic spaces" have arisen as an apparent resolution to the crisis of the "'public realm' of Western cities" (19): grounded and non-grounded cities. Non-grounded virtual cities merely use the metaphor of a city to arrange an array of services and features, without being intended to represent any single city. Grounded virtual cities are meant to represent particular sites and may be publicly or privately sponsored. Indeed, any single city may boast multiple Web sites, each claiming to be the virtual shadow of the real city. Graham and Aurigi point out that the city of Bristol in England has at least six virtual Bristols online (38). In fact, the region of South Carolina in which I used to teach (known as the Upstate) likewise boasted at least six sites purporting to cover the area, though three focus on particular towns in the region (Clemson, Anderson, and Greenville).

> Such virtual cities can be configured either as glossy advertising and promotional spaces, with no useful information for residents, or as civic services, providing "public electronic spaces" that support political and social discourses about the city itself.
>
> (Graham and Aurigi, 36)

However, even these latter sites tend to be "urban databases," providing a great deal of varying information for residents and tourists but few means for the citizen either to talk back or engage in discussions with others on issues.[4] The information is "uni-directional" (37). The issues with such virtual cities are twofold. One is that of access. Though such communities may make more information conveniently available, they make it available for what is still only a small proportion of the community at stake (though a few elite communities are exceptions). The second issue is that of community itself. Though these sites seek to represent communities (groups of people), can they create community (the quality of the relationship)? Graham and Aurigi question whether virtual communities can re-create the felt, affective experience of community. In Komito's terms, they doubt that an online community can combine the qualities of both proximate and moral communities. But perhaps grounded communities might be our best shot at this combination. Indeed, it is Andrew Shapiro's argument that community networks should focus first and foremost on enhancing—rather than replacing—the physical local communities from which they arise and that they purport to represent.

Finally, Komito presents a fourth version of community—*the fluid community* or *foraging society*—as an alternative to those versions that arise out of "an ethnocentric and restrictive view of community based on limited comparative examples from industrial and agrarian societies" (102). The foraging society is a nomadic one. Though a foraging group might exhibit patterns of seasonal migration, they are not tied to any particular plot of land or any larger macrosocial structures on which they depend. Therefore "foraging communities are temporary aggregations of individuals. There is often little sense of collective identity. . . . Membership in a community is voluntary and temporary, and individuals move and groups are redefined, depending on ecological and personal factors" (103). Though this image of community may not fit the idealized version of a moral, proximate community so often assumed in discussions around cyberspace, Komito argues that it actually might better describe the experience of online groups: the unstable membership in discussion groups, the easy ability to leave the group, membership in multiple groups, and so on.

This account of virtual communities is admittedly brief. Other chapters in this volume explore virtual communities and community networks in more detail. But what I would like to point out is that though we may idealize proximate, moral communities, what are most often produced on the Net are foraging communities and commercialized virtual cities. We also learn from these discussions that "affect" is as much of a god term in these discourses as "community" is, and as such the term bears some examination. In the remainder of this essay I will explore the idea of affect and its relation to the virtual, to technology, and to what I will term the digital sublime. In the end I will argue that it is the flow and capture of affect that grounds the virtual community and that represents its potential for both freedom and domination.

## AFFECT

What happens when affect is appealed to in most accounts of cyberspace and virtual communities is that the debate is drawn into the terms and political episteme of the modern. In most general discussions, "affect" and "emotion" are considered nearly synonymous. In addition to this, affect and emotion are said to oppose rationality. Also, they are said to arise from individuals (radically separate and self-contained beings each capable of providing a unique and essential point of view). The appeal to affect, then, is an appeal to authenticity. This sense of affect is often viewed as individualistic and resistant because it is not cognitive (and therefore not ideological). One's affective attachments are said to be a source of personal decision and personal strength. Affect is not regarded as being structured or overdetermined. This version of affect, perhaps, plays into the sense of libertarianism that is prevalent on the Net.

It has been argued elsewhere (by myself and others such as Stephen Doheny-Farina) that the two main political positions on the Net are libertarian and communitarian, though these overlap in interesting ways. The libertarians are most often noticed around the original *Wired* magazine (what we might call the Wired School: including John Perry Barlow, Kevin Kelly, Nicholas Negroponte, and the Electronic Frontier Foundation). They follow a certain reading of Marshall McLuhan and argue that the Net is (and should be) the domain of—if not the extension of—the rational individual and a bastion of the civil rights arising from this episteme, freedom of speech being primary. The communitarians see in the Net the potential for a resurgence of community, goodwill, and democracy. The positions overlap in some respects, since on the one hand, cybercommunities are often viewed as consisting of libertarians, and on the other hand both share a commitment to the sovereignty of the individual—the communitarians merely argue for a balance between individual rights and community responsibility. Both positions have more recently been overtaken in the corporate marketing reterritorialization of the Net—especially the Web—evidenced by the 1998 sale of *Wired* to Condé Nast. Echoes of these ideological debates (centered around freedom-of-speech issues) still linger in public discourse about children's access to violent or pornographic or hate sites (especially since the Columbine High School shootings) but these debates turn into arguments about media in general (for example, crackdowns on unaccompanied minors seeing "R"-rated films), and the Net's technological specificity—and hence its specific politics—is lost.

But perhaps such politics no longer matter and the representatives of such positions are mere holdovers from the politically—and affectively—charged 1960s (indeed, tracing *Wired*'s connections to the San Francisco counterculture is hardly difficult). For as Fredric Jameson has argued, apart from the destruction of the grand narratives (and with them ideology), one of the hallmarks of the postmodern era is the waning of affect. Following on from this logic, it makes sense that people are fleeing to cyberspace to find the affect and community that are so absent in their lives, to find something that matters (or something that matters for longer than the standard TV commercial or mass media feeding frenzy). It also, in a way, lets the Internet off the hook because the waning of affect is everywhere; it is not just a Net effect.

Both Brian Massumi and Lawrence Grossberg, however, have argued that perhaps there hasn't been a waning of affect at all; indeed, perhaps there is an *excess* of affect in society. It is just that we lack the appropriate critical-cultural vocabulary to notice and examine it. To understand affect, then, we must parse and refine the term, much as we did with the term "community" above. Otherwise we end up collapsing too many different meanings into the term. In exploring and redefining the term we will run counter to the assumed, modernist view set out at the start of this section, and argue that affect is neither personal nor individual.

So what do we mean by "affect"? Affect is not the same thing as emotion; affect refers to intensity. As Grossberg has written,

> affect identifies the strength of the investment which anchors people in particular experiences, practices, identities, meanings and pleasures, but it also determines how invigorated people feel at any moment of their lives, their level of energy or passion. (82)

Obviously this is not merely one's emotional commitments. Massumi writes:

> An emotion is a subjective content, the socio-linguistic fixing of the quality of an experience which is from that point onward defined as personal. Emotion is qualified intensity, the conventional, consensual point of insertion of intensity into semantically and semiotically formed progressions, into narrativizable action-reaction circuits, into function and meaning. (221)

Emotions are post hoc narrativations of experience and intensity, and as such are subject to ideological structure and direction. This means that we should look more carefully at the structure of emotions around the Internet and cybercommunities, because the identification and narrativation of emotion might reveal a broader social territorialization. In doing so we note that the types of emotions discussed by Howard Rheingold (caring, joy, grief, and the occasional need to bop someone on the head), for example, seem to map quite cleanly onto the middle-class baby boom family-picnic reconstruction of community evidenced in the communitarian movement (see Derber). In other words, emotion is used to support a particular value structure and version of community at the expense of other possibilities.

While emotions are nameable, graspable, affect is not. Indeed, affect—as intensity—is asignifying and preconscious. Affect is a gap (when words and conscious reactions fail), but it is a gap overflowing with energy and intensity, its potential. Affect occurs before the structuring of experience by language—indeed, experience is the retrospective patching over and narrativizing of the aporias of affect. Affect escapes language. "If some have the impression that affect has waned, it is because affect is unqualified. As such, it is not ownable or recognizable, and is thus resistent to critique" (Massumi, 221–222).

This does not mean that affect cannot be put to political uses. While affect qua affect simply is (and therefore cares not about ideology or individuals), once affect enters the realm of the human and is actualized it is no longer innocent and it is definitely not random. Our passionate need to buy a Saturn automobile (why that particular car?) or to purchase a faster modem attests to this. There are two moments of affect, if not two types. What we might call in the first moment the plane of affect (an eruption of affect) becomes in the second moment, to some extent, organized (e.g., focused on the purchase of something). We must recognize that the resources that act upon the plane of affect are not randomly distributed but act according to what Pierre Bourdieu called objective structures, but what Gilles Deleuze and Félix Guattari would call (much more dynamically) a differentiating machine. But objective structures do not necessarily parallel, mirror, or determine our affective reactions (just as affect and language are often at odds).

> The affective plane is organized according to maps which direct people's investments in and into the world. These maps are deployed in relation to the formations in which they are articulated. They tell people where, how and with what intensities they can become absorbed—into the world and their lives. This "absorption" constructs the places and events which are, or can become, significant. They are the places at which people can anchor themselves into the world, the locations of the things that matter.
>
> (Grossberg, 82)

These mattering maps do not correspond neatly with the structures of ideology where one can read one's investments based on how one is spoken (articulated) by ideology (just as one cannot specify someone's ideology based solely on that person's class position; there is a non-necessary correspondence). The potentials that make up the intensive moment follow tendencies based on traces of past action (Massumi, 223–224). Affects follow habits (rather than following ideological or objective structures). Habitual action does include traces of contexts (and structures), but habit in itself is not determining either. In each iteration of a habit, in each repetition, is difference.[6] On the one hand, context has shifted and so the iteration has altered, and on the other, each iteration opens up onto chaos, a hesitation where the potential of myriad habits arises, though only one is chosen. Brian Massumi argues that Ronald Reagan was such a successful president and political and ideological leader not because of eloquence or nonverbal skill but because of the continual production of gaps, of hesitations in speech and style in which the potentials welled up, the potential to head in any number of directions, to follow any number of habits. It wasn't what he said, or even how he said it, but rather the potentials he produced.

Our lack of appropriate political response to the Reagan hegemony, the postmodern political scene, and cyberspace itself is the result, in part, of not being able to recognize this affective dimension, and in part of working with an excess of affect rather than a dearth. Affect no longer maps as cleanly as it used to onto political, ideological, or even class frameworks, and so it does not act like it is "supposed" to. But rather than blaming the ideology or political position or even the citizen, one should follow the affect to understand what's going on.

Another part of the problem in our lack of appropriate response is that, especially in debates over surveillance and privacy (prominent in cyberspace discourse), we assume that we are still under what Foucault termed a disciplinary society, in which subjects are constructed through disciplinary apparatuses. The disciplinary society posits a central state apparatus, though the workings and effects of power are distributed and internalized. However, Deleuze has argued in his essay "Postscript on Control Societies" that Foucault's description of the disciplinary society was meant to be historically specific, and now new regimes of power are arising. We are moving toward, Deleuze writes, a control society, in which power has dispersed. There is no center to society. The control society is a massive deterritorialization, the creation of a smooth space crossed by intensities and speeds, but not distributed and structured as it had been. Speed is key as the society moves ever faster on the backs on new communication and information technologies. A control society doesn't hold people still (in lockdown), but accelerates them to its speed. This does not mean that disciplinary apparatuses no longer exist—they do, and in force; it merely means that there are other regimes of power at work in society. The nature of a virtual public under such a regime is quite different from what we may be used to. Again, this is a society without the familiar landmarks—so one declares the waning of ideology, of class, race, and gender (e.g., claims that there is no race or gender on the Internet), but what is left is speed and affect.[7] It is crucial, then, to understand how affect works and how it is structured, for the Internet is far from being the smooth space it purports to be.

To understand cyberspace it is not enough to understand the discourses that swirl through, around, and about it and how these discourses are distributed and structured (around god terms such as "community," "affect," "democracy," and "freedom," but also around such concepts as efficiency, decorporealization, and speed). And it is likewise not enough to understand the embodiment of cyberspace, the technological and corporeal, the distribution of machines, people, and jobs. Or even to understand the stratification of these two (language and technology), their double articulation.[8] What is also important is to understand the organization of mattering maps, the distribution of intensities, the territorialization of cyberspace. If we understand how affect (once it is actualized) is organized, and how affect itself functions, circulates, and emerges, we can begin to see a possible politics of resistance.

## VIRTUAL

Deleuze and Guattari argue that there are machinic processes that work to organize (and disorganize) the world. Machines are functions that work immanently and can be observed only by noting their effects. Affect is acted upon by, and acts like, such a machine. Machines do not exist in the actual, but in the virtual—and note that by "virtual" I no longer mean in the digital computer realm but am introducing a very different definition of the term.

The virtual is a concept originally from Bergson, which Deleuze took up and reread. Deleuze's concept of the virtual has had some influence on contemporary theories of space and culture. Elizabeth Grosz explains the concept of the virtual as follows: "The virtual is the space of emergence of the new, the unthought, the unrealized, which at every moment loads the presence of the present with supplementarity, redoubling a world through parallel universes, universes that might have been" (78).

This is not to say that the virtual is not real; rather the virtual is not actual. Likewise, the virtual is not merely the possible. To quote from Grosz again:

> The possible is an already preformed version of the real. The transition from the possible to the real is a predictable one, not involving anything new or unexpected. The relationship between the virtual and the actual is one of surprise, for the virtual promises something different to the actual that it produces, and always contains in it the potential for something other than the actual. (12)

I would like to approach the idea of the virtual through the findings of chaos theory,[9] because this approach yields concepts such as the singularity that will be useful in describing the actions and shaping of affect.

Chaos theory concerns itself in part with self-organizing processes, a concept based on the discovery that apparently chaotic activity (the turbulent flow of a liquid, for example) is actually highly organized. Self-organization occurs when seemingly random elements (molecules, insects) reach a transition point (a certain speed or density, perhaps) and suddenly become coordinated, organized. As Manuel De Landa has explained, such events are studied by means of a phase diagram, which is an attempt to map an event as it unfolds over time. The space of the phase diagram consists of *n*-dimensions, where *n* is the number of aspects or variables of the event that you are measuring. For example, if you are measuring height and distance of a ball rolling down a hill, you would map that on a two-dimensional plane. Add speed as a variable and it's a three-dimensional diagram, and so on (one needs advanced computers as the number of dimensions increases). The space of the map is phase space, the event as it unfolds in *n*-dimensions is represented by a line. The space of the map is the virtual, the line of the event is the actual. What has been discovered about such maps is that there seem to be points at which the path of the actual changes course, or circles back, or is drawn toward or away from a certain point. Such points are called singularities. They affect the event like gravitational fields, but they are not the event itself (not the actual); they are rather potentials (a potential outcome).

Affect is a singularity (Massumi, 226). It affects and shapes events, but is not the event itself. Affect is the two-sidedness of the emergence of an event: "the simultaneous participation of the virtual in the actual and the actual in the virtual, as one arises from and returns to the other" (228). We should be concerned with the virtual, affect, and singularities because the "seeping edge" where the virtual "leaks into the actual" is where potential is found (236). Potential triggers change and the emergence of the new. Grosz links the virtual with futurity: "The virtual is the realm of productivity, of functioning otherwise than its plan or blueprint, functioning in excess of design and intention" (130).

Perhaps we should think of the title of this collection, *Virtual Publics*, (at least for the purposes of this essay) as a description of the potentiality of publics more than simply digital or computer-based publics. To do so would be to focus on the emergent processes of technology and community: how the digital can stimulate discussion, social change, and material and political transformation. We cannot assume that it will automatically do so. But to simply state that the potential for change is there (where?) is clearly not enough. Affect is continually being captured, channeled into commercial sites or old patterns of consumer culture or preexisting structures. On the one hand, the task is to understand the capture of affect, once it has entered the human realm, and how singularities are organized into mattering maps. On the other hand, the task is to understand the circulation of affect within, between, and outside of communities and the seeping edges where the potential for change can be found.

To provide an example of the capture of affect, I will turn to a discussion of the idea of the technological sublime, which is an affective singularity, an attractor that draws us toward technologies and guides our investments in them. The sublime has been a point about which much of American technological history has been structured. I take a historical turn here to indicate how the sublime might function to organize a virtual public.

> The sublime underlies this enthusiasm for technology. One of the most powerful human emotions, when experienced by large groups the sublime can weld society together. In moments of sublimity, human beings temporarily disregard divisions among elements of the community. The sublime taps into fundamental hopes and fears. It is not a social residue, created by economic and political forces, though both can inflect its meaning. Rather, it is an essentially religious feeling, aroused by confrontation with impressive objects, such as Niagara Falls, the Grand Canyon, the New York skyline, the Golden Gate Bridge, or the earth-shaking launch of the space shuttle. The technological sublime is an integral part of contemporary consciousness, and its emergence and exfoliation into several distinct forms during the past two centuries is inscribed within public life. (Nye, xiii)

David Nye, in the above passage, attempts to structure and put into words moments of the eruption of affect: the desire to visit the Empire

State Building, or to flood onto the Golden Gate Bridge in 1987 on its fiftieth anniversary (causing worry that the bridge might collapse). In a moment of the sublime one is without words (a mark of affect), in awe. The moment of the sublime is an affective gap through which pour intensity and energy. These energies are subsequently captured, organized, narrativized, labeled (as emotion). But the energies are not *necessarily* captured, and the simple emergence of affect is the possibility of change. The affective gap of the technological sublime is significantly overcoded with references to religion and transcendence, but also to progress. A major theme with regard to technology in modern culture is the relation of technology to progress (and the idea of progress is invested with this affective energy). Technology, in this view, moves us as a society forward and upward. This articulation of technology to inevitable progress is deeply entrenched in American culture. New technologies are said to inevitably make the world a better place. The idea of technological progress can be found in the frontier myth of America,[10] is justified by an evolutionary view of technology, and has been central to international modernization and development efforts.

Both the idea of technology and the idea of progress are deeply embedded in the American national consciousness. The concurrence of the American Revolution (the creation of what was assumed to be the ideal society based on democratic ideals) and the Industrial Revolution are not to be ignored. Indeed, Europeans of the eighteenth and nineteenth centuries viewed America as the place where technology and nature would come together to form the perfect society (what Leo Marx has termed the "machine in the garden," the mechanical sublime). Such ideas undergirded manifest destiny and the drive westward into the supposedly uncivilized wilderness. As Merritt Roe Smith explains, the railway especially took on the embodiment of progress and the sublime. Historian Richard Slotkin has shown that the frontier myth has been the cover for capitalist territorialization, turning the wilderness into resources for the factories back East.

James Carey and John Quirk argue that this ideology was fundamentally challenged by the blatant destruction of the landscape by the railroads and mines, the rise of industrial slums, and the chaos of the Civil War. The New World proved to be much like the Old World, and the mechanical sublime became bankrupt. However, discoveries about electricity (in terms of both electrical power and the power to communicate by telegraph and later telephone) soon replaced the mechanical sublime with the electric sublime. Electricity was seen to be separate from mechanical technology, somehow transcendent, pure, and clean, and the electric revolution (telegraph, electric light, telephone, and so on) carried forward the utopian vision of the technological fix.[11] This ideology was upheld in the twentieth century by such projects as the Tennessee Valley Authority and such thinkers as Marshall McLuhan. McLuhan, now again a key figure in discourses on cyberspace, prophesied a global village made possible by these technologies; electrical technologies would enable a world of great personal freedoms (decentralization, democracy, and a cultural revival). However, these technologies are also connected with expansion and control over territory and favor the establishment of commercialism, empire, and eventually technocracy (Carey and Quirk, 133–134). Rather than freeing, such technologies are even more binding and controlling (indeed, since most were invented in order to enhance the idea of control,[12] it seems ironic to have them viewed as enhancing freedom).

The electric sublime is still with us to a certain extent, though it has become tarnished by pollution and the specter of nuclear technologies. But at the waning of this singularity comes yet another rearticulation of the sublime, this time in the pure, noncorporeal realm of digital bits: the digital sublime. The digital sublime is evident in the works of such authors as Nicholas Negroponte (*Being Digital*, the key work on the new sublime) and William Mitchell (*City of Bits*). The digerati, as they are called, advocate the abandonment of atoms to play in the clean, free, world of bits. Cyberspace is the new frontier (indeed, the subtitle of Howard Rheingold's book is *Homesteading on the Electronic Frontier*). Again, we are not talking about the rhetoric that is used to organize and sell plots of land in cyberspace, nor are we talking about the real possibilities of the technologies themselves. Indeed, the promises of decentralization, democracy, cultural revival, and individual freedom to be had in cutting edge technology mask the growth of electronic networks of surveillance and control, not to mention the fragmentation of the workforce into temporary just-in-time services and the movement of exploitative factories overseas and out of sight. And like the mechanical and electric frontiers before it, cyberspace is thoroughly permeated by capital.

What we *are* talking about is that the digital provides an eruption point for affect, the intensity of investment and mattering maps. For example, the early *Wired* magazine seemed to generate a great deal of affective response (channeled into both love and hate and sometimes from one to the other). Perhaps this might have been because the magazine revealed a gap, an interruption, a lurch as the society's technological gears shifted, and in that gap potentials welled up. Though the magazine captured that affect and stretched it over a corporate-libertarian frame ("cyber-rights now!"), enough affect leaked out to make the magazine captivating, even if one disagreed with its politics. Another example was the seemingly disproportionate flood of popular enthusiasm in 1993 at the mention of a National Information Infrastructure (never have so many been so excited about a rather rarefied government policy proposal) and the phenomenal growth of online services and the World Wide Web over the next few years. Widespread acceptance of the NII (especially in its more popular consumerist form of the Information Superhighway) consequently helped rev up the control society (the new regime of power). In a society of control we are swamped with data, overloaded with information, we are forced to speak, to produce more and more information until nothing means anything anymore. The drive for speed, Andrew Ross has argued, is a drive to increase scarcity and as a result to increase profit. And Deleuze wrote that communication is now thoroughly permeated with money ("Post-script").

What we are seeing is a corporate-consumerist territorialization of cyberspace, channeling affect into profit. Of course, virtual communities are not exempt from these processes, from the sale of the WELL to the establishment of "community components" at commercial sites. There are many reasons why people are online; the attraction of the digital sublime is just one. We must remember that corporate capital did not create this eruption of affect, but is beginning to manage it. The singularity is still there, though, as a gravitational point on our mattering maps. Affect before capture is not political or ideological, it is simply wild power.

How does one build a community in a society of control? What would such a community look like against a landscape of pure speed and circulating affect? One description is that of the nomadic migrations of Komito's foraging communities, communities contingent on resources and the ebb and flow of territories. Though that is a fairly accurate description of most online communities generally, as we have seen, this formation feeds all too easily into the corporate territorialization of cyberspace (indeed, it matches the needs of this territorialization: without long-term commitments individuals can easily move from one product to the next [improved] product). Another possible way of building community can be found through interrupting and redirecting the flows, tripping them up (as it were) by articulating speed and affect to the local, to specific territories (after all, Deleuze and Guattari once wrote that when territorializing and deterritorializing you should always carry a fresh plot of land with you[13]), to community networks. But to do so successfully means to use the local not as a receptacle for flows of investment and affect but as a lever to maximize and diversify affect (before its capture) by creating ruptures, gaps, and stutters.

Grosz identifies an additional community to which we must pay attention, one not mentioned by Komito or by discussions of community networks.

> There is a community, a collective of those who have nothing in common. This concept of a community of the lost, of strangers, of the marginalized and outcast is borrowed from the work of Alphonso Lingis, and especially from his concern with community not as that which is united through common bonds, goals, language, or descent, but as that which opens itself to the stranger, to the dying, to the one with whom one has nothing in common, the one who is not like oneself. (151–152)

Communities consist not only of what they include but also what they exclude, what is seen as unassimilable. The left out form an excess, an excess that both defies the community (the community doesn't work for or with the other) and constitutes it. The excess is not just people, but things, even technologies. And it is this excess that can cause ruptures, gaps, and stutters. Where Grosz argues for an architecture of excess that places excess at its core to create more fluid and more productive spaces (163), could we create virtual communities of excess to unlock the flows of communication and power?

It means to create communities of change, which is always a dangerous proposition, because change doesn't provide guarantees. It means to embrace the paradox of creating a community that is both fluid and proximate, to struggle with the articulation of the group of people and the quality of the relationship in search of a community that is both emergent and participatory.

Our task, then, is to produce a critical vocabulary with which to analyze these singularities, to analyze affect as Deleuze, Guattari, Grossberg, Massumi, and Grosz have done. I have begun to do so in this essay by rewriting key terms in the debate over communities and cyberspace. Whereas we started with the statement "*The debate over the authenticity of online community is a debate over affect, whether one can match the intensity of real-life experience in a virtual realm*," we conclude with the statement "*The debate over the authenticity of the democratic ideal online is a debate over the capture of affect and the singularities that structure the social realm.*" So by the term "virtual publics" I now mean something quite different from the way that phrase is being used to structure the rest of this volume. The virtual public is a shadow public, the realm of potential and possible paths immanent to the actual public. And the political tasks of the virtual community are these: to learn how to create "vacuoles of non-communication" (Deleuze, "Control") within the smooth space of cyberspace, to unleash the potential intensity buried under reams of data, and to build communities that are just and convivial.

## NOTES

My thanks to those who gave me feedback and constructive criticism on previous versions of this essay: Steve Jones, Beth Kolko, Gilbert Rodman, and Gregory J. Seigworth. Their input has made this a stronger and clearer essay. All errors remain solely my own.

1. See Wise, chapter 6, where I develop this further, and also James Brook and Iain Boal's preface to *Resisting the Virtual Life*.

2. See Jim Cashel, "Community Is a Commodity."

3. On community networks, see Mark Jones's and David Silver's essays in this volume.

4. See David Silver's essay in this volume for the discussion of the Blacksburg Electronic Village and the tensions between the village as a civic space and as a space of consumption.

5. Both Massumi's and Grossberg's discussions about affect derive from the work of Deleuze and Guattari, therefore their positions have much in common. Nevertheless, there are still some significant differences between their arguments, though these need not concern us for the purposes of the essay at hand. The account of affect that follows is something of a hybrid of their work. My deepest thanks to Gregory J. Seigworth for his commentary on an earlier draft of this section.

6. See Deleuze, *Difference and Repetition*.

7. The notion of a society of control has been expanded on by Michael Hardt (see also Hardt and Negri). I explore these issues in more depth in my essay, "Mapping the Culture of Control."

8. I set out this double articulation much more fully in my book *Exploring Technology and Social Space*.

9. The description of phase space that follows derives from De Landa's account, but see also Brian Massumi's essay "The Autonomy of Affect," as well as Félix Guattari's book *Chaosmosis*.

10. On this, see Thomas Tierney's *The Value of Convenience*.

11. See, for example, Carolyn Marvin's *When Old Technologies Were New*.

12. See James Beniger, *The Control Revolution*.

13. "Lodge yourself on a stratum, experiment with the opportunities it offers, find an advantageous place on it, find potential movements of deterritorialization, possible lines of flight, experience them, produce flow conjunctions here and there, try out continuums of intensities segment by segment, have a small plot of new land at all times" (Deleuze and Guattari, 161).

## REFERENCES

Beniger, James. *The Control Revolution: Technological and Economic Origins of the Information Society*. Cambridge, Mass.: Harvard University Press, 1986.

Bourdieu, Pierre. "Social Space and Symbolic Power." In *In Other Words: Essays Toward a Reflective Society*, 123–139. Stanford, Calif.: Stanford University Press, 1990.

Brook, James, and Iain A. Boal eds.. *Resisting the Virtual Life: The Culture and Politics of Information*. San Francisco: City Lights, 1995.

Carey, James, and John J. Quirk. "The Mythos of the Electronic Revolution." In James Carey, ed. *Communication as Culture: Essays on Media and Society*. Boston: Unwin Hyman, 1989.

Cashel, Jim. "Community Is a Commodity." *New Media*, August 1999, 38–43.

De Landa, Manuel. *War in the Age of Intelligent Machines*. New York: Zone, 1991.

Deleuze, Gilles. *Bergsonism*. Trans. Hugh Tomlinson and Barbara Habberjam. New York: Zone Books, 1988.

——. "Control and Becoming." In *Negotiations, 1972–1990*, 169–176. Trans. Martin Joughin. New York: Columbia University Press, 1995.

——. *Difference and Repetition*. Trans. Paul Patton. New York: Columbia University Press, 1994.

——. "Postscript on Control Societies." In *Negotiations, 1972–1990*, 177–182. Trans. Martin Joughin. New York: Columbia University Press, 1995.

Deleuze, Gilles, and Félix Guattari. *A Thousand Plateaus: Capitalism and Schizophrenia*. Trans. Brian Massumi. Minneapolis: University of Minnesota Press, 1987.

Derber, Charles. "Individualism Runs Amok in the Marketplace." *Utne Reader*, November–December 1994, 111–117. Reprinted from *Tikkun* 8.4.

Doheny-Farina, Stephen. *The Wired Neighborhood*. New Haven, Conn.: Yale University Press, 1996.

Graham, Stephen, and Alessandro Aurigi. "Virtual Cities, Social Polarization, and the Crisis in Urban Public Space." *Journal of Urban Technology* 4, no. 1 (1997): 19–52.

Grossberg, Lawrence. *We Gotta Get Out of This Place: Popular Conservatism and Postmodern Culture*. New York: Routledge, 1992.

Grosz, Elizabeth. *Architecture from the Outside: Essays on Virtual and Real Space*. Cambridge, Mass.: MIT Press, 2001.

Guattari, Félix. *Chaosmosis*. Trans. Julian Pefanis and Paul Bains. Bloomington: Indiana University Press, 1995.

Hardt, Michael. "The Global Society of Control." *Discourse* 20, no. 3 (1998): 139–152.

Hardt, Michael, and Antonio Negri. *Empire*. Cambridge, Mass.: Harvard University Press, 2000.

Jameson, Fredric. "The Cultural Logic of Late Capitalism." In *Postmodernism: The Cultural Logic of Late Capitalism*. New York: Verso, 1991.

Komito, Lee. "The Net as a Foraging Society: Flexible Communities." *Information Society* 14, no. 2 (1998): 97–106.

Lingis, Alphonso. *The Community of Those Who Have Nothing in Common*. Bloomington: Indiana University Press, 1994.

Marvin, Carolyn. *When Old Technologies Were New*. New York: Oxford University Press, 1988.

Marx, Leo. *The Machine in the Garden*. New York: Oxford University Press, 1964.

Massumi, Brian. "The Autonomy of Affect." In Paul Patton, ed., *Deleuze: A Critical Reader*, 217–239. Malden, Mass.: Blackwell, 1996.

McClellan, Faith. "'A Whole Other Story': The Electronic Narrative of Illness." *Literature and Medicine* 16, no. 1 (1997): 88–107.

Mitchell, William J. *City of Bits: Space, Place, and the Infobahn*. Cambridge, Mass.: MIT Press, 1995.

Negroponte, Nicholas. *Being Digital*. New York: Knopf, 1995.

Nye, David. *The American Technological Sublime*. Cambridge, Mass.: MIT Press, 1994.

Rheingold, Howard. *The Virtual Community: Homesteading on the Electronic Frontier*. New York: Harper Perennial, 1993.

Ross, Andrew. *Real Love: In Pursuit of Cultural Justice*. New York: NYU Press, 1998.

Sclove, Richard E. "Making Technology Democratic." In James Brook and Iain A. Boal, eds., *Resisting the Virtual Life: The Culture and Politics of Information*, 85–101. San Francisco: City Lights, 1995.

Shapiro, Andrew L. "The Net That Binds: Using Cyberspace to Create Real Communities." *The Nation*, 21 June 1999, 11–15.

Slotkin, Richard. *The Fatal Environment: The Myth of the Frontier in the Age of Industrialization, 1800–1890*. New York: Atheneum, 1985.

Smith, Merritt Roe. "Technological Determinism in American Culture." In Leo Marx and Merritt Roe Smith, eds., *Does Technology Drive History?: The Dilemma of Technological Determinism*. Cambridge, Mass.: MIT Press, 1994.

Thompson, Kenneth. *Key Quotations in Sociology*. New York: Routledge, 1996.

Tierney, Thomas F. *The Value of Convenience: A Genealogy of Technical Culture*. Albany: SUNY Press, 1993.

Williams, Raymond. *Keywords: A Vocabulary of Culture and Society*. Rev. ed. New York: Oxford University Press, 1983.

Wise, J. Macgregor. *Exploring Technology and Social Space*. Thousand Oaks, Calif.: Sage, 1997.

——. "Mapping the Culture of Control: Seeing Through The Truman Show." *Television and New Media*, 3. no. 1 (2002): 29–47.

5

# Securing Trust Online: Wisdom or Oxymoron?

HELEN NISSENBAUM

## INTRODUCTION

This essay is about trust in the online world. It is not a manual on how to achieve trust, nor an empirical study of trust's presence or absence online. Rather, it is an attempt to show that the way we stipulate the conditions of the online world may be decisive for whether or not trust is achieved. Applying this perspective to a dominant vision of trust as security, the essay argues that if conditions are wrongly stipulated, then efforts to achieve trust may be misdirected—indeed, even thwarted.

The value of trust for a robust online world is obvious. Trust is a key to the promise the online world holds for great and diverse benefits to humanity—its potential to enhance community, enliven politics, hasten scientific discovery, energize commerce, and more. Trust in the layered infrastructures of hardware, software, commercial and institutional presences, and its people is a necessary condition for benefits to be realized. People shy away from territories they distrust; even when they are prepared to engage voluntarily, they stay only as briefly as possible. Without people, without participants, many of the visions will be both literally and figuratively empty. Trust would invigorate the online world; suspicion and insecurity would sap its vibrancy and vitality.

In exploring the issue of trust online, I turned to the work and insights of two communities of researchers, writers and practitioners. To learn about concerns relating specifically to trust *online*, I found much discussion "in the air" and also in an extensive literature spanning scholarly and trade publications, the popular media, government reports, and the Web itself. I found a second source of insights in the considerable works on trust by philosophers, social scientists, and social theorists. These expanded, clarified, and enriched the commonsense conception of trust with which I began this exploration.

Animating the literature on the subject of trust *online* were two concerns. One, usually expressed by technical experts in security, was a concern over the fragility of technical systems. These experts worried that our vast networked information system—the network of networks including local private systems as well as public systems like the Internet, the Web, cyberspace—is vulnerable to technical failure as well as malicious attack.[1] The second concern was over the success of e-commerce if consumers balk because they are fearful that they will be cheated, defrauded, have their credit card numbers stolen, or receive poor-quality goods, or if businesses stay away, fearing costly losses from such actions as failure to pay, repudiation of commitments, and so on.[2]

Although inspired by distinct sources, the proponents of these two concerns converge in their vision of the likely shape of a solution—namely, a particular suite of technical security mechanisms that they believe will induce users to trust these networked information systems. Through strong mechanisms of security and security-oriented practices, we should seek to create "trusted" or, rather, trustworthy,[3] systems that would, in turn, induce consumers to trust providers of goods and services, providers to trust consumers, and in general engender a climate of trust online.[4] So conspicuous has been the vision of trust through security portrayed by these two groups that it currently occupies the mainstream—in part because there are no equally persistent, competing interpretations, and in part because talk of trust online is relatively new and the mainstream view relatively uncontested. Later in this paper, I shall say more about these mechanisms, but here I would like to label this common vision with a slogan: trustworthiness as security, or trust through security.[5]

This essay is an evaluation of the vision of trust through security. Its thesis, guided by conceptions of trust developed in the theoretical and empirical work of social scientists and philosophers, is that the online landscape thus envisioned will not be conducive to trust and trustworthiness; trust online will not be achieved through security because that vision is founded on a misconstrual of trust, missing the point of why we care about trust and making mistaken assumptions about human nature along the way. Before attending to this central thesis, we must first set realistic boundaries for the scope of this essay. Because the technological realm of which we speak is so extensive and intricate, and the conceptual domain of trust so broad and varied, we must make some qualifications and simplifying assumptions.

## CONCEPTUAL AND TECHNICAL SCOPE

In its broadest sense, the online world we speak of could cover the entire technological system, vast and powerful, that sits at the hub of almost all other parts of the critical infrastructures of society, controlling, and in some cases conjoining energy, commerce, finance, transportation, education, communication, and more, and as such, affecting almost all modes of social, community, cultural, and political life.[6] This essay does not address the system as a whole—the vast and powerful grid that connects and controls satellites, nuclear devices, energy, the stock exchange, and so forth. Instead, it focuses on those parts of the system directly experienced by the ordinary people, who in increasing numbers, use it to talk, conduct business transactions, work, seek information, play games, and transact with public and private institutions. At present, this means the World Wide Web (the Web) and the various servers (computers), conjoined networks, people, and institutions that constitute it. It means the realm that at times interacts with the realities of the offline world, and at other times, fragments into an apparently independent and separate reality that some writers and participants have taken to calling cyberspace, or the "virtual" world.

Neither does this essay cover everything that *trust* could mean. Trust is an extraordinarily rich concept covering a variety of relationships, conjoining a variety of objects. One can trust (or distrust) persons, institutions, governments, information, deities, physical things, systems, and more. Here, I am concerned with two ways that trust is used. One is as a term describing a relationship between one person (a trustor) and another (the trustee). Although, in practice, the trustee position could be filled by almost anything, here I limit consideration to cases where the trustee is a being to which we are willing to attribute intentions, motivations, interests, or reasons, and might also refer to as "agents." Central to this category, I would place people—individually and in groups; I would also be willing to include organizations, communities, and institutions. However, I exclude from my discussion at least one quite common reference to trust in the online context: trust in the networked, digital information systems themselves, in the layered hardware and software that individually constitute the micro-systems and the macro-system that is formed by these. This is not because of any deep-seated disagreement with those who write about trust in relation to networked information systems or information and communications technology and worry about the dependability of these systems, their resilience to various forms of failure and attack, and their capacity to protect the integrity of online interactions and transactions. My reasons are pragmatic. These cases are sufficiently distinct from one another that they deserve separate (but equal) treatment. Following others, I use the term "confidence" to refer to trust in systems, recognizing that trust in the online world begins with confidence in systems but does not end there.[7]

## THE FUNCTION OF TRUST

Why we care about trust online is a question that provokes several lines of response. One is to seek an explanation for why the online realm appears especially problematic, that is, why we worry particularly about trust *online*. We shall return to this later, but first let us consider why we might care about trust at all. I treat this daunting question in a more limited way by thinking about trust's function in order to generate a sense of the ways in which trust contributes in positive ways to our lives. Even in this limited sense, I can give here only a compressed and selective account, merely sampling from the extensive literature on the general subject of trust and its value, allowing my account to be shaped by the particular focus of this essay.

We might quickly agree with the general view that trust is good, though a more considered reaction is likely to yield the view that trust is good for certain ends. It is an instrumental good whose ends, in our common experience, are usually good, but need not be. Scholarship endorses this qualified position on trust as a phenomenon that is implicated in the achievement of many valued aspects and institutions of individual and social life.[8] This work has revealed the benefits of trust for individuals (both those who trust and those who are trusted), for relationships, and for communities. In the case of individuals, there are the psychological benefits both of being trusted and of trusting, of not being stricken with paranoia and suspicion. Clearly there is a lot to say about all these benefits, but I would particularly like to draw attention to one aspect of the value of trust for individuals observed by Niklas Luhmann, a social theorist whose profound work on trust has been widely influential.

Luhmann characterizes trust as a mechanism that reduces complexity and enables people to cope with the high levels of uncertainty and complexity of contemporary life.[9] Trust makes uncertainty and complexity tolerable because it enables us to focus on only a few of the possible alternatives.[10] Humans, if faced with a full range of alternatives, if forced to acknowledge and calculate all possible outcomes of all possible decision nodes, would freeze in uncertainty and indecision. In this state, we might never be able to act in situations that call for action and decisiveness. In trusting, Luhmann says, "one engages in an action as though there were only certain possibilities in the future."[11] Trust also enables "co-operative action and individual but coordinated action: trust, by the reduction of complexity, discloses possibilities for action which would have remained improbable and unattractive without trust—which would not, in other words, have been pursued."[12] According to this account, trust expands people's capacity to relate successfully to a world whose complexity, in reality, is far greater than we are capable of taking in.

The rewards of trust extend beyond the individual, leavening many important relationships. Some, like the relationships between friends, lovers, siblings, husbands and wives, parents and children, mentors and students, are predicated on trust. But even in impersonal and formal relationships, trust plays a critical role: for trade and commercial transactions, for relationships between professionals (caregivers, healers, lawyers, and so on) and their clients, between employers and employees, between constituents and their political representatives.[13]

The possibilities for action increase proportionately to the increase in trust—trust in one's own self-presentation and in other people's interpretation of it. When such trust has been established, new ways of behaving become possible; jokes, unconventional initiatives, bluntness, verbal shortcuts, well-timed silences, the choice of delicate subjects, and so on. When trust is tested and proven in this way, it can be accumulated by way of capital.[14]

This idea of trust as capital—social capital—has been developed and popularized by Robert Putnam in his study of Italian communities and in his later work suggesting a decline in social capital in American society.[15] With each trust-affirming action, trust accrues in communities as capital, to stabilize, to exert control, and to induce cohesion and solidarity, to be there to tap in troubled times. The value of trust in social and associational life, not necessarily mediated through social capital, is something that other political philosophers have endorsed. Philip Pettit, for example, stresses the strength and solidarity that trust can engender, concluding, like Putnam, that "trust is a precious if fragile commodity in social and political life";[16] it is characteristic of flourishing civil societies.[17] Trust among citizens may be the magic ingredient that helps undergird political and civil stability in multicultural societies;[18] trust is an "important lubricant of a social system";[19] it is the basis for modern solidarity.[20] Trust by individuals of such institutionalized authority as government may sustain a citizenry's engagement in a social system, and may even stave off highly volatile and disruptive reactions that one might normally expect in the wake of harms that citizens believe to have been caused by these authorities.[21]

From these and other works we learn that trust is especially important in complex, varied, and somewhat unpredictable personal, social, and political contexts where much is at stake. Trust facilitates cooperation and success within civil and political society; it enriches individuals' lives by encouraging activity, boldness, adventure, and creativity, and by enriching the scope of individuals' relationships with others. It is not surprising, therefore, that an interest in trust should grow just as the realm we know as cyberspace, the Internet, the Web, the Global Information Infrastructure burgeons, just as it is beset by deep and difficult questions about authority and governance,[22] just as it crosses a threshold of complexity where participants, in increasing numbers, turn to the online world for many of the experiences, relationships, community-life, information, and commercial interactions that once they lived entirely in so-called "real" space.

Before turning attention to the online world, though, I note two qualifications. As an instrumental good, trust may, on occasion, serve evil ends. Trust between partners in crime increases the chances of criminal success, and social solidarity among oppressive communities strengthens their efficacy.[23] The same might be said about other instrumental values, even privacy and freedom, which we see as overwhelmingly positive even as we seek ways to limit their exercise for the sake of evil ends. A second qualification is that trust is not appropriate for every situation and relationship. In negotiating with a used-car salesman or with a sworn enemy, both of which may be necessary at some time, we prefer strategies other than trust. In choosing a bank or a bakery, for example, trust also may not be crucial.

Returning to the online world, we would expect that trust here holds a key to similar good ends: improving the quality of personal experiences, relationships, and communal and civic life, and stabilizing governance. We can expect that more people and institutions will "buy in" to the online world, will engage with others online, if there is sufficient trust. If a climate of trust can be established on the Net, if attitudes of trust toward partners in electronically mediated transactions can be achieved, then the online world will thrive, it will attract information, it will be lively with interaction, transaction, and association. This will attract further investment of all kinds, which in turn will fuel participation, and so on. Conversely, if people do not trust interactions mediated electronically, they will minimize them; they will be cautious and suspicious in their dealings, they will not place information and creative works on the Web, they will not engage in e-commerce, they will not indulge in MUDs, MOOs, e-lists, b-boards, listservs, chat rooms, buddy lists, electronic banking, and more. A great resource will be wasted.

## CONDITIONS OF TRUST

At the same time that proponents of the Internet acknowledge the role of trust as a key to flourishing activity, interaction, and institutional growth, they recognize certain distinctive features of the online realm that may interfere with building and sustaining trust. To see how these features may interfere, let us think first about conditions that generally have been associated with the formation of trust. We initiate this inquiry by asking about the mechanisms that govern trust. To what factors are tendencies to trust (or not to trust) systematically responsive? What factors influence the tendency to trust other people, groups, and institutions? One may sensibly ask these questions whether one holds that trust is a species of belief (or expectation) or that it is a noncognitive attitude, a matter of some disagreement among theorists and social scientists. Those, like Baier, who assert a version of the former view ask about reasons that may systematically undergird trust, and may even subject it to judgments of rationality or irrationality.[24] Those, like Becker, who defend a noncognitive account of trust can nevertheless agree that trust is systematically responsive to a variety of factors.[25] For purposes of this essay, it will not be necessary to settle the question, as long as our agnosticism does not prevent us from drawing on empirical and analytic work that links trust with a variety of phenomena that function systematically as its cues, clues, or triggers, whether these function as reasons or merely as causes.

Admittedly, the factors listed below reflect my interest in the relevant distinctiveness of the online context and should not be taken as a complete theory of the causes of trust. My efforts may also rub against views on trust, like Adam Seligman's, that would reserve the concept of trust for an even more qualified subcategory of attitudes than the one I have articulated. Seligman, for example, prefers to use a term like "confidence" for cases in which similarity, or roles and other structured relationships, induce a positive expectation with respect to the other.[26] To engage further on this point of disagreement—interesting as it is—would deflect us too far from the main subject here. It is important, though, to acknowledge the difference between my more ample and Seligman's more austere concepts. One way to reconcile the difference would be to suggest that followers of Seligman's usage recast the concern of this paper as being one of trust, faith, confidence, and familiarity online.

## History and Reputation

One of the most convincing forms of evidence that others merit trust is their past behavior. If they have behaved well in the past, protected our interests, have not cheated or betrayed us, and, in general, have acted in a trustworthy manner, they are likely to elicit trust in the future. If they have disappointed in the past, then we will tend not to trust them. Where we have not built a history of direct interaction with others, we may refer to the experiences of others who have; that is to say, we may be influenced by their reputations.

### Inferences Based on Personal Characteristics

A trusting attitude may be triggered by the presence of perceived qualities in the other. Philip Pettit identifies four: virtue, loyalty, prudence,[27] and a desire for the good opinion of others,[28] all qualities that influence whether a person will trust those who are seen to have them. Pettit writes: "To be loyal or virtuous or even prudent is, in an obvious sense of the term, to be trustworthy. It is to be reliable under trust and to be reliable, in particular, because of possessing a desirable trait."[29] The fourth quality, namely a desire for the good opinion of others, although less deserving of our admiration, is nevertheless a powerful mechanism for preventing betrayals of trust.[30] Accordingly, Pettit recommends against calling the person who chases good reputation trust*worthy*, preferring a more modest commendation of trust-*responsiveness*, or trust-*reliance*.[31] Though not in direct disagreement with Pettit's characterization, Adam Seligman offers a different perspective, drawing attention to the importance of familiarity, similarity, and shared values as triggers of trusting attitudes.[32] What we know about someone, what we may infer on the basis of "their clothing, behavior, general demeanor,"[33] may lead us to judgments about their values and moral commitments, especially telling if we judge them to be similar to ours. A common religious background, high school, neighborhood, or traumatic experience (e.g., having fought in the same war) affects how confident we are in predicting what others will do and how inclined we are to rely on them. Though related to loyalty, these considerations are not identical. When one depends on a loyal cousin, for example, one counts on the family relationship to induce trust-reliance in one's cousin. Where trust is triggered by familiarity and, perhaps, a perception of shared values, a trustee does not necessarily count on these qualities to cause trustworthy behavior; the trustee merely forms expectations regarding the likely actions of these others.

### Relationships: Mutuality and Reciprocity

Aside from personal qualities, the relationship in which one stands to another may bear on the formation of trust. The presence of common ends can stimulate trust. Such cases of mutual ends occur when a person is "in the same boat" as another. When I fly in an airplane, for example, I place trust in the pilot partly because he is in the plane with me and I presume that we have common, or confluent, ends; our fates are entwined for the few hours during which we fly together.

Reciprocity is slightly different, but it, too, can be grounds for trust. In a reciprocal relationship, we trust others not because we have common ends, but because each of us holds the fate of the other in our hands in a tit-for-tat manner. This may occur, for example, when people are taking turns. The agent whose turn is first deals fairly, reliably, or responsibly with the other because soon the tables will be turned. The relationship of reciprocity admits of great variability. In some cases there is clear and imminent reversal of roles (this year I am chair of our department, next year you take over); in others it is more generalized (I might donate money to cancer research hoping that when I become ill, these funds will somehow help me). Reciprocity is evident in communities that are blessed with a climate of trust, helping those in need and trusting that when they themselves are in need, others will help them.[34]

### Role Fulfillment

There is another, perhaps more compelling reason for trusting the pilot of my airplane. After all, the pilot would not trust me, in spite of our common interest in staying alive. Crucial to my trusting the pilot is that he is a pilot, and being a pilot within the framework of a familiar system has a well-articulated meaning. I know what pilots are supposed to do; I am aware of the rigorous training they undergo, the stringent requirements for accreditation, and the status of airlines within a larger social, political, and legal system. Several of the authors already mentioned have discussed the importance of roles to the formation of trust.[35]

### Contextual Factors

One of the most intriguing factors to affect our readiness to trust, beyond those that are tied to what we know about the other, is the nature of the setting in which we act.[36] Such settings can be construed quite locally as families, communities, and towns or can extend to such large and diffuse entities as nations and countries.

Four elements seem relevant. The first is publicity: a setting in which betrayal and fidelity are routinely publicized is likely to be more conducive to trust-reliance, and consequently trust, than a setting in which people can effectively hide their deeds—especially their misdeeds. The second is reward and punishment: settings in which rewards and sanctions follow trustworthiness and betrayal, respectively, are likely to induce trustworthiness and trust. Third, where reward and punishment for fidelity and betrayal are not systematically available, promulgation of norms through other means can effectively shape behaviors and establish a climate of one sort or another. What norms are conveyed through parables, education, local lore, songs, fables, and local appraisal structures? Do they condemn betrayal and celebrate fidelity or do they mock gullible marks of confidence tricks and disdain cuckolded spouses while proffering admiration to the perpetrators?[37] Finally, a society can nurture a trusting climate by setting in place, through public policy or other means, various forms of "trust insurance," to provide safety nets for those whose trust is betrayed.[38] A simple example of such a policy is the current arrangement of liability for credit card fraud, which must surely increase people's willingness to engage in credit transactions.

## OBSTACLES TO TRUST ONLINE

Knowing a little more about trust, we return to trust online. To begin, we observe that the online world is relatively new. Novelty, or unfamiliarity, can in itself stall the formation of trust. Beyond sheer novelty, however, there are more specific features of the online world that bear on the formation and sustenance of trust, which cloak many of the aspects of character and personality, nature of relationship, and setting that normally function as triggers of trust or as reasons for deciding to trust (or distrust).

### Missing Identities[39]

In its current design, the medium allows agents to obscure identity. In many of their online transactions, agents are not compelled to relinquish the identities of their offline selves. Although this ability to engage online anonymously is beneficial in a number of ways, it shrinks the range of cues that can act as triggers of trust or upon which people base decisions to trust. If we imagine identity as a thread upon which we string the history of interactions with others, then without that thread we lose the ability to learn from past experiences of either vindicated trust or betrayal. Lacking information about sustained identity means we are also deprived of the means of learning from the experiences of others whether an agent is trust-reliant, as the construction of reputation is hampered—if not precluded altogether—where identity is unknown.

Lacking knowledge of an agent's sustained identity also means that we may not have the information necessary to recognize the nature of the sustained relationships in which we stand, for example, whether it is reciprocal or cooperative. Finally, because identity is also bound up with accountability, people might presume that anonymous agents are less likely to act responsibly. As a result, they would be less inclined to trust.

## Missing Personal Characteristics

There is an opacity not only with respect to others' identities but also with respect to many of the personal characteristics that affect (heighten or diminish) attitudes of trust. Online, we are separated from others in time and space; we lack cues that may give evidence of similarity, familiarity, or shared value systems. We may not know the other's gender (male, female, or "other"), age, race, socioeconomic status, occupation, mode of dress, or geographic origins. We lack the bodily signals of face-to-face interaction. Are we communicating with a fourteen-year-old girl or a fifty-seven-year-old man posing as a fourteen-year-old girl? Are we selling a priceless painting to an adolescent boy or to a reputable art dealer?[40] Are we sharing a virtual room with an intriguing avatar or a virtual rapist?[41] We must conduct transactions and depend on others who are separated not only by distance but also by time, who are disembodied in many of the ways that typically contribute to our sense of their trustworthiness.

## Inscrutable Contexts

The novelty and difference of the online environment lead not only to the veiling of properties that affect the formation of trust: the settings themselves are frequently inscrutable in ways that affect readiness or inclination to trust. One casualty is role definition, because, at least for now, we cannot rely on traditional mechanisms for articulating and supporting social, professional, and other roles. Even with roles that appear equivalent to offline counterparts—for example, "shopkeeper"—we lack the explicit frameworks of assurances that support them. As for the roles that have emerged in cyberspace (like "sysops," avatars, bulletin board moderators, and so on) that do not have obvious counterparts offline, their duties and responsibilities are even less clearly defined and understood.

Just as roles are still relatively unformulated, so are background constraints and social norms regarding qualities like fidelity, virtue, loyalty, guile, duplicity, and trickery. Are we sure that betrayal will be checked, that safety nets exist to limit the scope of hurts and harms, and so on? Although there is evidence of various groups—social groups, interest groups, cultural groups—vying for domination of their norms, the territory remains relatively uncharted, further compounded by the global nature of the medium. Participants, especially the majority, who are not strongly identified with any one of these groups, can rightly be confused. For them, the most rational stance may be one of caution and reserve.

It is important to note that what I call inscrutability of contexts has a double edge. Many people have observed that it is precisely this quality of cyberspace that is so liberating, enticing, promising. Enthusiasts invite you to participate *because* it is new, different, better, seamless, immediate, unstuffy, truly democratic, and so forth. I am not sure, therefore, that the immediate solution to the problem of inscrutability is a wholesale transfer of existing norms, even if we could effect that.

## THE SOLUTION: SECURITY

Given that we are deprived of the usual cues and triggers, what steps can we take to sustain trust? A cohort of security experts, security-minded systems managers, government oversight bodies, and proponents of e-commerce advocate developing a particular suite of security mechanisms that would assure freedom from harm for online agents by allowing them to act and transact online in safety. The idea is that safety will build trust.

Computer security is not a new concern, but rather has developed alongside the development of computing itself, responding to changes in the technology and the needs of its rapidly expanding range of applications. What is relatively new, however, is the close linking of the purposes of security with the idea of trust. There are, no doubt, a number of reasons why trust has entered the picture as one of the values that guides security. There are the historical and sociological reasons mentioned above; there are the ubiquity and power of the technical infrastructure; there is the fundamentally open (or insecure) architecture of the technical infrastructure. In this essay, we focus on the part of the picture that links security mechanisms to trust via the missing clues, cues, and triggers. Or, rather, we explore the security mechanisms developed in the name of trust—those that function, in part, to restore the missing cues, clues, and triggers.

What follows is a brief overview of some of the efforts in answer to this call, which I have organized according to three categories: (1) access control, (2) transparency of identity, and (3) surveillance. The categories, which are largely my own construction, are an obvious simplification of the broad range of work in computer and network security. My intent is not to describe categories explicitly adopted by computer security experts themselves, nor to suggest that there is a monolithic effort of people and projects, but to provide explanatory clarity relevant to the purposes of discussing trust. The categories reflect functionality, not underlying structural similarities, and, as we shall soon see, are highly interrelated.

## Access Control

One of the earliest worries of computer security, from the time when computers were stand-alone calculators and repositories of information, was to guard against unwanted access to the computer and its stored information, to maintain the integrity of the information, and to control distribution of the valuable and limited resource of computational power. Early on, the security mechanisms developed to prevent illegitimate and damaging access involved everything from passwords to locked doors.[42] The demands on computer security mechanisms expanded and became more complicated as networks and interactivity evolved. Vulnerability to intrusion increased because networks opened new means of infiltration—e-mail, file transfer, and remote access—that could not be stemmed by locked doors. The infamous Morris Worm, which received widespread national attention, jolted all users into noticing what security experts must certainly have feared: that it was merely a matter of time before vulnerabilities in theory would be exploited in practice.[43]

The Internet, and in particular the Web, has further expanded the modes and extent of interactivity while, at the same time, exposing participants to new forms of unwanted access and attack. The old fears remain: namely, infiltration by unauthorized persons (hackers, crackers, and so on), damage to information and systems, disruptive software flowing across the Net, information "stolen" as it traverses the networks, terrorists and criminals invading the infrastructure and bringing down critical systems. And new fears emerge: "evil" Web sites that harm unsuspecting visitors, Web links diverted from intended destinations to others, and disruptive applets—mini applications that visitors to Web sites can download onto their own systems to enable them to enjoy more extensive services from that site. Khare and Rifkin note, "While doing nothing more serious than surfing to some random Web page, your browser might take the opportunity to download, install, and execute objects and scripts from unknown sources."[44] To view a video clip, for example, visitors might need to download a player program in addition to the video files themselves; they may download a mini-spreadsheet program to view and interact with financial information provided by a financial services company. In the process of downloading the appropriate application, however, the user's computer system is infected with a harmful and often devastating applet. Greater interactivity spells greater vulnerability and a need for more extensive protections. Bruce Schneier, a computer security expert, comments on the level of vulnerability after one particular round of attack-and-repair:

> Looking back to the future, 1999 will have been a pivotal year for malicious software: viruses, worms, and Trojan horses (collectively known as "malware"). It's not more malware; we've already seen thousands. It's not Internet malware; we've seen those before, tool [*sic*]. But this is the first year we've seen malware that uses e-mail to propagate over the Internet and tunnel through firewalls. And it's a really big deal.

> What's new in 1999 is e-mail propagation of malware. These programs—the Melissa virus and its variants, Worm.ExploreZip worm and its inevitable variants, etc.—arrive via e-mail and use e-mail features in modern software to replicate themselves across the network. They mail themselves to people known to the infected host, enticing the recipients to open or run them. They don't propagate over weeks and months; they propagate in seconds. Anti-viral software cannot possibly keep up. . . .
>
> One problem is the permissive nature of the Internet and the computers attached to it. As long as a program has the ability to do anything on the computer it is running on, malware will be incredibly dangerous.
>
> And anti-virus software can't help much. If a virus can infect 1.2 million computers (one estimate of Melissa infections) in the hours before a fix is released, that's a lot of damage. . . .
>
> It's impossible to push the problem off onto users with "do you trust this message/macro/application" messages. . . . Users can't make good security decisions under ideal conditions; they don't stand a chance against a virus capable of social engineering. . . .
>
> What we're seeing here is the convergence of several problems: the permissiveness of networks, interconnections between applications on modern operating systems, e-mail as a vector to tunnel through network defenses as a means to spread extremely rapidly, and the traditional naivete of users. Simple patches won't fix this. . . . A large distributed system that communicates at the speed of light is going to have to accept the reality of viral infections at the speed of light. Unless security is designed into the system from the bottom up, we're constantly going to be fighting a holding action.[45]

Working within the constraints of current network and system architectures, security experts have developed a tool kit of mechanisms to protect people and systems against unwanted and dangerous access. One reason why demands on such a tool kit are considerable is because the agents of unwanted access may be not only people but also bits of code, like applets. Standard techniques like passwords remain in use, fortified where needed by such mechanisms as "firewalls," which are software barriers built around systems in order to make them impermeable except to people or code that is "authorized."[46] Cryptographic techniques are used to protect the integrity and privacy of information stored in computers; such techniques also protect against theft and manipulation as information travels across networks. Some protection is offered against treacherous applets—for example, one that might reformat a user's hard drive or leak private information to the world—through security features built into Java that limit what applets can do. There are, however, regular announcements of flaws in this security.[47] There is fundamentally no known technical means of differentiating "good" from "bad" applets. How could there be, except in some possible future when computers would be able to discern categories of human values?

## Transparency of Identity

The people and institutions of the online world have diverse tastes when it comes to identification. Some are happy to link themselves to their full-blown offline identities, while others prefer to maintain independent virtual selves. Among the second group, some are happy to maintain consistent identities represented by "handles" or pseudonyms, while others prefer full anonymity. The goal of security efforts in this category is to give more transparent access to online agents in order to stave off at least some of the threats and worries that follow from not knowing with whom one is dealing. Identifiability is considered particularly useful for recognizing malevolent or mischievous agents. And in general, it helps answer some of the questions that trust inspires us to ask: is there a recognizable and persistent identity to the institutions and individuals behind the myriad Web sites one might visit? Can we count on agents online to keep their promises? For the sake of e-commerce, how do we prevent malicious agents from posing as legitimate customers or service providers and conducting bogus transactions, tricking and defrauding legitimate participants? In other words, we strive to reintroduce identifying information, at least as much as is needed to create a history, establish a reputation, hold agents accountable, and so on.

Security efforts have focused on the task of making identity sufficiently transparent to protect against these and other betrayals and harms in an effort to build what Lawrence Lessig has called "architectures of identification."[48] Mostly, they are interested in developing a strong link between a virtual agent and a physical person through a constellation of information that is commonly seen as proving identity even offline.[49] Security experts are investigating the promise of biometric identification—for example, through fingerprints, DNA profiles, and retinal images. Cryptographic techniques are deployed to authenticate users, computers, and sources of information by means of digital signatures and digital certificates working within a socially constructed system of Certification Authorities, trusted third parties who vouch for the binding of cryptographic keys to particular identities—persons and institutions. These same mechanisms are intended to prevent repudiation by agents of commitments or promises they may have made.

Schemes of identification, even the attenuated forms, work hand in hand with access control, because controlling access almost never means preventing everyone from using a system or the information in a system. It almost always means distinguishing the sanctioned, legitimate users from the illegitimate ones. In the case of applets, because direct examination can provide only imperfect evidence, we may rely on what is known about who sent them for another source of discrimination between "good" and "bad" applets.[50] "Trust management systems" are offered as integrated mechanisms for identifying and authenticating the identity of those people, information, and code that affect us, and they are also supposed to authenticate an applet's origins. The Snow White fairy tale offers an irresistible comparison: if Snow White had known the true identity of the bearer of the apple, she could have avoided the fateful bite.

Security experts seem always to be engaged in a Sisyphean battle, warding off attack, repairing system flaws, closing up loopholes and "backdoors," and devising new layers of protection; a process that ends, temporarily at least, until the next attack occurs. Outspoken security experts accept that this is an inevitable consequence of the "open" architecture of the Internet and Web, which many consider to be fundamentally insecure.[51] As a result, we live with an unstable equilibrium of relative comfort until the latest, more devastating intrusion is made public; there is a flurry of reaction, followed by relative comfort, and so on.

## Surveillance

A third layer overlaid upon the security offered through access control and transparency of identity is surveillance: we keep an eye on things in order both to prevent harms and to apprehend perpetrators after harm has been done. Surveillance can involve active watching and tracking, which can be fairly fine-grained, as demonstrated by the monitoring software that many business organizations have installed on their computer systems. Or it can be relatively coarse-grained, as are some "intrusion detection" systems, where real-time monitoring issues an alarm in response to suspicious or unusual activity, to be further investigated if necessary.[52] Surveillance can also involve passive recording (reifying) of digital trails. Popular means include logging and auditing, which creates records of activity through which authorities can sift at a later time. Logging and auditing helped authorities identify David Smith as the creator of the Melissa virus.[53]

## CAN TRUST BE SECURED?

The claim we must examine is that through an array of mechanisms, such as firewalls, biometrics, digital signatures, intrusion detection, auditing, and so forth, trust will be secured online. We might adjust the claim slightly to apply to an idealized world in which we have perfected these mechanisms of access control, establishing reliable markers of identity and maintaining a watchful eye through surveillance. Will we thus secure trust?

Given the framing of the problem of trust online that we have seen so far, the claim has prima facie plausibility because the mechanisms in question appear to be a means of restoring some of the triggers of trust that elude us online. Strong and smart walls, and limits on the flow of information and the range of interactivity establish "safe" zones; greater transparency of identity through authentication allows participants to steer clear of "suspicious" agents. By exposing identities or, at least, crucial dimensions of identities, agents—individuals, organizations, and computers—may more effectively make judgments about trustworthiness and decide whether others are "safe bets." Mechanisms of nonrepudiation restore accountability. This, then, is the compelling current generated by the proponents of security and e-commerce.

I will argue, however, that in spite of its prima facie plausibility, security—or rather the particular vision of security occupying the mainstream—will not, as promised, bring about trust. I argue this not because I think security is unimportant but because the ends of trust online are not well served by this mainstream vision of security. The rhetoric is misguided because when the proponents of security and e-commerce try to bind trust too closely to security, they threaten to usurp a concept as rich and complex, as intensely social, cultural, and moral as trust, for merely one slim part of it. The mistake is not merely semantic; it has a weighty practical edge. Pursuing trust online by pursuing the complete fulfillment of the three goals of security would no more achieve trust and trustworthiness online—in the full-blown sense of these qualities—than prison bars, surveillance cameras, airport X-ray conveyor belts, body frisks, and padlocks could achieve it offline. This is the case because the very ends envisioned by the proponents of security and e-commerce are contrary to core meanings and mechanisms of trust.

Security misses the mark in two ways: it overshoots trust and it undershoots it.

## Securing Trust Versus Nourishing Trust

Let us begin with the first critique—namely, that security as commonly prescribed may actually quash trust. Here, an excursion back to theoretical and empirical studies of trust is useful. Trust, we learn, is an attitude. It is almost always a relational attitude involving at least a trustor and a trustee. In this relation of trust, those who trust accept their vulnerability to those in whom they place trust. They realize that those they trust may exercise their power to harm, disappoint, or betray; yet at the same time they regard those others "as if" they mean well, or at least mean no harm. Trust, then, is a form of confidence in another, confidence that the other, despite a capacity to do harm, will do the right thing in relation to the trustor. For the philosopher Annette Baier, trust is "accepted vulnerability to another's possible but not expected ill will (or lack of good will) toward one";[54] trust is the "reliance on others' competence and willingness to look after, rather than harm, things one cares about which are entrusted to their care."[55] For Russell Hardin, "trust involves giving discretion to another to affect one's interests."[56] In a similar vein, Adam Seligman holds trust to be "some sort of belief in the goodwill of the other, given the opaqueness of other's intentions and calculations."[57] Francis Fukuyama adds a social dimension to his account, describing trust as the "expectation that arises within a community of regular, honest, and cooperative behavior, based on commonly shared norms, on the part of other members of that community."[58]

Usually trust involves more than the trustor and trustee; there is almost always an object with respect to which the trustor trusts the trustee.[59] For Annette Baier, this is demonstrated in her example of trusting the plumber to take care of the pipes in her home but not to take care of her daughter—and trusting a baby-sitter to take care of her daughter but not to take care of the pipes.[60] A person might entrust even her life to a friend, but not her heart. In the online world, there is similar discretion about not only whom one is prepared to trust but with what one is prepared to entrust them; for example, many consumers have learned that they can trust Amazon.com to deliver their orders but not trust it with their personal information.[61]

Most relevant to our concern here, however, is a theme common to all the works that I have studied, namely the essential connection between trust and vulnerability. When people trust, they expose themselves to risk. Although trust may be based on something—past experience, the nature of one's relationships, and so on—it involves no guarantees. As Hardin writes, trust is "inherently subject to the risk that the other will abuse the power of discretion."[62] In trusting, we are acknowledging the other as a free agent, and this is part of the exhilaration of both trusting and being trusted. Where people are guaranteed safety, where they are protected from harm via assurances—if the other person acted under coercion, for example—trust is redundant; it is unnecessary. What we have is certainty, security, and safety—not trust. The evidence, the signs, the cues and clues that ground the formation, that give evidence of the reasonableness of trust must always fall short of certainty; trust is an attitude without guarantees, without a complete warranty.[63] When we constrain variables in ways that make things certain—i.e., safe—we are usurping trust's function. Trust is squeezed out of the picture.

No loss, some, like Richard Posner, would say: "But trust, rather than being something valued for itself and therefore missed where full information makes it unnecessary, is, I should think, merely an imperfect substitute for information."[64] According to Posner's position, if we must choose between trust—and, consequently, vulnerability—on the one hand, and certainty on the other, then certainty must win.

In practice, however, such a choice has significant consequences, which are as evident online as off. In a world that is complex and rich, the price of safety and certainty is limitation. Online, we do not have the means at our disposal of assuring safety and certainty without paying this price: a streamlining and constraining of the scope and nature of online interactions, relationships, and community; a limiting of the range and nature of allowed activity and scope and nature of interaction; a need to make a priori judgments about with whom we will or will not interact; and an acceptance of greater transparency and surveillance.[65] In general, then, we trade freedom and range of opportunity for this certainty and safety.

The link between trust and vulnerability seems to be both conceptual and empirical. The conceptual claim is that whatever the feeling or attitude one experiences when acting and anticipating in a context of certainty and safety, it cannot be trust; this is not what trust means. The empirical conjecture, which has occupied the work of several scholars, is that in a context of complete certainty, the material conditions needed to induce and nourish trust are absent.[66] Trust does not flourish in a perfectly secure environment for reasons that are very different from the reasons for which trust does not flourish in a hostile, threatening environment. For trust to develop between an individual and either another individual or an organization, the trustor must somehow have had the opportunity to test the other agent and have had that agent pass the test. Luhmann explains the crucial role of uncertainty in the process of building trust:

> First of all there has to be some cause for displaying trust. There has to be defined some situation in which the person trusting is dependent on his partner; otherwise the problem does not arise. His behaviour [*sic*] must then commit him to this situation and make him run the risk of his trust being betrayed. In other words he must invest in what we called earlier a "risky investment." One fundamental condition is that it must be possible for the partner to abuse the trust.[67]

When we are placed in a context in which we depend on others for our well-being and are assured, guaranteed by whatever means, that these others are prevented and restrained and therefore incapable of harming us, then the context, though safe and secure, is not one that nourishes trust. No test has been given; none has been passed. The variables that theorists and empirical scientists have identified as trust-inducing may signal the reasonableness of trust in a particular setting, but when grounds are transformed into guarantees of good behavior, trust disappears, replaced not by distrust but perhaps by certainty. In the presence of a violent psychopath whose limbs are shackled, one feels not trust but, at best, safety.

Another empirical basis for doubting the efficacy of security to deliver trust is that boxing people in is a notoriously bad strategy for inducing trustworthiness or even trust-reliance. Constraining freedom directly or indirectly through, say, surveillance may backfire and have the opposite effect. Roderick Kramer, in reviewing empirical work in the social sciences, notes:

> Ironically, there is increasing evidence that such systems can actually undermine trust and may even elicit the very behaviors they are intended to suppress or eliminate. In a recent discussion of this evidence, Cialdini (1996) identified several reasons why monitoring and surveillance can diminish trust within an organization. First, there is evidence that when people think their behavior is under the control of extrinsic motivators, intrinsic motivation may be reduced (Enzle & Anderson 1993). Thus, surveillance may undermine individuals' motivation to engage in the very behaviors such monitoring is intended to induce or ensure.[68]

Philip Pettit's observations reinforce this result:

> Certain intrusive forms of regulation can be counter-productive and can reduce the level of performance in the very area they are supposed to affect. . . . If heavy regulation is capable of eradicating overtures of trust, and of driving out opportunities for trusting relationships, then it is capable of doing great harm.[69]

The many inducements at the disposal of individuals and institutions to encourage trustworthiness are most effective when they operate indirectly. Above all, people need to perceive a choice. By means of these inducements, including sanctions and rewards, clearly articulated norms, education, character development, and so on, we may increase the incidence of trust as well as trust-reliance. On the other hand, if we go too far, and deny the possibility of choice, we deny what is fundamental to trusting relationships and climates of trust. Symbols of trust can be exhibited in small but clear ways, as illustrated at the service counter of a popular downtown café. A discreet sign says: "At our busy times, please be respectful of those waiting for tables." We trust, we do not coerce; we cannot assure decency, but we offer patrons an opportunity to demonstrate their trustworthiness.

## Security Is No Panacea

If the earlier criticism was that security, following the trajectory of development described above, overshoots the mark and creates an environment that does not allow trust to take root and flourish, then the alternative criticism is that security does not go far enough. For even though security mechanisms promise to reduce our vulnerability in some ways, they leave us vulnerable in other ways that are relevant to the prospect of trust online. This loophole is all the more worrisome because, having achieved some modes of safety through security, we might fail to notice its significance until considerable damage is done.

To clarify, it will be useful to set in place a simplification, framing what is at stake in terms of "insiders" and "outsiders." Experts in computer security are worried about outsiders: malicious, avaricious, incompetent, or simply unauthorized outsiders who may break into our online space, damage or steal information, and destroy or compromise our systems. They develop security mechanisms to keep outsiders where they belong—outside—and to help spot or identify outsiders in order to take appropriate—preventative or punitive—action.

Far less systematic attention is paid to the threat of insiders, those agents—individuals and organizations—who, by degrees, have sanctioned access to our space. These agents, who count among the respectable, socially sanctioned, reputable members of online society, engage in actions that many citizens of the online world dislike, resent, or even consider harmful. They track our Web activities, they collect and use personal information without our permission, they plant "cookies" on our hard drives, they hijack our browsers while they download ads, they fill our mailboxes with spam, and they engage in relentless commercialism. Some of these insiders—perhaps not the "respectable" ones—"troll" our discussion groups, afflict us with hateful, inflammatory, mean-spirited e-mails ("flame" us), send us threatening chain mail, and even attack our virtual selves.[70] In other words, even if the walls of security effectively keep outsiders outside, they do not curtail the agents and activities that, behind the veil of respectability and legal sanction manage to make online citizens skittish, cautious, and resentful. Such security barriers do not address various forms of activity that are fully capable of engendering a climate of suspicion and distrust online even if we are successful in our projects to secure the online world.

Even in the physical world, attention only to the threats of outsiders misses a universe of possibility linked closely with the presence of trust and trustworthiness. Consider the more familiar case of physical safety. To protect ourselves from bodily harm, many of us go to great lengths: we stay clear of dangerous parts of town, we affix padlocks to our doors and install burglar alarms in our homes, and we support the use of closed-circuit television (CCTV) in public spaces. Homicide statistics, however, tell a curious story: when the relationship of the killer to victim is known, we find that only 22 percent of killers are strangers—the proverbial outsiders.[71] Others are spouses, friends, and acquaintances. Betrayal comes from those who are allowed within our spheres of safety, within our safe zones.

My intention is not to launch into paranoiac realms of suspicion and universal distrust. It is to illustrate that keeping outsiders out need not assure safety. A wall of defense against malicious outsiders does not defend against the threats posed by sanctioned insiders, who energetically defend their "right" to exercise online freedoms—by means of cookies, misleading registrations, matching, mining, and so on. They are, arguably, chipping away at trust just as surely as amoral hackers are. As much as the latter, they are capable of causing a dangerous ebb in the abundant social capital we currently enjoy in life online.

Because it is in the nature of trust to be conservative—both to ebb and to grow—the results of these transgressions may not be immediately evident.[72] That the transgressions I speak of are capable of undermining trust, however, is implied by several of the works that have shaped this essay. One example is found in a long-term study of e-commerce, which shows that consumers' trust is related to their understanding of how information about them is treated; it wanes if they think that it will not be held in confidence.[73]

Another important insight that explains why interventions like the familiar suite of security mechanisms cannot fully induce trust is that trust is as sensitive, if not more so, to motives and intentions as it is to actions and outcomes. It is in the goodwill of the other, Lawrence Becker has argued, that we trust or fail to trust, not necessarily their actions.[74] As long as we believe that others are well intentioned toward us, our trusting attitude toward them will survive a great deal of bad news: "incompetence, mendacity, greed, and so forth."[75] This holds for the relation of citizens to government as well as among persons. According to Becker, only when citizens begin to attribute the poor performance of governments to deviant motivations—e.g., corruption or inappropriate power seeking—will they "respond in ways that are . . . volatile and disruptive."[76] Citizens' trust, it seems, is able to survive incompetence, at least for a while. In a similar vein, Paul Slovic, an expert on risk assessment, reports that the extent to which citizens are willing to accept societal risk resulting from technological innovation is related to their degree of confidence in the motives of those in charge.[77]

Similar ideas emerge in Tom Tyler's research on public trust of police and the courts. Tyler is interested in variables that affect citizens' confidence in legal authorities, their readiness to accept outcomes, and their evaluation of the quality of decision making and fairness of procedures.[78] He finds that the most important variable is trust in the motives of authorities.[79] This he calls "motive based trust": "Motive based trust is distinct from judgments about whether or not authorities behave as anticipated. It involves an inference about the 'spirit' or 'motive' that will shapes [*sic*] behavior, not what specific behavior will occur."[80] One of Tyler's somewhat surprising findings is that in brushes with law enforcement and legal authorities, people's positive reactions are tied more strongly to inferred motives than even to whether or not the outcomes of their cases were favorable to them.[81]

The significance of these ideas for the purposes of this section is to emphasize that the behavior of many sanctioned, established, powerful individuals and organizations is capable of undermining trust even when the actions they undertake, such as Web tracking, for example, are not immediately aggressive or harmful. In these cases, when we learn of such activities we may find them ambiguous. What would matter to us for purposes of trust would be the motivations behind the behaviors. As long as we are not able to read people's minds, it is difficult, often impossible, to assess motives and intentions directly. So we usually find ourselves drawing on as many indirect sources as possible, sometimes resorting to subtle detection and artfulness.

One important indirect source of others' intentions is their interests. When, for example, a politician seeking office expresses concern for a particular situation, voters might attribute the expression not to genuine feeling but to an interest in being elected. In a case of this type, as much as we welcome and praise the action, it may not serve as grounds for trust as long as we see it emanating from a motive of vote seeking. In the case of Web tracking—and more generally, information gathering and commercialism—we might initially be willing to read positive meaning into such practices. As time goes by, and we take measure of the distance between our own interests and those of the trackers (profit and potency), we begin to reinterpret those same actions as forms of betrayal. Actions that at first seem neutral or even friendly can come to be seen as sinister when interpreted in light of inferred motives and intentions.

We all need to interact, even cooperate, with others whose interests are not consistent with our own and may even conflict with ours. In such cases, we transact cautiously, ever on the lookout for betrayal, sometimes seeking protections from the most egregious harms, betrayals, and exploitation. So trust remains elusive.

If we choose not to pursue policies for the online world that aim to contain the pursuit of avaricious interests that are contrary to those of the citizens of the Net, we are, I fear, planting the seeds of general distrust. People may continue to participate in this arena, but will do so with caution and a sense of wariness—wisely so, in interactions with those whose interests run contrary to our own, and whose actions may be annoying, bothersome, intrusive, or even threatening. Guardedness will be the norm.

Those who would pursue security in the name of trust do us this disservice. They focus on the outsider, the aberrant individual or organization, the trickster, the evil hacker, and the scam artist. These are the villains from whom security would protect us. In proportion to actual harm done to individuals online, too much attention is paid to the aberrant individual, the trickster, and the evil hackers lurking outside the borders of civilized society online. The media play up dramatic cases: the Melissa virus, spies who infiltrate systems and sell secrets to our enemies, or hackers who distribute unauthorized copies of intellectual works. These techniques do nothing against agents acting behind the veil of respectability who invade our privacy and offend us by turning cyberspace to their own interests and not ours.

We should take greater heed of the sanctioned harms of respectable insiders; we should question the systemic imbalances between the individual citizens of the online world and the organizations that create it with little sense of the interests of the individuals. For the vast majority of Net users, it is the second group and not the first that is the significant danger; it is the second, at least as much as the first, that affects our attitudes of trust online. Powerful security mechanisms may keep us safe from malicious outsiders at the cost of our online experience, but such mechanisms still leave us vulnerable to those agents. We can keep out the aberrant individuals, but we remain powerless against those parties that are poised to systematically exploit their positions. If we care about developing a climate of trust online—full-blown trust, not a thin substitute—we must address these conditions of imbalance between individuals and institutions. Evil hackers are not the only, nor are they the most important, barriers to trust online. If we do not address the systemic problems, trust will erode and we will not easily recover from a sense of wholesale exploitation.

## CONCLUSION: STRUGGLE FOR THE SOUL OF CYBERSPACE

I am not opposed to computer security. Underlying security mechanisms are diverse and can be shaped in an enormous variety of ways. The specific shape they take can have a significant impact on the shape of the online world and the experiences possible within it. Security technology does not, in general, necessarily lead to the state that appears at the end of the current trajectory, which would limit the complexity, richness, intensity, and variety of experience online without assuring us protection from a range of sanctioned predatory activities. Developed wisely, computer security may be able to produce a measure of safety with sufficient degrees of freedom to nourish trust. Cryptography is a good example: it can be used in service of transparent identification, but it may also be used to protect individual interests in privacy, freedom of association, and free speech.

Yet even the security mechanisms I have questioned here, namely, those that enable surveillance, sustain identifiability, and form selectively permeable fortresses—let us call this "high security"—are not in themselves objectionable. High security is good; it is even necessary for a great many settings: for airplane flights, military compounds, national secrets, nuclear power plants, banks, prisons, and more—all places where we welcome Richard Posner's vaunted certainty.[82] If the arguments of this essay have succeeded, they will have convinced readers that the pursuit of trust must be decoupled from the pursuit of high security; trust will not ride in on the coattails of security. But these arguments do not in themselves provide an answer to the further question of what course of action we, the virtual agents, people, institutions who populate the online world, or they, influential parties involved in building and governing the technical infrastructures, ought to pursue. This we must recognize as a value about what we envision for the online world.

A highly secured cyberspace offers a good climate for activities like commerce and banking, and for established commercial, public, and governmental institutions. The interests and modes of interactions that would not flourish are likely to include the creative, political, unusual, freewheeling, subversive, possibly profane, possibly risky modes and activities of individuals. For airplane flights, we may welcome security checks, but for these kinds of activities and interactions, for the virtual hustle and bustle that has come to resemble (and in some cases replace) much of our common experience, people avoid brightly lit scrutiny. To express the trade-off in terms offered by Luhmann, we may say that while both trust and security are mechanisms for reducing complexity and making life more manageable, trust enables people to act in a richly complex world, whereas security reduces the richness and complexity. Which one of these alternatives ultimately characterizes the online world—a virtual Singapore or, say, a virtual New York City[83]—should be a matter for full and deliberate consideration and should not follow merely as an accidental consequence of immediate technological imperatives and hasty policy choices.

In holding fast to the progressive social vision of cyberspace, my choice would be an insistence on preserving the degrees of freedom that trust needs, while continuing to support a path of technical development in which security would ideally aim both to construct pockets of high security and to maintain minimal protections—safety nets to prevent catastrophic harms—in the realms outside of these pockets. If we set these as our goals, then we will have set the stage for trust. But we will *only* have set the stage. The work of nourishing trust and trustworthiness remains and calls for a familiar range of complex responses, including the promulgation of norms, moral and character education, and comfort for the hurt.

## NOTES

This paper is an outgrowth of a collaborative project with Edward Felten and Batya Friedman, and owes much to them. The work was supported by grants from the National Science Foundation, SBR-9729447 and SBR-9806234. I am enormously grateful to colleagues for probing questions and suggestions: Tamar Frankel, Jeroen van den Hoven, Rob Kling, and Mark Poster; for editorial and research assistance: Beth Kolko, Helen Moffett, Michael Cohen, and Hyeseung Song, Sayumi Takahashi, and Robert Young. Earlier versions of the paper were presented at "Computer Ethics: Philosophical Enquiry 2000," New York University School of Law Conference on a Free Information Ecology, and Boston University School of Law Conference on Trust Relationships. This version of the paper was published in 81 B.U. L. Rev. 635 (June 2001).

1. See, e.g., Commission on Information Systems Trustworthiness, National Research Council, Fred B. Schneider, ed., *Trust in Cyberspace* (1999), 1: "The widespread interconnection of networked information systems allows outages and disruptions to spread from one system to others; it enables attacks to be waged anonymously and from a safe distance."

2. See, e.g., James P. Backhouse, "Security: The Achilles Heel of Electronic Commerce," *Soc'y* 35 (1998): 28 (discussing security issues in e-commerce); Donna L. Hoffman et al., "Building Consumer Trust Online," *Communications of the ACM* (April 1999): 80 (addressing the trust issues between consumers and businesses in e-commerce); Robert Moskowitz, "Ask Yourself: In Whom Can You Really Trust?," *Network Computing* 1, 1 (15 June 1998). http://www.networkcomputing.com/911/911colmoskowitz.html (discussing the doubts that plague e-commerce); Pauline Ratnasingham, "Implicit Trust

Levels in EDI Security," *J. Internet Security* 2, no. 1, 1 (1999). http://www.addsecure.net/jisec/1999–02.htm (arguing that trust is an "important antecedent" for successful business relationships); Karl Salnoske, "Building Trust in Electronic Commerce," *Business Credit* 100 (January 1998): 24. http://www.nacm.org/ bcmag/bcarchives/1998/articles1998/jan/jan98art2.html (commenting that both businesses and consumers regard transaction security as their biggest concern); Dennis D. Steinauer et al., "Trust and Traceability in Electronic Commerce," *Standard View* 5 (1997): 118 (exploring "technology or other processes that can help increase the level of confidence . . . in electronic commerce"); David Woolford, "Electronic Commerce: It's All a Matter of Trust," *Computing Canada* 25 (7 May 1999): 18, 1. http://www.plesman.com/Archives/cc/1999/May/2518/cc251813b.html (arguing that electronic deals suffer from the problems of "authenticity and integrity").

3. A misuse of language persists within the technical computer security community: proponents of a particular security device invariably use the term "trusted" to signal their faith that the system in question is trustworthy. This usage is misleading, as it suggests a general acceptance of the device in question when in fact it is the duty of the proponents to argue or prove that it is indeed worthy of this acceptance.

4. See, e.g., Alfarez Abdul-Rahman and Stephen Hailes, "A Distributed Trust Model," in *New Security Paradigms Workshop* 48 (1998) (discussing the weaknesses of current security approaches for managing trust); Department of Defense Trusted Computer System Evaluation Criteria (visited 1 July 1999), http://www.all.net/books/orange (classifying computer systems into four divisions of enhanced security protection); Rohit Khare and Adam Rifkin, "Weaving a Web of Trust" (visited 13 January 2001), http:/www.w3journal.com/7/s3.rifkin.wrap.html (1997) ("develop[ing] a taxonomy for how trust assertions can be specified, justified and validated"); Michael K. Reiter, "Distributing Trust with the Rampart Toolkit," *Communications of the ACM* (April 1996): 71 (describing group communication protocols that distribute trust among a group).

5. Although I do not discuss their work here, I must acknowledge another community of researchers—namely, those interested in computer-human interaction, who are concerned with ways to elicit trust through the design of user interfaces. See, e.g., Ben Schneiderman, "Designing Trust into Online Experiences," *Communications of the ACM* (December 2000): 58–59 (outlining certain steps, such as disclosing patterns of past performance and enforcing privacy and security policies, that designers can take to encourage trust in online relationships).

6. See Schneider, *Trust in Cyberspace*, 12–23 (evaluating whether and to what degree we can rely on existing networked information systems that support

our critical infrastructures). This report urged a set of actions to increase trustworthiness and limit our vulnerability to harm, even catastrophe, that might result from failures due to malfunction or malicious attack. See 240–255 (outlining the commission's conclusions and recommendations).

7. See Adam B. Seligman, *The Problem of Trust*, 19 (1997) (arguing that trust in systems entails confidence in a set of institutions).

8. See, e.g., Annette Baier, "Trust and Antitrust," *Ethics* 96 (1986): 232 ("There are immoral as well as moral trust relationships, and trust-busting can be a morally proper goal").

9. Niklas Luhmann, "Trust: A Mechanism for the Reduction of Social Complexity," in *Trust and Power: Two Works by Niklas Luhmann*, 8 (1979; photo. reprint, 1988) ("Trust constitutes a more effective form of complexity reduction").

10. See ibid., 20 (noting that trust evolves from past experiences that can guide future actions).

11. Ibid.

12. Ibid., 25.

13. See generally Francis Fukuyama, *Trust: The Social Virtues and the Creation of Prosperity* (1995), 7 (illustrating examples of the need for trust in economic life); Baier, "Trust and Antitrust," 239 (commenting that ordinary individuals must trust the mailman and the plumber to do their jobs properly); Lawrence C. Becker, "Trust as Noncognitive Security About Motives," *Ethics* 107 (1996): 51 (discussing trust of government officials); Russell Hardin, "Trustworthiness," *Ethics* 107 (1996): 33 (explaining how economic institutions are trustworthy with their customers); Philip Pettit, "The Cunning of Trust," *Phil. and Pub. Aff.* 24 (1995): 204–205 (discussing the trust placed in a city bus driver).

14. Luhmann, "Trust," 40 (footnote omitted).

15. Robert D. Putnam, *Making Democracy Work: Civic Traditions in Modern Italy* (1993), 169 (arguing that social capital increases when it is used and diminishes when it is not used).

16. Pettit, "The Cunning of Trust," 225.

17. See ibid., 202 (arguing that society where people trust one another will most likely function "more harmoniously and fruitfully" than society devoid of trust); see also Fukuyama, *Trust*, 47 (arguing that "sociability is critical to economic life because virtually all economic activity is carried out by groups rather than individuals"); Putnam, *Making Democracy Work*, 170 (asserting that trust is an "essential component" of social capital).

18. See Daniel M. Weinstock, "Building Trust in Divided Societies," *Pol. Phil.* 7 (1999): 263–283.

19. Kenneth J. Arrow, *The Limits of Organization* (1974), 23.

20. See Seligman, *The Problem of Trust*, 73 (arguing that solidarity must include some element of trust).

21. See Becker, "Trust as Noncognitive Security About Motives," 51 (voicing that the majority of U.S. citizens trust the motives of public officials enough to combat the effect of receiving negative information about them).

22. Consider, for example, controversies over governance of a range of issues, from speech and gambling to the allocation of domain names. For one of the classic (and controversial) positions on Internet governance, see David R. Johnson and David Post, "Law and Borders: The Rise of Law in Cyberspace," 48 Stan. L. Rev. 1367, 1367 (1996) (arguing that cyberspace requires different laws than the laws that govern geographically defined territories).

23. For a similar critique of social capital, see Alejandro Portes and Patricia Landolt, "Social Capital: Promise and Pitfalls of Its Role in Development," *J. Lat. Am. Stud.* 32 (2000): 546 (commenting that "one must not be over-optimistic about what enforceable trust . . . can accomplish").

24. See Baier, "Trust and Antitrust," 259 (arguing that in some instances it is more prudent to distrust rather than to trust).

25. See Becker, "Trust as Noncognitive Security About Motives," 58 (noting that a "proper sense of security is a balance of cognitive control and noncognitive stability").

26. See Seligman, *The Problem of Trust*, 16–21 (explaining the difference between trust and confidence).

27. See Pettit, "The Cunning of Trust," 210 (arguing that the mechanisms of trust can explain why "trust builds on trust").

28. See ibid., 203 (commenting that many are not proud of this trait).

29. Ibid., 211.

30. See ibid., 203 (arguing that people regard their desire for the good opinion of others as a disposition that is hard to shed).

31. See ibid., 207 (arguing that "where trust of this kind materializes and survives, people will take that as a token of proof of their being well disposed toward one another, so that the success of the trust should prove to be fruitful in other regards").

32. Seligman, *The Problem of Trust*, 69 (arguing that familiarity relates to the "human bond" rooted in identity).

33. Ibid., 69.

34. See Putnam, *Making Democracy Work*, 172 (arguing that reciprocity undergirds social trust, which facilitates cooperation in communities).

35. See, e.g., Seligman, *The Problem of Trust*, 22 (arguing that the concept of social role has been "fundamental to modern sociological analysis"); Baier, "Trust and Antitrust," 256 (arguing that people trust others to perform their roles in society); Pettit, "The Cunning of Trust," 221 (arguing that divisions

among people in a community are likely to reduce the chances of people from different sides trusting one another).

36. See Luhmann, "Trust," 78–85 (discussing the conditions necessary for trust to be formed); Russell Hardin, "The Street-Level Epistemology of Trust," *Pol. & Soc'y* 21 (1993): 514 (asserting that the "terrible vision of a permanent underclass in American city ghettos may have its grounding in the lesson that the children of the ghetto are taught . . . that they cannot trust others"); Pettit, "The Cunning of Trust," 222 (arguing that a society in which trust is found only in small family groups might become very cynical); Weinstock, "Building Trust in Divided Societies," 263–283.

37. See Luhmann, "Trust," 84 (commenting on how "complex and richly varied the social conditions for the formation of trust are").

38. See Hardin, "The Street-Level Epistemology of Trust," 522 (discussing social mechanisms that generate trust); Pettit, "The Cunning of Trust," 220 (arguing that the "trust-responsiveness mechanism" has implications for institutional design); Weinstock, "Building Trust in Divided Societies," 263–283.

39. There is far more complexity to this issue than I need, or am able, to show here. See, e.g., Helen Nissenbaum, "The Meaning of Anonymity in an Information Age," *Info. Soc'y* 15 (1999): 141 (discussing anonymity and what it means to protect it); Kathleen Wallace, "Anonymity," *Ethics and Info. Tech.* 1 (1999): 23 (offering a definition of anonymity).

40. In 1999 a thirteen-year-old boy from Haddonfield, N.J., participated in eBay auctions, bidding away $3.2 million on items like a van Gogh sketch and a 1971 Corvette convertible. His parents were successful in freeing themselves from responsibility for these transactions. See "Boy Bids $3M at Online Site," AP Online (Haddonfield), 30 April 1999, available in 1999 WL 17062405 (reporting the exploits of the eighth-grade online bidder).

41. See Julian Dibbell, "A Rape in Cyberspace; or, How an Evil Clown, a Haitian Trickster Spirit, Two Wizards, and a Cast of Dozens Turned a Database Into a Society," in Mark Dery, ed., *Flame Wars: The Discourse of Cyberculture*, 237–240 (1994) (describing a fictional virtual rape in an online multiuser domain).

42. This is what I mean by organizing according to functionality. Structurally, a password is a very different device than a locked door is, but in relation to this aspect of computer security, namely access control, they are effectively the same.

43. See Ashley Dunn, "Computer World Battles Faster-Moving Viruses Technology," *Los Angeles Times*, 4 October 1999 (reflecting on the "notorious" outbreak of the Morris Worm and explaining that an Internet security clearinghouse was created in response to the damage done by the worm).

44. Khare and Rifkin, "Weaving a Web of Trust" at 4.

45. Bruce Schneier, "Risks of E-mail Borne Viruses, Worms, and Trojan Horses," *Risks Digest* 20, no. 2, 1, 6, 9, 11, 12, 13 (17 June 1999), http://catless.ncl.ac.uk/Risks/20.45.html.

46. See, e.g., Schneider, ed., *Trust in Cyberspace*, 134–137 (defining firewalls and identifying them as one of the mechanisms used to prevent unwanted access to computer systems).

47. See, e.g., Gary McGraw and Edward Felten, "Understanding the Keys to Java Security," *Javaworld*, 1 May 1997, available in 1997 WL 28334788 (reporting that a "code-signing hole" had been found in Java software); Richard King, "Java Sun's Language Is Scoring Some Early Points with Operators and Suppliers," *Tele.Com*, 1 May 1996, available in 1996 WL 16760663 (noting that "several security flaws have been reported since Sun [Microsystems, Inc.] announced Java").

48. See Lawrence Lessig, *Code and Other Laws of Cyberspace* (1999), 34–35 (identifying three common architectures of identity used on Internet as passwords, "cookies," and digital certificates).

49. But cf. Helen Nissenbaum, "The Meaning of Anonymity in an Information Age," *Info. Soc'y* 15 (1999): 143 (arguing that the capacity of the information age to aggregate and analyze the data necessary to identify an individual, even without access to a name, presents a new challenge to protecting anonymity, where society desires to do so).

50. Microsoft Explorer's security is based on this principle.

51. See Schneier, "Risks of E-mail Borne Viruses, Worms, and Trojan Horses," 9 ("One problem is the permissive nature of the Internet").

52. This seems to be the form of the Federal Intrusion Detection Network (FIDNet) system proposed by the National Security Council and endorsed by the Clinton administration to protect government computers. See Marc Lacey, "Clinton Outlines Plan and Money to Tighten Computer Security," *New York Times*, 8 January 2000 (identifying FIDNet as part of the Clinton administration's larger computer security plan); see also "White House Fact Sheet: Cyber Security Budget Initiatives," *U.S. Newswire*, 15 February 2000, available in 2000 WL 4141378 (outlining the Clinton administration's budget initiatives related to cybersecurity for fiscal year 2001); The White House, "Defending America's Cyberspace: National Plan for Information Systems Protection, Version 1.0: An Invitation to Dialogue," *Executive Summary* 15 (2000) (discussing various government intrusion detection systems). The FIDNet proposal has met with significant opposition from various civil liberties groups. See, e.g., John Markoff, "The Strength of the Internet Proves to Be Its Weakness," *New York Times*, 10 February 2000 (noting that FIDNet caused alarm among civil libertarians, who said it would be used to curtail privacy on the Internet); see also Patrick Thibodeau, "Senate Hears Objections to Cyber-

alarm," *Computerworld*, 7 February 2000, 25, available in Lexis, News Library, U.S. News, Combined File (reporting on privacy group's testimony before the U.S. Senate Judiciary Subcommittee on Technology, Terrorism, and Government Information).

53. See John Leyden, "Melissa's Creator Faces 'Hard Time,'" *Network News*, 14 April 1999, 7, available in Lexis, News Library, U.S. News, Computing and Technology file (reporting that America Online assisted federal and state law enforcement agents in identifying David Smith as the creator of the Melissa virus); Lee Copeland, "Virus Creator Fesses Up—Admits to Originating and Disseminating Melissa," *Computer Reseller News*, 6 September 1999, available in Lexis, News Library, Newspaper Stories, Combined Papers (noting that America Online tracked Smith down by tracing the virus to a list server in New Jersey); Hiawatha Bray, "N.J. Man Charged in Computer Virus Case," *Boston Globe*, 3 April 1999, available in Lexis, News Library, Newspaper Stories, Combined Papers (noting that America Online assisted the government agents in identifying Smith).

54. Baier, "Trust and Antitrust," 235.

55. Ibid., 259.

56. Hardin, "The Street-Level Epistemology of Trust," 507.

57. Seligman, *The Problem of Trust*, 43.

58. Fukuyama, *Trust*, 26.

59. See Baier, "Trust and Antitrust," 236 (analyzing trust as a relationship in which "A trusts B with valued thing C," and in which B is given discretionary powers with respect to C); Hardin, "The Street-Level Epistemology of Trust," 506 ("To say 'I trust you' seems almost always to be elliptical, as though we can assume some such phrase as 'to do X' or 'in matters Y'"); Weinstock, "Building Trust in Divided Societies," 263–283.

60. Baier, "Trust and Antitrust," 245 ("We take it for granted that people will perform their role-related duties and trust any individual worker to look after whatever her job requires her to. The very existence of that job, as a standard occupation, creates a climate of some trust in those with that job").

61. See Goldberg et al., "Trust Ethics and Privacy," 81 B.U. L. Rev. 407 (2001) (discussing changes to Amazon.com's privacy agreement, protecting customer information, that resulted in reduced protections).

62. Hardin, "The Street-Level Epistemology of Trust," 507.

63. See Luhmann, "Trust," 20 (noting that trust is based in part on familiarity, history, and past experiences); ibid., 24 (arguing that trust always involves the risk that the harm resulting from a breach of trust may be greater than the benefit to be gained by trusting); Pettit, "The Cunning of Trust," 208 (arguing that irrespective of how one defines risk-taking, trust always involves putting oneself in a position of vulnerability whereby it is possible for the other

person to do harm to the trustor); Weinstock, "Building Trust in Divided Societies," 263–283.

64. Richard Posner, "The Right of Privacy," 12 Ga. L. Rev. 393, 408 (1978).

65. There has been discussion in the media about the Clinton administration's proposals to monitor both governmental and private networks for signs of terrorist and criminal activity. See, e.g., Robert O'Harrow, "Computer Security Proposal Is Revised: Critics Had Raised Online Privacy Fears," *Washington Post*, 22 September 1999, available in Lexis, News Library, Newspaper Stories, Combined Papers (reporting that civil liberties groups welcomed changes to the Clinton administration's original proposals, in particular limitations on automatic data collection); see also note 52 above (discussing the Clinton administration's proposal for, and reaction to, enhanced computer network security programs).

66. See Luhmann, "Trust," 15 (noting that "trust increases the 'tolerance of uncertainty'" and explaining that "mastery of events" (i.e., knowledge) can replace trust).

67. Ibid., 42.

68. Roderick M. Kramer, "Trust and Distrust in Organizations: Emerging Perspectives, Enduring Questions," *Ann. Rev. Psychol.* 50 (1999): 591.

69. Pettit, "The Cunning of Trust," 225.

70. See Dibbell, "A Rape in Cyberspace," 239–242 (describing a fictional virtual rape in an online multiuser domain).

71. See U.S. Department of Justice, *Bureau of Justice Statistics: Selected Findings, Violent Crime* 3 (1994) (reporting that "in murders where the relationship between the victim and the offender was known, 44% of the victims were killed by an acquaintance, 22% by a stranger, and 20% by a family member").

72. See Becker, "Trust as Noncognitive Security About Motives," 50 (noting that "ordinary life" provides substantial anecdotal evidence that most people have personal relationships in which they remain "trustful despite the known untrustworthiness of others"); cf. Paul Slovic, "Perceived Risk, Trust, and Democracy," *Risk Analysis* 13 (1993): 677 (describing trust as fragile and identifying "the asymmetry principle," by which trust is usually created slowly but destroyed in an instant, often by a single event).

73. See Hoffman et al., "Building Consumer Trust Online," 82 (concluding that the primary barriers to consumers' providing demographic data to Web sites are related to trust and noting that more than 72 percent of Web users indicated they would provide demographic data if the Web sites would provide information about how the collected data would be used).

74. See Becker, "Trust as Noncognitive Security About Motives," 59 (arguing that a person's loss of confidence in another person's motivations does

more harm to the relationship than when the other person proves to be "merely unreliable or not credible").

75. Ibid., 51.

76. Ibid., 59.

77. See Slovic, "Perceived Risk, Trust, and Democracy," 680 (contrasting the reactions of French and American citizens to risks associated with nuclear power and noting that the French public's acceptance of the risks is partly related to the public trust in the state-run nuclear program, which has a reputation for emphasizing public service over profits).

78. See Tom Tyler, "Trust and Law Abidingness: A Proactive Model of Social Regulation," 81 B.U. L. Rev. 361 (2001) (advocating a "*proactive model of social regulation* that is based upon encouraging and maintaining public trust in the character and motives of legal authorities").

79. Ibid., 366 ("Motive based trust is central to situations in which people rely upon fiduciary authorities"); see also ibid., 376 (summarizing results of an empirical study and concluding that trust is an important factor in shaping people's reactions to their experience with legal authorities because (1) "people who trust the motives of the authority with whom they are dealing are more willing to defer to that authority" and (2) "trust leads to more positive feelings about the legal authority involved").

80. Ibid.

81. See ibid., 396 ("In the context of a specific personal experience with a legal authority, people are willing to voluntarily defer based upon their belief that the authorities are acting in a trustworthy manner. They infer trustworthiness from the justice of the actions of the authorities"); see also ibid., 398 (discussing the opportunities police officers and judges have to develop public goodwill by justifying outcomes by reference to the public's moral values, in the outcome context, and treating people fairly in the procedural context).

82. See note 64 and accompanying text.

83. I am grateful to Beth Kolko for suggesting this metaphor. When I presented a version of this paper in September 1999 at The Netherlands Royal Academy of Arts and Sciences, a thoughtful audience argued that Amsterdam served better as a contrast.

# Part 2

# TECHNOLOGY AND THE STRUCTURE OF COMMUNITIES

6

# TV Predicts Its Future: On Convergence and Cybertelevision

TARA MCPHERSON

## THE DEATH OF TELEVISION?

A special panel at New York's 1997 International Radio and Television Society Industry Conference found "new media" upstart and editor of the *Silicon Alley Reporter* Jason Calacanis pronouncing the "death of television." Neil Braun, president of NBC, shared the dais with Calacanis and appeared relatively unconcerned. Still, the conference played out in miniature an increasingly weighted confrontation between television and the Internet in contemporary U.S. culture. Although TV has long portrayed itself as the most timely and immediate of media, always ready to bring the world *live* into our living rooms, the industry was clearly anxious about how new technologies would affect television and its audiences throughout the late 1990s. Doomsday headlines like the one emblazoned upon a November 1995 *USA Today* piece announcing HOME PCS DRAW VIEWERS AWAY FROM TVS and magazines from *Wired* to *FamilyPC* offered up new technologies as an answer to the evils of television. Even though television audiences actually appeared to be growing, there did seem to be some cultural consensus at the millennium's close that TV and the Internet are waging war against each other.

While articles like the one from *USA Today* (and my own first paragraph) suggest that a battle was brewing between TV and the Internet, a closer examination actually shows that the relations between TV and the Web were shaping up in boardrooms, not on battlefields. Witness the strategic merger of media giants Microsoft and NBC, which, in July 1996, announced their partnership in MSNBC, a venture designed (in the words of a press release) to "marry TV and the Internet" through the joint development of a cable news station and a large-scale Web site. While MSNBC is interesting purely at a formal level, this union also has much to tell us about the limits of certain theories of emerging technologies and about the possible future of the Web, at least from the perspective of television.[1]

Though I will spend some time in this essay detailing what the cable channel and especially the Web site of MSNBC looked like in their first few years, I also want to use this specific investigation to pursue some larger questions about what this joint enterprise might suggest for the future development of new technologies in the United States. For instance, what kinds of knowledges, practices, or habits of thought enabled the emergence of a hybrid like MSNBC and shaped its development? By this, I do not mean only or primarily the corporate discussions of NBC and Microsoft or even the will to power of Bill Gates, but rather the nexus of discursive practices that fostered a seemingly natural alliance between broadcast television and the Web. What strategic enactments of certain ideals and values does a project like MSNBC foster? And what enactments are foreclosed, made hazier, and pushed to the margins by this rhetoric of convergence? Why *TV* and the Web?

Think about the very moniker "MSNBC." More than just the name of a cable news station and a growing Web site, it also represents a powerful melding of the broadcast/cable tradition to emerging technological practices. The five letters *M, S, N, B, C* thus bring forth a new media entity (one with particular textual and ideological takes on the global, the national, and the local) and simultaneously shape the very terrain in which we can imagine media practices. Put differently, MSNBC can be thought of as both a combination TV station/Web site and a central emergent mode of conceptualizing consumer and industrial relations on the Web and on TV. Accounts of the early years of television and radio by scholars like Bill Boddy, Jeanne Allen, and Tom Streeter underscore that the turn of these media toward unidirectional commercial broadcast had less to do with their actual technological capacities than with their very narration. That is, early discursive constructions of these media powerfully circumscribed their potential development, creating an environment in which some regulatory and corporate structures were more possible than others. Today's popular narratives of convergence work in a similar fashion, limiting the field of possibility in relation to the future of the Internet.

New technologies evolve via a process of selective adaptation that often has very little to do with the inherent physical properties and capacities of the technologies themselves. Communications scholar Dan Schiller argues that we now inhabit an era of digital capitalism that powerfully shapes how telecommunications technologies are conceived of and developed. A hallmark of this historical moment is the ascendancy of the transnational corporation and the concomitant ceding of the ownership of networks and airwaves to business interests. Schiller's point is further driven home by our government's recent sale of the public airwaves to the highest corporate bidders. The emergence of this neo-Fordist system of production is underwritten by and simultaneously underwrites the project of neoliberalism, and the rhetoric of convergence works to naturalize both neoliberal philosophies and the workings of digital capitalism.[2]

The stakes in this battle around convergence extend far beyond the mere popularity of a hybrid form like MSNBC. The corporate and journalistic conversations around convergence also leave several propositions unexamined. First and perhaps foremost, the union of the computer and the television is not simply about the marriage of computing and televisual technologies, that is, the marriage of machines. Rather, this union brings together computing technology with the American broadcast system, a very particular articulation of television technology: commercial, unidirectional broadcast. Thus, "convergence" as it is playing out today already presupposes the commercial nature of the Internet as a medium. While this might not seem particularly surprising, it is important to remember that the initial popularity of the Internet and, more specifically, of the World Wide Web, as communications media was not inextricably wedded to the system's commercial viability, despite the origins of the network in the military-industrial complex. In the mid-1990s, the Web was often celebrated for its "bottom up" possibilities, its capacity to make us all producers of media, implying elements of universal access and distribution. The current rhetoric about convergence shies away from this vision, replacing it with the notion of "consumer choice," mapping the model of cable television over the Net and, in Schiller's language, deepening the market (88).

This shift from producer to consumer is an important one, a move that might also be described as going from citizen to consumer, from virtual public to consuming publics. As the Internet increasingly adapts the commercial forms of media like television, other modes of expression become harder and harder to conceptualize and advocate for. The supposed anarchic or rhizomatic nature of the Web becomes less and less prominent as corporate Web site architectures and commercialization increasingly map our paths through cyberspace in fairly rigid ways. The very nature of interactivity narrows as well. This is not simply an argument that the Internet needs a kind of PBS or public access "channel" of its own; rather, I want to underscore that we should not de facto imagine cyberspace as a commercial zone. As Schiller notes,

> if the present trend is not comprehensively interrupted, the extent to which cyberspace becomes a commercial consumer medium will very largely be determined by profit-seeking companies themselves. Non-profit prospectors of alternative visions of cyberspace will . . . be marginalized. . . . [To date], the debate over commercialism in cyberspace has been a nonstarter. (128)

Developments like MSNBC and the Oxygen network, another combination Web site/cable channel, received substantial press, helping to cement the "natural" link between the two technologies in the public eye. While such hybrids claim to offer an almost unending array of choices to their users, those choices still largely comprise *consumption* choices, and, more important, choices made available only to choice customers. Much has been made of the Internet's capacity to narrowcast, that is, to select precise target audiences. We should be concerned about just how narrow that casting actually will be. Though the rhetoric of convergence calls for an alliance of two media forms, both will be reshaped by the merger. Just as we should be wary of the language of convergence, we should also guard against easily casting television as the bad object in this scenario. For all of its problems, television is at least a *mass* medium. Ellen Seiter reminds us that as a relatively cheap and available technology, television has brought communities together and given us things to talk about, creating the space for sociality and serving as a kind of lingua franca. There is, however, no promise that the current developments in new technology will result in a new media network readily available to everyone. Cable television still does not reach one third of U.S. households. As we watch the links between cable and the World Wide Web strengthen, there is little reason to believe that computer technologies will inherently broaden access.

Nonetheless, I do not think a cynical pessimism takes us very far in imagining other possible futures for the Internet. The remainder of this essay pays careful attention to narratives of new technology emerging from the corporate world, questioning the oft-told tale of convergence through an examination of the early days of MSNBC. In confronting the myth of convergence head on, we might begin to discern other paths in cyberspace, paths charted by many of the essays in this volume. We need both a public conversation about the possible forms the Internet might take and carefully articulated policy decisions that move beyond the desires of the neoliberal project. Raymond Williams once argued that "the moment of any new technology is a moment of choice." We need to act now before that moment passes us by.

## THE PEACOCK GETS WIRED

MSNBC is neither the Web site nor the cable channel but, rather, some conglomeration of the two, and, from the very first PR, the link between the platforms was promoted as the unique element of MSNBC. Though the cable channel originally competed with CNN and later with Fox News, MSNBC hawks the convergence of Microsoft and NBC as the true cachet of its enterprise. On cable, MSNBC took over NBC's *America's Talking*, giving the new station an initial subscriber base of 28 million, with plans to reach more than 55 million by the year 2000, while the Web operation consistently has been ranked the "number one general news site" on the Internet. Though the numbers that MSNBC-TV pulled in early on were minuscule in terms of the big broadcast picture (less than 100,000 households watching during the third quarter of 1997, as compared to CNN's 766,000), the channel did begin to make a name for itself in its coverage of both the O. J. Simpson civil trial verdict and the death of

Princess Diana (when network cross-promotion led to a 35 percent increase in the channel's viewership). In both cases, the ability to program across platforms—network, cable, and Web—proved central to ratings success (Jensen and Sandberg; Landler; Pope).[3]

MSNBC's initial slogan was "It's time to get connected," and the TV channel was hyped as the first to "use the look of computer graphics," though in practice this often translated into the use of split screens, quick-cut video, and quirky camera angles (and it hardly represented the first use of computer imagery on television).[4] Early programming included *The Site*, a show centered on issues of new technology and pitched to the younger crowd, which was seen to be deserting network news in droves, and most series both heavily promoted the Web site and also included e-mail and chat connections to let the home viewer "participate" in the show. Other original programs, like Jane Pauley's *Time and Again* cleverly repackaged old NBC news footage to create hour-long (and relatively cheap) shows on topics ranging from Watergate to White House pets to sex and the 1970s. In order to cement relationships with the more than two hundred local NBC affiliates, MSNBC programming also allows for a three-minute local cutaway during each half hour of airtime, a move that permits NBC to promote both national and local broadcasts within a cable venue while also hyping MSNBC's local and national Web sites.

Formally, the television channel incorporates the look and "feel" of the Web via several formats, some more successful than others. One 1997 human-interest story had anchor Lori Stokes chatting live in the studio (a "hip," edgy space deliberately structured to appear less formal than most news studios) with "Internet correspondent" Mary Kathleen Flynn. While describing the release from Seaworld into the Pacific of a young gray whale, J.J., Flynn surfed Seaworld's Web site, instructing viewers in what they might find there. In a visually bizarre moment, TV viewers were subjected to minutes of a small, grainy, almost indiscernible, quicktime video image as it played live on the Seaworld site, inadvertently (or not) highlighting the diminished video capacities of the Web in relation to television. Other "hybrid" formats include shows like John Gibson's *Newschat*, a kind of visual talk radio that devotes a good portion of screen space to replicating and displaying viewer e-mail (via a "Windows" format). Perhaps not surprisingly, the most successful examples of the inclusion of computer imagery occur in commercials, particularly in an ad featuring Brian Williams and trumpeting the Web site's News Alert feature, a browser update service designed to "bring the latest news to you," allowing you "to stay on top of the news while . . . at your computer." Visually, the advertisement utilizes the device of the cursor, seemingly moving from image to image via some imagined surfer's desire and quick clicks. These formal techniques echo the language of convergence spewing forth from corporate headquarters and the pages of *Wired*, the *Wall Street Journal*, and the *New York Times*, structuring a visual equation between the Web and TV (though, as the Seaworld example illustrates, not always a seamless and enticing one).

Although the cable channel was expected to turn a profit before the year 2000, and did so, despite lagging behind CNN and Fox News in ratings, the Web channel, like most Internet developments, still struggles to break even, a fact that suggests that both NBC and Microsoft see the Web site as building a crucial "brand" identity (and as providing valuable market research) despite losses in the millions. A quick surf around the Web site also reveals one thing very quickly: *this is not TV*, though we can fairly easily find aspects of the site that forge links between the two media. In early theoretical investigations of television, work that labored to distinguish television from film, Jane Feuer observed that "the differences between TV and . . . cinema are too great not to see television as a qualitatively different medium" (12), but granted this, she queried what *was* specific to TV, both as a form and as an ideological and industrial practice. Her answer, of course, was liveness (or, more crucially, the illusion of it), and liveness is indeed a key dimension of the experience of the Internet, which also promotes itself as essentially up to the minute (one need only hit "reload" or sign up for News Alert), ideology again masquerading as ontology. But this is liveness with a difference.[5]

How does the Web, as a medium, in its own practices, insist upon "an ideology of the live, the immediate, the direct" (Feuer, 14)? At a site like MSNBC, the self-reflexive constructions of "liveness" are manifold. From the "instant" traffic maps, which, the copy tells me, "agree within a minute or two" with real time, to my personalized front page, which greets me with the "current" weather conditions and individualized news bits, the Web site repeatedly foregrounds its currency and timeliness. A frequently changing ticker-tape scroll bar updates both headlines and stock quotes, and a flashing target signals "breaking news" whenever my PC is on, whether or not I've got my Web browser open. Even the blinking ads for an ISP that pop up in my browser insist that I can "get it NOW . . . Just click." I am also told I can instantly affect the news by participating in one of the numerous polls or surveys that dot MSNBC's electronic landscape (they're called "live votes"); I get the results immediately, no need to wait for the 10:00 P.M. broadcast. Just click. Instant gratification.

This sense of being in the moment is further enhanced by the chat rooms built into the site, forums designed to wed the Web site more securely to the TV schedule, allowing the computer user to join the television audience by asking questions to talk show guests in real time. Heated chats on topics like Zippergate tend to scroll by faster than they can be read, creating not only a sense of "being there" but also of the inexorable speed of the present, linking presence and temporality in a frenetic, scrolling now. We feel time move.

Of course, as with television, this much-touted liveness is actually the *illusion* of liveness: though the traffic conditions may indeed be up to date, most of the "breaking news" I access via my personalized front page is no more instant than the news I would watch at 6:00 P.M. on KTLA. Indeed, many of the stories on my front page right now have been there for days, and many of the new headlines simply refer me to older stories. But with this venue, as with television, what is essential is not so much the *fact* of liveness as the *feel* of it. MSNBC's Web site (representing a clear trend in commercial site development) presents liveness as a given, indeed as the very raison d'être of the medium; to paraphrase Feuer on TV, the site "as an ideological apparatus positions the [surfer] into its imaginary of presence and immediacy" (14).

Yet this is not just the same old liveness of television; it is a liveness that also foregrounds volition and mobility, a liveness on demand. Thus, unlike television—which parades its liveness before us—the Web structures a sense of causality in relation to liveness, a liveness that we navigate and move through, often structuring a feeling that our own desire drives the movement. Interestingly, as we imagine ourselves *navigating* sites, the Web *feels* more mobile than television, even though it relies largely on text and still images rather than the moving video of TV. Furthermore, this is a sense of a connected presence in time: connected to the machine, to data, and to others, from the auction venues of eBay to the chat rooms of MSNBC to the financial parlors of E*TRADE. The Web's forms and metadiscourses thus generate a circuit of meaning not only from a sense of immediacy but also through yoking this presentness to a feeling of choice, structuring a mobilized liveness, which we come to feel that we invoke and affect, in the instant, in the click, reload.

If television news, in the words of Bob Stam, obliges the telespectator "to follow a predetermined sequence" exhibiting "a certain syntagmatic orthodoxy" (32), the Web appears to break down the preordained sequencing of the TV news report, allowing the user to fashion his or her own syntagmas, moving from news bit to news bit with a certain degree of volition. Our choices, perhaps our need to know, our epistemophilia, seem to move us through the space and time of the Web, and this volitional mobility implies our transformation, shimmering with the possibility of change, difference, the new and the now. From the dress-up mannequins of the Gap to the instant quizzes and horoscopes of sites like MSNBC, the click propels us elsewhere. The vast database capacities of the Internet structure the field upon which this sense of volition and movement unfolds, permitting the Web surfer to move back and forth through history and geography, allowing for the possibility (both real and imagined) of accident and juxtaposition to an even greater degree than television.

This back-and-forth movement occurs at a number of levels, ranging from the ease with which my personalized front page allows me to skip from local to national to international news, alternating between accounts of a car wreck (or a car chase) on an L.A. freeway to reports on the progress of the Irish peace talks. A concrete example of the Web's capacity to structure a sense of volitional spatial and temporal mobility is found on MSNBC's "Kennedy Remembered" page. Here, a real-time plug-in called SurroundVideo allows me to move around Dallas's grassy knoll in a 3-D representational space via a fairly seamless patching together of digital photographs, navigating actual footage of the area. Once the image loads (waiting is also one of the Web's temporalities), I am able to explore this Texan geographic terrain, moving back and forth between the road, the book depository, the grassy arena. The space is in full color, and I am able to choose my own path with a click and drag of the mouse, zooming in and out for different perspectives and "edits." The sense of spatiality and mobility is fairly intense and certainly feels driven by my own desire. An even odder experience is created by clicking a button that maps black-and-white images of the 1963 assassination of the president *over* the color images, a slightly surreal collapse of space and time, still navigable. An archive of video and audio clips, various articles about JFK, transcripts of debates and speeches, and Web visitors' own stories structure a roam-able space of JFK, evoking mediated memories of Camelot and a poignant affect of national loss and nostalgia.[6] I am able to be both here (in L.A.) and there (in Dallas), both then (1963) and now (1999), but I am always present, moving, live. For those not moved by mobile history, other SurroundVideo sites also allow users to surf the solar system and tour the White House, each positioning the national via specific moments of geography and movement.

At one level MSNBC's Web pages are able to create this feeling of a willed, real-time movement through the news and the nation by eliminating a visible anchor. In television news, as Feuer notes, the anchor wields the ideology of liveness to structure a unity that overcomes fragmentation. The anchor acts "as a custodian of flow and regularity," mediating all discourse (16–19). Moving through the various twists and turns of MSNBC's site, the user can imagine that she has become the anchor, making sense (or not) of the vast archive of information with intentional clicks of the mouse. In chat rooms, participants often reject the anchor-moderator, refusing to stay on topic and redirecting the conversation. For instance, in one MSNBC chat space, a live forum with a pet psychic followed a three-hour discussion of Zippergate the day after the Willey story broke; the moderator valiantly tried to change topics and generate questions for her guest, but "audience" participants refused to yield the "space," busily typing in comments like "most pets have more control over their libidos than bubba does."

Of course, the mediation of information has not really disappeared; rather, the author or anchor function has simply gone underground, below the code. The news stories on MSNBC are highly mediated (and generally well under 750 words); vast parts of the world simply are not accessible or represented; and very few links exist to sites other than those on MSNBC, thus eliminating much of the "intertextuality" and rhizomatic structure so often praised on the Net. The site is highly controlled, and yet the promise and feeling of choice, movement, and liveness powerfully overdetermine its spaces. MSNBC self-consciously constructs itself as a projected fulfillment of what seems missing in the status quo (both on TV and in real life), becoming a solution to the oft-voiced dilemma of having 100 channels and still nothing to watch.

## RETHINKING CONVERGENCE

So what might we learn from MSNBC's promotion of itself as a site of liveness and volitional mobility? It would seem to suggest that the Web as a formal system is different from television, and, certainly at an experiential level, it is easy to support this point of view. Yet, despite these clear differences and despite the difficulty that MSNBC has experienced in creating a computer-centric cable channel (*The Site*, for instance, was canceled, and the station has experimented with a look that more closely parallels CNN's, slightly modifying its "edgier" style), at both formal and metadiscursive levels, the two media are still tightly linked.

Formally, the Web site and TV station endlessly reference each other, and the content of the Web site is heavily skewed toward features on new technology that stress the coming convergence of television and the Web. Stories detail the technological advances in interactive television, hyping "custom viewing from ACTV" (a system that allows viewers to choose angles in sports broadcasts), as well as endlessly reporting on set-top boxes and cable Web access. That Microsoft, a corporation not widely recognized for playing fair, is willing to foreground even its competitors' Web-TV projects suggests a powerful motivation to create a seemingly natural link between TV and the Internet. The bulletin boards on MSNBC endlessly query their visitors about what they want in interactive TV technology, simultaneously gathering free research data while framing questions in such a way as to suggest that the only real dilemma is *what* TV-Internet technological hybrid we should choose, obscuring larger questions about whether or not the Internet is really (or really should be) tied to the commercial traditions of television. In his work on early radio, Streeter reminds us that a similar logic of functionality worked to close down alternative, grassroots forms of radio, bringing broadcast firmly under corporate control in less than thirty years and diminishing its potential as a democratizing technology. Allen notes the early two-way potential of television and documents a similar loss of possibility, underlining the lack of an effective public discourse for protecting the interests of amateur "ham television" operators in the face of corporate interests.[7]

The illusion of a mobilized liveness in a Web site like MSNBC actually masks the degree to which the site is already moving toward a linear, largely unidirectional model of the Internet, a model predicated on contemporary broadcast modes of information delivery and encouraged in recent Web design manuals. The same 1997 IRTS conference at which the young computer entrepreneur predicted the death of television also offered up another vision of the Internet's future, a future that looks a lot like TV. During a panel discussion that brought together representatives of AOL, Prodigy, and the big three networks, a future model of Internet access based on TV's network structure was introduced to sound approval. This model, predicted to come online in less than a decade, would limit Internet access to three or four providers or portals that would function much like networks, offering their own programming, directing users to approved parts of the Web, and limiting the capacity to post a home page or Web program to specialized producers. While this may sound far-fetched, small steps in this direction are already under way. For instance, if you want to cruise around the grassy knoll in MSNBC's re-created Dallas, you had better be using a Microsoft Internet Explorer browser. Netscape can't take you there.

The interfaces deployed by MSNBC (and most other commercial Web sites) suggest a sense of liveness and movement even while the very programming that underwrites them works to guide and impede the user's trajectory. The increasing popularity of "portal" sites often works to constrict the surfer's movement, effectively detouring users along particular paths or containing them within particular sites. For instance, both MSNBC and AOL work as portal sites, which makes it hard to leave their confines and allows them to function as the kind of locked-in channel that television executives have long dreamed about. The ideological implications of actual interfaces and other programming choices need to be investigated and theorized; we need to foreground the political effects of burying the author function within the code. The standardization of temporality and style via channels, regular programming, and published schedules is a central part of the history of television and radio commercialization. Television's much-heralded "flow" works to move viewers through chunks of televisual time, orchestrating viewership, and Web programming allows for an even more carefully orchestrated movement, all dressed up in a feeling of choice.[8]

"Convergence" executives have recently taken to trumpeting what they term "lean-back interactivity," which provides "little snippets of interactivity to enhance the broadcast experience" (Pillar). Also described as "minimal interactivity," this mode largely "enhances" broadcast by offering consumers a wider array of click-and-buy shopping. A "give the buyer what he wants" logic underwrites the move, as Wink Communications chairman and chief technology officer Brian Dougherty maintains: "If the interactivity is so complex . . . consumers aren't going to want it." Another chairman proclaims that "the really cool digital application turns out to be about TV" (Pillar). This could simply be dismissed as so much corporate grandstanding, but the ways in which meaningful interactivity has been threatened by recent commercial developments on the Web need to be taken seriously. "Lean-back interactivity" could still provide me with a feeling of volitional mobility as I gleefully click my way toward a roomful of furniture from my favorite sitcom or voice my opinion on a variety of timely topics, but there is a political liability to this illusion of volition. Feeling as if we have a world of choices makes it all that much harder to recognize the meaningful choices we haven't been allowed to make. I may move through the Web with a sense that I am clicking my own path, but this is a volition to do precisely what? Who's moving whom?

While we might be tempted to read the ability of the MSNBC Web site visitor to choose her path through the day's news stories or to personalize her own front page as empowering and preferable to TV's reliance on anchors, this focus on choice conceals those choices that are being foreclosed, including a notion of interactivity that extends beyond "live votes" and mouse clicks. What happens when we stop making our own home pages and instead rely on the "personalized" front page that MSNBC willingly creates for us? Though the ability to move at will from the global to the local is a real promise of the Web as we know it today, the personalized front page might seriously curtail this potential, limiting the news we come in contact with to a very narrow frame. Moving from the global space of NASDAQ to the local traffic and weather reports may be convenient, but it hardly propels us along toward an idealized global village. Databases are not all equal, and MSNBC's ontology of volitional liveness conceals the ideological limits of the options it does offer us.

Of course, cultural studies scholarship serves to remind us that users are not entirely held captive by the technologies and narratives they encounter in a commercial broadcast medium. Viewers can creatively engage with mainstream forms, making meanings that are often at odds with the original text and the constraints of digital capitalism. Nonetheless, the promise of new interactive media like the Web (like the promise of many of the technologies that predate it, from radio to television to cable) is that they might retain a more democratic, bottom-up capacity, allowing an authorship in which volitional mobility remains in the user's control. Put differently, the development of these media should allow us the possibility for something beyond poaching, however pleasurable such interloping might be.[9]

Much of the current academic theory about new technologies focuses on the new media's narrative strategies and modes of address (including their propensity to multiply or fragment identity) and on their ability to foster new experimental cultures and objects (from MUDs to CD-ROMs), and this work has produced important insights in terms of the specificities of these technologies. Still, there is too often a gap between such investigations and larger public and corporate discussions about where new technologies are headed, a gap between our formal analyses and the larger cultural and economic discourses in which new technologies are embedded and which powerfully affect their development. Understanding MSNBC and the rhetoric of convergence might help us to resist the pull of these discourses by taking on their vision of the future, situating our readings of the Web's structures within a more complex examination of the dreams of digital capitalism.

## NOTES

I would like to thank several people for their contributions to this essay. Beth Kolko offered valuable comments on an early draft, Ethan Thompson provided helpful research assistance, and both Mark Williams and Tom Streeter shared their own insightful and interesting scholarship (as well as their friendship) at just the right moments.

1. Even Jason Calacanis has changed his tune about the "death" of television. In the late 1990s he began publication of the *Digital Coast Reporter*, noting that "broadband is not five years away, it is today." His first editorial went on to celebrate content, "the 'Digital Coast' (f.k.a. Los Angeles) and the CONVERGENCE industries," singling out a list of companies, including DEN, which are developing cybertelevision. Television's annihilation by new media has been supplanted by a seemingly easy marriage of the two forms.

2. In addition to Schiller's work, also see Tom Streeter's essay "That Romantic Chasm" for an excellent examination of the rhetoric of neoliberalism. While Streeter is rightfully critical of the neoliberalist project, he traces its ties to the romantic libertarianism of many of those involved in computing culture in order to suggest what we might learn—both as scholars and as activists—from these two very popular paradigms.

3. By the summer of 2001, MSNBC.com had enjoyed five years at the top of the General News Category for online users. According to Media Metrix, a ratings service, the Web site logged 11.5 million unique users during the month of July. The site also garnered critical praise, winning the top prize for general excellence in online journalism for the year 2000 from the Online News Association (in association with the Columbia University Graduate School of Journalism). On November 8, 2000, the Web site's coverage of the presidential election, "Decision 2000," garnered 6.9 million unique users.

The television channel continues to grow its audience even as it ranks third among cable news stations, trailing CNN and the Fox News Channel. In August 2001, CNN averaged 606,000 homes, up one percent from August 2000, while the Fox News Channel averaged 498,000 homes, up 72 percent from a year earlier. MSNBC averaged 285,000 homes, an 8 percent increase. MSNBC did score very well in its target demographic of young viewers, leading company president Erik Sorenson to suggest that advertisers were happy with the ratings numbers (Huff; Rutenberg).

4. For a detailed and interesting exploration of the use of computer imagery in commercial television, one need look no further than John Caldwell's provocative *Televisuality*. Caldwell's book weds a consideration of actual production practices to an analytical investigation of television's aesthetics and ideology, noting the degree to which digital culture affected television's style, even before the widespread use of the World Wide Web.

5. In an article that greatly enriches the scholarship on television and liveness, Mark Williams reminds us that "liveness, though long considered to be a defining and natural characteristic of [television], may best be recognized as a historically specific and perhaps even situational affect which continues to play a crucial role in delineating TV's mediation of the real and the real world" (1). He goes on to illustrate the importance of historicizing television's various

appropriations and deployments of liveness, and this essay builds on his work to examine the Internet's relationship to this historical trajectory.

6. This SurroundVideo experience is archived on MSNBC's Web site and is available at http://www.msnbc.com/onair/msnbc/timeandagain/archive/jfk/dealey.asp.

7. In fact, the similarity between the early development of and public discourse around technologies from radio to television to video to cable should give us pause as we flip through the pages of *Wired*. Our investigations of digital technologies require an understanding of this history. See work by Streeter, Freedman, Boddy, Mellencamp, and Allen.

8. The best delineation of television's "flow" remains Raymond Williams's *Television: Technology and Cultural Form*.

9. For more complete discussions of the concept of poaching, see the works by de Certeau and Jenkins.

## REFERENCES


Allen, Jeanne. "The Social Matrix of Television: Invention in the United States." In E. Ann Kaplan, ed., *Regarding Television: Critical Approaches, An Anthology*, 109–119. Los Angeles: AFI, 1983.

Boddy, William. *Fifties Television: The Industry and Its Critics*. Champaign: University of Illinois Press, 1992.

Calacanis, Jason. "Another Big Step . . . Digital Coast Weekly!" E-mail to *Silicon Alley Reporter* subscribers. 8 July 1999.

Caldwell, John. *Televisuality: Style, Crisis, and Authority in American Television*. New Brunswick, N.J.: Rutgers University Press, 1995.

De Certeau, Michel. *The Practice of Everyday Life*. Berkeley: University of California Press, 1984.

Feuer, Jane. "The Concept of Live Television: Ontology as Ideology." In E. Ann Kaplan, ed., *Regarding Television: Critical Approaches, An Anthology*, 12–23. Los Angeles: AFI, 1983.

Freedman, Eric. "Citizen's Arrest: Public Access Cable Television in the Digital Domain." Paper presented at the 1999 Society for Cinema Studies Conference, West Palm Beach, Florida.

Huff, Richard. "CNN Ratings Down Despite Condit Case." *New York Daily News*, 29 August 2001.

Jenkins, Henry. *Textual Poachers: Television Fans and Participatory Culture*. New York: Routledge, 1992.

Jensen, Elizabeth, and Jared Sandberg. "NBC, Microsoft Face Hurdles in New Venture." *Wall Street Journal*, 15 December 1995.

Landler, Mark. "The Logic of Losing at All-News TV." *New York Times*, 22 June 1997.
Lieberman, David. "Home PCs Draw Viewers Away from TVs." *USA Today*, 16 November 1995.
Mellencamp, Patricia. "Video and the Counterculture." In Cynthia Schneider and Brian Wallis, eds., *Global Television*, 199–224. Cambridge, Mass.: MIT Press, 1988.
Pillar, Charles. "Improved Technology May Finally Make Interactive TV a Go." *Los Angeles Times*, 16 November 1998.
Pope, Kyle. "As the Focus Shifts, the Picture Brightens at MSNBC." *Wall Street Journal*, 28 October 1997.
Rutenberg, Jim. "At MSNBC, a Young Anchor for Younger Viewers." *New York Times*, 29 October 2001.
Schiller, Dan. *Digital Capitalism*. Cambridge, Mass.: MIT Press, 1999.
Seiter, Ellen. "TV and the Internet." Talk given at University of Southern California, Los Angeles, 1998.
Streeter, Thomas. *Selling the Air: A Critique of the Policy of Commercial Broadcasting in the United States*. Chicago: University of Chicago Press, 1996.
——. "'That Deep Romantic Chasm': Libertarianism, Neoliberalism, and the Computer Culture." In Andrew Calabrese and Jean-Claude Burgelman, eds., *Communication, Citizenship, and Social Policy*, 49–64. New York: Rowman and Littlefield, 1999.
Stam, Robert. "Television News and Its Spectator." In E. Ann Kaplan, ed., *Regarding Television: Critical Approaches, An Anthology*, 23–43. Los Angeles: AFI, 1983.
Williams, Mark. "History in a Flash: Notes on the Myth of TV 'Liveness.'" In Jane Gaines and Michael Renov, eds., *Collecting Visible Evidence*, 292–312. Minneapolis: University of Minnesota Press, 1999.
Williams, Raymond. *Television: Technology and Cultural Form*. New York: Schocken, 1975.
——. *The Year 2000*. New York: Pantheon, 1983.

7

# Women Making Multimedia: Possibilities for Feminist Activism

MARY E. HOCKS AND ANNE BALSAMO

## FEMINIST TECHNOLOGICAL ACTIVISM

Our essay rests on a simple premise: feminists can design and deploy technologies for activist goals to accomplish important, even essential, cultural and political work. We ultimately believe that feminist teachers and scholars need to use new media and communications technologies to build applications that promote research and action in the interest of women. As designers of technological artifacts, we believe we can imagine and create, at least temporarily, notions of activism, agency, and community that are then employed via these technological artifacts. We can also avoid the traps of technological determinism, neo-Luddite anxieties, or simple cause-and-effect equations between ideologies and technologies when we develop a more complex notion of how technologies function in our culture. A carefully articulated theory of technology actually frees us to see the empowering potential of particular technologies and design processes within specific contexts. Our Women of the World Talk Back project, designed for the specific historical moment of the United Nations Fourth World Conference on Women, helped us to enact and explore the possibility of cross-cultural dialogue and exchange in an international feminist context. As an instance of digital political activism that later became an evolving presentation with multiple audiences, this project underscores for us the understanding that technological activism will be politically effective only in the context of transformed institutionalization, cultural narratives, and agency that are structured and disseminated by digital technologies.

A grant to attend the 1995 United Nations Fourth World Conference on Women as an official delegation became the perfect vehicle for putting our ideas into practice. Here we were, two feminist scholars, working at institutions in programs blessed with rich technological resources, wondering how to use those resources specifically in the interest of educating and engaging women with new technologies. We both had explicit pedagogical purposes for involving ourselves and our students in the design and critique of new media. Mary worked at Spelman College, a historically black women's institution, directing a technology-rich writing program. As project director of a Mellon Foundation grant, she wanted to design collaborative educational projects that integrated multimedia technology meaningfully into the curriculum (see Hocks and Bascelli). Anne worked across town at the more conservative, male-dominated Georgia Institute of Technology, where she helped design a graduate curriculum in information, design, and technology. She was especially interested in finding ways to combine feminist cultural theory with the development of new media in the service of feminist pedagogy (see Balsamo, "Teaching in the Belly of the Beast"). Thus, we brought to this project a shared interest in the design and analysis of new media and a sense of the pedagogical potential of these emerging media forms.

In preparation for attending the UN conference in Beijing, we decided to create an entire booth devoted to the topic of women in science and technology that we could present at the accompanying NGO (Nongovernmental Organization) Forum held in Hairou, a small resort town forty miles outside of Beijing. With the booth as a showcase, we designed an interactive multimedia project, called Women of the World Talk Back, that was aimed at the international feminist audience that was also participating in the NGO Forum. Created with Macromedia Director to run on a desktop Macintosh system, the project featured the perspectives of the conference organizers and longtime activists from various global women's organizations, such as Women in Development and OXFAM International. The version we presented included videotaped statements about the global political situation of women by international spokespeople, several of whom gave plenary addresses at the forum. As the title of the project implies, we then invited other NGO participants to "talk back" to the global leaders featured in our presentation. Thus, we used this multimedia project as a way to stimulate communication with the women we met at the forum. For images, please see our Web site at http://www.gsu.edu/~engmeh/mmdoc.html (Balsamo and Hocks).

Originally, we conceived of Women of the World Talk Back as a video-based CD-ROM project. In early 1995 the World Wide Web was still a relatively novel and limited medium. While we have since watched with interest the growth of feminist resources on the Internet, when we began the project there were far fewer Web sites or CD-ROM titles that specifically addressed feminist concerns.[1] A couple of notable exceptions do stand out: the late Christine Tamblyn's self-published CD-ROM, *She Loves It She Loves It Not: Women and Technology*, explored a feminist's ambivalence about technology; Brenda Laurel's early work at Purple Moon resulted in the first non-Barbie-based games for girls.[2] Taking inspiration from these pioneers, we wanted to design a project that explored the communicative possibilities and organizing potential of these information technologies.

We then discovered an archive of forty hours of videotaped interviews with international spokespeople and heads of state conducted by the Georgia Tech Telephoto Division. These interviews had taken place in connection with previous UN conferences—the UN Conference on Population and Development in 1994 and the UN Conference on Environment and Development, or Earth Summit, in 1992. The interviews included a wide range of material concerning the global situation of women. In screening these video archives, we began to conceptualize the construction of a series of "talking head" dialogues that would present one side of a conversation—the official spokesperson's views about the global politics of women. Indeed, we were able to extract from these video interview archives several dozen sound-bite statements that we eventually edited together to create the main video pieces for our project. We also conducted additional interviews with the 1995 UN conference and NGO Forum organizers. Thus the version of the project that we took to Hairou included statements culled from the video archive, as well as statements from Gertrude Mongela, Irene Santiago, and Patsy Robertson, three well-known organizers of the 1995 UN conference and NGO Forum.

This project became our first opportunity for making feminist multimedia and exploring their political potential within several specific theoretical contexts. An instance of using technology, and specifically a work of feminist communication as a social and political force, the initial project featured digitally designed public narratives about women's global economic and political situations. Those narratives were intended to inspire and activate a community of international feminist activists and educators—the "live" audience for the original conference presentation. However, we also designed these public narratives as open-ended statements that needed completion in electronic format so that they would have an even broader virtual audience: an evolving, electronic archive that ushered in and coalesced an electronic community, a virtual public. We envisioned these statements as political interventions within the broad international political and academic discourses about women. As an evolving work that has been presented in numerous contexts over several years, Women of the World Talk Back serves as an evocative meditation on the relationships among technology, culture, and power for our American academic audiences as well as an instance of digital political activism.

Our project was initially designed to serve as a ritualized form of invocation inviting response from other participants at the NGO Forum. The model of communication we used to conceptualize the project was based on James Carey's elaboration of a ritual model of communication. Carey views the purpose of communication as directed toward the representation of shared beliefs across time and across space. He describes this model as a way to conceptualize the "act" of communication that refuses to see communication as mere "transmission" or the "transportation" of information from a sender to a receiver. Although Carey's broader point is to elaborate a specifically cultural theory of communication, in describing the notion of communication as ritual he elaborates an alternative model of the communicative act that resonates with feminist ideals. In Carey's words, communication as ritual is "the sacred ceremony that draws persons together in fellowship and commonality . . . and it focuses on the construction and maintenance of an ordered, meaningful cultural world" (18–19). As an invitation to dialogue, our multimedia presentation literally became an occasion for a conversation and a means for establishing that commonality in a well-defined context. We wanted to create a communication experience that brought people together to meditate on and discuss the conference themes, especially women's use of technology around the globe. By thinking of the act of communication in a ritualistic and dramaturgical mode, we considered the new information technologies more as a reality engine than as a message transmitter. Not only did we actively engage in diverse conversations with the women we interviewed, we were also able to videotape and record them performing their "talk back" statements. (We include excerpts of those statements on our Web site, http://www.gsu.edu/~engmeh/talkbackstate.html.) We hoped to bring back video statements from different women about the situation of women in their communities with respect to technology access and education. Although we were able to videotape only a dozen women, we spoke with many others who visited the booth and who, in effect, provided us with a rich education about the global situation of women and technology.

## PARTICIPATING IN REPRESENTATIVE GLOBAL POLITICS

We traveled to the NGO Forum as a delegation of female students and faculty to discuss with others the gendered impact of new communication technologies and to promote the education of women in science and technology. The UN conference brought together heads of state and government officials to debate and draft a platform for action that would reinforce the resolutions outlined during the 1985 Third World Conference on Women in Nairobi. The Beijing conference exerted pressure on global governments to enact the objectives and policies suggested in the Nairobi document. The conference worked toward consensus among official government delegations about the objectives and defining language outlined in the platform for action. The draft platform for action outlined "critical areas of concern" that included several key topics for U.S.-based feminist scholars and teachers: women and the media, and the education and training of women in science and technology. Running concurrently with the official UN conference, the 1995 NGO Forum provided individuals and representatives from global women's organizations an opportunity to network and to influence their delegates attending the political conference. Those who participated in the NGO Forum in Hairou gained opportunities to lobby the delegates from their countries and offer statements of support for various parts of the draft platform for action. The final platform for action was then published in print and on the Feminist Majority's World Wide Web site ("Beijing Declaration and Platform").

By organizing and sending a delegation, we wanted to lend intellectual support and offer arguments elucidating the importance of statements about women and media in the draft platform for action. These statements addressed issues pertaining to women's education in science and technology and their preparation for careers in mass media. We recognized that our participation in the forum would present us with a rare opportunity to take part in discussions on the global level about the education of women in science and technology and their training in mass media. Indeed, we did have the opportunity to lobby several members of the official U.S. delegation to the UN conference directly, among them Donna Shalala, Veronica Biggens, and Elizabeth Coleman. (Donna Shalala served on Clinton's Cabinet, Elizabeth Coleman founded the Maidenform Corporation, and Veronica Biggens, an executive from NationsBank in Atlanta, organized the United States delegation for the conference.) We presented a position paper titled "The Education of Women in Science and Technology," which was circulated among the U.S. delegates. During our meetings with them, we presented a letter of endorsement that strongly urged U.S. delegates to support several "planks" in the draft platform for action that dealt specifically with women and media. In particular, we argued for an expanded definition of the term "literacy," to include both scientific and technological literacy. Moreover, we encouraged U.S. support for the policy statements that outlined the importance of the media as a powerful socialization device that shapes the expectations and treatment of women worldwide.

Although the platform for action is not a binding document, governments are expected to commit resources to enact on the national level the policies it outlines. Thus, the document serves as a guide for national legislation and for helping to shape international priorities in the future. Political follow-up work since the conference has continued through teleconferences, meetings, and additional conferences, both internationally as well as nationally, in the form of published and online reports from the President's Interagency Council on Women (Women

Watch). Women's representation in the media and access to forms of technology have continued to remain areas of focus in the United States since the conference.

Now, by choosing to present our work on technology and design (and writing about it) in academic feminist forums, as well as to students in various courses, we underscore the importance of making technology integral both to feminist activism and to a women's studies curriculum. When we use this project to demonstrate an example of high-tech multimedia that is also historically situated, we encourage students to imagine the social and political possibilities of new media. As a feminist project, it reminds students of the broader global context discussing the relationships among women, science and technology, as well as the reality that there is no single global feminist agenda about technology (see Balsamo, "Teaching in the Belly of the Beast"). The political context also provides a bridge to broader, economic analyses of technologies as commodities designed to be consumed. In discussing the design of our project, and our reasons for attending the NGO Forum, we hope to suggest ways that feminist thinking can intervene, and complicate, dominant cultural narratives about technology. A self-consciously feminist design, for example, might strive to be collaborative and open-ended, rather than fixed and prescriptive. Technological artifacts can be built to facilitate dialogue and exchange among people in a specific context rather than for the simple circulation of a message from a sender to a passive receiver. We aimed to design things differently with the technologies we had access to, both to address the broader global situation we found ourselves facing (as delegates and lobbyists) and to help develop new ways of thinking about technology from a feminist perspective. To this end, we have worked to elucidate a new theory of technology that would help us describe our process of new media design.

## TECHNOLOGY AS ARTICULATED ENSEMBLE

The purpose of invoking a theory of technology in the context of discussing Women of the World Talk Back is to illuminate the complex definition of technology that underscored our design and our production process. We challenged ourselves to design a technological experience based both on feminist principles and on insights drawn from recent cultural studies. This project is thus centered around a critique of the commonsense notion of technology as simple artifact, machine, device, or software application. We began, instead, with the understanding that technology is a postdisciplinary object that many disciplines across the academy have taken up as a subject of scholarly inquiry. "Technology" is no longer the province of a select group of academic and professional disciplines; especially in the 1990s it became a topic of contemplation across the humanities, sciences, social sciences, educational fields, and professional programs in medicine, law, engineering, and business. These disciplines are actively engaged in discussions about the relationship of traditional disciplinary topics to technological issues. In this sense, the object-status of "technology" is under debate. It no longer "sits" still while the developers and analysts circle the machine puzzling over its "nature." While some may argue that the machine never sat still—that it was always a dynamic entity, manifesting cultural values and social practices—most commonsense understandings of technology rarely acknowledge this dynamic nature. Nor have our theories of technology reliably taken into account its cultural dimensions. But this is not an argument about the limitations of earlier analyses of technology nor about the way our common sense falls short. Rather it is an attempt to sketch a feminist theory of technology that will necessarily build on notable attempts to construct a critical philosophy of technology, but also extend them in important directions.[3]

There is a broader consensus now among scholars and professionals in various disciplines that technologies manifest cultural values. These values are embedded in the design, the deployment, the development, the dissemination, and the material effectivity of technology. Such an understanding of technology implies a definition of technology that considers it to be *both* an object and a subject. As an object, it is produced and constructed either by human practices and labor or by mechanized routines. As a subject it is a form of knowledge and a determining condition. But what is the nature of this object/subject?

A useful way to think of technology, drawing inspiration from recent cultural theory, is to consider it an ensemble or an articulation.[4] In this sense it is an ensemble of objects, knowledge, practices, and effects. What is called "a technology" is, according to this understanding, a structured amalgamation of different things, things that include *material* objects such as devices and artifacts, but also *discursive* moments such as communication practices and forms of knowledge. A simple way to express this definition of technology is to view it as a relationship among material objects and discursive practices.

TECHNOLOGY AS ARTICULATED ENSEMBLE

| | |
|---|---|
| Devices and Artifacts | Cultural Values |
| Material Conditions | Forms of Knowledge |
| Aesthetic Properties | Cultural Narratives |
| Human Practices | Social Relations |
| Institutional Forms and Policies | Ideological Systems |

The organization of a technological ensemble is not random. Using terminology borrowed from Gramscian cultural theory, a technology is an "articulated arrangement." As an articulation, a technology is "built" in certain ways. In that technologies are constructed, we can discern an order and an organization among the articulated elements. The process of critically analyzing a technology involves identifying the constitutive elements of the articulated arrangement and specifying the relationship among them. Analyzing a technology, or technological formation, involves describing the elements of the articulated ensemble.

Probably the most critical element of any articulation is the way in which human practices and the human body are implicated in it. Technologies both embody *reified* human practices and enable *new* human practices. The incorporation of human practice and the empowerment or disempowerment of bodies distributes a measure of agency to a technological arrangement. In this way, technologies are also structuring entities in that the structure of the technological arrangement influences the subsequent use of the technology. This assertion is distinct from an argument for technological determinism. Technologies do not, in a simplistic sense, determine forms or practices of human life. Although they do have a determining influence on the structure and texture of our lives, the nature of this determination is complex. We suggest that any given technological articulation includes several forces of determination, such as economic, political, and institutional, that can combine to invest determining "agency" in the technological device or object. An analysis that stops there, however, recognizes only the determinant agency of the technological object. Technological agency is always *shared*, albeit unevenly, with the people who design the device, program it, engineer it, manufacture it, buy it, use it, and abuse it. This understanding—that technological agency is differently distributed throughout a technological formation—offers a point of entry for the elaboration of a feminist theory of technology.[5] Determining the points of agency becomes an important feminist enterprise. We can ask such questions as: Where are the places within a given formation that the technology is given meaning or shape? At what point is the technology designed to serve certain ends and not others? Who benefits from specific technological designs? At what moments do decisions get made to pursue one technological research program and not another? These kinds of questions, contextualized within the technological articulation, become the points for feminist intervention.

## TOOLS OF MASTERY OR OF COMMUNICATION?

The dominant meaning of new information technology typically includes reference to computer hardware, peripherals, and networks. Occasionally people will remember to include reference to the more immaterial elements of computer systems, such as software applications, databases, and interface designs. These elements are highly fetishized and, indeed, circulate as highly desirable commodities that even when they are distributed for free (such as is the case with software applications available via the World Wide Web), have a discernible commodity form. They are "produced" by recognizable corporate agents, be it large entities like Microsoft or small start-up companies. They are "marked" with a trade name that establishes a marketplace identity. And like all successful commodities, their primary effect is to stimulate future consumption of other commodities: version 1.0 is built to be consumed and discarded when version 2.0 arrives. Although these elements are key parts of the technological ensemble called "information technology," they are not really the main goods in circulation. The marketing of new information technologies is more centrally concerned with the circulation of a set of ideas *about* information than about the selling and buying of hardware, software, and services. This set of ideas—or guiding myths—is built on the following axioms: (1) that data equal information, (2) that information equals knowledge, and (3) that access to information represents power. These ideas serve as the foundation for the development of our commonsense understanding about personal computers and informational services: computer components and related networking peripherals are sold as tools that provide information access, which in turn holds the key to greater power.

The dominant articulation steadfastly rehearses the equation: the use of new information technologies offers greater access to a greater quantity of information, which translates into greater personal power. Upon closer examination, there is ample evidence to suggest that networked information services often serve a broader capitalist project of creating new marketing avenues for the generation of "good old-fashioned" surplus value. As one example, we know that interactive Web sites—where users leave identity tracks when they visit—have proliferated wildly and are in great demand by corporate clients, in part because they can be used to gather information about individual consumers. That information, in turn, can be organized into databases that are then accessed by or sold to other corporate customers seeking to sell other goods to consumers whose tastes and habits seem predictable and can ultimately be manipulated. The promise of enhanced information access for individual users in this scenario serves as an alibi to divert discussion about how practices of digital information exchange and interactivity create a surplus of capital—now defined in terms of "information"—that can be bought, sold, rented, or analyzed for the additional information it offers about things like trends, tastes, buying habits, and consumption patterns. As everyday users who encounter and are cajoled to enjoy (and, indeed, to *need* access to) the vastly distributed network of information resources, we are subtly promised the wealth of total knowledge. This promise of total knowledge is impossible, of course, not primarily for technological reasons but because of the institutionalized limitations on what is deemed important or marketable to record and archive in the first place.

Thus, in this articulation, the computer is redefined as a tool of power that provides mastery for users, both over information and over other people. We wrestled with whether this "information as mastery" definition was inherent in the technology or appropriate for our project. In designing our project, we envisioned a more collaborative, participatory, and open-ended use for the technology. Our goal was to explore the social use of these technologies for reasons other than those that sought mastery of information or people. In theoretical terms, we took on the task of *rearticulating* the technological ensemble. To put it another way, we were interested in designing another use for these new information technologies, a use that would have an impact that would be different from the dominant articulation. More specifically, our hope was to design a use for these new technologies that would actually facilitate communication and the exchange of information among people.

The belief in the possibility of rearticulation is critical here. We rehearse these theoretical formulations about articulation theory and technological formations to suggest a way for feminists to intervene in dominant arrangements that define the meaning and "proper" use of various technologies. Our position implicitly takes issue with one common feminist response to technology that rejects it as an inherently patriarchal and masculinist tool. We argue instead that the meaning of any technology is a result of an elaborated articulation among various elements. This is not to say that technologies have no inherent meaning but rather to suggest a more complex understanding about where their meaning inheres. In positing the notion of a "technological articulation," we are suggesting that the meaning of any particular technology is actually a consequence of several determining factors. This notion provides for the theoretical possibility for political intervention. In order to know how to *redirect* the meaning of technology, one must first understand how the technological articulation is organized. In order to redesign a particular technology, one must understand the mechanism whereby the meaning of that technology is already set in place. In this way, the process of *rearticulation* then becomes a practice of political intervention such that cultural theory is used overtly as a guide for action that can be strategic and effective.

How can the process of rearticulation occur? As discussed earlier, technological formations include dispersed agency, and agency is a dynamic force. Regardless of how solidly real or timeless they appear, articulations are themselves dynamic formations that are inherently unstable. Specific articulations must be constantly reproduced in the face of incomplete forms of determination and as a consequence of human characteristics of entropy, decay, and forgetting. In the case of new information technologies, for example, the task of changing institutions that structure the distribution of machines and regulate things like computer access is daunting. As this analysis should suggest, the problems of a divided society now stratified on the basis of computer access are not going to be solved simply by giving machines to those who currently have none. At the base level, the simple redistribution of machines means that more people will be targets for those guiding myths that promote the information surveillance and the technological colonization of daily life. An effective plan of intervention would begin by investigating the multiple ways in which the meanings of the machines are constructed and consequently institutionalized. In this example, changes in distribution will be politically effective only when accompanied by changes in forms of institutionalization, in the cultural narratives that are disseminated via new technologies, and in the way in which agency is structured and enacted by all participants.

## DESIGN OF THE WOMEN OF THE WORLD TALK BACK PROJECT

Technological design processes became the central way for us to try and create new narratives and to structure agency. We thought a great deal about the political possibilities of multimedia development conceived as a project that involved the process of explicit rearticulation. Multimedia technologies—by this we mean desktop computer systems that integrate the expressive production of graphics, sound, animation, video, and text—offer rich opportunities for the design of multi-modal communication. The process of designing multimedia involves the selection of hardware and software, the development of novel content and interfaces, and the integration of multiple forms of digital material: text, graphics, sound, and animations. It also offers the opportunity to design modes of connectivity, modes of communication, and modes of address. The challenge inherent in multimedia design is tied to the explosion of meaning that accrues as a consequence of each and every design decision, from the selection of hardware and software (platform issues and processor speeds) to the model of communication implied by the information design (telephony or shared ritual). While many can understand the cultural implications that arise in the context of content development discussions, few appreciate that every *element* of multimedia development has cultural implications in that every design decision implies a set of expressive values, modes of sociability, and restrictions on user accessibility.

We wrestled with these challenges most overtly in the context of content development for an international audience as we selected images, cultural references and symbols, verbal cues and intonations (see figure 7.1). Even before we delved into the issue of content development, we had invoked a host of cultural issues by designing this project as a computer-based multimedia presentation. The very notion of mouse-based computer interaction is a fully enculturated habit of technological engagement. In making explicit design decisions to use a point-and-click interface, and to use English as the only language of address, we had already situated this project within the confines of the dominant computer culture of the United States. We modulated this set of design decisions with a different set of decisions that reflected a more interna-

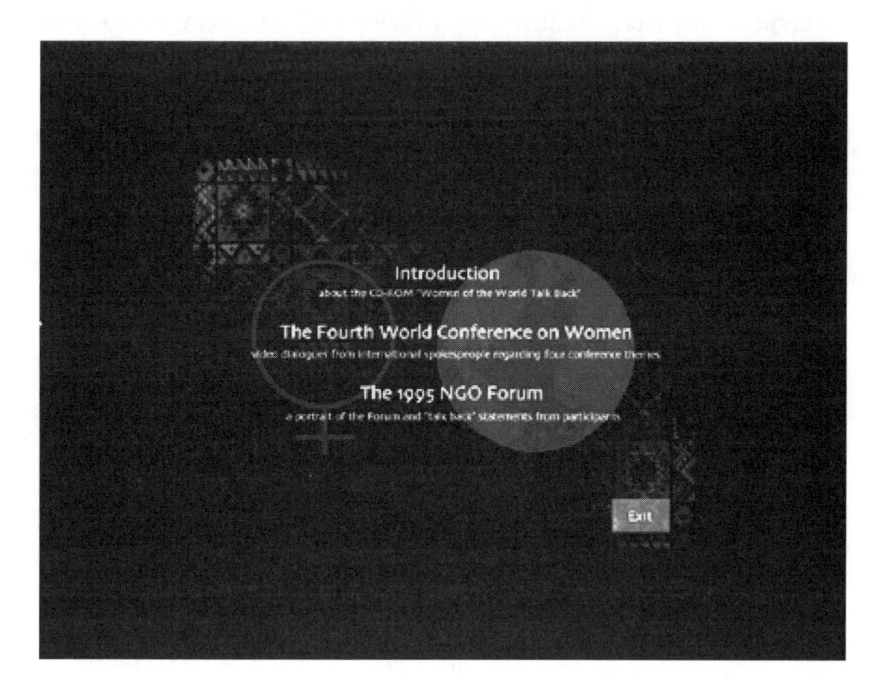


FIGURE 7.1. Opening screen of Women of the World Talk Back.

tional sensibility. The project used minimal text for either navigation or content delivery. Thus, for example, we used particular pieces of world music as aural cues for different sections. The video pieces were designed to look televisual, like international public service announcements. To achieve this style, we made ample use of close-up interview shots, or "talking heads," animated still images, and background video footage obtained from the video archives of the UN. These media constituted our "found" material that we rearticulated in a feminist context.

In many ways, the Women of the World Talk Back project was designed to exemplify how feminists can rearticulate technology on several levels when they have the opportunity to use high-tech resources.[6] We explicitly used feminist cultural theory based on feminist work in aesthetics, narrative theory, and documentary video. Those theories helped us generate a design paradigm to then create the symbolic language that appears throughout the project. A situated theory of women's material culture inspired our use of symbols, colors, textures, and interactivity, as well as the design of the content and the overall narratives presented. The narratives, which we crafted from interviews into what we called "video dialogues," put in circulation theoretical insights about the global situation of women politically, economically, and socially. We designed and organized the "Video Dialogues" section to address the major themes of the conference. The titles suggested emphatic answers: "What Do Women Want?" "Access to Education," "Economic Opportunities," "Empowerment." The resulting videos are short, two-to-three-minute movies that constitute a dialogue of voices. For example, the video dialogue called "Access to Education" offers a concise theoretical statement about the importance of the education of the girl-child across broad cultural contexts and ends with a call for a change in curriculum at all levels. We designed it to invite specific statements from our audience about the importance of education in particular communities. In accounting for multiple voices that are culturally situated, the interactive design is sensitive to differences in perspective between developing and developed countries, to the insights of women situated in different national contexts, and to the impossibility of representing a single narrative about the global situation of women. In addition to the narrative structure, the design paradigm draws on the insights of women's material culture. The look and feel of the interface itself draws inspiration from a richly textured piece of fabric. Textile art is a global women's art that takes very specific cultural forms. The symbolic design of the multimedia thus invokes a feminist aesthetic through the use of textiles and symbols.

During our production process, we used a collaborative team model that is commonplace in multimedia development.[7] Although our project construction process was entirely collaborative, there was an institutionalized, hierarchical relationship among project team members. For example, the two of us served as project directors, while three Georgia Tech graduate students were employed as multimedia authors, graphic designers, and interactivity architects. As the project directors, we provided the design, information structure, and content for the project, as well as some of the labor involved in video editing, graphic production, and interactivity authoring. The bulk of the multimedia production work, however, was done by the students under our supervision. The total cost of the project amounted to approximately $10,000—not including the *many* hours of labor donated by project team members at various times during its development. Given the typical costs of building professional multimedia projects, this one was created very inexpensively. We kept costs down by using "found" video footage, free B-roll footage, and donated labor. Thus, we began this project as an example of the kind of desktop multimedia presentation that can be built by nonprofessionals with a modest budget.

The project was well received during the NGO Forum, and we believe that it accomplished its communicative objective. We met dozens of NGO participants through the "invitation" of the multimedia piece, which gave us the opportunity to talk with people about their specific objectives in participating in the forum. We were especially interested in hearing about how women across the globe are using media to serve their political aims and to enhance the quality of life of women and their families. The people who visited our booth provided us, in turn, with an education about the diverse global situation of women and technology. We talked informally with publishers of women's newsletters from Haiti, artists from Mexico, and television producers from India. In several cases, we were able to videotape interviews with women who had their own electronic artwork or media-oriented projects to discuss (see figure 7.2). We learned that women are using many types of traditional media—from video to print—to educate themselves and their communities about everything from political

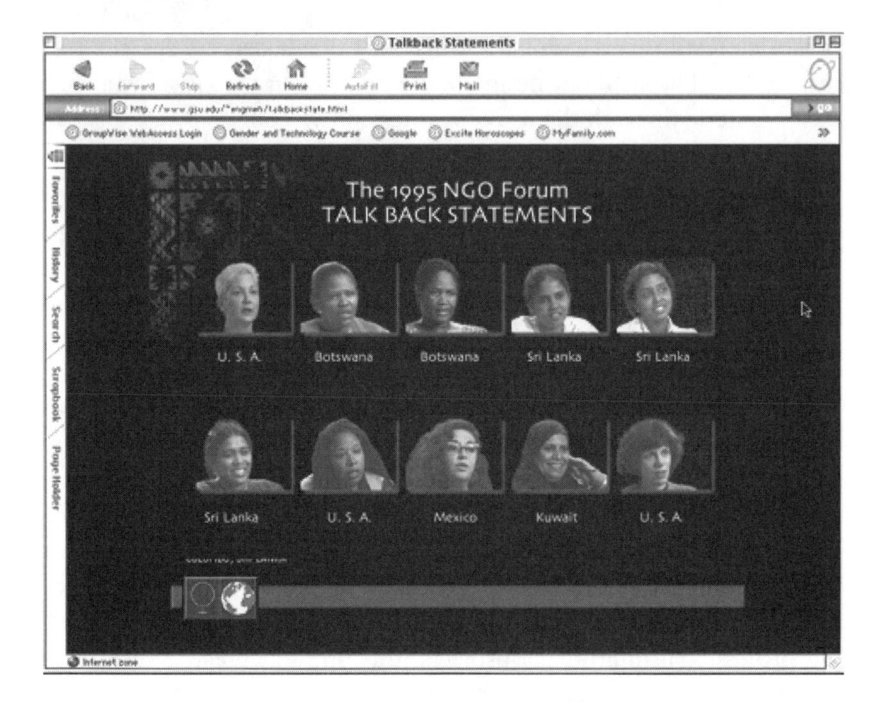


FIGURE 7.1. Talk Back Statements by NGO Forum Participants. The design of this section was influenced by other UN-related projects.

rights to health issues. We met women from around the world who are eager for access to new information technologies for grassroots organizing and educational efforts. Whether it was in a discussion about the use of the fax machine as an organizing tool in a suburb of Brazil or through an explanation of the importance of videocassette recorders as an educational technology in a rural village of Botswana, we learned that women around the globe have similar objectives concerning new and old communication technologies: they seek access to these technologies because they are a means of community building and political organization across great divides, especially for women separated by economics, geography, education, and politics. To this end, our project could be considered in the same spirit as an attempt to use new communication technologies in the service of similar feminist goals.

The intended audience for the presentation included not only the people we would meet at the NGO Forum but also those we would meet when we returned: scholars and teachers in women's studies, as well as new media producers who are interested in alternative design paradigms. By the end of our three-week stay, we had begun a series of conversations and realized that our initial communication project could now develop into a documentary project that included the media coverage of the event and a narrative based on our own experiences. In this way, our assumptions about audience were designed and projected in specific technological artifacts as new communicative forms that can then intervene within particular electronic environments. By involving a wider range of colleagues and students in the production and consumption of these technologies, academic feminists and designers can imagine and help create new audiences for this kind of work (see Hocks, "Feminist Interventions"). The Women of the World Talk Back project now includes the material that we gathered while in China, in the form of a documentary video on the NGO Forum, and a narrated headline review of the political controversies and logistical events during the months leading up to the forum. We also provide biographical information on the speakers from each video and their organizations, as well as the collection of "Talk Back" statements by people we interviewed at the forum.

We returned from Beijing with a sense of a new focus for the project—to document our participation in the NGO Forum as well as the global activism possible via media forms. We used a new sense of audience and genre to create a design that actively engages our colleagues and students. We also committed ourselves to presenting our work and elaborating our design process for the purpose of inspiring other multimedia developers who have the privilege of access and want to find ways to use new media to serve feminist ends.

## WHAT WE LEARNED

Technological access remains one of the central issues of concern among women across the world. The paradox we heard was that while there remains a striking global imbalance in the distribution and access to new communication technologies such as fax machines, video players, computers, and network connections, there is also increasing interest among women from all parts of the world in the use of new information technologies for grassroots organizing and educational efforts. For example, we met one woman from Tanzania who produces educational television programs for women. She wanted to know if we planned to distribute our multimedia project in video form so that she could run it on her television station. Other women who had access to computer networks encouraged us to develop the Web site based on the project. Yet other women told us that the acquisition of a fax machine in their community was a more pressing need. We discussed issues of distribution and access to the project quite extensively, both before and after the forum. To be truthful, we didn't imagine that we would distribute the project very widely after the conference. It was, from the beginning, thought of as a communication event that would be tied to the moment of the NGO Forum. We imagined that it would be an educational project for ourselves and our women's studies colleagues and students. But after our conversations with several women at the forum, we began to think about how we might make the project available to other people. This idea raised questions about who we thought would be the long-term audience for the project. The question of audience, in turn, sent us back to consider the foundational purpose of the project, including its design. This changing image of a primary audience, along with our ongoing interactions during presentations, is intimately connected to visual rhetoric and other fundamental design choices: those assumptions about audience, in fact, help us to define the kinds of feminist interventions possible in various forms of digital media (Hocks, "Feminist Interventions"). After the conference, Women of the World Talk Back became a multimedia documentary, a genre of new media presentation that engages with a live audience.

Based on our professional positions in technological and educational institutions in the United States, we believe that one of our most important audiences remains other educators in similar institutional positions who might also have access to rich technological resources. As we mentioned in the introduction, our aim was to produce a high-tech multimedia presentation about feminist issues, targeted for an international feminist audience. We wanted to stage a communication event that would be educational for all participants and create a temporary moment of cross-cultural communication. To this end, we believe that we were successful. We know that multimedia projects are costly operations. They require deep resources of equipment, design skill, and production time. Precisely because of our institutional locations, we were able to garner the resources for this project. In turn, the resources we had available enabled us to critically rearticulate the meaning of these new technologies as well as the institutions that produced them. Although it was only one project, with limited impact, it did demonstrate that machines, laboratories, production time, and talents could be deployed for purposes other than the continued accumulation of capital. While we understand the privilege of our positions, we also hope the project will continue to demonstrate the benefits of deploying privilege for broader feminist goals.

## NOTES

1. See, for example, the Internet site developed by Joan Korenman on gender-related electronic forums; *Womenspace Magazine* online by the Canadian feminist organization E-Quality; the Feminist Majority Foundation Online; and the UN "Women Watch" site for conferences and events. The Feminist Majority's Web Site provided essential information and ways to prepare ourselves for the conference (http://www.feminist.org).

2. Purple Moon eventually developed such CD-ROM games as *Rockett's Tricky Decision* (1997), a "friendship adventure" intended to encourage preteen girls to participate in a collaborative technological environment. For more information, see the Purple Moon Web site at http://www.purple-moon.com/.

3. Landon Winner, for one, addresses the lack of attention that philosophers pay to developing a philosophy of technology straightforwardly in his book *The Whale and the Reactor*. Andrew Feenberg, in *A Critical Theory of Technology*, elaborates a critical theory of technology that suggests a similar formulation of technology that we propose in this essay.

4. The notion of articulation comes from Gramscian social theory and has been applied to the discussion of new technologies. See Ernesto Laclau and Chantal Mouffe, *Hegemony and Socialist Strategy: Towards a Radical Democratic Politics*.

5. The feminist engagement with technological issues is quite varied and ranges over many disciplines. Two landmark texts include Joan Rothschild, ed., *Machina ex Dea: Feminist Perspectives on Technology*, and Judy Wajcman, *Feminism Confronts Technology*. For a discussion of the gendered nature of communication technologies, see especially Lana Rakow's "Women and the Telephone: The Gendering of a Communications Technology." For other studies of the gendered nature of computer use, see Sara Kiesler, Lee Sproull, and

Jacquelynne Eccles, "Poolhalls, Chips, and War Games: Women in the Culture of Computing"; and Ruth Perry and Lisa Greber, "Women and Computers: An Introduction."

6. The design of the Women of the World Talk Back project uses a simple point-and-click navigational strategy that presents a main menu and a set of video clips, called "Video Dialogues," that are the heart of the original project. The main menu displays the logo—the symbol for female and a globe next to one another—and a simple text list to access the different videos and textual information. The large logo becomes an icon on later screens for navigating back to this main menu. The introduction displays a short video with dramatic music that was designed to capture people's attention and draw them to the screen. We constructed this video using brief, emphatic statements from international spokespeople and designed it to resemble a public service announcement about the importance of the conference. See our Web site for more information on the project. Available at http://www.gsu.edu/~engmeh/mmdoc.html.

7. Our original design team consisted of seven people: ourselves; three graduate students in the Georgia Institute of Technology's M.A. program in information, design, and technology; one professional TV producer; and one professional musician. The graduate students were Kelly Johnson, a multimedia producer; Mary Anne Stevens, a graphic designer; and David Balcom, a multimedia author. They all contributed to the design and authored the modules during the initial development process. Phil Walker, a professional TV and video producer, produced the interviews and the music sound tracks used in the project. With the help of a local musician, Bryan Arbuckle, Phil cowrote the music used in the project. On new modules, Sandra Beaudin and Ellen Strain contributed additional graphic design and multimedia authoring.

## REFERENCES

Balsamo, Anne. "Teaching in the Belly of the Beast: Feminism in the Best of All Places." In Kim Sawchuk and Janine Marcessault, eds., *Wild Science: Reading Feminism, Medicine, and the Media*, 184–214. New York: Routledge, 2000.

Balsamo, Anne, and Mary E. Hocks. Women of the World Talk Back: A Multimedia Documentary on CD-ROM. Online. Internet. Available http: www.gsu.edu/~engmeh/mmdoc.html.

"Beijing Declaration and Platform for Action." *Women's Studies Quarterly* 24, nos. 1–2 (Spring/Summer 1996): 154–289.

Carey, James W. *Communication As Culture: Essays on Media and Society*. Boston: Unwin Hyman, 1989.

Feenberg, Andrew. *A Critical Theory of Technology*. New York: Oxford University Press, 1991.

Feminist Majority Foundation Online. Internet. 6 September 2001. Available http:// www.feminist.org/.

"Gender-Related Electronic Forums." Online. Internet. 6 September 2001. Available at http://research.umbc.edu/~korenman/wmst/forums.html.

Hocks, Mary E. "Designing Feminist Multimedia for the United Nations Fourth World Conference on Women." In Pamela Takayoshi and Kristine Blair, eds., *Feminist Cyberscapes: Essays on Gender in Electronic Spaces*, 285–296. Stamford, Conn.: Ablex, 1999.

——. "Feminist Interventions in Electronic Environments." *Computers and Composition* 16 (1999): 107–119.

Hocks, Mary E., and Daniele Bascelli. "Building a Writing-Intensive Multimedia Curriculum." In Donna Reiss, Dickie Selfie, and Art Young, eds., *Electronic Communication Across the Curriculum*, 40–56. Urbana, Ill.: National Council of Teachers of English, 1998.

Kiesler, Sara, Lee Sproull, and Jacquelynne Eccles. "Poolhalls, Chips, and War Games: Women in the Culture of Computing." *Psychology of Women Quarterly* 9, no. 4 (December 1985): 451–462.

Laclau, Ernesto, and Chantal Mouffe. *Hegemony and Socialist Strategy: Towards a Radical Democratic Politics*. London: Verso, 1985.

Perry, Ruth R., and Lisa Greber. "Women and Computers: An Introduction." *Signs* 16, no. 11 (Winter 1990): 74–101.

President's Interagency Council on Women. "U.S. Follow Up to the U.N. Fourth World Conference on Women." Pamphlet. Washington, D.C.: U.S. Government Printing Office, 1996.

Purple Moon Company. Online. Internet. 28 June 1999. Available at http://www.purple-moon.com/.

Rakow, Lana. "Women and the Telephone: The Gendering of a Communications Technology." In Cheris Kramarae, ed., *Technology and Women's Voices: Keeping in Touch*, 207–228. Boston: Routledge, 1988.

Rothschild, Joan, ed. *Machina ex Dea: Feminist Perspectives on Technology*. New York: Pergamon, 1983.

Tamblyn, Christine. "She Loves It She Loves It Not: Women and Technology." In Jennifer Terry and Melodie Calvert, eds., *Processed Lives: Gender and Technology in Everyday Life*, 47–50. New York: Routledge, 1997.

United Nations Development Fund for Women. *Putting Gender on the Agenda: A Guide to Participating in U.N. World Conferences*. Pamphlet. New York: United Nations, 1995.

Wajcman, Judy. *Feminism Confronts Technology*. University Park: Pennsylvania State University Press, 1991.

Winner, Landon. *The Whale and the Reactor*. Chicago: University of Chicago Press, 1986.

*Womenspace Magazine*. Online. Internet. 28 June 1999. Available at http://www.womenspace.ca/.

"Women Watch: UN Conferences and Events." Available at http://www.un.org/Women Watch/confer. Accessed 14 Jan 2003.

8

# Is It Art, in Fact?

MITCH GELLER

> Some impose upon the world that they believe that which they do not; others, more in number, make themselves believe that they believe, not being able to penetrate into what it is to believe.
>
> —Montaigne, "Apologies"

Deeper than factual information, closer to the core of that which makes us human, of more importance than instincts, related to our collective experience—arguably that which affects what we think and do more than anything else—lies what we each believe. As an artist, I have found that my interests and the focus of my work drift from topic to topic, pausing for a moment on the political, social, religious, ethical, or situational facets of my subject. Yet beneath every subject, at the core of each of the works I produce, is an intense and deeply held series of beliefs. As I focus, I find that while the subject of these beliefs is what first attracted me . . . it is the intensity with which a series of beliefs is held that forms the true subject of my work.[1]

> Nothing is so firmly believed as what we least know.
>
> —Montaigne, "Divine"

## IS IT ART . . . IN FACT?

The concept of truth as a construct that is at once familiarly perceived as both a malleable form and a fixed and ineffable quality has a long history in nearly every form of academic endeavor. This somewhat contradictory state of being has led to a range of works by artists—both popular cultural iconographies and some fairly pedantic attempts at

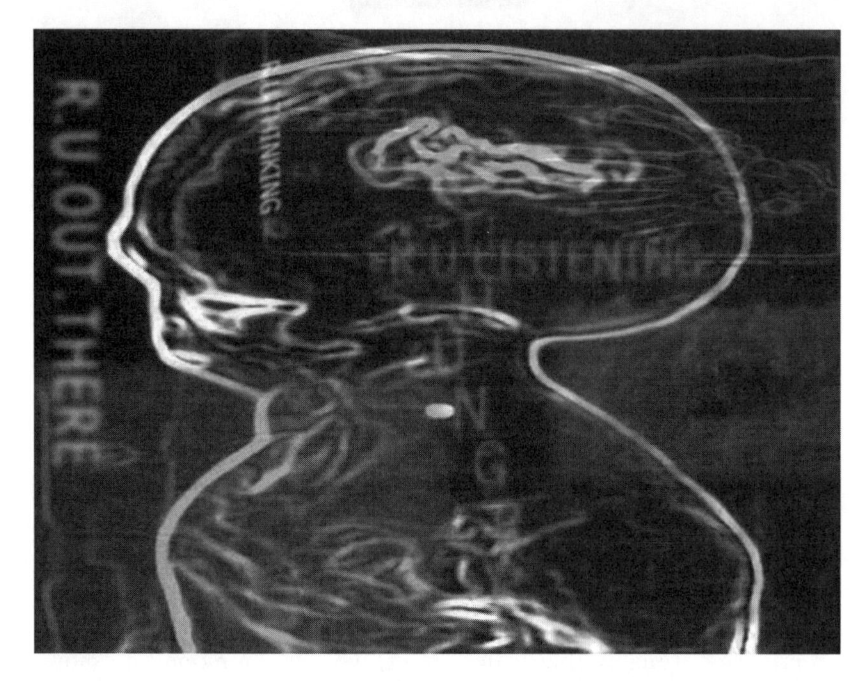


FIGURE 8.1. Head Alien image from *R.U.OUT.THERE*. The aesthetic characteristics of the image mirror the conceptual underpinnings of the piece. Image by Kelly Hart.

socialization and normalization of the identification and interpretive strategies that are applied to "the real."

Rather than add to the already well-documented literature on the history of the way truth has been defined, interpreted, and analyzed, this essay will instead generally recount the sometimes unique, often exaggerated, and occasionally borrowed experiences that have led to a body of artistic work that at its core uses the trappings of veracity as its primary materials of construction. As an example, we will examine *R.U.OUT.THERE*, my most recent interactive work of art. Fueled by the mechanics of reproduction technologies, artists create virtual worlds that depend on internal consistency in their structure to lend validity without foregrounding the fact that their external accuracy has been altered. This approach has facilitated the creation of compelling works that slice across time, space, and the restrictiveness of sequential history in order to cut right to the core of complex issues.

It is arguable that since the early 1960s, television, more than any other influence, has shaped the minds of children as they develop their primary intellectual foundation. As I try to think back to when I first became interested in the idea of the actual validity of supposed facts, I am reminded of several key television events.

I remember being about twelve years old and being forced to watch what seemed to be nothing more than a bunch of old men conducting some sort of long, dull ceremony that unfortunately preempted (although I'm not sure that was a TV word yet) the programming on all *three* channels. The rationale presented by my upper-middle-class parents was that this was *history* and that I would be glad that I had watched what I later came to understand was the Nixon impeachment/resignation television event (again, this phrase is probably an anachronism in this context). Even with bugging and espionage, the stuff that spy novels are made of, it seemed mundane and, to a twelve-year-old, really boring. It wasn't until years later that the term "plausible deniability" retroactively surrounded the event.

Upon re-analysis, I have realized that this television broadcast pinpoints the exact moment when I began to understand the power of *the truth*. Not the actual truth, (for discussion on the existence of said truth there are volumes upon volumes), but what we might call the *teletruth*, or what might be described as the illusion of factuality as ascertained by watching a television broadcast. The relationship of the *teletruth* to the actual truth has several describable aspects but is not altogether predictable. Of primary importance is that this version of the truth must have a sense of plausibility, not altogether accurate but at least reasonably credible. Achieving an air of factuality on television involves elements of style and content. Stylistically, what appears credible on television is dependent upon what is in fashion at the moment.

Cut to a white man in his early forties. He has short, neatly styled dark hair and is clean-shaven. He is in good physical shape, has a slight tan, perfect white teeth, and is wearing a white lab coat and a tie. "When one of my children feels ill, I want the best medicine available. That's why I only trust the Algood Pharmaceutical Laboratory, where we use the latest medical research to make Algood Children's Aspirin. Nine out of ten doctors use it on their own families." (Brief Dramatic Pause) "Shouldn't you?"

This type of traditional television advertisement plays on our notion of plausible believability, and in 1961 it worked extremely well. Brand loyalties were formed that carried through generations of customers. Which nine out of ten doctors? And were they given free samples? But all that doesn't matter, so long as the style is right and the content *seems* believable.

> Digital crosshatch dissolve (with squiggles and jitter) to a crisply shot black-and-white image of a thirtyish man in a starched white dress shirt and black Kenneth Cole slacks. He is rowing an old wooden boat across what seems to be an endless and windless lake. The sun beats down, and while he is not sweating, he does appear to be a bit uncomfortable. The sound track, "*Rockefeller Skank*" by Fatboy Slim. . . . "Right about now . . . funk soul brother . . ." mirrors the redundancy of his strokes. A whispering female voice with a bit of reverb: "Feel bad . . . doc says . . . it's all good" accompanies a half super of the Algood Aspirin logo.

In 1999 the ad is a bit faster-paced and less direct and has much more concern for style, but the same basic message remains. We might now call it *casual credibility*.

Also important, and often overlooked, is the aspect of shared reality. With the concept of *teletruth* there is something to the idea that we're all watching it at the same time. Obviously, when there were only three channels and the VCR was something out of a sci-fi film, this idea of shared reality was much easier to imagine. Conceptually, the idea helps to create what we might consider somewhat of a self-perpetuating truth. Most people at work or school saw it on TV, and those who didn't actually see it heard about it from a variety of sources. The power of this shared experience harks back to the original conception of the television apparatus. Initially, television was to provide a way essentially to collapse distance—for people in remote locations to share an event or experience in real time. Although storage and replay technologies are widely available now, we still see the vestige of this as many choose the serendipity of broadcast . . . still rushing home to watch something when it is "on."

Recalling once again the Nixon broadcast mentioned earlier, I remember feeling bad about what was happening. At twelve I didn't having any real understanding of the political ramifications of what was going on. But I remember feeling that the fate Nixon was suffering was quite undeserved. In retrospect, my sincere belief was much the same as that feeling you get when the known hero of a superhero show is wrongly accused of a crime. You know that while it may be a convoluted story, in the end our hero will be vindicated.

Remember *The Rockford Files*?[2] Now *there* was some really practical use of deception. Recall that the show opened with James Garner's voice on an answering machine[3] (which was at the time a fairly high-tech gadget) serving to remind us that he was hip to the latest technology.[4] From a practical standpoint, the show was created using very traditional *cookie-cutter, assembly-line* production techniques, which served to minimize costs while allowing rapid production of multiple episodes without compromising continuity or the illusion of continuous reality (Zettl, 129). In this vein, the answering machine was an important plot device that allowed the rapid interjection of plot points, characters, and essential backstory without additional production expenses or continuity hassles.

> We distinguish among three types of time: (1) objective time (clock time), (2) subjective time (or psychological time), and (3) biological time. The objective and subjective time[s] are especially important for television and film. . . . The screen event . . . becomes a new construct with its own objective and subjective times. (Zettl, 253–254)

As a programmatic construct, this now mundane device was in a sense an early example of the introduction of virtuality into an otherwise reality-bound program. Unlike the simple crosscut phone call insert, which on larger-budget productions actually shows the callers while they speak, the use of the electromechanical answering machine device provided not only a faceless voice that never even implied that images of the caller were needed or missing but also, and more significantly, the ability to introduce *voices from the past*. Unlike the commonly utilized flashback, which takes the viewer to a present that existed at an earlier time, the virtual voice from the answering machine seamlessly allowed faceless characters from some unspecified time in the past to communicate with a character in the presesnt. Of course, in non-science-fiction genres, this communication is one-directional (although in *The Rockford Files* the protagonist often *spoke* to his answering machine or in actuality spoke to the audience through this device).

There is, however, a much more central issue brought up by the dramatic role that was assigned to Rockford's answering machine in the plot of nearly every episode. Surprisingly out of sync with the doctrine of the rest of the series, the answering machine became a sort of oracle of truth. Every call that came through (with the exception of the stereotypical *anonymous thug call* and the occasional comically obvious caller masquerading as another character) was unquestionably taken at face value. It was assumed that all callers were either recognizable by voice or would accurately identify themselves during the message. In light of the almost effortless ways in which Jim Rockford assumed various identities in nearly every episode, one would expect that he would question all but the most familiar callers[5].

> I always speak the truth. Not the whole truth, because there's no way, to say it all. Saying it all is literally impossible: words fail. Yet it's through this very impossibility that the truth holds onto the real. (Lacan, 3)

Critical to our sense of understanding of our world is some means of believing that there are discernible *truths* that exist in the universe. In contemporary society, where the average individual has little control over much of what occurs in his or her day-to-day life, the ability to analyze information and determine its legitimacy is valued. As technology has advanced, so has the quantity of information that bombards us in a constant yet fluctuating stream. But what aspects of this information do we actually use in our quest to authenticate the factual correctness of our data? As we explore incoming information, we find that there are many different means of authentication. Certain elements are easily eliminated because of their sheer distance from what it is that we consider plausible. As we dig deeper, we begin to realize that, with Marshall McLuhanesque finesse, we often base these decisions less on the information itself and more on the form that it takes. Determining the value of something by its packaging reminds us of both the genius and the frightening effectiveness of modern commercialism.

> The medium is not the message in a digital world. It is an embodiment of it. (Negroponte, 71)

In the digital era, it has become rather difficult to ascertain both the source and the credibility of most forms of evidence. The types of images, documents, and recordings that we tend to consider accurate can easily and convincingly be created, manipulated, and reattributed with only limited skill and inexpensive, *off-the-shelf* technologies. If a fourteen-year-old with a home computer and an Internet connection can convincingly forge evidence of nearly anything, how can we consider any tangible evidence as legitimate? Of course, professionals use sophisticated technologies that can help to detect forgeries and alterations in digital evidence. But for the average individual, raised to believe what we see and hear, this inability to weight credibility accurately has far-reaching implications.

> Like traditional folklore, [urban myths] . . . are narratives crafted by the collective consciousness. Like traditional folklore, they give expression to the national mind. And like traditional folklore, they blend the fantastic with the routine, if only to demonstrate, in the words of University of Utah folklorist Jan Harold Brunvand, the nation's leading expert on urban legends, "that the prosaic contemporary scene is capable of producing shocking or amazing occurrences. . . . Shocking and amazing, yes. But in these stories, anything can happen not because the world is a magical place rich with wonder—as in folk tales of yore—but because our world is so utterly terrifying. Here, nothing is reliable and no laws of morality govern." (Gabler, 21-A)

The Internet has probably done more to propagate the urban myth[6] than any previous means of communication. Through various Web sites, chat groups, private and group e-mail, and listservs, the speed of global dissemination of information has increased exponentially.

Anyone who has an e-mail account cannot help but come into contact with these sorts of contemporary urban myths. Some of the more widely disseminated ones include the story of the woman who bought the chocolate chip cookie recipe from Neiman Marcus, and became distressed when she found that it cost her $250 (instead of the $2.50 that she thought she had heard). She decided to distribute it on the Web. Note that before the proliferation of e-mail, variations of this story with the same recipe were distributed by fax and multigeneration photocopy. Another is the story of a man who is found/wakes up with a pain in his back, in a hotel room bathtub surrounded by ice, and finds that one or more of his internal organs have been stolen. Or the one about the bones of a diver found smoldering in an extinguished forest fire because when water was picked up in a large trough carried by a helicopter, he somehow was trapped inside (the trough, not the helicopter—at least in the versions that I have seen). My most recent favorite refers to a little-known betatest program by Microsoft that involves tracking software that is already on your computer. The message goes on to explain that if you simply forward this e-mail to others Microsoft will pay you five dollars per message. It then recounts the tale of *someone I know personally* who has received a check for eight hundred dollars just for sending out this e-mail. The best part for me is that two relatively intelligent college-educated people that I know have told me in all sincerity that they actually know the person who received the eight hundred dollars!

What these stories share is that they are bizarre, unusual, or far-fetched and yet they all contain elements that are somewhat believable. Like all good fiction, they contain a twist that makes them worth retelling. And—most important—they are difficult to trace. The details may change, as slight alterations creep into successive versions (called "noise" in some of the more popular communication models), like a global instance of the children's game *Telephone*, but the essential information is passed on. At the heart of these stories, something is awry with our society—globally, strange things are afoot. And like the all too familiar *rubberneckers* who line the constantly tightening periphery of any traffic accident, we strain for just a glimpse of catastrophe—to see something outside the ordinariness of our everyday experience, whether horrific, quirky, or just plain strange to us.

> It is not just our fears, then, that these stories exploit. Like so much else in modern life—tabloids, exploitalk programs, real-life crime best-sellers—urban legends testify to an overwhelming condition of fear and to a sense of our own impotence within it. That is why there is no accommodation in these stories, no lesson or wisdom imparted. What there is, is the stark impression that

> our world is anomic. We live in a haunted forest of skyscrapers or of suburban lawns and ranch houses, with no one to exorcize the evil and no prince to break the spell. Given the pressures of modern life, it isn't surprising that we have created myths to express our malaise. But what is surprising is how many people seem committed to these myths. (Gabler, 21-A)

A comprehensive review of Web-disseminated urban myths shows that there are several commonly traveled pathways to legitimacy. One of the most frequent errors is that of cross-verification without consideration of the validity of the source. The "Yeah, I heard about that, too" validation is passed along with the story and, without documentation, many falsely assume that receiving the same information from multiple sources in some way confirms its accuracy.

In the popular media, this phenomenon of assuming credibility based on unverified information is regularly brought into sharp focus on *The Late Show with David Letterman* (formerly *The David Letterman Show*) during the weekly Viewer Mail segment, when Dave repeats the mantra "If these weren't actual letters from viewers, could I do this?" while bending the purported actual letters to show that they are in fact "real viewer mail." His not-so-subtle parody highlights the casualness with which we treat the verification of that which we read, watch, and hear.

In *The Rockford Files* credibility is a valuable commodity upon which the outcome of the entire episode often hinged. Mostly, the agents of this credibility were manufactured in the trunk of the protagonist's trusty gold 1974 Pontiac Firebird.[7] Using a portable printer, James Garner conveniently produced new identities in the form of forged business cards, which allowed him almost to magically assume the virtual identity of choice. As viewers, we were in the unique position of *seeing both identities at once*, which allowed us to interpret the dialogue from simultaneous multiple points of view. At the time the technology to create this sort of fictitious document was not easily accessible, and we never imagined that it would one day be available in nearly every home in the form of the personal computer.

A voice inside screams, "But of course we're more sophisticated than that. *I* wouldn't be fooled by something so obvious as a fake business card." And you're right, most of us probably wouldn't. Not because we are that much more perceptive or because we are conscious of the possibilities of forgery, but simply because for most of us there are few times in life when we will allow a stranger with nothing but a business card for identification to have access to our confidential information. "I would ask for proper ID!" we'd say. But how many of us know what a real FBI ID actually looks like? Even so, how hard is it for someone to create a convincingly realistic facsimile? Or to get hold of a credible-looking badge[8] and police uniform[9] (or even a squad car,[10] for that matter)?

It is easier than most of us want to think about to use this contemporary (and often digital) technology to create convincingly credible artifacts of *the truth*, and it's probably much more widespread than we might imagine. After all, the stories from the Web are just for amusement, and we're too smart to believe any of those scams anyway. Right?

> Shortly after the March 30th [1981] attempt on . . . President . . . [Reagan's] life, the major television news programs played an excerpt from a videotape produced at station KYNV. The section was from a show entitled *Dick Maurice and Company*, and his guest was a Hollywood "psychic," Tamara Rand, who predicted that at the end of March President Reagan would be shot in the chest. It was claimed that the interview had taken place on January 6th, 1981, but apparently this interview (only the relevant portion was shown on television news programs because of its sensational nature) had originally been produced on March 31st, the day after the shooting, and had been inserted into a tape produced at an earlier time. . . . Tamara Rand continues to proclaim her amazing predictive abilities. (Gumpert, 46)

But of all the urban myths, of all the stories that are passed on electronically or otherwise, one topic outlasts them all, one that is the subject of numerous radio call-in shows, white papers, investigative reports, special series, films, Web sites, books, and magazines. Of course, we're talking about aliens, Martians, UFOs, extraterrestrials, visitors, or whatever terminology is in vogue at the moment. In the public eye for well over a century, this enduring subject of varying public interest enjoys a constant fluctuation between being just a molecular speck floating in the great biochemical environment that is our collective consciousness and being something that *everyone* is talking about. The most recent resurgence, beginning a few years back as evidenced by the appeal of shows like *The X-Files*, has included *alien* episodes on a number of popular shows (much like the prevalence of the Elvis impersonator episodes that accompanied the resurgence of the Elvis Presley phenomenon in the early 1990s). Further reading of our pop culture foregrounds the *alienhead* symbol in its various forms. Examining the imprints on such diverse items as disposable pens, T-shirts, notebooks, toys, backpacks, bumper stickers, and caps yields a rapid and fairly accurate measure of the recent tidal activity of the alien issue. At times the expression of this issue takes the form of UFO and occasional alien sightings, sometimes including minimal contact. At present, we more frequently encounter a different and more frightening expression, that of abduction. Examples of abduction stories can be found throughout the popular media, the most significant of which has been *The X-Files*. As the level of societal paranoia rises, we find that the expressions of our shared urban mythologies tend to become much more focused on harm from an outside and uncontrollable source. As a theme, alien abduction fills all the necessary requirements. It is difficult to verify, has plenty of room for government conspiracy and mistrust, and elicits an almost religious fervor on the part of those who believe. In a world where individuals increasingly feel that they have no control, worrying about alien abduction helps to distract us from those aspects of the world that each of us, deep down inside, knows we should do something about and yet painfully knows that we won't. (Sorry, I must have been abducted for a brief moment there; now back to the less painful truth and how we can create our own.)

> Formula for a *credible* abduction video: One of the most important elements in manufacturing a video that you want to appear to be credibly real is to choose or simulate the appropriate video format, meaning that grain, texture, and overall look of the footage must be carefully controlled. For something that appears older, 1970s for example, the appropriate choice would be super 8 film, while for a piece to appear more contemporary, use small-format video like VHS, Hi8, or DV. Shoot your footage handheld (rather than with a tripod)[11] and make sure to overexpose the image a bit. If you remember, leave the date superimposed on top of the image. Make sure to look around (through the camera) in response to environmental noise and to bring the image out of

> focus occasionally. Running with the camera tends to lend a bit of credibility as well. Add a few glitches, a few "incidental" background ambient noises, and you've got something as credible as the rest. Make sure to generate a list to accompany the footage which includes the names and ages of all that were supposedly present, and include something irrelevant but rather specific about the camera operator, like that he weighs 220 and is diabetic or that she is in her second trimester. Also include a description of the *exact time, location, and atmospheric conditions*. An anomaly is good here too, for example, the temperature being unseasonably hot or cool. Add this text in an *official-looking* format, and you're ready to begin to disseminate.

When I initially considered doing a project on aliens and UFOs I thought of it first as a way to contextualize this sort of manufactured evidence and then as a means of getting at how our various notions of truth and credibility were intertwined. I knew even from childhood that there was something powerful about aliens and UFOs,[12] that these issues seemed to enjoy cycles of popular interest but that they were always a part of our culture, lurking somewhere at the edge of our collective attention.

An earlier project, *TexChrisT*, explored Christianity and notions of "the West" as they were intertwined in the state of Texas. The framework for the project was the creation of a fake radio station (called TexChrisT, which is an acronym for Texas Christian Talk radio) complete with station IDs, commercials, and excerpts from programming. This was the common thread that wove together the various elements of the piece. At an opening in a small gallery in Texas, people mentioned that they frequently listened to religious broadcasts and asked about *TexChrisT*. Several asked about the broadcast frequency and seemed surprised when I told them that it was entirely fictional. One woman was quite adamant in her demand for the station and refused to believe that it didn't exist. I wondered what it was that had been so convincing, and then she said, "I saw the radio dial right there on screen." It took several minutes of repeating that I had simply pointed a camera at the radio dial in my office and then added my own sound before she started to accept my explanation. As I began to plan my project on Aliens, I remembered this lesson on creating credibility and internal factual consistency.

FIGURE 8.2. Still from *TexChrisT*, a video installation about religion intertwined with notions of "the West." This image, shot from an old clock radio in my faculty office, helped to convince a number of viewers that Texas Christian Talk was actually a real station.

Adopting a pseudonym and attending Alien Encounter Group meetings, I learned that the frequently repeated mantra on *X-Files*, "I want to believe," is *not* an exaggeration. Here I found some who so desperately wanted to believe that they were willing to spend inordinately large sums of money on grainy photocopies of *secret proof* (which was documented only by the solemn word of the seller and was being made available *only* in this single instance and with no profit whatsoever), while others chose selectively from the facts to avoid any sense of cognitive dissonance. Many recounted story after story, but the most highly regarded in the group were those who were silent yet somehow implied that they had stories that they could tell, secrets that they knew but kept inside. I watched as several members pleaded with a silent older gentleman to tell them what he knew. He quietly and unemotionally refused, and I learned how much more powerful the implied possession of knowledge was. (When I was asked about my attendance I mentioned passionlessly that something had happened that I knew I needed to talk about, but that I wasn't ready yet and that hearing the stories of others would eventually make me secure enough to speak with them. I was strongly encouraged to attend all the meetings.)

Soon my alien project became *R.U.OUT.THERE*, and I started to develop characters and an internal structure:

> You take your first step into the virtual datascape of R.U.OUT.THERE, a fictionalized UFO encounter group, and are confronted with unusually high security. . . .
>
> Make your way past authentication sequences and tests, avoid the security traps, and you're in a virtual datascape of video, recorded sightings, secret government documents, group histories and records, failed UFO products, and a quirky collection of real and fictional UFOlogists. . . .

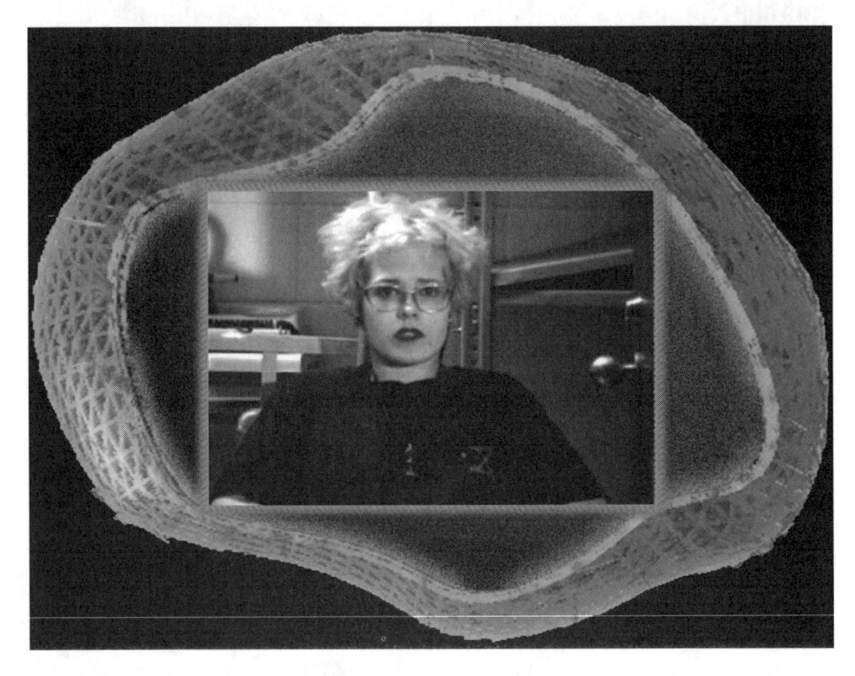

FIGURE 8.3. Alien Video Viewing Device with an interview with one of the major characters in *R.U.OUT.THERE.* The unassuming background paired with the fact that the person playing the role is actually telling us her real ideas about extraterrestrials play further with our notions of what is "real."

> As you grasp at the sometimes contradictory threads of the elusive and challenging narrative, you are privy to the carefully guarded secrets of the group members . . . and you begin to figure out what is really going on . . .
>
> R.U.OUT.THERE . . . a question . . . a statement . . . an obscure URL.[13]

Describing the piece as a virtual datascape implies both that there will be information in a variety of media formats and that it is explorable by the user rather than presented as a fixed temporal experience. To accomplish this we gathered, created, and manipulated elements in a range of media, including VRML (virtual reality rooms), video, Web sites, Web links, letters, photographs, documents, audio recordings, music, essays, x-rays, and so on. Once we had all the elements, we spent months creating a complex web of what are essentially hyperlinks within the elements of the piece. Many portions are fragmented or incomplete, and some elements are hidden rather carefully. Live Web links, externally updateable information, and some careful data mining on the user's hard drive lend each experience a bit of uniqueness. Web-based mechanisms allow users to contribute elements and information that may be added to the piece.

Throughout *R.U.OUT.THERE* the sightings, reports, Web sites, and government documents seem to be credible. As we examine these convincingly realistic pieces of *evidence*, the nature of truth is called into question, and we are graphically shown the ease with which our *credible* sources are imitated and manipulated. In actuality, the piece is filled with examples of what we might call *stylized legitimacy*—elements that utilize the look and feel that we associate with *real* evidence to imply that they are credible. Obviously, (as discussed earlier) the societal implications are staggering.

For example, to manufacture a convincingly realistic government UFO document one might simply search the FBI archives[14] and find a packet of declassified documents. Find a seal and header (if it's got artifacts of multiple generations of photocopying, that adds to the credibility) and paste it into your new document. Add text in a typewriter font and apply various grain and distortion filters to simulate age and multiple copies. I also like to go into the document with a digital paintbrush and add some irregularities by hand. This hides the uniformity that results from using digital filters to simulate age. Finally, and this is possibly the most important step, provide the right context so that your fake document seems to come from a legitimate source. In this case, placing our manufactured document into a group of actual declassified FBI documents will work perfectly.

Now to get our manufactured document into the hands of others. In the case of the UFO phenomenon, adding a bit of mysteriousness will only add legitimacy. First sign up for two or three different free e-mail accounts.[15] Then mention the supposed existence of the document and, using the various e-mail accounts, support and contradict your initial posting bit. Make sure to include a bit of the exact wording in a

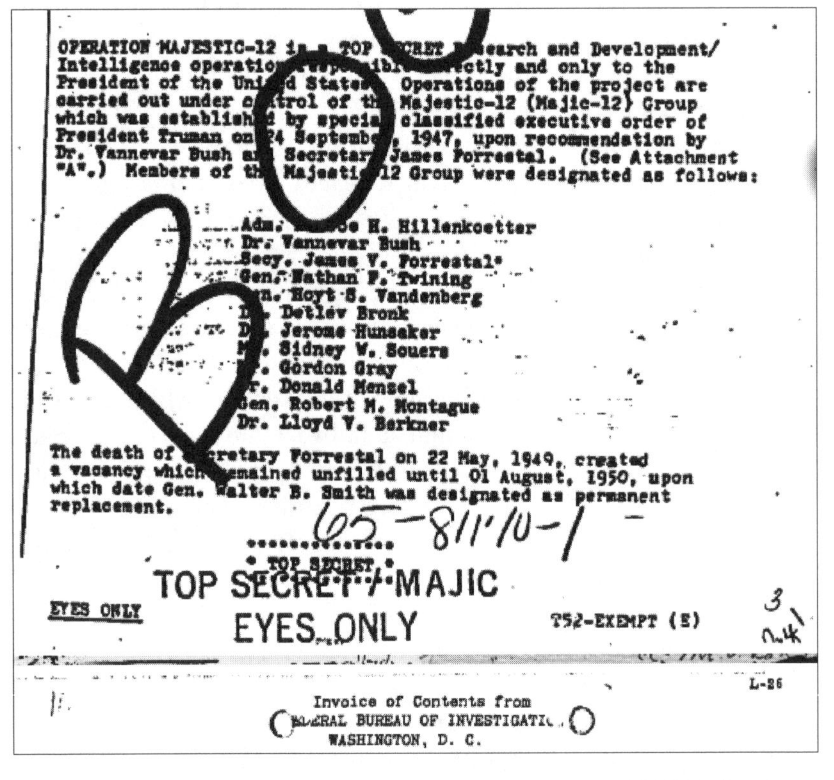
OPERATION MAJESTIC-12 is a TOP SECRET Research and Development/ Intelligence operation responsible directly and only to the President of the United States. Operations of the project are carried out under control of the Majestic-12 (Majic-12) Group which was established by special classified executive order of President Truman on 24 September, 1947, upon recommendation by Dr. Vannevar Bush and Secretary James Forrestal. (See Attachment "A".) Members of the Majestic-12 Group were designated as follows:

Adm. Roscoe H. Hillenkoetter
Dr. Vannevar Bush
Secy. James V. Forrestal*
Gen. Nathan F. Twining
Gen. Hoyt S. Vandenberg
Dr. Detlev Bronk
Dr. Jerome Hunsaker
Mr. Sidney W. Souers
Mr. Gordon Gray
Dr. Donald Menzel
Gen. Robert M. Montague
Dr. Lloyd V. Berkner

The death of Secretary Forrestal on 22 May, 1949, created a vacancy which remained unfilled until 01 August, 1950, upon which date Gen. Walter B. Smith was designated as permanent replacement.

65-81110-1

* TOP SECRET *

TOP SECRET / MAJIC

EYES ONLY

EYES ONLY

T52-EXEMPT (E)

L-26

Invoice of Contents from
FEDERAL BUREAU OF INVESTIGATION
WASHINGTON, D. C.

FIGURE 8.4. Government document viewer from *R.U.OUT.THERE*, showing a piece of a manipulated government FOIA document.

posting or two. Add the document to an archive or Web site, or post it to a chat group, and watch the results.

Throughout *R.U.OUT.THERE*, there are links that open Web sites. They all appear within a custom browser that restricts what you can do and where you can go. There isn't even a URL input because we'll take you where you need to go. This adds another layer of potential deception. If you are not in control of the browser, how do you know that you are looking at an actual Web site and not a fabrication? One of the best examples is our use of the FBI Web site. As you read the home page, you are actually on the real federally controlled Web site. If you follow the link to the FBI's Top Ten Most Wanted list, nine of the ten are actual felons, while the last has been replaced by Alpha, the fictional leader of the R.U.OUT.THERE group, who is under investigation for fraud and other confidence activities.

You might wonder, What if I don't choose that link? Will I miss an important part of the story? This begs the issue of nonlinearity and hypermedia. Much like our interpretations of truth or history, there is no single point of viewership like there is in traditional media. Instead, each reader of the text becomes a collaborator in the creation of meaning. The elements of the piece create many stories, in many different voices that are dependent both on the chosen pathways and on what the "reader" brings to "the story."

For example, the Alpha character is a charismatic yet enigmatic leader—someone who seems to say a lot, and who says it in an interesting and powerful manner, yet who really isn't saying anything that we can specifically nail down. Someone who can take even the most mundane statement and make it sound truly brilliant. Someone who can make us feel that we are a part of something that is of the utmost importance. Someone who can make us believe without even really understanding what it is that we are committing to. And most important, someone who can appeal to that specifically American need that we each have to believe that we are special; others may be ordinary, but we are unique and are doing something that is truly of the utmost importance. Is he a scam artist, is he a religious huckster known as Ozzie D. Lyte, is he working to sell alien technology for the government, is he really in contact with what he calls *the Os*, was he hiding in an insane asylum or is there good reason for him to be committed? The

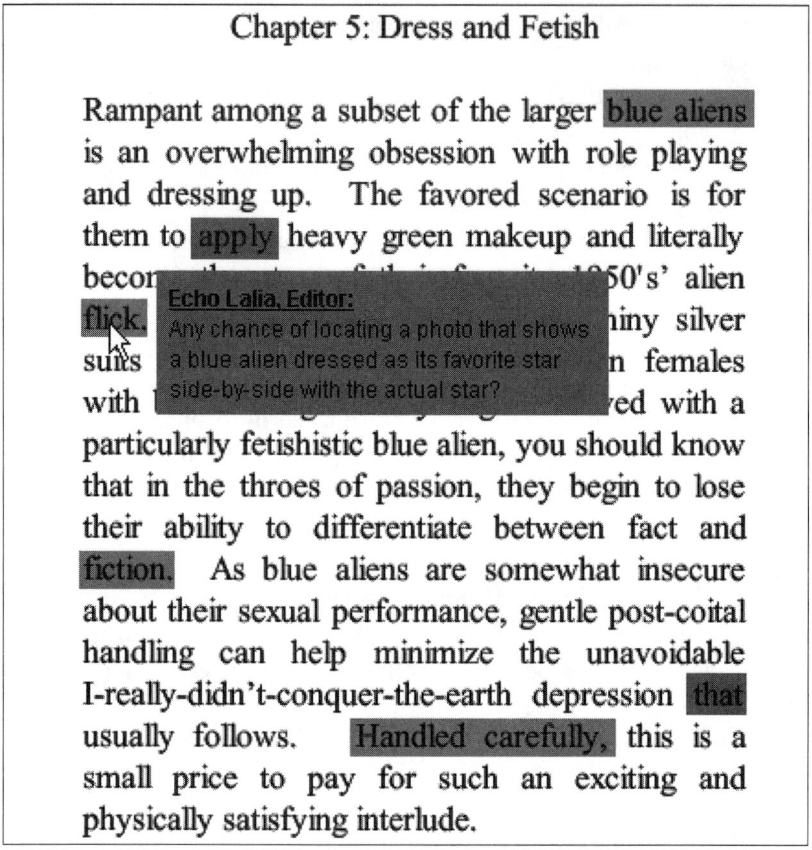

Chapter 5: Dress and Fetish

Rampant among a subset of the larger blue aliens is an overwhelming obsession with role playing and dressing up. The favored scenario is for them to apply heavy green makeup and literally becon … 50's' alien flick. … iny silver suits … n females with … ed with a particularly fetishistic blue alien, you should know that in the throes of passion, they begin to lose their ability to differentiate between fact and fiction. As blue aliens are somewhat insecure about their sexual performance, gentle post-coital handling can help minimize the unavoidable I-really-didn't-conquer-the-earth depression that usually follows. Handled carefully, this is a small price to pay for such an exciting and physically satisfying interlude.

Echo Lalia, Editor:
Any chance of locating a photo that shows a blue alien dressed as its favorite star side-by-side with the actual star?

FIGURE 8.5. Excerpt from "How to Make Love to an Alien: Everything you always wanted to know about extraterrestrial sex but were never abducted to ask," a fictional text by one of the characters in *R.U.OUT.THERE.* Taking credibility to the next level, the highlighted sections of text are mousecovers that bring up comments from another character, the editor Echo Lalia, which were written by an actual editor in the same manner in which she normally works with real authors.

answers, of course, depend on what you see, hear, and read, and, more important, how you interpret the pieces of evidence that you discover.

Adding another level of reality, (or unreality, as the case may be), I recorded interviews with witnesses, believers, skeptics, and curiosity seekers at the fiftieth anniversary celebration of the incident at Roswell,

FIGURE 8.6. Front and back of virtual (VRML) character trading card from *R.U.OUT.THERE*. Velma Elliot, granddaughter of the founder of the group, turns out throughout the piece, and elements like these trading cards provide readers with clues that help them to figure out "what is really going on."

New Mexico. As you discover these video clips it becomes difficult to decide which are actual people who are expressing their own beliefs, which are fictionalized people, and which are just people that I asked to repeat a story that someone else really seems to believe as if it were their own. Most of the "actors" also brought their own stories, and with a bit of direction, wove them seamlessly with the fiction of R.U.OUT.THERE.

> That newscast into which you tuned which turned out to be a drama about the world of television journalists now turns out to actually be part of a documentary that is comparing images of practicing television journalists with fictional portrayals. Scenes of each have been included in the program. What is the context of the unfolding exposition and how are those scenes to be interpreted. (Gumpert, 47)

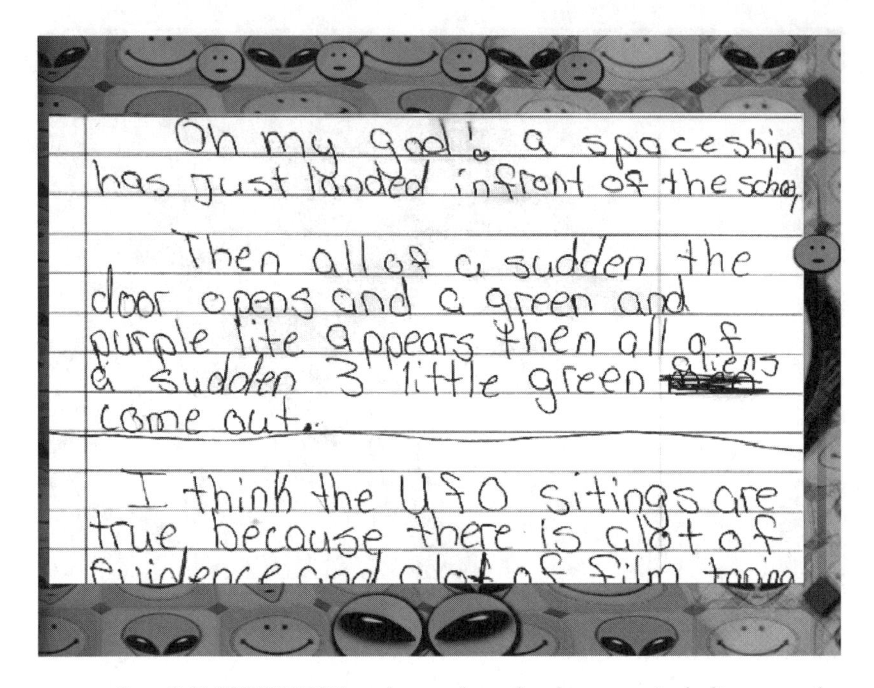

Oh my God!. a spaceship
has just landed infront of the scho
Then all of a sudden the
door opens and a green and
purple lite appears then all of
a sudden 3 little green aliens
come out.
I think the UFO sitings are
true because there is alot of

FIGURE 8.7. *R.U.OUT.THERE* used a number of real sources, including essays by junior high students concerning their beliefs about aliens and UFOs. In order to maintain the illusion of credibility, original and manipulated essays were presented in "original" handwritten form and are seen above in an RUOUTTHERE viewer.

According to what we have learned from the popular media, a twelve-year-old can launch a nuclear missile using his Atari, we can defeat a technologically advanced race of alien aggressors with a laptop computer, and *the Truth is Out There*. Think about *War of the Worlds*, *Capricorn One*, or even *The Blair Witch Project*. What happened at Roswell? How will we ever really know?

## NOTES

1. Mitch Geller, excerpt from the Artist's Statement distributed with a tryptich of works titled *A Series of Beliefs*, which starts out with *So Few Scarletts*, a work that examines the historical and contemporary contradictions of

being *Southern* through the eyes of a small group of white Southern women, including the city manager of a tiny rural town, a columnist for the *Atlanta Journal-Constitution* who knew Margaret Mitchell, an artist who runs her own company in a gentrified section of Savannah, a young secretary, and a shopkeeper who leads a struggle to defend her heritage against accusations of racism. The center piece, *TexChrisT*, examines the ways in which Christianity and notions of *the West* intertwine in the state of Texas. The final piece, titled *R.U.OUT.THERE*, is an interactive work of art that deals extensively with UFOs and our various notions of *The Truth*.

2. *The Rockford Files* premiered on NBC on 27 March 1974, and ran for six seasons. The final episode was aired on 10 January 1980 and has been followed by eight made-for-TV movies to date, with the most recent premiering on 20 April 1999 and rerun on CBS on 1 August 2001.

3. Retrieved 20 July 1999 from the World Wide Web at http://www.thesandbox.net/arm/rockford/multimedia. This link contains a grainy recording of the actual answering machine message that was used on most of *The Rockford Files* episodes and is best known from the original opening to the series.

4. Retrieved 20 July 1999 from the World Wide Web: http://www.thesandbox.net/am/rockford/answering_machine/ index.html. Provides a comprehensive listing of answering machine messages from all episodes of *The Rockford Files*.

5. Acknowledging, of course, that one of the ways that the show appealed to viewers is somehow related to this disruption in the normal rules of logic. If I got *roughed up by thugs* on my way into my trailer home each week, I would certainly move, install an alarm, get a watchdog, or at least park down the street and approach quietly to make sure that I *had the jump* on anyone who was *waiting in the shadows*. But that is part of the charm: although the protagonist is *our hero*, he is still an *everyman*. His car breaks down, he gets beat up and falsely arrested, clients don't pay their bills, people lie to him and use him, yet still he stays true to his values, does what's right, and, often without credit, brings the scofflaws of the week to justice.

6. Lost Legends, Urban Myth, and Nostalgic Disaster Web page, http://www.intercall.com/kimchee/. Contains shared information and links covering a wide variety of unusual subjects that fall loosely within the categories of Popular Legends, Urban Myth, and Forgotten History.

7. Retrieved 1 August 1999 from the World Wide Web, http://www.maada.com/museum/popcult/correct.htm. These sites contain reference information and photographs detailing the automobiles that appeared in many popular TV shows, ads, and films.

8. Retrieved 20 July 1999 from the World Wide Web, http://www.

stonerconnection.com/pagejewelry.htm. These companies sell pins, badges, and other ornamentation commonly used by police officers, firefighters, and other official organizations.

9. Retrieved 20 July 1999 from the World Wide Web at http://www.uniwearonline.com. This is one of a number of companies that sell both *off-the-rack* and custom-made uniforms of all types.

10. Retrieved 4 August 1999 from the World Wide Web: Movie Time Cars, Inc., 759–63 Riverside Ave., Lyndhurst, N.J. 07071; Picture Cars East, Inc., 72 Huntington St., Brooklyn, N.Y. Primarily serving the film and television industries, these companies can provide nearly any official vehicle and in some cases will customize the vehicle as needed.

11. A relatively recent example of this use of handheld point of view (indicating that we as viewers are looking at something that is really happening and that we are aware that we are seeing it through the lens of a camera held by one of the participants as opposed to the less self-reflexive POV shot in which we are seeing the action *through the eyes of one of the characters* and the camera is never acknowledged directly) is the popular film *The Blair Witch Project*. The premise that drives the plot is that the film we see is actually the discovered footage of three students who disappeared while making a documentary. Several fake Web sites, each in a different style, were quietly published to provide curiosity seekers with reasonable reassurances that this fictional film was actually a true story. Not surprisingly, many people have turned up in the town where the story was based to search for real evidence. Ironically, in addition to the fact that the story is fiction, only a few moments of the footage were even shot in that town.

12. As a sophomore in high school, not particularly motivated about my schoolwork, I remember waiting until 5 A.M. on the due date to begin my research paper. As was my habit, I hadn't done any research ahead of time or even selected a topic. Digging quickly through some old books, I found a collection of UFO stories that were written on about a fifth-grade level. Perfect! I churned out a quick term paper with numerous references to this book, using it as my only source. I turned it in sheepishly, thinking that I would be grounded again when grades were returned. A week later, sitting in the back of my Honors English class, I daydreamed absentmindedly as the teacher rattled on and on about one outstanding paper. When she mentioned UFOs it caught my attention but only added several weeks to my assumed punishment, as I imagined a well-done paper on the same topic making mine seem even worse than it already was. As the teacher handed out the papers, she mentioned that I was the only one who had received an A. In retrospect I wonder about the power of alien intervention.

13. Mitch Geller, excerpt from the press release for *R.U.OUT.THERE*, an interactive work of art.

14. http://www.fbi.gov, the official site of the Federal Bureau of Investigation. The site contains a wealth of information about the FBI in its current state, as well as historical documentation. Many of the documents and images that are available are found on sites throughout the Web that are dedicated to providing documents retrieved from various federal organizations through the Freedom of Information Act.

15. http://www.yahoo.com, http://www.hotmail.com, etc. Several of the ever-increasing number of sites that offer free e-mail that you can obtain without any real form of personal identification. Of course, to be truly anonymous, you must also be concerned about the identifiability of the computer that you are using. To avoid leaving digital fingerprints, one can either use computers that are publicly available without personal login names (as in some universities and libraries) or use services such as remailers, which allow one to send and receive mail without being identified by routing electronic transactions through complex global pathways that render them untraceable. Although as hacker (in the original positive sense of the word, which brings to mind open-source software and a spirit of global research cooperation) and Internet pioneer Charlie Lindahl recently pointed out, there are now pages on the Internet that allow you to log in and use anyone's Hotmail account with only their e-mail address. Even knowing about only this one example, how can we ever again look at the "*From:*" line on an e-mail and not wonder if it really indicates who sent the message?

## REFERENCES

Gabler, Neal. "How Urban Myths Reveal Society's Fears: Tales May Be Our Most Genuine Folklore," *Star Tribune*, 19 November 1995.

Geller, Mitch. Excerpt from the Artist's Statement distributed with a triptych of works titled *A Series of Beliefs*.

——. Excerpt from the press release for *R.U.OUT.THERE*, an interactive work of art. 1998. Available at http://www.ruoutthere.com.

Gumpert, Gary. *Talking Tombstones and Other Tales of the Media Age*. New York: Oxford University Press, 1987.

Lacan, Jacques. *Television: A Challenge to the Psychoanalytic Establishment*. New York: Norton, 1990.

Montaigne, Michael de. "Apology for Raimond Sebond." In *The Essays*. Ed. and trans. George B. Ives. New York: Heritage, 1946.

——. "Of Divine Ordinances." In *The Essays*. Ed. and trans. George B. Ives. New York: Heritage, 1946.

Negroponte, Nicholas. *Being Digital*. New York: Knopf, 1995.

Zettl, Herbert, *Sight, Sound, Motion: Applied Media Aesthetics*. Belmont, Calif.: Wadsworth, 1990.

# 9

## Making the Virtual Real: University-Community Partnerships

ALISON REGAN AND JOHN ZUERN

A peeling but still-vibrant mural on the east wall of the community hall at Kuhio Park Terrace and Kuhio Homes, the largest public housing facility in Hawaii,[1] offers the viewer at least five perspectives on the idea—and the ideal—of a community. In the far left panel, boys and girls of different races play basketball in shirts emblazoned with the initials *KPT*. One of the facility's two apartment towers rises in the background; the foreground is luxuriant with carefully rendered tropical plants, among them taro, a food central to the cultures of the Hawaiians and Samoans who make up the highest percentage of the project's residents. Next to the basketball court, a group of children and adults carry rubbish to a large bin, among them a little boy who trundles his load in a red wagon. In the center of the mural, a couple with three children stand in front of a single-family house surrounded by a white picket fence. They look toward a small group of teenagers hunkered down to listen to a large portable stereo. In the final panel, four Samoan elders are gathered on a fine mat woven with intricate geometric patterns. Here, as in the first panel, the human figures are positioned between the looming apartment block and a row of blossoming local plants, so that the entire sequence of scenes is framed by distinct references to the architecture of the housing project and the environment of Polynesia.

These images represent a particular social group in a particular place, and at the same time attest to an ideal vision of a community sustained by solidarity, stewardship, communication, and continuity within change. Painted by members of the KPT community in 1987 during a period that saw a high incidence of drug trafficking, gang activity, and domestic violence in the project—all of which were significantly reduced throughout the 1990s (Franco and Aga, 189)—the figures on the community hall appear now less as documents of their time than as avatars of a collective hope.

As an intersection of the real and the ideal, of the actual and the virtual, the mural is emblematic of the kind of community we ourselves hoped to foster when we launched the Going to Class, Getting Online, and Giving Back community service learning project in 1997. The project seeks to establish an ongoing partnership between undergraduate students in the Department of English at the University of Hawaii at Mānoa and residents of Kuhio Park Terrace and Kuhio Homes. Each fall semester for the past two years, students in a new advanced writing course, "Rhetoric, Composition, and Computers," have met regularly with KPT residents in a small computer facility on the KPT grounds to provide individual tutoring in a variety of computing tasks, including basic keyboarding, word processing, spreadsheets, Internet searches, and e-mail. Students augment this direct personal assistance by producing computer-related educational materials in a variety of formats—print, World Wide Web, and most recently video—which they use during their tutoring sessions and which remain as resources for the KPT community after the semester is over. Additionally, students conduct research projects in order to prepare Web-based public information resources on subjects such as health care, employment, and the U.S. immigration and naturalization process—all topics that KPT residents identified as relevant in focus group discussions before the project began.

The goals of Going to Class, Getting Online, and Giving Back are twofold. We want to provide our students opportunities to strengthen their skills in computer-mediated communication by having them engage in real projects for real audiences with specific needs, and we want to work against the still-persisting "digital divide" by extending technology skills to members of our local community who at present have little access to computers or to technology training. When we began to plan this project in 1996, we envisioned our students collaborating with members of underserved communities to build community information networks, in effect virtual communities in which information relevant to the lives of the project participants, students and public housing residents alike, would be produced, exchanged, and openly discussed. Although we believe our project to be successful in a number of important ways, we have only begun to lay the groundwork for a functional virtual community of the kind we set out to create.

Our aim in what follows is to outline the challenges we faced in bringing our university-community partnership into its present form, to assess its outcomes up to this point, and to project a critical but still hopeful vision of a future for our initiative and for others like it. As our title suggests, our emphasis will be on the paradoxes involved in *realizing* a virtual public space in which public institutions—in our case, a housing project and a public university—can join in a mutually productive, interdependent, and sustainable relationship.

## COMMUNITY COMPUTING AND COMMUNITY SERVICE LEARNING: AN OVERVIEW OF THE PROJECT

While planning the Going to Class, Getting Online, and Giving Back project, we imagined our own and our students' work fitting into several important contexts. First, our goals meshed with the goals of what is loosely termed the "community computing movement"—that is, the movement whose objectives consist of bringing information and communication technology to individuals and groups who have limited access to digital resources and "using the technology to support and meet the goals of the community" (Beamish, 366). Second, our project combines three important areas of research and teaching in English studies: literacy, computer-mediated communication, and community service learning.

As faculty, our first responsibility is our students' learning. Following the lead of other faculty involved in community service learning projects, we turned to David Kolb's work on experiential education. Kolb supplies a model of pedagogy in which learners engage in active experimentation in order to apply, explore, and test abstract concepts, then reflect upon these experiences in order to reformulate their initial conceptions (see Kolb, 33). Our commitment to developing our students' and our own analytical capacities in the face of social disparities also led us to the scholarship of educators committed to critical pedagogy. Henry Giroux's emphasis on the "importance of naming and transforming those ideological and social conditions that undermine the possibility for forms of community and public organized around the imperatives of a critical democracy"(151) serves as a cogent summary of what we hoped to accomplish in the area of technological literacy and access to information technology. Two further theoretical models that proved useful to us are teacher research, the "systematic and intentional inquiry about teaching, learning and schooling carried out by teachers in their own school and classroom settings" (Cochran-Smith and Lytle, 27), and action research, "the systematic collection of information that is designed to bring about social change" (Bogdan and Biklen, 215).

Within the framework provided by these philosophies of teaching and learning, we sought to develop a course that would encourage students to learn about contemporary literacy and technological literacy issues through hands-on efforts to address literacy problems in the local community. We hoped for nothing less than to provide a context in which our students could make the important transition from students to writers, teachers, and caring citizens. The design of "Rhetoric, Composition, and Computers" incorporates five major activities: (1) research and argumentative writing relating to literacy, computer literacy, and the closely related issues of access to rights and privileges of citizens in a democratic society; (2) hands-on participation in community service learning focused on building technological literacy in an underserved population; (3) research and Web development to produce computer-related educational materials and public information resources for the target community; (4) reflective writing on experiences in the course, especially in the community service learning component; and (5) regular and active participation in an online class discussion list—an ongoing, collective dimension of reflection.

All student writing is submitted electronically and published on a course Web site, where it is read and discussed by members in all course sections. As the semester progresses, students increasingly work on teams that are reconfigured at least once to give the students the opportunity to work with a range of classmates. We have found that teamwork not only builds students' skills in collaborative thinking and writing but also creates an environment for the rapid dissemination of technological skills among class members, with the more adept students teaching their less experienced classmates as they all prepare to share their knowledge with others.

As professors in the Department of English at the flagship institution of the University of Hawaii System, we recognize that our students themselves qualify as both "haves" and "have-nots" in terms of their access to the benefits of information technology. Compared to most U.S. research universities of similar size and scope, the technology resources available to our mostly working-class, ethnically diverse student body, which also includes a large number of nontraditional students, are frustratingly limited and exasperatingly dated. Educational resources in public institutions have always been scarce in Hawaii, where, historically, a large proportion of middle-class and wealthy families have paid tuition at local private secondary schools and continental U.S. colleges instead of relying on or supporting public education. This situation has worsened considerably in the wake of the state budget crisis of 1995 to the present, in which the university's general operating budget has been cut by more than 15 percent, and further restrictions are anticipated in coming years. Consequently, at the same time as many state-supported and private institutions of higher education in the rest of the United States have been able to increase their modem pools, add networked classrooms, and provide information technology training for students, staff, and faculty, technology initiatives in Hawaii have been paralyzed by lack of funds.

Nonetheless, compared with members of economically distressed communities in the state, undergraduates at the University of Hawaii are clearly in a privileged position. They are also in a position to share their knowledge and skills with others, although they are often at a loss as to how they might do so. Rather than asking our students to seek out their own service learning projects, we chose to select a single community site at which all students would be able to contribute time and knowledge. We found that providing a common set of community participants and institutional structures led to a sense of a focused collective project. Our initial contact with Parents and Children Together (PACT), the social service agency that administers the computer facility in the Learning Center at KPT, came through our university's service learning coordinator. In the months preceding the first semester of the project, we conducted a series of focused discussions with PACT staff members and residents to identify the needs of the community and the most effective ways for us to meet those needs within the parameters of our proposed project.[2]

What we discovered about the circumstances in which PACT was endeavoring to provide much-needed access to computers and basic technology training confirmed the recent findings of the National Telecommunications and Information Administration (NTIA) inquiry into penetration levels for telecommunication resources in the United States:

> Despite . . . significant growth in computer ownership and usage overall, the growth has occurred to a greater extent within some income levels, demographic groups, and geographic areas, than in others. In fact, the "digital divide" between certain groups of Americans has increased between 1994 and 1997 so that there is now an even greater disparity in penetration levels among some groups. There is a widening gap, for example, between those at upper and lower income levels. ("Falling Through the Net II")

The general profile of the KPT community fits two of the major categories of the country's "least connected" groups: central city minorities and female-headed households. With reference to these groups, the policy implications of the NTIA report state that "these populations are among those . . . that could most use electronic services to find jobs, housing, or other services. Because it may take time before these groups become connected at home, it is still essential that schools, libraries, and other community access centers ('CACs') provide computer access in order to connect significant portions of our population" ("Falling").

The KPT residents' interests in technology were quite varied, but some clear objectives emerged through our discussions. Members of the PACT-sponsored Job Club sought experience with word processing and spreadsheets that would help them secure entry-level positions with a range of employers. The many members of the community who had family in other parts of the Pacific region or in the continental United States were attracted to free e-mail accounts on the World Wide Web. A number of people wanted to learn how to browse the Web for entertainment and to pursue their hobbies, which included soccer, reggae music, French antiques, Chinese calligraphy, and kabuki theater. An important and especially challenging goal—one that we had anticipated and that was emphasized in our focus groups, was that we "teach the teachers": that we provide sufficient training in basic computing to those residents who served as volunteer computer monitors in the Learning Center that they would be able to assist users in our absence.

Even before our project began, *absence* had become one of the crucial determining factors in the realization of our plans. The needs of the community did not slot neatly into the schedule of the academic year. We conducted our focused discussions in the spring, and the discovery that our project would not actually start until September was met with some disappointment among the participants. We could not be there soon enough, and, as we quickly learned, we could not be there often enough or long enough to have the kind of impact we had idealistically anticipated. With those limitations in mind, we scheduled two-hour sessions for two afternoons a week for ten weeks of our sixteen-week semester.

In spite of the serious time constraints and significant limitations in technical infrastructure at KPT as well as on campus, at the end of the semester both students and residents registered a high level of satisfaction with the project. Over the past two years, sixty-two students have taken part in Going to Class, Getting Online, and Giving Back. We estimate that in the course of forty visits to KPT (twenty in each semester), our students have conducted individual or small-group tutoring sessions with fifty members of the KPT community. For some of these residents, the sessions have had concrete results: the coordinator of the Job Club reports that a number of our students' tutees have secured employment based, at least in part, on their ability to claim fundamental skills in computing. In their final evaluations of the class, many students commented on what they had gained from their work with these learners. "I really think I benefited from them more than they benefited from me," one student wrote. "I learned to be humble, patient, semi-responsible, a leader, and made new friends in the process. I learned about how these people see the world and sometimes it was really different from how I see things. I also learned the importance of cooperation with fellow classmates."[3]

Our assessment of student surveys, student work, and our own participant observations throughout the past two semesters of the project assure us that class members are making tangible gains in a number of areas, including basic skills in communication technology such as HTML scripting, information architecture, and Web site management; rhetorical sophistication in both written and spoken discourse, as well as increased sensitivity to the communication needs of specific audiences; skills in traditional and online research techniques and in the critical analysis of their findings; and experience in collaboration.[4] Improvements in students' capacities to communicate effectively and ethically can be realized in technology-based community projects that are continuing to work toward fuller access for all project participants. We concur with Kathleen Tyner's suggestion that

> a broader concept of "technology infrastructure" beyond hardware and software is one step beyond access. Infrastructure can be expanded in an organizational and systems approach to include curriculum, instruction, policy, and the roles of the people involved. Another way out of the "access" cul-de-sac is to steer the discussion about technology and schooling away from its focus on tools, in order to frame the debate in terms of literacy. (90)

We remain committed, however, to keeping the discussion from straying too far from the question of basic access, particularly for communities on the far side of what Manuel Castells has described as "the truly fundamental social cleavages of the Information Age" (*Information Age*, 346). While we are pleased with our preliminary successes, we also recognize that our project continues to be haunted by absences in a variety of forms. Most significant to us are those absences that impede the formation of a virtual community that is true to its name: at once *really* virtual, sustained within functional computer networks, and *really* a community, a group of people united over time by collective concerns and expectations, affection, and trust.

## THE COSTS OF ABSENCE

In his often-cited 1991 essay "Cyberspace: Some Proposals," architect Michael Benedikt makes a lapidary statement that in its context seems almost to be a non sequitur: “Absence from cyberspace will have a cost” (161). In this section of the essay, Benedikt is describing what he calls the “Principle of Indifference,” which

> states that the felt realness of any world depends on the degree of its indifference to the presence of a particular “user” and on its resistance to his/her desire. The principle is based on a simple phenomenological observation: what is real always pushes back. Reality always displays a measure of intractability and intransigence. One might even say that “reality” is that which displays intractability and intransigence relative to our will. (160)

The intransigence of a reality that continues to exist regardless of the presence or absence of any particular individual is one of the features of the “real” space of human experience that Benedikt believes should be preserved as we construct versions of virtual space. Absence from cyberspace will (and ought to, according to Benedikt) have a cost, because real life goes on even if some people or groups of people are not “there.” Not being there has consequences, but the events that individuals and or groups of people might miss are themselves largely indifferent to those who are not present.

In the context in which we and our students have been working, Benedikt’s 1991 observations on the Principle of Indifference take on a disturbing resonance. As the NTIA report has revealed, the gap between the residents of KPT and the many people in our society who enjoy the benefits of connectivity has not been shrinking over the course of the decade. As the virtual spaces Benedikt theorizes proliferate, aggregating into the “real virtuality” that Castells views as a key component of the network society in which many of us increasingly live, “switched-off territories and people will also be found everywhere, albeit in different proportions” (*Information Age*, 354). The absence of these “discarded individuals” (346) from the virtual spaces into which political, cultural, and economic power is now moving has real costs. While Castells recognizes that some individuals freely choose to exclude themselves from a culture dominated and enabled by communication technology, he stresses the likelihood that the lives of those shut out from participation in the new society will be marked by escalating anxiety, danger, and frustration in the face of political impotence.

"With no Winter Palace to be seized," he muses, "outbursts of revolt may implode, transformed into everyday senseless violence" (352). Enormous costs accrue on the other side as well, in terms of cultural diversity, the productive social energy generated by the ongoing attempt to create an inclusive society, and the immeasurable, unpredictable contributions that any individual might make, given the chance.

The absence of spatial constraints, a key factor determining the virtuality of any virtual community, is a paradoxical characteristic. We recognize, of course, that the celebrated virtues of a cyberspace unbounded by the geographical and less tangible barriers of physical and social space (race, gender, and class, for example) are themselves contingent upon entities that in obvious and less obvious ways take up space in the socioeconomic domain: computers, cables, electricity. For those of us who are "haves," even if we do not enjoy top-of-the-line resources, it becomes relatively easy to view this contingency as a technicality. Working on a recent grant proposal to establish networked classrooms in Hawaiian-language schools on the neighbor islands brought home to us the *constraints* of existing material conditions on possibilities for cyberspace: most of the school buildings, it turned out, not only did not have air conditioning (a condition that in the humid climate of Hawaii has a significant impact on the maintenance of computer equipment), but their transformers could not handle the line load of even a modest ten-station computer lab.[5] The costs of refurbishing the technical infrastructure—before any consideration of telecommunication resources—quickly became staggering for the small nonprofit educational organization with which we hoped to collaborate and which would have to come up with a substantial portion of the cost sharing for the grant.

Facing the day-to-day dilemmas brought on by time constraints and a lack of technical resources, students working on the Going to Class, Getting Online, and Giving Back project quickly gained an appreciation for the complex material and institutional factors that determine any individual's access to information technology. In the second year, one of our students developed a phrase that encapsulates a number of our challenges: "It's almost like we're saying, 'Send us an e-mail if you want to learn how to use e-mail.'" In their written work for the community, many students paid careful attention to the means by which their materials would—could—be disseminated to members of the community. One group produced a pamphlet about where to find free and low-cost access to the Internet in Honolulu. They published the pamphlet as a PDF file on our project Web site so that PACT and other agencies could download, print, and make it available to people who did not themselves have ready access to the Internet. Another team produced an entertaining video on basic computing that could be circulated among residents or shown during meetings of the Job Club or other organizations.

Through such materials, as well as our twice-weekly presence in the Learning Center lab, our project has introduced a number of KPT residents to basic computing skills. We are still addressing the serious question of sustainability, however, a question that must be approached from a variety of angles. We must continue to identify community members who are interested in information technology, adding to the pool of individuals who regularly visit the Learning Center. We need to encourage their interest and build their skills with appropriate expert training that has some degree of continuity. That training must be hands-on, requiring adequate technology resources that are upgraded at a reasonable rate. While it is true, as Beamish argues, that community computing is more than "hardware and software, or access, or a Web site, or wiring, or information" (366), successful community computing projects do in fact depend upon those material things. But technology resources and skills are not all it takes. While a functional technical infrastructure is crucial for the success of technology-based community service learning projects such as ours, technical difficulties are not the only, and perhaps not even the most significant, obstacles to the formation of a viable virtual community in which people in the university and in the housing project could meet on common ground.

## BLANK MESSAGES: PARTITIONS OF THE PUBLIC SPHERE

Aside from persistent frustrations with connectivity and with the complex logistics of moving groups of students back and forth across town twice a week, one of our major challenges lay in students' perceptions of the housing project. While our own preliminary visits to the project fully alleviated our concerns about safety, the reputation that KPT had acquired in the larger Hawaii population during the 1970s and 1980s, when the project was plagued with violence and drug- and gang-related crime, has proved hard to shake. The KPT community of the late 1990s is very different from that of the previous decades, but the remarkable gains in safety and community life have received far less publicity than the earlier problems.

A number of our students were literally absent from the service-learning component of our course. In some cases, their failure to participate had to do with insurmountable scheduling problems, but in several other cases their reluctance was directly related either to their own perceptions of what KPT was like or to the perceptions of authority figures in their lives. One student's parents forbade her to participate when they learned that KPT was our community partner; another reported being advised by a member of the English department staff to "try to get out of" the project because we would be taking him into a "rough area." The reluctance to participate became a recurrent topic on the course-based listserv discussion, with actively participating students encouraging their less active peers to join them:

> Hello everyone. I just wanted to encourage everyone to keep on coming out to KPT if you've already made a visit. For those of us who haven't, it isn't as intimidating as you think! On Monday, about 11 people showed up for our help. As more people are becoming involved, they are spreading the word and encouraging their friends to come. As a matter of fact, one guy named Tony had three of his friends waiting for us outside the room. . . . They are eager to learn and they are appreciative of the help. Not too many people give them any type of attention because of all the negative perceptions that surround KPT. Once you make the first visit, I am sure you will find that a second one will be on its way. I hope to see more of you out there, they are counting on us! Thanks.

For the vast majority of students who did overcome these resistances and fears, the confrontation with social differences and disparities proved to be a rewarding experience. Having to speak and write to people whose lives were in many respects unlike their own, whose ways of seeing the world, expectations for the future, and styles of communication were quite different from theirs, situated traditional problem-solving tasks of composition and rhetoric within a constellation of emotional, ethical, and political challenges. It often struck us that what was really new and scary about our course from our students' perspective was much less composing in electronic media than composing for a living, breathing, and sometimes cantankerous audience.

A lengthy report to the discussion list from Carolyn, one of our students in the first semester of the project, incorporates issues that we see as central to the kind of learning we want our project to facilitate:

> At first KPT is a little intimidating (I just didn't know what to expect). Also, I was wondering how people would react to us. I was thinking, if I was in the income bracket of these people and a group of college students (probably living at home with mommy and daddy in decent to nice houses walked in to "help" me . . . I don't know how I would treat them or how I would react. Most of the people in there were very nice. Most of them wanted our help . . . but some didn't. I guess what I'm saying is, one cannot expect to be a "god" when helping these folks. It's not a good idea to say "oh, just open this icon and click that, open Word . . ." and assuming they should know how to do that. I was careful about how I worded things . . . I didn't want to come across like we were better than them. We are not. Simply lucky. I guess that's what I learned yesterday . . . to be humble and not take so many things for granted. Most of the people that I met in KPT yesterday were VERY polite with wonderful hearts. No matter what their social condition may be, most had a more positive attitude than I did. I always thought that by my visiting KPT I would help "those people," but I never guessed that "they" would end up helping me so much more. If you haven't yet gone to KPT . . . PLEASE PLEASE try and fit it into your schedule . . . if you only go once (as may be the case with me . . . my job simply doesn't allow me to attend) you'll be so glad you did. I'll never forget what I was taught by the people of KPT.

In reflecting on her care in "wording things," Carolyn identifies the central course-related component of the project: rhetoric in its fullest sense, not only the effective arrangement of words but an engagement with the social, cultural, and psychological dimensions of human communication. Carolyn's ability to imagine the position of her audience, as well as her willingness to acknowledge and critique the assumptions she brings to this new social situation, help her to confront the implicit paternalism of the project and to negotiate the sometimes uncomfortable ethical position of the helper. This combination of real-world practice in targeted skills and thoughtful personal reflection on the student's orientation to a diverse social world seems to us exemplary of the goals of service learning, which cannot simply be an exercise in doing good but rather must integrate service with the production of knowledge.

Garry Hesser views the benefits of service learning as a continuum. "At one end, experience-based learning enables one to work on very personal agendas. At the other end, there are agendas that strengthen the community. The question is, How do you keep that teeter-totter balanced so that it's feeding us as individuals yet not making us self-centered, reminding us of the community that's enabled us to be here?" (quoted in Stanton, Giles, and Cruz, 212). None of our students have displayed any form of overt self-centeredness in their work with the project. In fact, many of them have gone to some trouble to be able to participate, reorganizing personal and job schedules and sacrificing time for extracurricular activities. An honest assessment of our overall accomplishments so far, however, must take into consideration the fact that while we have abundant student commentary on their experiences, we have very little first-person documentation of the experiences of KPT community members. If our efforts had been as successful as we had initially hoped, this chapter would be filled with quotations taken from lengthy e-mail exchanges between community members and our students. This lack speaks volumes to the difficulties of realizing goals for interactive university/community partnerships.

One of the students who had grown up in Kalihi offered a description of her initial experience at the project that is indicative of these difficulties in establishing lasting communication links:

> I got back from my first time up at KPT. Strange, since I am a few minutes walk and really across the street from there. (I even found a shortcut over the bridge thing.) I doubt anyone else lives in Kalihi like me. Anyway. I had a good time. I liked meeting the people, especially Sam. I already received the email that he tried

> to write to me. It was a blank message but at least I have his email now and I can write to him (which I already did).

Not quite real, lacking substantial content, and not quite virtual, either—although at least it indicates an open channel—the "blank message" turned out to be a common unit of exchange in the relationships our students established with KPT residents. A few students did exchange messages with residents over a short period of time. That these online relationships did not develop is not only a function of the semester drawing to a close just as they were beginning. Learning about technology was what brought the students and KPT residents together, but apart from a few messages from residents thanking students for their help and student replies encouraging them to persevere, the technology did not make for exciting e-mail conversations. It takes time for people to find points of common interest, especially when they have to negotiate the spaces, imaginary and real, that separate their worlds. Finding shortcuts across this terrain continues to prove immensely challenging; our whole project can be summed up as a search for "the bridge thing."

Two stories drawn from student writing and the field notes we collected during our tutoring sessions at KPT illustrate the sometimes unexpected ways in which technology can throw complex social problems and divisions into relief. In the first year of the project, one of our students posted the following report to the class list:

> The work that I actually did [during that day's tutoring session] was to help a woman named Melinda enter information into a genealogy program that the center bought for the residents. All she had to do was point and click on added siblings, children, spouses, etc. And the program views the work that she has accomplished in a family tree type display. By the time 4:00 rolled around, she wasn't completed but she was enthusiastic to continue. I also look forward to coming back and seeing how much her project has come along. I recommend to others in the class to try and make it out there—it really changes your perspective on the way you live and the way others live.

The genealogy generator was the focus of a number of fascinating and often moving encounters between our students and the residents of

KPT. As genealogy is a central component of Pacific Island culture and personal identity, the software promised to engage many learners at KPT in an activity that was more culturally relevant than using such software as the Mavis Beacon typing tutorial or Microsoft Excel. The personal stories that emerged while our students worked with residents on their family trees, ranging from harrowing tales of the immigration experience to amusing anecdotes of cultural adjustment, opened lines of communication and exchange that appeared to contribute to a greater sense of community. Our students' backgrounds (Chinese, American Samoan, Native Hawaiian, Filipino, Japanese, Korean, Portuguese, German, and English) proved just as diverse as those of the community members they tutored.

The narrative of Melinda's experience with the genealogy program has an illuminating continuation, one that inspired a stimulating class discussion. In the first year both of us accompanied our students during every visit to the project. We happened to be sitting with Melinda when she encountered some difficulty with the family tree generator. She had finished entering information about herself and had clicked the "Build Family Tree" button to check her overall progress. The program returned the following error message: "Melinda seems to have been born before parents' marriage. No marriage has been recorded." Melinda's confusion was apparent. "Well, that's true," she said. "My folks didn't get married until after I was born." Then she turned to us and asked, "What did I do wrong?"

Melinda's question opens a whole range of inquiries into the hard-wiring of values in our digital world. Telling her that she hadn't made a mistake, that the problem lay in the way the genealogy program had been designed, and that furthermore she could ignore the message, clearly did not fully alleviate her sense that the program had identified an *error* in her family tree. As do most learners confronting computer technology, she attributed a measure of authority to the program. Like teachers and government officials, computer programs present a set of instructions, instructions that individual users need to follow in order to achieve the desired results. The possibility of *making a mistake* is one of the most powerful sources of anxiety for many novice computer users, who frequently inflate the potential consequences of the errors they might make. The program's message to Melinda was certainly not blank, and the message it sent failed to foster an inclusive sense of family or spirit of community. Rather, it reinforced a particular image of a community made up of officially sanctioned nuclear families, an image that is no more adequate to the configurations of the KPT community than it is to contemporary American society at large. The programmers of the family tree generator had determined a definition of the family and had structured the system so that information that does not conform to that definition is marked as aberrant, as problematic, as a faux pas. In this case, the Principle of Indifference operates to resist individual wishes—the wish to represent intimate relationships accurately—in a manner that must be viewed as a mode of discursive violence. Is indifference about and hostility toward *difference* a feature of our real societies that we really want to import into our virtual spaces? Michael Benedikt certainly does not think so, but Melinda's experience points to the subtle ways in which the architecture of digital environments can restrict access to certain members of our societies.[6]

Questions about the relationship between virtual social spaces and actual social environments arose again in another encounter, this one in the project's second year, between Carl, one of our students, and Kawika, a teenager from KPT. Our group was visiting the Learning Center in the early afternoon, during hours when classes at local schools were still in session. Kawika was in the lab playing a computer game when Carl engaged him in a conversation. Carl describes what followed in his final reflective essay:

> He told me that he was fourteen and that he loved computers. I asked him, "If you love computers so much, why aren't you in school?" He replied to me, "I no like." That really hurt me to see a young boy who is interested in computers not getting an education to help him learn more about the world and computers. I think that he didn't know that there was a world besides the rock that we live on now. So I hooked us both onto the internet and showed him some stuff that was not in Hawaii: Notre Dame football, NBA, and other big sports sites sparked a lot of interest in him. I could tell by his eagerness to search for more things over the internet. Then I hooked up to Hawaii Chat Universe, and started the beginning of the end of my time with him. Being such a dolt, I forgot how kids at that age are so playful. He started swearing at people and even observed a verbal fight on the screen.

> I logged off and talked to him about the dangers of internet use. . . . As we were leaving, I was left wondering to myself if the words I spoke fell on deaf ears.

This story of a tour through cyberspace is saturated by its geographical and historical context. It is significant that Carl refers to Hawaii as "the rock that we live on *now*"[7]; in the past decade, the literal insularity of life in Hawaii has been coupled with decreasing opportunities for employment, leading many people to make the often painful decision to leave the state to seek jobs on the more prosperous mainland or, in some cases, in countries of the Pacific Rim. As is increasingly true for all job seekers, obtaining a relatively secure and adequately compensated position anywhere is all but impossible without at least an undergraduate degree. Although the sites they visit are all oriented toward entertainment, Carl is clearly concerned to stress to Kawika the educational value of the Internet, and by extension the value of education itself. "I asked him if he thought about going to college," Carl told us in the car on the way back from that session. "He said 'yes,' and I asked him how he thought he was going to go to college if he didn't go to school now."

As is evident in his narrative, Carl was discouraged by the way his encounter with Kawika played itself out. His canny attempt to use sports and a chat room to expand the young man's notions of what computers can do seemed to him to have backfired. It isn't obvious to us that Kawika's online behavior was all that inappropriate; from our own observations of the incident we gather that the tone of that particular chat session was already fairly combative when Carl and Kawika joined in. For Carl, however, the online experience reflected badly on his capacity as a mentor and guide to the younger man. (The fact that his professor and another faculty member were in the room observing him quite likely reinforced this sense.) The institutional spaces of the Learning Center and our project—itself an extension of the university—with their hierarchies of age and institutional position all shaped Carl's understanding of what had happened in Hawaii Chat Universe.

Although we did our best to reassure Carl at the time, his written account shows that he retained his own version of our concerns over blank messages: "I was left wondering to myself if the words I spoke fell on deaf ears." Service learning initiatives generally incorporate reflective writing precisely for this purpose, as a means of working out the various responses to the service experience, not all of which are warm and fuzzy. Reflection "regards one's views as perpetually open to challenge, as choices entailing a responsibility toward the effects of one's arguments on others. This sort of critical reflection is quite difficult to exercise entirely on one's own; we are enabled to do it through our conversations with others, especially others not like us" (Burbules and Berk, 61). Though brief and not especially satisfying for him, Carl's exchange with Kawika was a real conversation about real issues. The challenge for us as designers of the project is to imagine an environment in which that conversation might be extended in time, deepened, and expanded to include other interlocutors.

We don't have nearly enough information to understand Kawika's resistance to school on that particular day, but we might consider his truancy in light of Castells's evaluation of schooling in the "dual city" of the Information Age: "Given that the school system is spatially segregated, public schools in devalued spaces become mechanisms of reproduction of social devaluation, unable to provide the necessary skills for the informational labor market, and becoming instead training grounds for survival in a world of social irrelevance" ("Informational City," 33). The most we can say is that Kawika's choice of a computer game over an afternoon in the classroom cannot necessarily be attributed to deficits in the young man's character or in his ability to perform a cost-benefit analysis. In exchange for a lesson on the dangers of the Internet, on what dangers could Kawika have schooled us?

Even a blank message bridges a divide. It is largely phatic gesture, marking the possibility of communication, saying, *I am here; I am trying to reach you*. Each of our visits to KPT opened up potential channels of communication and cleared preliminary spaces for community building. Our problem is not so much how to "get through" to the people at KPT, but rather how to keep the channels and spaces open. "The leverage is in the dialogue, not in the action," argues Judy Sorum Brown. "It's not what the individual student does for the client; it's in the conversation that the relationship makes possible. If you bring students into dialogue on what they observe and what questions that raises for them, and make that a community conversation within the academy, that would have remarkable transformative power" (quoted in Stanton, Giles, and Cruz, 218). To bring this community conversation, which is hard enough to accomplish within the academy, back into the community in which it originated requires a high level of commitment from all participants in the university-community partnership.

## DEDICATED LINES

In one of her reports to the class discussion list on her service learning experience in the KPT computer lab, one of our students identified a basic restriction on the formation of the virtual communities toward which we were working:

> There were greater limitations on members' accessibility to cyberspace because there were limitations on a computer's accessibility to a line needed to connect to cyberspace. Often times when members and I tried to access the Internet, we would hear fellow members say, "They're turning it on." So we would wait until "they" turned "it" on and then we were able to make the steps necessary to connect to Hawaii On-Line in order to access the Internet. Through this experience, I was able to truly realize the meaning of what I had mentioned briefly in my first paper: that a citizen's access to computers and computer programs depended on his/her social contexts.

The fax machine in the PACT office shared the single phone line that supplied the Internet connection for the five-station computer network in the KPT lab, so whenever PACT staff members needed to send or receive a fax, they would have to disconnect the network. This arrangement testifies to PACT's shoestring budget as well as to the willingness of the PACT administrators to go out of their way to provide connectivity, intermittent though it necessarily may be, to the Learning Center lab. On the basis of our extensive observations of the social dynamics of the Learning Center, the perception among residents in the computer lab that the PACT office had the power to "turn on the Internet" reflects an acceptance of severely limited resources more than any resentment of the agency's control over their connectivity. The idea that the Internet can be switched on and off does, however, point to the complex circuits along which power can be distributed in administrative structures that seek to provide public access to information technology. It indicates, too, the degree to which the execution of technology literacy projects are dependent upon basic technical infrastructures that cannot be taken for granted, and that in fact often have to be fought for continuously and on multiple fronts.

One of the 1989 Wingspread Report's Principles of Good Practice for Combining Service and Learning calls for an effective program to expect "genuine, active, and sustained organizational commitment" (Honnet and Poulsen, 1). Elaborating on this principle, the report's authors state that service learning programs "must receive administrative support, become line items in the organization's budget, be allocated appropriate physical space, equipment, and transportation, and allow for scheduled release time for participants and program leaders" (Honnet and Poulsen, 1). An additional phone line, an amenity that at the university—not to mention in many of our homes—can be secured with relative ease, presents a substantial hurdle to communities with sharply restricted funds and many pressing needs. Social service agencies like PACT, which receive the bulk of their funding from the federal government, frequently cannot employ existing funds as cost sharing for future federal grants. On the university side, participating in grant-writing initiatives with such agencies can be frustrated by the reluctance of the university to share costs in a project for which the university will not itself receive benefits in the form of indirect costs or actual grant monies. A conference at Wingspread in 1997 produced a similar set of guidelines for campus-community partnerships, including the recommendation that "partnerships should involve institutional structures that promote institutional change and ongoing innovation, as well as cooperation and collaboration among partners" (Lisman, 128). For us in Hawaii, actualizing the potential of university-community partnerships in a time of severe economic crisis requires that we take creative approaches to generating funds, securing equipment, compensating community members for their contributions of time, labor, and good faith.

By working directly with residents in the Learning Center at KPT in their own real space, we hope to create the conditions of possibility for a virtual community in which membership is not predicated from the start on constant access to or great facility with computers and the Internet. Following the 1997 Wingspread principles, laying the technical foundation for such a community must go hand in hand with establishing "long-term, serious, and sustained" connections between the university and the housing project, "involving multiple sectors in deepening and broadening relationships" (Lisman, 128). We have developed strong relationships with the PACT administrators who oversee the Learning Center as well as those who run the economic development program for the community. A number of the residents attend the tutoring sessions regularly; through the Job Club, we have been able to follow the progress of those who are employed.

Partnerships such as the one we are trying to build require an open structure that allows for a variety of modes of participation. Our partnership must come to terms with the nature of a community whose members are transient and interchangeable. Communities certainly transcend individual members; any community is somehow larger than the sum of its parts. But as places like KPT have all too directly experienced, if too many of the parts are not working, the community as a whole begins to falter. An institutional commitment must clear a space for the development of individual, personal commitments that can address the various functions of the various parts. A space must be made ready for community, dedicated to a community of the future. Another student analyzed this situation:

> Thanks to the donation made by the Bank of Hawaii, the Kuhio Park Terrace Learning Center has five computers to work with. I can't help but imagine the progress that could be made if they had more computers, more programs, more people involved and more respect. Money may be the central problem but I believe there [are] ample monies out there that could be designated for this community. The lives of the parents, the children and possibly further generations along the line are at stake. To all those that I worked with at the Kuhio Park Terrace Learning Center, thanks for reminding me of my responsibility to my community. Work hard, keep the hope alive and keep in touch through email!

That the final lines of this message are directed not to us as teachers or to the writer's fellow students but to the residents of KPT is the source of great satisfaction for us. This simple rhetorical gesture bears witness to a belief that the channel is open, and will remain open, for messages that are not blank. The following passage comes from a far more typical, though certainly no less insightful, final assessment of the project:

> The hard thing is that you get attached to the residents after the time you spend with them. We relate one-on-one, we encounter difficulties together, and discover new things together. But when the project is done, we have to part. What we leave behind is new skills and new knowledge. It's up to them to retain and practice it. We can help by keeping in touch with the residents we've worked with through email messages that we've helped them set up free accounts for. We can also give them special online resources to browse through on their own, and to further learn from. But who can honestly promise them that we'll be back?

As we have discovered in the course of our project, keeping in touch is a profoundly complex dimension of community life, regardless of the medium. Getting connected is not as hard as staying connected. "The passing on of technological know-how was the easy part," one of our students writes in her final reflections on her service learning work. "The hardest thing, and by far the most gratifying, was learning how to relate to the participants on the same level—it was then that I found in myself the emergence of compassion and sensitivity." Further on in her essay, this student described a painful moment when she had to say good-bye to a young person at KPT with whom she had established a warm relationship during the semester. "It's enough to make you think about the consequences of working too closely with people who start out as being just another workshop participant. But friendship can't be a bad thing. In time, that youth will remember the things we shared. Hopefully, they will be good memories. And that may be enough."

The connectivity crisis is not over. One of the values of engaging in projects such as Going to Class, Getting Online, and Giving Back is that it compels us to toggle between the exhilarating—and sometimes giddy—utopianism that attends much of the discourse on virtual spaces and the gritty, often frustrating material and social realities that continue to steer the wiring of the world. Our experience over the past two years has convinced us that university-community partnerships organized around technological literacy provide significant benefits for the learning and development of university students. To a more limited degree, our project has indicated that members of the target community can also enjoy a return on the investment of time and trust that their participation in such projects requires. We also feel that we have gained a more nuanced understanding of what it takes to create and to sustain a virtual community that lives up to its name. We will continue to work toward the realization of a functional community information network that will open a dynamic and productive space for public debate over public concerns as well as for the welter of individual exchanges that make up the real life of any community, virtual or actual. For the time being, the cracks, peels, and missing pieces of the community hall mural at KPT, its contingency on the conditions of the material world, make it a fitting representation of the kind of community that in the course of our project *really* formed among ourselves, our students, and the wide variety of people who live and work at Kuhio Park Terrace and Kuhio Homes: incomplete, vulnerable, but still recognizable, both as a tangible presence and as a promise.

## NOTES

1. Kuhio Park Terrace and Kuhio Homes is located in Kalihi, a heavily built-up area west of downtown Honolulu. "Authorized" residents number approximately 2,400; the population also includes a significant number of temporary residents, usually members of extended families and visitors. The physical structure of KPT includes two high-rise towers and a cluster of low-rise buildings totaling 748 units. For an analysis of the impact of the project's Western-style urban architecture on traditional structures of Pacific Island societies, see Franco and Aga.

2. Our focused discussions were part of our attempt to adhere to the Wingspread Group's fourth Principle of Good Practice for Combining Service and Learning, which states that "an effective program allows for those with needs to define those needs" (Honnet and Poulsen).

3. On the basis of our agreement with our students, we will not identify them by name. The names of all project participants in this article have been changed.

4. For a more detailed analysis of the learning outcomes of this project for students, see Regan and Zuern, "Community Service-Learning and Computer-Mediated Advanced Composition: The Going to Class, Getting Online, and Giving Back Project," *Computers and Composition* 17 (2000): 177–195.

5. Beamish refers to a 1995 investigation of ten thousand American schools by the U.S. General Accounting Office, which discovered that the poor material conditions of school buildings are a frequent impediment to networking initiatives (356).

6. Anna Cicognani's essay in this volume, "Architectural Design for Online Environments," provides a detailed examination of the design challenges facing architects of virtual spaces.

7. A common phrase in local discourse, "the rock we live on" is more an expression of ambivalence than one of despair. The Hawaii writer Milton Murayama titles his 1994 novel *Five Years on a Rock*; the slogan of a local rock-and-roll radio station, KPOI, is "the Rock You Live On."

## REFERENCES

Beamish, Anne. "Approaches to Community Computing: Bringing Technology to Low-Income Groups." In Donald Schon, Bish Sanyal, and William J. Mitchell, eds., *High Technology and Low-Income Communities: Prospects for the Positive Use of Advanced Information Technology*, 349–369. Cambridge, Mass.: MIT Press, 1999.

Benedikt, Michael. "Cyberspace: Some Proposals." In Michael Benedikt, ed., *Cyberspace: First Steps*, 119–224. Cambridge, Mass.: MIT Press, 1992.

Bogdan, R. C., and S. K. Biklen. *Qualitative Research for Education: An Introduction to Theory and Methods*. Boston: Allyn and Bacon, 1982.

Burbules, Nicholas C., and Rupert Berk. "Critical Thinking and Critical Pedagogy: Relations, Differences, and Limits." In Thomas S. Popkewitz and Lynn Fendler, eds., *Critical Theories in Education: Changing Terrains of Knowledge and Politics*, 45–65. New York/London: Routledge, 1999.

Castells, Manuel. *The Information Age: Economy, Society, and Culture*. Vol. 3. *End of Millennium*. Oxford: Blackwell, 1998.

——. "The Informational City Is a Dual City: Can It Be Reversed?" In Donald Schon, Bish Sanyal, and William J. Mitchell, eds., *High Technology and Low-Income Communities: Prospects for the Positive Use of Advanced Information Technology*, 27–41. Cambridge, Mass.: MIT Press, 1999.

Cochran-Smith, M., and S. Lytle. *Inside/Outside: Teacher Research and Knowledge*. New York: Teachers College Press, 1993.

Franco, Robert, and Simeamativa Mageo Aga. "From Houses Without Walls to Vertical Villages: Samoan Housing Transformations." In Jan Rensel and Margaret Rodman, eds., *Home in the Islands: Housing and Social Change in the Pacific*, 175–193. Honolulu: University of Hawaii Press, 1997.

Giroux, Henry A. *Schooling and the Struggle for Public Life*. Minneapolis: University of Minnesota Press, 1988.

Honnet, Ellen Porter, and Susan J. Poulsen. *Principles of Good Practice for Combining Service and Learning*. Racine, Wis.: Johnson Foundation, 1989.

Lisman, C. David. *Toward a Civil Society: Civic Literacy and Service Learning*. Westport, Conn.: Bergin and Garvey, 1998.

Lockard, Joseph. "Progressive Politics, Electronic Individualism, and the Myth of Virtual Community," In David Porter, ed., *Internet Culture*, 219–232. New York: Routledge, 1997.

Murayama, Milton. *Five Years on a Rock*. Honolulu: University of Hawaii Press, 1994.

National Telecommunications and Information Administration. *Falling Through the Net II: New Data on the Digital Divide*. http://www.ntia.doc.gov/ntiahome/net2/falling.html. 25 June 1999.

Regan, Alison, and John Zuern. "Community Service-Learning and Computer-Mediated Advanced Composition: The Going to Class, Getting Online, and Giving Back Project." *Computers and Composition* 17 (2000): 177–195.

Stanton, Timothy K., Dwight E. Giles Jr., and Nadinne I. Cruz. *Service-Learning: A Movement's Pioneers Reflect on Its Origins, Practice, and Future*. San Francisco: Jossey-Bass, 1999.

Tyner, Kathleen. *Literacy in a Digital World: Teaching and Learning in the Age of Information*. Mahwah, N.J.: Lawrence Erlbaum, 1998.

10

## Where Do You Want to Learn Tomorrow? The Paradox of the Virtual University

COLLIN GIFFORD BROOKE

Given the slow pace of change in higher education, the speed with which distance learning has captured the attention of colleges and universities in this country is remarkable. This shift has been even more notable considering the overwhelming lack of consensus about what constitutes an effective distance learning program.[1] Distance education has not spread as a result of a few pioneers enjoying success and engendering imitators; in the United States at least, the vision of a virtual university seems to have sprung fully grown from the heads of thousands of administrators at roughly the same point in time. Substantial portions of college and university budgets are now devoted to capitalizing on that vision, while most of us who teach for these schools struggle to comprehend the change.

To date, the differences between traditional and distance education have been measured only in the most limited fashion, by student surveys and cost-benefit analyses. Many of those who are assessing the potential of distance education do so because of the stake they have in its success, and as a result, much of the scholarship about distance learning is celebratory. While student satisfaction and cost-effectiveness may be important considerations, it is foolish to assume that the long-term effects of distance education will be similarly limited. This is not to suggest, however, that we must simply control for more appropriate variables. By the time distance education has become sufficiently commonplace for properly controlled study, it will already have become ubiquitous. Distance education is not simply the superior packaging of traditional education; rather, it is symptomatic of a shift in our thinking about education, and it should be treated as such. The practices and attitudes implied by distance education represent a significant challenge to the contemporary university.[2]

I am tempted to suggest that the shift to a virtual university is all but inevitable, but I believe that the form such change will eventually take is less certain. If we as educators wish to intervene in the implementation of the virtual university, we cannot delay in doing so. Partly out of our own fear of technology, distance education is being realized as an administrative rather than an educational project, which has made it easy for educators to ignore the potential change that a fully virtual university will bring. We will not be able to ignore it for much longer, however. Distance education will not supplement the university; it will transform it. There is certainly some usefulness in the empirical study of distance education programs, for that may give us some idea of what to expect, but such studies require other kinds of inquiry at a time when it is the original vision itself that is at issue. That is, by the time we might conclusively determine that the traditional university is worth preserving, we are likely to find that its time has passed.

The approach that the following essay takes, therefore, is grounded in two assumptions. The first is that distance education is here to stay, and although it doesn't represent the end of education as we know it, there should be little question that the university as an institution will change in significant ways as a result. The second is that we should accept this inevitability only insofar as it allows us to concentrate our efforts on shaping it. To do so, our present universities must themselves become objects of our investigation. There have always been critiques of the university system, for its profligacy, exclusivity, and/or bureaucracy, but more rare, I think, are claims that the university itself is obsolete. Arguments that it performs its functions poorly have been made at times, but the functions themselves have not been called into question. We should not, however, therefore conclude that they never will be.

Here I attempt to examine the university (and its status as an institution dependent upon print technology) in terms of what it purports to accomplish. Such a topic is far too broad for a single essay, but I hope to sketch out and describe one part of it, namely the relationship between the university and the public sphere. How has the university served the interest of the public? Can the virtual university provide analogous service? Will the gains of distance education be sufficient to replace what we might lose with the abandonment of the traditional university? To answer these kinds of questions we must turn to the history and philosophy of the university. The answers will provide us with the means of asking better questions and making better decisions regarding distance education than we have done up to this point.

As administrators across the country race to implement distance education, we are called upon to imagine the possibilities far more than we are to consider the history of the institution that the virtual university claims to replace. With the advent of the Internet, the historical study of information technology has enjoyed a resurgence. Many of these studies, however, attempt to isolate technology from its social and cultural context; their focus is on the relative (dis)continuities among technologies. Claims of radical revolution on behalf of the Internet outnumber those that minimize its novelty. And yet when we consider the possibilities of the virtual university, we are not talking about solely technological change, for distance education is more than a change in information technology. Asking students to meet online rather than in a classroom does indeed involve different technologies, but it also requires us to rethink the idea of an educational community, an idea informed by more than technological difference. It is not unusual to see analyses of our social and cultural institutions viewed through the lens of technology, but we need to nuance such analyses, to consider the interaction between institution and technology mutually constitutive. George Landow offers an example of this sort of analysis:

> One can point out several other crucial facts about the changing ways people have encountered the word, perhaps the most important of which for this examination of future universities is that each information technology, each form of the word, has created its own characteristic educational institution and educational practice. Each of these technologies of cultural memory, furthermore, becomes naturalized. Each, in other words, becomes so expected and obvious a part of its culture that it appears inevitable, natural, *what one expects*, and therefore all but invisible,

> particularly to those who rely upon it most and whose thoughts and attitudes have been most shaped by it—that is, students, teachers, researchers, and theorists of education. (340)

A statement like this cuts both ways when we consider it in terms of the distance education debate. On the one hand, Landow's statement might be employed to explain the kind of faculty resistance that distance education has encountered on numerous campuses. If we assert that distance education is incapable of adequately meeting our pedagogical goals, it could be argued, it is only because our own perceptions of those goals are warranted by technological assumptions that have become invisible to us. On the other hand, as Linda Carswell notes, "Universities make the assumption that providing distance education is a simple process of translating from one medium to the next" (1). In other words, advocates of distance education approach the opposite extreme; because the technology is naturalized, they assume that it has no impact whatsoever on education. If faculty are bound too tightly to potentially obsolete models of information technology, we might argue that administrations are not sufficiently bound to them.

Neither argument is entirely incorrect. There are doubtless those faculty members who equate any sort of change with an increase in responsibilities or duties, and such an increase is rarely accompanied by improved status or salary. And as Andrew Feenberg suggests, there are "too many administrators [for whom] the big issues are not educational. The fiscal implications of electronic distance learning are what is interesting to them." One of the problems with the way these positions have polarized is the degree to which it isolates those of us who do not find the prospect of instructional technology to be an all-or-nothing issue. Increasingly, we find ourselves in the paradoxical position that Feenberg describes: we have to defend distance education against its faculty detractors at the same time that we try and preserve it from its advocates among administrators.

Ultimately, both of the positions described above share a common warrant, the invisibility that Landow cites with respect to current applications of technology. Opponents of distance education need to explore the degree to which their resistance is grounded in a particular instantiation of information technology, so that those points of resistance that are legitimate can form a basis for dialogue. On the other side of the debate, the context dependency of education needs to be examined in greater detail. To believe that education can be reduced to raw quantities of information that remain unaffected by differing media is to risk education itself. As Sir John Daniel, vice chancellor of England's Open University, points out,

> Much of the commercial hype and hope about distance learning is based on a very unidirectional conception of instruction, where teaching is merely presentation and learning is merely absorption. The Open University's experience . . . suggests that such an impoverished notion of distance education will fail—or at least have massive drop-out problems. (Quoted in Gladieux, 16)

While this is precisely what distance education detractors wish to hear, it is important to note that Daniel's experience has included successful distance education as well. That is, there are some advocates of distance education who have managed to navigate a middle path between the polarized positions of this debate. In the United States, with its elaborate and extensive system of universities, colleges, and community colleges,[3] such a middle path presents a much more serious challenge.

## WWW.UNIVERSITY.GOV

The relationship between information technologies and higher education is complex and requires extensive examination. But in keeping with the theme of this volume, I would like to sketch out the portion of that argument that relates to the university as a public institution. In short, I will claim that the advent of print texts and the modern university provide the conditions of possibility for a particular articulation of the "public interest," an interest that our current universities serve. That role, whether it is necessary or even desirable, is one that distance education calls into question in substantial ways.

According to Bill Readings, Immanuel Kant "founds the modern University on reason, and reason is what gives the University its universality in the modern sense. . . . The life of the Kantian University is therefore a perpetual conflict between established tradition and rational inquiry" (56–57). In many ways, though, it is the printing press that enables this dialectic to take place. The printing press keeps the modern university from simply propagating local, regional, and national traditions. The development of a Habermasian "public sphere in the world of letters," strongly tied to the mission of this modern university, occurs in no small part thanks to the (relative) explosion of information that the printing press enables.

Although we are less interested today in writing history as a narrative of progress and development, earlier historians labored under no such restriction. One such scholar, French historian Antoine-Nicolas de Condorcet, goes to great lengths to credit the printing press in particular with the "means of accelerating, assisting, [and] ensuring the forward march of the human mind" (101). Condorcet's "forward march" takes place in a public sphere that transcends both the "tyranny" of the Church and national borders. With printing,

> men found themselves possessed of the means of communicating with people all over the world. A new sort of tribunal had come into existence in which less lively but deeper impressions were communicated; which no longer allowed the same tyrannical empire to be exercised over men's passions but ensured a more certain and more durable power over their minds; a situation in which the advantages are all on the side of truth, since what the art of communication loses in the power to seduce, it gains in the power to enlighten. The public opinion that was formed in this way was powerful by virtue of its size, and effective because the forces that created it operated with equal strength on all men at the same time, no matter what distances separated them. (100)

Certainly, Condorcet's account of the various effects of printing is idealistic; he discounts the degree to which "lively impressions" may deepen or persuasiveness might lead to enlightenment. He separates content from delivery and attributes to orality a subordinate, less rational position with respect to print. Nevertheless, insofar as the printing press is a vast improvement in the distribution of knowledge, the implications of Condorcet's account remain with us today. Tenure and promotion guidelines require faculty to publish, to make public their research in forums that represent the kind of public tribunal that the printing press enables. The relative weight that universities place upon activities that result in print and those that result in oral performance coincide easily with Condorcet's conclusions.[4]

As Roger Chartier notes, however, Condorcet's vision is incapable of transcending two important limitations. If universities allow for the exercise of reason and join together into a network of knowledge production that stretches beyond national borders, access remains an issue. Chartier names this as the problem of public instruction, which "would break the Church's control over education and would give to everyone the necessary competence to read the books" (10). Access is a problem that must be answered by more than improvements in information technology, though. There are social and economic factors that have restricted access to the university and its public sphere of letters, factors that the ready availability of printed texts cannot address. Even within purely technical parameters, the printing press represented a substantial improvement rather than a complete solution. William J. Mitchell describes this problem of distribution as "Gutenberg's gotcha": "Paper documents can be mass produced rapidly at centralized locations, but they must then be warehoused, transported, stocked at retail outlets, and eventually hand carried to wherever they will be opened and read" (50).

A second, obvious difficulty with Condorcet's vision relates to distribution/access and its claim to transcend national boundaries. Ironically, the printing press itself is one of the causes of this difficulty, as readily accessible and reproducible texts allowed scholars to move away from Latin toward their own national tongues. As a result of this shift, Chartier explains that "there must be established a common language, one capable of eliminating the contradiction implicit in a formulation such as 'the universality of people who speak the same language'" (10). The inevitable delay of publication, compounded by the potential problems of translation, seem far less tolerable to us today than they probably did for Condorcet himself, who claims that printing allows "any new mistake [to be] criticized as soon as it is made, and often attacked before it has been propagated" (100). It is also important to note here that the issue of translation is not simply a matter of transposing research from one language to another. As research has become increasingly specialized, the public sphere in the world of letters, once cloistered by Church and geography, is now similarly fragmented by department and discipline. Given these two problems, of access and of a common language, it is certainly debatable whether contemporary universities sit closer to or further from the "public opinion" that is central to Condorcet's understanding of human progress. If Condorcet's notion of a "public tribunal" is scarcely able to transcend boundaries of departments, much less nations, and if access to the university remains restricted by numerous factors, how can we describe the university as a public institution?

Part of the answer to this question lies in the nexus of meanings that have been ascribed to the very idea of a "public," as Habermas explains in the introduction to *The Structural Transformation of the Public Sphere*, describing it as a "clouded amalgam" of competing meanings. According to him, "We call events and occasions 'public' when they are open to all, in contrast to closed or exclusive affairs—as when we speak of public places or public houses" (1). Even as universities have opened their doors wider to applicants, and in some cases declared "open admissions," they remain institutions that are decidedly less than public in this sense. A second category of definitions, closer to Condorcet's, is also offered by Habermas, in which for a particular institution, "its function as a critical judge is precisely what makes the public character of proceedings—in court, for instance—meaningful" (2). While universities, like courts, are not open to all, there is nevertheless a sense in which they operate for the public interest. In the case of the legal system, issues of public safety, embodied in the enforcement of law, are paramount; in the university, it is the development of knowledge, and the dissemination of that knowledge to the citizens of a community or nation, that justify its public status (and often, its subsidization by the state).

While this account of the university's public status may seem obvious to many and implied by accounts like Condorcet's (whose "universality" is largely restricted to citizens of a certain race, gender, and class), it creates an aporia of the sort described by Jacques Derrida in his book *Logomachia: The Conflict of the Faculties*. If the university is established as a place of reason, independent of any religious or political claims to authority, how can its mission be one of "public interest," insofar as that interest is represented and enacted by the state? Bill Readings summarizes this conflict:

> [Kant's text] argues that one of the functions of the University is to produce technicians for the state, that is, men of affairs. . . . So

> on the one hand, the state must protect the university in order to ensure the rule of reason in public life. On the other hand, philosophy must protect the University from the abuse of power by the state, in limiting the rule of established interests in the higher faculties. This unlimited right of reason to intervene is what distinguishes legitimate conflict, *concordia discors*, from illegitimate conflict (which is the arbitrary exercise of authority by the established powers of the higher faculties and the state). (58)

The modern university as a site for the exercise of reason, rather than Condorcet's "tyrannical empire" of superstition and tradition, nevertheless contains the seeds of the very traditions that it seeks to escape. As Readings asks, "How can the reason embodied in the University not come to be the object of a superstitious rather than rational respect" (58)? For the Kantian university, this problem is analogous to the pressures that the contemporary university feels with respect to market forces. That is, how can a university meet the needs of an increasingly specialized (and technologically sophisticated) marketplace without giving itself over entirely to market forces in the determination of its curriculum?

> Kant's answer to this dilemma is to transfer responsibility for it to the subject: Kant seeks to do so by producing the figure of the *republican subject* who incarnates this conflict. If the regulative principle of the Kantian University is the *sapere aude* of reason, the problematic of institutionalization is circumvented in the figure of the subject, who is rational in matters of knowledge, republican in matters of power. (Readings, 59)

In other words, according to Readings, the university "only institutionalizes reason fictionally"—that is, decisions occur according to custom or tradition *as if* the people on whose behalf those decisions are made had arrived at such choices via autonomous, rational means. "A heteronomous power is invoked in order to give to a people the laws that it would give itself *if it were autonomous*" (59). The modern university, then, prepares subjects to act in the public sphere along similar lines, to exercise power only to establish those conditions that a universally educated and rational populace would choose for themselves.

This "rationalization" of the public sphere, according to Habermas, is grounded in "the fictitious identity of the two roles assumed by the privatized individuals who came together to form a public: the role of property owners and the role of human beings pure and simple" (56).

Whether or not such an ideal was ever possible, much less desirable, we must consider the extent to which the development of the modern university is grounded in that ideal. Certainly, the popularity of polemics such as Allan Bloom's *The Closing of the American Mind* and E. D. Hirsch Jr.'s *Cultural Literacy* can be traced back to this ideal. Both Bloom and Hirsch propose the kind of education that they assume everyone would rationally choose. The resurgence of core curricula at universities also speaks to the notion of tradition imposed in the name of reason. While we may not wish to identify ourselves politically with thinkers like Bloom and Hirsch, or to invest ourselves in the existence of a core curriculum, we cannot so easily dismiss such projects. The proliferation of diversity requirements on campuses across the nation is evidence that this Kantian ideal is still active at the contemporary university. The political ends of such requirements may be radically different, but the contemporary university employs the same mechanisms to accomplish those ends. In this model, the traditional university seems a less than desirable place, with its production of Enlightenment subjects. If indeed the mission of the university as a public institution is to produce such subjects, who will act in the public sphere according to what is admittedly an exclusionary model of the rational subject, we might easily answer the question of whether this kind of university should be replaced. Before we address that question more directly, however, it will be worthwhile to complicate our picture of the traditional university. For while the university is as conservative as any large-scale institution must be, it also provides for the possibility of critique, the kind of critique that Condorcet attributes to the emergence of the printing press.

## WWW.UNIVERSITY.ORG

The university produces a particular type of subject, but it is reductive to consider it nothing more than the site of that production. There is a particularity about the site itself, the university *qua* physical space, and that particularity should form an integral part of any understanding of the university. John Henry Newman's series of essays titled *The Idea of a University* begins, first and foremost, with the notion that the university is a specific place (cf. Landow). William J. Mitchell elaborates upon this: "Schools, colleges, and universities are spaces that exist primarily to bring students and teachers together so that this sharing of a corpus can take place. . . . The demand that colleges and universities typically make is to be 'in residence'—to be part of the spatially defined community" (67). This spatiality of the university as Mitchell describes it also articulates some of the principles with which Harris Breslow defines the space of "civil society," and it is as an exemplum of civil society that the university's public mission seems least adaptable to distance education.

According to Breslow, four principles are operative in the classical model of civil society. The first is *spatio-social contiguity*, which the university fulfills in the act of "bring[ing] students and teachers together," in Mitchell's words. Breslow explains that "it is the point of contact between the private and the public, between the individual and the social" (239), or between the student and the various bodies of knowledge represented by the faculty. The second condition, *socio-spatial density*, is implied in the gathering of which Mitchell speaks (and embodied in the minimum number of students required for any given course). A certain number of people must be gathered in a particular place for it to be an active site of civil society. The third principle, *information/communication*, ranges from the pedagogical act itself to the various codes of conduct imposed upon members of the university community to the network of research and scholarship in which the faculty are involved and to which the students are exposed. The "sharing of a corpus" is primarily a communicative act. Finally, civil society is characterized by *socioeconomic struggle/competition*. While the university is not a free market in the strictest sense, the symbolic capital of student grades, faculty evaluations, departmental credit hours and majors, and such do constitute a competition sufficient to name the university as a site of civil society.

This characterization of the university has been a part of the American cultural landscape for some time. As Breslow notes, "[For John Dewey,] education provides the subject with a sense of purpose and place. As such, education enables the subject to express him or herself to others, and thus to participate—socially, politically, culturally—within the community" (244). Unlike Kant's rational idealism, then, the university as a model of civil society maintains a more pragmatic relationship with the public sphere. The subject produced by the university, particularly as the institution has moved away from the Kantian paradigm, is not so much a subject of privilege who will enter the public sphere to make decisions on behalf of the excluded; rather she is one who has gradually learned how to be with others, how to participate in the broader community. While the opportunities for participation are undoubtedly less immediate and plentiful than they may be outside the university, they do exist within higher education, and it is in this sense that the university can be said to introduce students to the public sphere.

The extent to which these two explanations of the university's public mission, rational idealism on the one hand and social pragmatism on the other, are integrated will of course vary from campus to campus. Civil society is not architectonic, according to Breslow; in fact, the very attempt to institutionalize civil society in the form of a university problematizes the simple equation of the two. Furthermore, the idea of the university graduate as a rational, self-possessed subject capable of political, cultural, and social action may seem hopelessly unrealistic. Finally, the suggestion that this idea can be tied to the emergence of the printing press (even as one of several causes) will probably seem to some to stretch the bounds of credulity. I would suggest, however, that this account of the university cannot be dismissed until it has been articulated in more detail than I have been able to provide here. Before we can responsibly take a position with respect to distance education, before we can begin to construct virtual universities, we must make our various assumptions[5] about the university (and the role that information technology plays in shaping them) more visible than we have done to date. In the final section of this essay, I hope to demonstrate the urgency of this project, particularly as it concerns distance education.

## WWW.UNIVERSITY.COM

While we may question the degree to which the university can serve as a microcosm of democracy or function as a repository for democratic values, there has been no shortage of this type of argument on behalf of distance education. If, as Chartier notes, the modern university still suffers from the problem of access, distance education advocates claim that the virtual university will provide the solution. Sondra F. Stallard, dean of continuing education at the University of Virginia, writes:

> To me, the greatest promise arising from the infusion of digital technologies in higher education is that it will enable us to open the doors of Thomas Jefferson's university to the world. With technology, high-quality courses can now be offered to persons who otherwise would not be able to study here in residence—senior citizens, working adults, inner-city minorities, and international students. This resonates loudly and clearly with Thomas Jefferson's notion of universal education as the keystone of democracy. . . . I strongly suspect that our founder would have embraced the notion of using technology to enhance teaching and learning on and off Grounds.

Nor is Stallard alone in describing the virtual university in such a democratic fashion. Mitchell suggests that "if a latter-day Jefferson were to lay out an ideal educational community for the third millennium, she might site it in cyberspace" (70). The optimism expressed in comments like these has been tempered recently with the realization that for many, the economic barriers to owning an Internet-ready computer are as substantial as the geographical limitations. Nevertheless, the political and commercial support for a computer "at every desk" or "in every classroom" is currently more pervasive than analogous support for financial aid.

Implicit in the traditional description of the university as a place is its temporal character as well. While the notion of the average college-going student as an eighteen-to-twenty-two-year-old who completes the degree in four years is more nostalgic than realistic at most schools these days, the time it takes to complete a degree is another "obstacle" to the universal access claimed on behalf of distance education.[6] As Stallard's comments above suggest, distance learning accommodates those potential students who can't take four years off from their jobs ("working adults") and those whose interests may not include a degree ("senior citizens"). Access to education, then, is figured as the ability to avoid the putatively restrictive model of the university resident who must make specific temporal and spatial investments to receive a degree.

The second shortcoming of Condorcet's vision of the public sphere, as Chartier explains it, is the absence of a common language, a problem that distance education promises to address, but in a manner far different than that imagined by Condorcet. This common language is not unique to distance education, but as I hope to show, it inheres to it. As I suggested above, the problem of a common language is now less a matter of translating between languages than one of translating between increasingly insular and specialized disciplinary discourses. Bill Readings's *The University in Ruins* suggests that the contemporary university has solved this problem through a process he calls "dereferentialization." Whereas the university of the past relied upon reason or culture as its ultimate reference, the contemporary university, according to Readings, grounds itself in the notion of "excellence," a criterion without content. In fact, "its very lack of reference allows excellence to function as a principle of translatability between radically different idioms: parking services and research grants can each be excellent, and their excellence is not dependent on any specific qualities or effects that they share" (24).

It is this principle of translatability that provides a common language in the contemporary university and allows comparisons not only of widely divergent functions within the university but also of the kinds of rankings performed annually by *U.S. News and World Report* and *MacLean's*. In this fashion, accountability for the quality of an education is translated into accounting, the language of capital. Readings notes how this dereferentialized University of Excellence fits part and parcel with a logic of consumerism:

> Choosing a particular university over another is presented as not all that much different from weighing the costs and benefits of a Honda Civic against those of a Lincoln Continental in a given year or period. . . . Fuel efficiency, whether calculated in miles per gallon or spending per student, is a growing concern when measuring excellence. (28)

That higher education is now subject to the logic of consumerism should not strike any of us as particularly newsworthy. Our students shop for courses and in many cases believe that the fact that they've paid tuition entitles them to a particular outcome. Course evaluations bear strong resemblance to consumer satisfaction surveys. Cost-effectiveness in terms of faculty/student ratio is a primary criterion for budget allocations.

While the university has operated according to a logic of consumerism for some time, distance education brings its own twist. Historian David Noble explains:

> The major change to befall the universities over the last two decades has been the identification of the campus as a significant site of capital accumulation, a change in social perception which has resulted in the systematic conversion of intellectual activity into intellectual capital and, hence, intellectual property. There have been two general phases of this transformation. The first . . . entailed the commoditization of the research function of the university. . . . The second, which we are now witnessing, entails the commoditization of the educational function of the university, transforming courses into courseware, the activity of instruction itself into commercially viable proprietary products that can be owned and bought and sold in the market.
>
> ("Digital Diploma Mills")

While some distance education advocates have dismissed Noble's claims as alarmist, he followed up his "Digital Diploma Mills" essay with a second one that detailed agreements between UCLA and The Home Education Network (THEN), the University of California at Berkeley and America Online, and the University of Colorado System and Real Education, Inc. The agreement between UCLA and THEN included a compulsory "Instructor's Agreement," "whereby instructors would be made to surrender their rights to UNEX [a division of UCLA's Continuing Education program] as a condition of employment."

I include Noble's claims here not to contribute to the general alarm over distance education but as evidence of the degree to which higher education is migrating to a retail model as a means of achieving a common language.[7] William Wulf offers an analogy that is rapidly becoming reality when he explains that "we 'manufacture' information (scholarship) and occasionally 'reprocess' it into knowledge or even wisdom, we warehouse it (libraries), we distribute it (articles and books), and we retail it (classroom teaching)." Significant in Wulf's account is the way that he casts all the various informational functions of the university as products that are simply manufactured, reprocessed, stored, distributed, and retailed. While the traditional university is conceived as an institution that performs a service in the public interest, the virtual university recasts itself as a site for the production of a public, consumable good. Also important is the role played by the student (the consumer) in Wulf's analogy, or rather the absence of such a role. Rather than positing education as an experience that the subject engages with and becomes responsible for, the student/subject in this retail model passively buys it.

This shift toward commercialization also has implications for the university as a model of civil society, implications that are not entirely incompatible with that model. Civil society possesses a mediatory function distributed along three dimensions: political, juridical, and—most important for our purposes—economic:

> Economically, civil society exists in the guise of the free market, a space within which competing private economic actors "rationally negotiate" their interests with one another. . . . The rational-critical function described of individuals as they act politically is relocated to the marketplace and redescribed as the capacity to rationally evaluate an item's exchange value against its use value in the public milieu of the market. (Breslow, 239)

The virtual university certainly meets the conditions of communication and competition necessary for civil society. If anything, the Internet expands upon the potential for communication to occur, unfettered by geographical or temporal boundaries. Similarly, the furor over distance education suggests that it is competitive. However, in fulfilling these criteria, the virtual university buys into what N. Katherine Hayles describes (and decries) as the "systematic devaluation of materiality and embodiment" (48), that is, it abandons the principles of socio-spatial contiguity and density.

There are many who would claim that advances in computer technology, particularly in the form of (text-based) virtual realities, both synchronous and asynchronous, make such an abandonment irrelevant, and even perhaps desirable. Feedback over e-mail can be nearly immediate, and it is indeed possible to conduct discussions in chat rooms and/or MOOspaces, electronic forums that enable a virtual presence on the part of the faculty and students.[8] Although optimism of this sort has been questioned in recent years, the earliest studies of networked classrooms, an important step in the direction of distance education, named such electronic spaces as potentially more egalitarian than their face-to-face counterparts. Whether or not that is an accurate assessment, there is little question that such spaces radically alter the structures of the educational experience. The added anonymity afforded to distance education students, it might be argued, temporarily allows students to escape the restrictions of physical and cultural markers. In short, we might understand contiguity and density not as conditions for civil society but as potential obstacles.

This is not Breslow's assessment of the Internet's potential, however; he argues that "it tends to amplify the sense of isolation" that is a result of the shift toward a "postcivil society." "In this sense," he writes, "the Internet is contributing to the dispersion of the social processes which make up civil society" (254). While there may indeed be "no significant difference" when difference is measured in terms of student performance on examinations, the ability of distance education to provide the same sort of social practice as the residential campus does is questionable at best. Too often, the sheer volume of activity on an e-mail list is taken to represent the type of community building that can take place in face-to-face encounters. Ed Neal elaborated on this problem in an essay for the Winter 1999 issue of *National Forum*:

> If one visits a typical course-discussion board to read the student postings, one finds that the students are not really having a discussion in the traditional sense of give-and-take; instead, they are simply making *sequential position statements*. Often, in response after response, students simply refine their initial position rather than modifying it in the light of what others have written. (43)

Instead of talking to each other, students in such an environment are often simply talking at their screens, and this is a problem in face-to-face courses with asynchronous elements. This reservation would seem to possess even more force in a course where classmates never have the opportunity to meet each other.

As I hope I have demonstrated here, the question of how the virtual university might achieve or supplant the public functions of the traditional university is a complicated one, with no easy answer. Many of these functions can be achieved through distance education, although perhaps not in the form in which we are accustomed to considering them. If the printing press represented a substantial improvement in terms of distribution and access, and made possible the vision of a public sphere governed by autonomous, rational subjects, the Internet may signify a quantum leap toward such goals. In the process, the university's primary contribution to the public sphere may shift from a democratic to a demographic one.

Ultimately, the relationship between education and the public sphere is the site of the paradox I name in my title to this essay. Supporters of the virtual university promise a realization of a particular democratic ideal for education. Yet distance education threatens to erase one of the longest-lasting institutions through which we've worked toward that goal. Some of the players in this game, chiefly administrators and private-sector corporations, see no contradiction here. As Noble suggests, "Some skeptical faculty insist that what they do cannot possibly be automated, and they are right. But it will be automated anyway, whatever the loss in educational quality. Because education, again, is not what this is all about; it's about making money."

For those of us whose first priority is education—those of us who perceive in distance education the kind of paradox I have tried to lay out here—a great deal of work needs to be accomplished in a relatively short time. We must begin to articulate a vision of the university that will compete with the retail or market model that has become pervasive; my sense is that it will be a vision that includes technology without being entirely determined by it. Furthermore, we need to reestablish a sense of public value in education that relies on criteria more concrete than "excellence." And finally, we must develop strategies to avoid the sort of de-skilling and displacement that the influx of technology has created in other industries. The integration of new information technologies into higher education is probably inevitable; how we position ourselves (or allow ourselves to be positioned) with respect to them remains an open question that we must begin to answer.

## NOTES

1. The question of effectiveness in distance education is premature, as there is significant debate as to how to define the term itself. The most general definition is any educational practice that does not require teachers and students to physically be in the same place at the same time. Beyond that general definition, however, distance education is implemented through a wide range of formats, from virtual reality and Internet technologies to the broadcast of videotaped lectures on local access cable television to the more "traditional" correspondence courses.

2. For the sake of convenience, I will be using the word "university" to signify all higher education institutions. I am mindful of the vast differences that can exist among universities, colleges, community colleges, and trade schools, but I would suggest that the issue of distance education creates similar concerns for all of these institutions.

3. While I do not make this argument in the body of the essay, I believe that it will be incredibly difficult to take a middle path toward distance education, for purely economic reasons. Murray Turoff writes that "the U.S. has invested sizable capital into trying to establish local colleges so everyone has easy geographical access" and that this economic infrastructure of higher education will endure "a tremendous long term shakeout." In the rush for market share, I have yet to see a persuasive account of how local economies would recover from a large-scale shift to nonresidential education. In this regard, it might prove instructive to consider those communities whose economic health depended upon military bases that were closed.

4. The degree to which technological context of these requirements has become naturalized is nowhere more clear than in the "controversy" over weighing electronic publications in the decision process for tenure. Despite the potential for a more rigorous process of refereeing, and more active and frequent engagement with a community of scholars, there are still many disciplines that refuse to acknowledge electronic publication as "real."

5. For example, I have not seen work that speculates on the relationship of athletics and academics at a potentially virtual university. The idea of a successful athletic program, which is financially important to many universities, depends upon a large residential population of supportive fans. While the relationship between academics and athletics can suffer from a lack of perspective at times, athletic programs in their own way provide tens of thousands of students with strong incentive for academic performance.

6. As someone who has taught at schools with significant "nontraditional" populations, I consider this argument to be less than persuasive. My evidence for this can only be anecdotal, but I find that students who have to overcome

the "obstacle" of time are often more motivated and ultimately successful than their "traditional" counterparts.

7. There is a sense in which detractors are scapegoating distance education, and I don't wish to contribute to such an argument here. While I find distance education to be symptomatic of the increasing commodification of education, that commodification (as Noble notes) began long before distance education provided a realistic alternative to the traditional university.

8. Here I am collapsing many technologies and techniques for instruction for the sake of convenience, ranging from the synchronous (lectures delivered over television, virtual classrooms/chat rooms) to the asynchronous (lecture notes posted on the World Wide Web, discussions conducted over mailing lists or bulletin boards) and from technologies that now seem commonplace (postal correspondence, radio, television) to those (streaming video, virtual reality) that were barely imaginable ten years ago. It is significant to note that AT&T's "You will" commercials of several years ago were capitalizing on images of distance education (virtual archives and synchronous video courses) long before the concept itself took hold in this country.

## REFERENCES

Bloom, Allan. *The Closing of the American Mind.* New York: Touchstone Books, 1998.

Breslow, Harris. "Civil Society, Political Economy, and the Internet."In Steven G. Jones, ed., *Virtual Culture: Identity and Communication in Cybersociety*, 236–257. Thousand Oaks, Calif.: Sage, 1997.

Carswell, Linda. "The 'Virtual University': Toward an Internet Paradigm?" *ACM SIGCSE Bulletin* 30, no. 3 (September 1998): 46–50. 1 May 1999. http//www.acm.org/pubs/citations/proceedings/cse/282991/p46-carswell/.

Chartier, Roger. *Forms and Meanings: Texts, Performances, and Audiences from Codex to Computer*. Philadelphia: University of Pennsylvania Press, 1995.

De Condorcet, Antoine-Nicolas. *Sketch for a Historical Picture of the Progress of the Human Mind.* Trans. June Barraclough. New York: Noonday Press, 1955.

Derrida, Jacques. *Logomachia: The Conflict of the Faculties*. Ed. Richard Rand. Lincoln: University of Nebraska Press, 1992.

Feenberg, Andrew. "Distance Learning: Promise or Threat? My Adventures in Distance Learning." 1 May 1999. http://www-rohan.sdsu.edu/faculty/feenberg/TELE3.HTM.

Gladieux, Lawrence E., and Watson Scott Swail. *The Virtual University and*

*Educational Opportunity: Issues of Equity and Access for the Next Generation.* Washington, D.C.: College Board, 1999. http://www.collegeboard.org/index_this/policy/html/April.pdf.

Habermas, Jürgen. *The Structural Transformation of the Public Sphere: An Inquiry Into a Category of Bourgeois Society.* Trans. Thomas Burger. Cambridge, Mass.: MIT Press, 1989.

Hayles, N. Katherine. *How We Became Posthuman: Virtual Bodies in Cybernetics, Literature, and Informatics.* Chicago: University of Chicago Press, 1999.

Hirsch, E. D., Jr. *Cultural Literacy: What Every American Needs to Know.* New York: Vintage Books, 1988.

Landow, George P. "Newman and Idea of an Electronic University." In *The Idea of a University, by John Henry Newman.* Ed. Frank Turner. New Haven: Yale University Press, 1996.

Mitchell, William J. *City of Bits: Space, Place, and the Infobahn.* Cambridge, Mass.: MIT Press, 1995.

Neal, Ed. "Distance Education: Prospects and Problems." *National Forum* 79, no. 1 (1999): 40–43.

Noble, David F. "Digital Diploma Mills: The Automation of Higher Education." *virginia.edu* 2, no. 2 (1998): 31 pars. 1 May 1999. http://www.itc.virginia.edu/virginia.edu/fall98/mills/home.html.

——. "Digital Diploma Mills, Part II: The Coming Battle Over On-Line Instruction." *virginia.edu* 2, no. 2 (1998): 26 pars. 1 May 1999. http://www.itc.virginia.edu/virginia.edu/fall98/mills/comments/c23.html.

Phipps, Ronald, and Jamie Merisotis. *What's the Difference? A Review of Contemporary Research on the Effectiveness of Distance Learning in Higher Education.* Washington, D.C.: Institute for Higher Education Policy, 1999. http://www.ihep.com/difference.pdf.

Readings, Bill. *The University in Ruins.* Cambridge, Mass.: Harvard University Press, 1996.

Stallard, Sondra F. [Response to David Noble's "Digital Diploma Mills"]. *virginia.edu* 2, no. 2 (1998): 12 pars. 1 May 1999. http://www.itc.virginia.edu/virginia.edu/fall98/mills/comments/c2.html.

Turoff, Murray. "Alternative Futures for Distance Learning: The Force and the Darkside." 1 May 1999. http://eies.njit.edu/~7Eturoff/Papers/darkaln.html.

*The Virtual University and Educational Opportunity—Issues of Equity and Access for the Next Generation.* College Board. April 1999. 1 May 1999. http://www.collegeboard.org/policy/html/April.pdf.

Wulf, William A. "University Alert: The Information Railroad Is Coming." *virginia.edu* 2, no. 2 (1998): 57 pars. 1 May 1999. http://www.itc.virginia.edu/virginia.edu/fall98/mills/comments/c1.html.

11

# Community-Based Software, Participatory Theater: Models for Inviting Participation in Learning and Artistic Production

SUSAN CLAIRE WARSHAUER

Community-minded software developers and theater artists share a common concern for community representation in learning and artistic production. This concern is evident in the heightened role given to the participant who is asked to contribute to the development of a software environment or a performance event. This essay examines the ExploreNet software program, models of literary narrative and dramatic interaction that it is based on, and a series of participatory performance trends from the 1960s onward. Ultimately, the essay investigates the phenomenon of increased representation of participants in the development process for software environments and theatrical events.

ExploreNet, a multiuser graphical program with a cartoon-like interface, was developed from 1991 to 1994 by Charles Hughes and Michael Moshell at the University of Central Florida (see "ExploreNet™"). The communitarian vision of the ExploreNet developers is conveyed in their desire to include in-school students, terminally ill students who are homebound, senior citizens, and college students and faculty in developing and interacting within an ExploreNet world based on an educational lesson plan. ExploreNet developers work directly with these groups to ensure their participation in the development process. The ExploreNet structure mirrors performance trends in the Americas and Europe from the 1960s onward that have stressed the heightened role of the audience in contributing to the performance event.

Happenings and Theatre of the Oppressed, for example, offer models for involving a community of people in the development of a performance and thereby offer insights to software developers who value community input. Indeed, Happenings have been referred to as precursors of online interaction in computer-generated environments, and they are comparable to ExploreNet in their inclusion of a minimal, pre-made script and involvement from a real-time audience.[1] Likewise, Augusto Boal's Theatre of the Oppressed uses input from a community of people to determine the shape and substance of the theatrical event. Boal uses the concept of the "spect-actor" to illuminate the increased input from the audience member, who should not only view but also participate in acting within the performance.

Community-based software development and participatory theater illustrate similar, graduated levels of involvement for the participant. While community members may be viewers, scriptwriters, and actors in collaborative performance events, they may be Cast Members, World Builders, and Tool Builders in ExploreNet. Although varied levels of interactivity are indicated by these disparate names for participants, the attempt to include people more actively in the development process for software or performance events—at any of these levels—attests to a shift in the balance of power between creator and participant. These parallel shifts can be read as part of a larger refiguring of community-based relations that is founded on a heightened respect for the input of a community of people by software developers and theater artists. This essay concludes with a consideration of how the specific strategies used by ExploreNet developers correlate with the community-based strategies of participatory theater.

## COMMONALITY BASED ON HEIGHTENED AGENCY OF PARTICIPANTS

This study assumes that trends toward more participatory involvement in the development of software environments and in the development of theatrical events are analogous. But what do theater and software have in common as they relate to a community of people? When considering participatory theater as it relates to a community, we may ask the following: who develops the theatrical work, who performs in it, for whom is it performed, where is it performed, and about whom or with what does it deal? For all of these agents or issues, to what extent are they part of or pertinent to a community? The same questions could be asked of software environments for multiple users (multiuser environments).[2] In both instances, we have at base a concern for the agency and representation of the participant. Participatory theater and the development process for ExploreNet worlds have in common an emphasis on the heightened agency of the participant, who should be able to represent herself or himself in the process of creating the production or environment.

Moreover, we may examine the relation of the individual in the software environment to a community of people: To what extent are the developers, participants, and audiences of the software environment part of a community?[3] Do the contents of an online environment relate to topics in a community or emerge from the thoughts of community members?

The concern for community participation in a computer-based simulation environment has infused the ideals of ExploreNet software developers Charles Hughes and Michael Moshell. Hughes and Moshell cast a wide net when they designed ExploreNet to serve in-school and homebound students of all ages (from kindergarten to twelfth grade and college students), faculty, parents, and senior citizens. Most importantly, they aimed to give these people the means to develop their own online "worlds," to break the cycle of passive viewing common in precursors to online media such as television. Their success in achieving this goal will be questioned in this essay, but that they set out to achieve it is at least admirable. A progressive political agenda resonates in the emphasis on a proactive, participatory role for people in ExploreNet worlds who would, according to the plan, be given the means to build their own worlds.[4]

## BACKGROUND ON EXPLORENET

Computer science faculty Charles Hughes and Michael Moshell developed ExploreNet in the SmallTalk programming language between 1991 and 1994 at the University of Central Florida (Hughes and Moshell, "ExploreNet"). A multiuser, two-dimensional graphical program with a cartoon-like interface, ExploreNet runs in Microsoft Windows as a client-server application. I studied ExploreNet version 3.5–014, which is dated 19 June 1997; as of February 2003 no subsequent version had been released.

## Objectives

ExploreNet is designed to support cooperative learning and educational role-playing games. The program is based on constructionist educational theory, which suggests that it is pedagogically productive for students to build "physical, working systems that embody their understandings of relationships" (Moshell, Hughes, and Kilby). According to constructionist learning theory, students should develop superior thinking skills when they build models of software, gadgets, or dramatic reenactments (Moshell and Hughes, "The Virtual Academy: A Simulated Environment").

Original design goals included making ExploreNet simple enough to be used by sixth graders or adults within a minute of using it, enabling it to work on 486 PCs running Windows and having Internet access, and making it sturdy enough to serve as its own authoring environment (Hughes and Moshell, "ExploreNet User's Manual").

The developers of early ExploreNet worlds took their inspiration from African American novelist and folklorist Zora Neale Hurston, and the program has been tested in an elementary school in her hometown of Eatonville, Florida (Moshell and Hughes, "Virtual Communities Experiments"). The character Zora, and scenery based on Hurston's autobiographical writing, appear in several ExploreNet worlds, including Zworld, which is pictured in figure 11.1.

## Virtual Academy

Ultimately, Hughes and Moshell aimed to "facilitate the creation of habitats in which virtual communities of learners and mentors interact" ("Shared Virtual Worlds"). They describe their educational model as the Virtual Academy. In the Virtual Academy model, teachers select the subject area to learn about and multi-age teams of mentors and students codesign and build the world that instantiates this subject in constructionist practice. Moshell, Hughes, and Kilby mention that one

^ if original art is needed, see www.cs.ucf.edu/~ExploreNet

FIGURE 11.1. A screen shot from an ExploreNet world called Zworld (Hughes and Moshell, "ExploreNet™").

"major product of students' work is a collection of virtual worlds intended as learning environments for younger students" ("Virtual Academy: The Educational Model"). Moshell and Hughes write that by students' "taking on responsibility for others' learning, the students would themselves learn more" ("Virtual Communities").

Hughes and Moshell liken the teaching model to that of the Girl Scouts or Boy Scouts: "Under the leadership of teachers and adult volunteers, students learn how to construct virtual worlds that teach specific (teacher-chosen) concepts to other students." They believe that the sense of control gained by students as they develop the worlds will increase their sense of ownership of the work: "The students themselves have a large amount of control over the kinds of situations and simulations that are constructed to convey these concepts. This gives the students an ownership stake in the work. The overall concept is referred to as *The Virtual Academy*" (Hughes and Moshell, "Shared Virtual Worlds").

The Virtual Academy model proposed by ExploreNet developers contrasts with traditional curriculum design by including students in the teacher's process of developing lesson plans. The extent to which students are involved in that process depends on their status within the ExploreNet world. For World Builders, the educational model is more inclusive in its incipient stages—when they make decisions about how to develop the worlds; in contrast, the Guest character who enters into an already existing ExploreNet world has little impact on the process of developing the lesson plan that is conveyed in the world. At the earlier world-building stage, the ExploreNet model could be viewed within a more discussion-based pedagogy that welcomes the World Builder's contributions, thereby allowing a greater sense of agency, unlike the presentational pedagogy that the Guest character experiences when she or he enters an already existing world.

## THE AGENCY OF THE PARTICIPANT

To gauge the extent to which ExploreNet empowers its users to participate and build worlds of their own, it is useful to examine the agency of the users. Any interface or computer-based representational medium that mediates people's interactions with each other through a simulated environment could be evaluated for how the technology situates the agency of the participant. Allucquère Rosanne Stone defines an "interface" as anything across which agency changes form (Lebkowsky, Nathan, and Stone). I abide by this definition in studying ExploreNet as an interface that offers varied options for participants to exercise their agency and have that expression recognized in the design and interaction within the program.

So I am using the term "agency" to refer to one's ability to make choices that have a meaningful impact on circumstances, events, people, avatars, and representations in an environment. For example, participants with a heightened sense of agency in a multiuser environment would feel that the choices they make affect the contents and potential narratives within the environment. The choices offered to people include their communication, representation, and navigation options, and these options are made meaningful by the response that people receive from the other people/avatars and the interface of the environment.

Moreover, agency relates to the extent to which one feels oneself to be present within a responsive environment, which is associated with the concept of interactivity. Because varied levels of interactivity exist in ExploreNet, varied levels of agency are available to its users. Two main levels of interactivity are evident:

- participating in the existing "world": communicating, navigating, acting, representing self, and having actions or input in the environment responded to graphically and textually within the environment.
- building the "world": contributing graphical characters, dramatic story line, scenery, dialogue, or even the software tools themselves that are used to build the worlds.

In this study, I will focus mainly on the Guest character, who is interactive on the level of participating in an existing world. I will also examine the narrative structure, the dramatic form, and the interface of ExploreNet in order to shed light on how the narrative and dramatic model of the program and its visual design affect the agency and interactive experience of the participant.

## LEVELS OF AUTHORSHIP, LEVELS OF AGENCY

The extent to which one feels a sense of agency in determining the narrative or scene elements in ExploreNet is related to one's role in the development process for the world. Likewise, programs such as HyperCard articulate discrete user roles that range from browsing to authoring and programming. Using HyperCard as an illustration, Espen Aarseth points out the hierarchical stratification in classes of users and developers of software:

> For the developers of Hypercard, I am a user. However, if I use Hypercard to write an application, I too am a developer—but on a lower level. . . . The end users . . . might also be differentiated by their ability to change or subvert the software. . . . And so we have both user strata and developer strata, overlapping each other but still in a hierarchical relationship. (174)

Aarseth's framework is analogous to the various levels of participation and authorship in ExploreNet, whose designers make explicit the distinctions among four levels of involvement: Guest, Cast Member, World Builder, and Tool Builder.

Moshell, Hughes, and Kilby explain that when a school joins ExploreNet, students become Guests in the world, meeting live human Cast Members who play roles in the world to enhance the simulation; finally, as they gain experience, they become Cast Members and World Builders themselves ("Virtual Academy: The Educational Model"). The World Builders script new worlds in which others can participate, and finally, the Tool Builders build tools with which to build the worlds.

## NARRATIVE AUTHORITY AND NARRATIVE STRUCTURE IN EXPLORENET WORLDS

These varied roles and levels of participation are implicit in the narrative structure in ExploreNet worlds. In three ExploreNet worlds—EggQuest, Autoland, and CAETI—a mentor figure (who is played by a Cast Member) is used to guide participants through the narrative (I studied six ExploreNet worlds that were downloadable from the ExploreNet site as of February 2003: Autoland, CAETI, Carland, Dinosaur, EggQuest, and Zworld). The objective in EggQuest is to locate and boil eggs, and Wise, the helpful owl, helps the participant in this scenario. The "mentor" figure who plays Wise is an experienced student or teacher (Hughes and Moshell, "Shared Virtual Worlds"). In Autoland, a character named Mentor helps "open the gates for learners" (written in the Mentor's online description); the Mentor assists participants who work collaboratively to gather resources to build a car. In the CAETI world, a dinosaur named Bronto offers assistance to Guests.

In these instances, the mentor figure occupies a dual position as both a character within the world who interacts in real time with Guests and Cast Members and the narrator who in fact knows the world's narrative before the quest has begun. I am using the term "narrative" here to describe all allowable actions in the world and the sequence of events that is necessary to achieve particular outcomes.[5] While being there to provide basic assistance like a human help file, the mentor figure also gives participants hints about the actions necessary to attain desired goals.

In addition to the narrative authority vested in an online mentor figure in these three ExploreNet worlds, the role of a guide figure is alluded to in the online informational files in worlds such as Carland: "Ask your guide how to pick something up" (Pathway description in Carland). In the Dinosaur world, Zora, the only human among the dinosaurs, is also described as a "God-like character who controls the coming of night and day" (written in the world description when one selects the textual title for Dinosaur world).

The presence of such a guide figure is further supported by the ExploreNet developers' philosophy of guiding newcomers through the various worlds via real-time human assistance, whether in the form of an online guide or a guide in the physical-space room in which students are logged on to ExploreNet.[6] So narrative authority is vested in these mentor figures who interact in real time, online or in physical space, with others who visit the environment. At the same time, because the story is constructed ahead of time by the World Builders, a layer of narrative authority is effaced; the presence of the scene elements, characters, and precoded responses is taken as a given when one logs on.

Thus, the programmers and World Builders constitute part of the narrative authority but the results of their work are seen asynchronously; in the real-time show, they remain hidden behind the curtain. It is possible for the Mentor character to be played by one of the World Builders, but this is not always the case; at any rate, the mentor figure possesses a different type of narrative authority than the programmer/World Builder, whose implied values, images, and messages must come across asynchronously rather than in real time.

For instance, if you click on the lantern object in Zworld, a pop-up menu will allow you to select the option "Information About Lantern," which offers the text file: "This lantern is used in the EggQuest world to . . . wait! We shouldn't give away the story line just yet! This lantern is useful. Let's just say that much right now." A story line is set in advance by the world developers and communicated asynchronously to the participant through hints and scenery items such as these.

Another instance in the Dinosaur world illustrates how the adventures of Guests are centered around the exploration and discovery of a preexisting script. If you are the dinosaur named Icet and you click on the dinosaur named Bigfoot, a pop-up menu (referred to as an action menu in ExploreNet) will open up, which allows you to select "Attack

This Dinosaur." After selecting this textual description of an action, a series of prewritten responses scrolls on the screen:

> BIGFOOT We try the raptorDefense [*sic*]
> BIGFOOT "Quit picking on me!"
> ICET I like to Win!

The words of your own character, IceT, are displayed across the screen without your writing them; words are put into your mouth. Your agency as a participant in the environment is reduced to selecting a precoded action and viewing the ensuing responses. Ultimately, you are enacting someone else's script.

In fact, the integral role of the mentor/narrator figure in these ExploreNet worlds replicates the narrator common in a work of prose fiction who knows in advance about a story and speaks with authority about what happens. I emphasize the mentor/narrator so much because reliance on this role keeps ExploreNet worlds from being as collaboratively developed through improvisational input as they could be. For the goals of having participants develop and teach lesson plans, however, this narrator role may be appropriate. The issue is this: at what stage of the development process does the designer want the participant to be most interactive? In the end, what needs to be considered is the delicate, strategic balance between interactivity and narrativity that must be struck to suit the aims of designers and/or participants of an environment.

Janet Murray, in *Hamlet on the Holodeck: The Future of Narrative in Cyberspace*, and Marie-Laure Ryan, in "Interactive Drama: Narrativity in a Highly Interactive Environment," have both noted the tension between narrativity and interactivity. Murray remarks on the tensions between author and participants in online environments that are both participatory and authored: "There will always be a trade-off between a world that is more given (more authored from the outside . . .) and a world that is more improvised (and therefore closer to individual fantasies)" (267).

To address the trade-off between controlled authoring and decentralized improvisation, Murray encourages "stories that are goal driven enough to guide navigation but open-ended enough to allow free exploration and that display a satisfying dramatic structure no matter how the interactor chooses to traverse the space" (134–135). Likewise,

Ryan formulates the concept of interactive drama to describe a genre of virtual reality applications that also balances the interactive options of the participant with a controlled environment. Ryan states that the classical spirit of interactive drama is the "opportunity to act within the constraints of a controlled environment" (703).

Moreover, Ryan describes a series of narrative structures for interactive dramas that involve different combinations of interactivity and system-designed narrativity; the combination of these elements is key to the success of such works. Ryan remarks that a "rewarding interactive experience . . . requires the integration of the bottom-up input of the user into the top-down design of the storyteller" (683). It is important to note that in Ryan's articulation of roles, the user and the storyteller are in distinctly different places, unlike in ExploreNet, in which classes of characters are separate but a fluid movement from one role to another is expected. In fact, Ryan faults the open-ended MOO environments for being insufficiently directive, even though the collaborative, improvisational aspects of MOOs are the reasons some participants like them so much. Ryan finds that MOOs "fail to provide narrative guidance," whereas interactive drama offers a script (682). Ryan supports the use of such a script since it "limits the freedom of the user, but it also maximizes the chances of a pleasurable performance" (682). So, too, ExploreNet would seem to offer such a script in its prewritten narratives.

Similarly, Murray emphasizes the narrative side of the balance between narrativity and interactivity by stressing the continued importance of the authorial role: "We like to know that there is a ruling power in control of an imaginary universe, and it makes us uncomfortable if the author seems to abdicate the role" (275). Precisely what role an author should take, however, is figured differently in various online environments.[7]

So both Murray and Ryan support maintaining some measure of narrative authority—almost as a bulwark against the threat of descending into the chaos of a fully improvisational online environment with a less clearly structured set of activities. Similarly, Moshell and Hughes, in supporting the development of educational lesson plans in ExploreNet—based on teacher-originated topics—ensure that participation by students does not derail the ultimate plans set out by the teacher. Input is asked for but in a measured way.

In the conceptualization of the current ExploreNet model of developing and teaching a lesson plan, developers seem to err too much on the side of controlling the narrative for the new Guest character. Given the goal of promoting the Guest to the role of World Builder, however, this could be compensated for (the Guest could gain agency at a later stage) once the Guest moves into roles higher up in the food chain. If the Guest character could truly move into the World Builder role with greater ease, if the identity categories were in fact more fluid in ExploreNet, then the asynchronous form of traditional story creation would not necessarily obstruct community participation. Because of the limitations of the current ExploreNet interface and the Guest's inability to gain sufficient agency to build her or his own world, however, the Guest remains in a somewhat traditional paradigm of guessing about someone else's story line—guessing what the moral or objective of the lesson plan may be, with the narrator-mentor standing in for the figure with superior knowledge. Unless the transition between roles can become more fluid, the current ExploreNet model will not serve the ultimate goals of ExploreNet developers to allow a group of participants greater agency in developing worlds.

Thus, given a spectrum of narrative authority ranging from a narrator who is in control of the story to no narrator in control of the story (in which case participants would sculpt and direct their own interactive fiction), one can identify a layering of narrative authority in the preexisting ExploreNet worlds that are accessible to people who download the program. The function of conveying a story in these ExploreNet worlds is divided between a visible real-time mentor figure and the offstage programmers/World Builders who work ahead of time to develop the world and its narrative possibilities. The programmers/World Builders are similar to the playwright and scene designers for a well-made play with a tight plot.

The potential for interactivity in ExploreNet and other multiuser environments—for inviting the input of a community of people in real time—is constrained by the perceived need for narrative control by literary theorists such as Ryan and Murray. My study of narrative authority in ExploreNet worlds indicates a similar desire among developers to encourage storymaking by drawing from a traditional realm of literary and dramatic creation, which I call asynchronous narrative development (presenting a narrative developed at one time to an audience at a future time, when the audience is not involved in the making of the pre-set narrative).

## ASYNCHRONOUS NARRATIVE DEVELOPMENT

Indeed, developers of ExploreNet worlds work according to a model of asynchronous narrative development, which is coded into a world, hinted at by mentor figures if they are part of the world and (hopefully) discovered by participants.

Although ExploreNet developers have mentioned how they are inspired by multiuser virtual environments such as Habitat, they have in fact modeled the narrative structure of the worlds that have been thus far developed according to the asynchronous development and delivery of print-based stories or plays.[8] (Habitat is a multiuser, graphical role-playing game developed in the mid-1980s by LucasFilm; see Morningstar and Farmer for background). The author or writer develops the story or play ahead of time, and at a designated future time, the reader/participant/interactor has the opportunity to experience it, with varying degrees of assistance in discovering the workings of the pre-made narrative.

Yet a precedent for this provisionally settled narrative structure (varying only according to the order of events or the straying from the plotline by online participants) may be found not only in print-based stories but also in computer games and game-playing MUDs (such as LP and Diku MUDs; MUD stands for Multi-User Domain or Dungeon). Like their print-based predecessors, game-playing MUDs have built-in, pre-defined narrative structures. Based on such settled narrative structures, ExploreNet worlds do not take full advantage of the improvisational potential of more collaborative online storymaking and interaction found in another subset of MUDs called TinyMUDs (with the most popular type of TinyMUDs being TinyMOOs, abbreviated as MOOs [MUDs Object Oriented]).

To clarify the types of narratives found in ExploreNet worlds, I have found it helpful to use graphical models. Chaim Gingold has proposed a black box metaphor for describing multiuser narrative design:

> A black box represents a story topology, interpersonal relationship, or mechanical machine to be explored by multiple users. This box represents an informational constraint, because neither user can see directly inside the box, but both users can experiment with its external behavior. This informational constraint implies a narrative progression between the black box and user. Traversal

of the story topology or discovery of the machine mechanics is equivalent to unraveling a narrative. (4)

In Gingold's depiction of multiuser narrative design, two users have knowledge of part of the world, partial information about the narrative, but they must explore further and collaborate or communicate to fill out the picture of the whole narrative.

Gingold's model would describe the narrative of an ExploreNet world in which no mentor is needed but the interactive story mandates cooperation between players in order to proceed toward a goal.

Although the developer of the narrative could be assumed to be in another area of the picture in figure 11.2, I find it helpful to add this

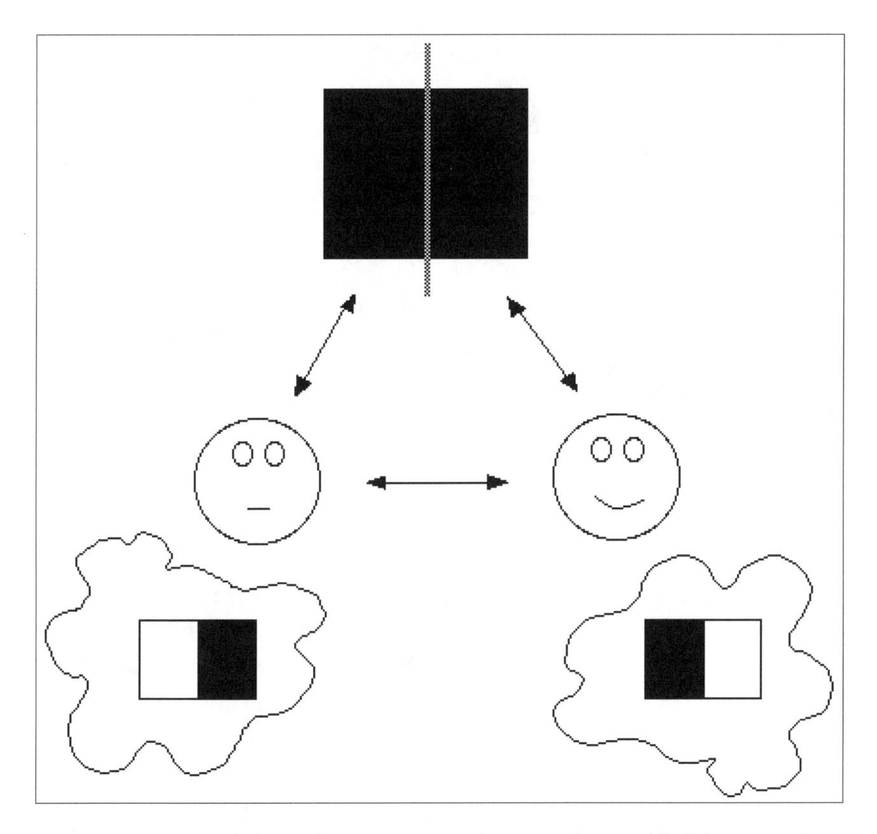

FIGURE 11.2. A model of multiuser narrative design, utilizing a black box metaphor, by Chaim Gingold.

representation to model the offstage or onstage role of the developer and/or narrator, since these roles are especially prevalent in the narratives of ExploreNet worlds. The shifting circular figure that I add below (figure 11.3) represents the offstage narrative developer at the top, the combined developer/online narrator character in the middle, and the fully online mentor figure in the circle within the box.

The vertical, shifting circular figures describe the varied locations (in relation to the online user) of those who are vested with narrative authority. In the combined developer/online narrator figure in the middle, with a half circle drawn above the box and a half circle drawn within the box, I indicate that the same individual who develops the narrative before the real-time interaction online—and who thus stands outside of the box—is also playing the role of narrator (or mentor in ExploreNet) in the real-time interaction with the participant—and is thereby also represented within the box.

Figure 11.3, when the narrator is fully within the box, models the narrative design of ExploreNet worlds such as EggQuest and Autoland, which are designed for a mentor figure to be online when Guests interact there. In addition, all predesigned narratives could include the figure of the developer in the circle that is fully outside and above the box.

## EMERGENT NARRATIVE STRUCTURE

Yet if the term "asynchronous narrative structure" describes the process of developing narratives in existing ExploreNet worlds such as EggQuest and Autoland, how might one characterize narrative structure in environments such as Habitat and MOO, which I have contrasted with ExploreNet?

Habitat and MOOs provide the platform for an "emergent narrative structure," which is developed collaboratively, either synchronously or asynchronously, by multiple users. To the extent that there is a narrative or story line, it is not typically pre-known by outside agents, and no one character has a view of the ultimate story line. Rather, each of them contributes to interactions that could be labeled "narrative," and the precise story line or dramatic interaction that emerges is dependent on the way those contributions build onto and merge into each other.

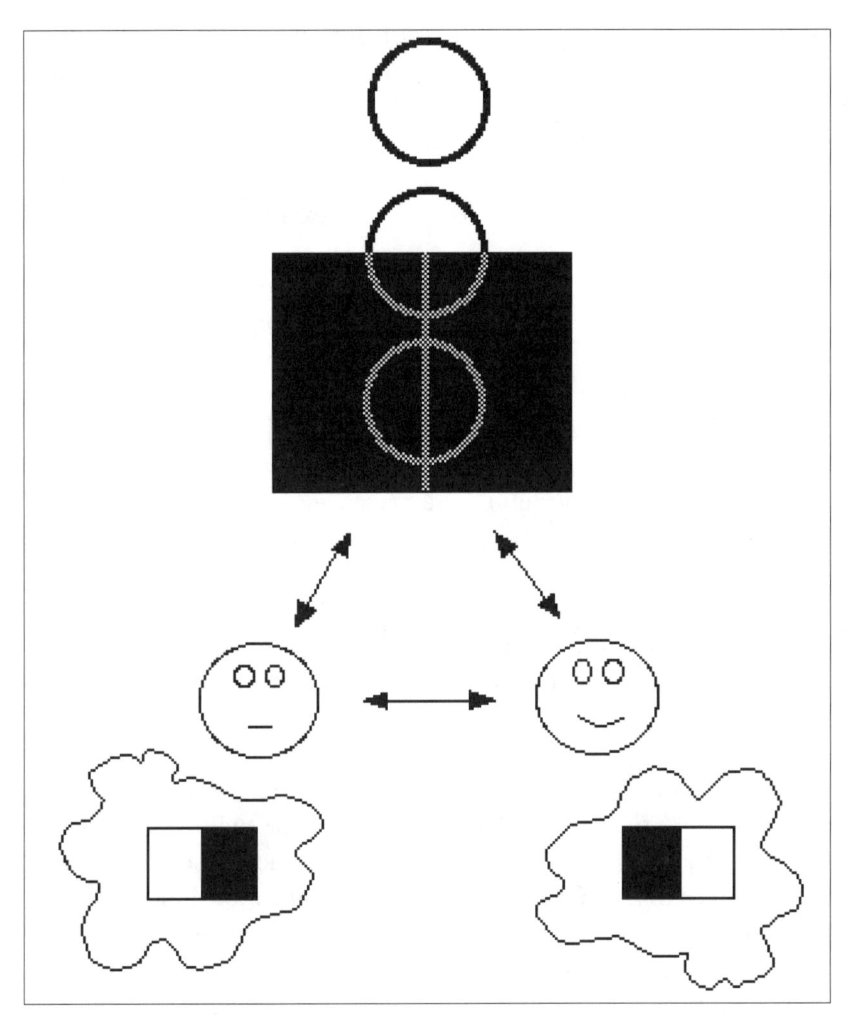

FIGURE 11.3. A model of multiuser narrative design with narrative authority represented, based on Chaim Gingold's narrative design model. Narrative authority figures added by Susan Warshauer.

It would be helpful to have a graphical model that could describe multiuser narrative design, which is emergent and collaboratively developed. One such model could simply replicate the smiley-face figures in the original black box picture in figure 11.2, such that we see multiple people with partial awareness of an overall narrative in the making.

But is collaborative, emergent narrative structure preferable to pre-scripted narrative? The decision to use a pre-set narrative is not in itself problematic, although one might interpret it as such if viewing ExploreNet worlds from the perspective of the new Guest. It would seem that new Guests don't have as much agency as others to determine the story line, lesson plan, identity, and visual representation of the characters; potentially, this could decrease motivation to participate in the environment.

The essential roles of the "super-teacher," the online mentor, and ExploreNet developers who do onsite training suggest the top-heavy reliance on technical and instructional expertise to facilitate the process of showing students how to develop their own worlds. The process of learning about ExploreNet and developing a world is constantly mediated by the expert strata of teachers and students who have been trained to have sufficient background. The presence of students in the strata that might have formerly been relegated only to teachers is indeed innovative, but a fundamental shift to a more discussion-based pedagogy and a literary or dramatic form that reflects such pedagogy is not evident. For the purpose of teaching and developing specific lesson plans within a presentational framework, however, ExploreNet provides a valuable platform.

Overall, abiding by a traditional model of asynchronous literary production (the text—or play—is developed at one time and read, seen, or experienced at a future time), ExploreNet offers the audience member or Guest the least amount of input into the production process; one must reach the position of Cast Member, World Builder, or Tool Builder to have more input.[9] To gain another perspective on participating in ExploreNet, we should consider its dramatic elements. In the same way that a literary paradigm based on models of asynchronous and synchronous, emergent narrative offers insight into ExploreNet, dramatic models based on asynchronous and synchronous, collaborative theater-making extend this analysis to shed further light on ExploreNet worlds.

## DRAMATIC MODEL

When Guests and Cast Members in the ExploreNet world are invited to play the role of predesigned characters whose visual representation and names are not alterable, they are invited to interact in the world but at arm's length. To people familiar with the customizable characters of other multiuser environments, such as Habitat, MOOs, Microsoft Chat 2.1 (comic view), and Microsoft V-Chat, the agency of the ExploreNet characters seems limited.

On a dramatic level, people's identification with the character in ExploreNet is similar to that in a play produced according to theatrical realism, in which a fourth wall separates audience and performer. In theatrical realism, the audience is supposed to be peeking in from behind an invisible fourth wall and the performers are ostensibly unaware of the audience's presence (see Worthen). The audience should get lost in the illusion of the onstage action by identifying with an already existing character.[10] For example, in ExploreNet one may be either Zora or Jake in Zworld. As Jake, one plays a dog. As Zora, one plays "the role of a nine year old girl named Zora" (Hughes and Moshell, "Using ExploreNet," 2). The look, age, and name of the Zora character are prescribed.

It is critical to note that the descriptions of all the existing worlds offered to the reader begin with "This world is inhabited by . . . " and then list a series of characters, from Zora and a dog named Zeke in Zworld to a worker named John in Autoland. What's not listed is "you," since to participate in the world, you must log in as a preexisting character. Thus, Guests and Cast Members who do not participate directly in developing a world could use more options to express themselves within their roles; customizable names and visual representations would help in this process.

In addition, the description of scenes might be amended for real-time input by a Guest character. Built into the ExploreNet interface is a button with the name of the current scene; the button is located on the top button bar and provides a pre-set description of the scene. In future development, to enhance the interactive potential of the environment to register the marks of multiple users, it would be useful to have a comparable text area that could be manipulable or extensible by other users who could leave their own mark on the environment by describing the scene themselves.[11]

Adding such options to allow Guests to provide their own scene descriptions and customize their names and visual representations would subvert the aesthetic of theatrical realism that keeps the audience at arm's length in affecting the onstage events. Theatrical realism is suited for a passive audience that sits in its seats. In contrast, an aesthetic of greater involvement and self-representation would enhance the interactive component of an online multiuser environment.

An assessment of the roles that participants play in the dramatic environment of ExploreNet must take into account the particular status of the contributor, from Guest to World Builder. Moshell and Hughes acknowledge the varied levels of interactivity allowed in the life cycle of the ExploreNet world and in different types of worlds and story lines. Moshell, Hughes, and Kilby describe how Guests may play a bit part in a drama and have no ability to change the storyline, how they may then move to a Quest and to an Exploratory world, and finally experience the construction of a world ("Virtual Academy: The Educational Model").

The agency of the participant is increased as Guests progress through the different player classes: "Quests are like railroads; there is a hidden 'right track' of ordered events, along which you proceed. You have at most a limited amount of control over the world's state." In exploratory worlds, participants have a goal but little guidance. Finally, Moshell, Hughes, and Kilby describe the "most interactive kind of experience" in the "construction of worlds" and state that "World builders progress from the guided construction of objects or worlds someone else designed, through the design of parts of objects and worlds, up to the design of whole worlds."

To meet the goals of ExploreNet's developers to involve players and enhance the beginning player's sense of immersion and presence, I would encourage developers of multiuser environments to increase the agency of the new participant earlier in the development cycle, during the real-time event whenever possible. While some agency will be deferred until sufficient skills are developed, a dramatic experience in real time will be enhanced by added options to express oneself and affect others and an environment. Such a move would also be consistent with modern performance art and performance trends that foreground the identity and expression of self of the performer (Carlson, 150–151).

## ASYNCHRONOUS THEATER PRODUCTION

The dramatic model I have associated with ExploreNet so far is asynchronous theater production, which has a distinct development and rehearsal stage followed by a presentational stage. ExploreNet developers, working with a group of participants, come up with a scenario for a world, and at a subsequent time an audience experiences the world; the irony is that the production is occurring in an environment that lends itself to collaborative real-time role-playing and storymaking.

While the development of an ExploreNet world is reminiscent of an asynchronous development cycle for a theatrical production, the interactive elements of the real-time ExploreNet event are suggestive of Happenings.

## HAPPENINGS

A performance movement of the late 1960s and the 1970s, Happenings are occasionally referred to as precursors of online interaction in multiuser environments, but such references are all too often clouded by generalizations about improvisation, collaboration, and non-scripted interaction.

In fact, the current version of ExploreNet is similar to a Happening because of its inclusion of a pre-made script as well as the limited involvement it offers to the real-time audience. Visual artist and "Happening" maker Allan Kaprow wrote in 1977 that most of the early Happenings were not in fact "participatory" and that the "artist was the creator and director, initiating audiences into the unique rites of the pieces" (*Essays*, 183–184).

Kaprow notes: "What was unusual for art was that people were to take part, were to be, literally, the ingredients of the performances. Hence instruction in participation had to be more explicit than in communal performances" (*Essays*, 184). Indeed, Kaprow seems to respect the agency of the participants by forecasting what they should do in the event:

> I think that it is a mark of mutual respect that all persons involved in a Happening be willing and committed participants who have a clear idea what they are to do. This is simply accomplished by writing out the scenario or score for all and discussing it thoroughly with them beforehand. In this respect it is not different from the preparations for a parade, a football match, a wedding, or religious service. It is not even different from a play.
>
> ("Excerpts," 240)

Kaprow, coming from a visual arts background, emphasizes how the innovation of the happening related to a more dynamic, interactive relationship between an observer and an art object. He indicates that the new aspect that people were not used to was the "real-time close physicality of the experience. They were accustomed to paintings and sculptures viewed from a distance" (*Essays*, 184).

Moving beyond the Happening in a theatrically innovative sense would involve moving into theatrical forms that emphasize improvisational and collaborative elements and a heightened agency for the real-time participant. MOOs and Habitat offer a fine model for such interaction within an online multiuser environment, and physical-space theater paradigms—in community-based theater—offer additional insights.

## COMMUNITY-BASED THEATER IN THE UNITED STATES

Theater may be "community-based"[12] in terms of:

- its content (the subjects it deals with)
- who develops its content and the production
- who performs in it
- where it is performed
- for whom it is performed
- methodology with which it is produced (such as participatory methodologies)

A classic example of community-based theater in the United States would be the Krigwas Players, formed in 1926 by W. E. B. DuBois to produce plays "about Negroes, by Negroes, for Negroes, and near Negroes" (Hatch, 773).

While mainstream, commercial theater also emerges from a particular community, it is not typically referred to as community-based, although the group of moderate- to high-income, Caucasian, middle-aged and older theatergoers from a similar geographical area could constitute a community. More often, community-based theater is perceived as an alternative to an elite form of mainstream theater and is frequently associated with activist theater that is oppositional to the political status quo; it may also emerge from identity-based communities of people who are in some manner marginal to other mainstream communities.

Community-based, activist theater from the 1970s onward in the United States, for example, includes the San Francisco Mime Troupe, El Teatro Campesino, the Free Southern Theatre, Bread and Puppet, and theater emerging from the women's, lesbian and gay, Asian, black, Native American, and Latino communities (some of which overlaps with the companies mentioned). This type of community-based theater, which included street theater and political theater, dealt with the civil rights movement, the anti–Vietnam War movement, the women's liberation movement, and union organizing, among other issues. In addition, by utilizing street theater in public protest events, groups such as ACT UP (AIDS Coalition to Unleash Power), which has emerged from the gay and lesbian and political activist communities, have continued the tradition of social change theater in the United States in the 1980s and 1990s. Overall, these community-based activist theater groups have developed a tradition of supporting social change through theatrical work in the United States that is parallel to a tradition of political theater in Augusto Boal's Theatre of the Oppressed in Brazil and other countries.

Moreover, one strand of community-based theater involves participatory theater methodologies in conjunction with an emphasis on the themes or context of a community.[13] Examining participatory strategies to involve a group of people in telling or acting their own stories should offer insights into designing interactivity in ExploreNet and other multiuser environments.

A number of different community-based theater groups have used participatory methods to involve an audience in an improvisational or collaborative way so that they have a fundamental impact on the direction of a performance. The following discussion surveys several types of community-based participatory theater that have in common a concern for turning spectators into active participants, for having a theatrical performance that springs from the interests and concerns of its participatory audience.

Theater designed to activate a community to tell its own stories includes Maryat Lee's EcoTheater, an indigenous Appalachian theater that has been active from the 1970s to the present and draws on local material for a performance (oral history or stories from the performers themselves, presented in the vernacular of the community). EcoTheater performances are followed by a discussion with the audience that sometimes lasts longer than the performance itself (French, 49–51). William French describes EcoTheater as a "simple, effective way of encouraging people to tell their stories and showing them ways to do it effectively" (74). For example, according to French, Lee advises those who interview people in a community to keep an open mind, since a person "may not want to tell you the story you're after, but they will probably come up with something even more valuable" (76). Other scripts emerge from improvisation after a group of people is asked questions about a community event such as a mine disaster or a flood (78). At the same time, this form of theater requires a "leader" for the seed groups; also referred to as the "playwright-director," the leader gathers a group of people, organizes the collection of oral histories and other material, and directs rehearsals. The group of performers may represent their stories directly (similar to World Builders in ExploreNet) or elicit them from other community members. The EcoTheater company comprises local, untrained nonprofessionals, so it is participatory in involving a community in both developing and performing its material.

Similarly, the International Playback Theater Network works with communities to elicit stories and play the stories back in dramatic form to encourage discussion and understanding about conflicts and common issues. Operating since the 1980s, the network has theater companies in the United States, England, Germany, Russia, India, Japan, Australia, and other countries.

Other community-based, participatory theater groups involve additional improvisational elements. The Living Stage Theatre Company in Washington, D.C., has since 1966 pioneered the use of improvisational theater in local community settings to encourage progressive social change. Affiliated with Arena Stage as a multiracial community outreach program, the Living Stage offers workshops for youth and adults who typically lack such opportunities. At the Living Stage, professional actors guide participants, who become immersed in the improvisational theater process and draw on material from their lives, including topics related to violence, poverty, racism, and substance abuse. Programs aim to "empower . . . [participants] to express themselves and to gain the self-confidence to explore new solutions to real life problems" (Living Stage).

Moreover, a valuable set of theater exercises related to participatory community-based theater is contained in Michael Rohd's Hope Is Vital theater program, and specifically his training manual, *Theatre for Community, Conflict and Dialogue: The Hope Is Vital Training Manual.* Rohd describes Hope Is Vital as community-based "because it's non-self-identified performers or artists coming together within a context of some commonality or common interest and making theater" (Rohd, personal interview). Influenced by a tradition of improvisational theater in the United States, particularly Viola Spolin's improvisational theater games, Rohd developed Hope Is Vital as a "community dialogue and outreach program that . . . uses theatre to work with youth and adults around social issues such as violence, HIV/AIDS, substance abuse, and diversity" (Rohd, "A Summer Hope Is Vital Institute"). Hope Is Vital workshops explore specific issues that are determined by community members, with the ultimate aim of using artistic expression to heighten people's awareness about how to solve problems, communicate better, and develop self-esteem.

Most important for its role as a participatory methodology that could be applied to the development of ExploreNet and other multi-user-environment worlds, Hope Is Vital offers exercises that encourage group work and elicit "activating material" (which forms the substance of performances) from workshop participants. By using improvisation and group work, Hope Is Vital workshops result in participants' developing stories based on their experiences and improvising to alter story lines to explore varied issues. For example, in group "Sculpting" exercises, which are used in Hope Is Vital, Living Stage, and Theatre of the Oppressed workshops, people gather in small groups, tell each other true stories about a group-determined topic such as discrimination or family and miscommunication, develop a single group image with their bodies that unites the themes from the stories (and complete this without speaking), and then develop an "activating scene" with speaking characters that is based on the image (Rohd, *Theatre*, 105–106). The point of many such exercises is to create a group fiction from individual truths so that people can integrate true stories from their lives into an imaginative group vision that generalizes beyond their individual experiences to give them perspective on these situations.

Other activating material for discussions emerges from improvisational means. For example, in a "Line Improv" exercise used in the Living Stage and Hope Is Vital, people form two lines that face each other and are given a relationship and an intention, such as siblings going to the same high school, one of whom believes the other has a substance abuse problem and plans to tell the parents unless the other goes to the school counselor that day (Rohd, *Theatre*, 86–88). The facilitator for the workshop asks participants to approach each other and improvise a conversation to explore the challenges of discerning whether someone has a substance abuse problem and how to address this issue. Some of the pairs may volunteer to present their specific scenario before the whole group, and people may discuss whether the conversation seems realistic, or they may substitute in for one of the characters to suggest other ways of handling a situation. In eliciting activating material, Hope Is Vital aims to develop scenes that pose questions rather than deliver answers.

Although Rohd's work also includes exercises drawn from Boal's Theatre of the Oppressed, it is important to note that Rohd's participatory theater methods and those of others are as indigenous to the United States as similar methods are to other countries. At the same time, theater artists working in participatory, improvisational theater gain insight from each other's work, particularly in an international context with increased telecommunications capabilities in the late 1990s. Moreover, because of the pervasive influence of Boal's principles of participatory theater on international theater trends, software designers who are interested in participatory, community input may also gain valuable insights from examining the activities and principles of his Theatre of the Oppressed.

## THEATRE OF THE OPPRESSED

As a model of physical-space theater, the Theatre of the Oppressed offers a helpful paradigm for the type of enhanced agency that participants enjoy in MOOs and Habitat—a type of involvement that ExploreNet designers hoped their players would achieve.[14]

The influence of theater artist Augusto Boal on political theater in the Americas and Europe in the late twentieth and early twenty-first centuries is akin to that of Bertolt Brecht in his time. Boal coins the term "spect-actor" to refer to the active spectator who takes part in the action (Boal, *Games*, xxiv). According to Boal, the spectator who is not allowed to act is "less than a man" and is someone "on whom the theater has imposed finished visions of the world" (*Theatre of the Oppressed*, 155). The Theatre of the Oppressed offers two fundamental principles—that "spect-actors must be the protagonists of the dramatic action" and that they "must prepare themselves to be the protagonists of their own lives" (Boal, *Games*, 242).

Moreover, Boal's Theatre of the Oppressed "asks questions without dictating the answers . . . it involves a process of learning together rather than one-way teaching; it assumes that there is as much likelihood of the audience knowing the answers as the performers" (*Games*, xxi). To the extent that Theatre of the Oppressed counteracts "one-way teaching," it is aligned with a discussion-based pedagogy in contrast to a presentational pedagogy. Instead of preaching to people, Theatre of the Oppressed should transform people into spect-actors who not only observe but also act.

Boal's theater aims for social change that will be carried into real life beyond the aesthetic experience, beyond the presentation of a narrative with a settled story line and ending. Boal stresses that a session of the Theatre of the Oppressed should never end because

> the objective of the Theatre of the Oppressed is not to close a cycle, to generate a catharsis, or to end a development. On the contrary, its objective is to encourage autonomous activity, to set a process in motion, to stimulate transformative creativity, to change spectators into protagonists. (Boal, *Games*, 245)

Boal is not interested in replicating an Aristotelian catharsis in which audience members pity a character and fear that they might experience the same plight as the character they identify with, but feel relief that the character has undergone the experience in place of themselves. Boal would argue that such a catharsis relieves the audience members of the need to act.

In contrast, to the extent that there is a catharsis in Theatre of the Oppressed, it is intended to purge people of the obstacles to taking action, thereby emphasizing even more strongly their agency and their ability to represent themselves and participate in society and politics. For example, in Forum theater (a type of Theatre of the Oppressed), participants perform a story that they have collaboratively developed and interrupt the action repeatedly by adjusting dialogue, movement, or scene elements to achieve a type of behavioral interaction that they find satisfying or expressive of their feelings. They are empowered to develop and then to alter a role-playing scenario until it is meaningful to them.

So Theatre of the Oppressed produces the desire to step in and change the course of action rather than to passively accept a dictated story line. Boal explains that the poetics of the oppressed, which he also calls the poetics of liberation, focuses on the action that emanates from the spectator:

> The spectator delegates no power to the character (or actor) either to act or to think in his place; on the contrary, he himself assumes the protagonic role, changes the dramatic action, tries out solutions, discusses plans for change—in short, trains himself for real action. (*Theatre of the Oppressed*, 122, 155)

Similarly, were ExploreNet or other software programs to model their worlds on Theatre of the Oppressed's Forum theater, participants would be given greater agency to develop and perform a story line or lesson plan in real-time as well as to spontaneously rework this story line or lesson as they see fit. Participants would not be playing the role of an existing character but would be representing themselves.

While the Theatre of the Oppressed aims toward participatory, real-time collaboration and contributions from "spect-actors" to constitute a performance event, the real-time interaction in an existing ExploreNet world is less open-ended. However, the earlier stages of developing an ExploreNet world (before it is placed online as a finished product) do offer the possibility of enhanced agency and contributions from a group of people to determine the content of a world and how it will convey educational material. Yet significant obstacles to realizing the potential of building an ExploreNet world remain. By articulating these obstacles, and potentially having them addressed in future versions of ExploreNet, we may be able to enhance people's agency in the program.

## INTERFACE

A significant obstacle to building in ExploreNet and similar multiuser environments resides in the limitations of the interface. The potential of real-time communication to add to the narrative and serve pedagogical purposes is not fully realized. The interface could better foreground communication options in a number of ways, by

- making the text input area larger
- putting a blinking cursor in the text input window
- leaving more than three dialogue segments onscreen simultaneously to enhance the conversational flow
- having real-time communication play a more integral role in the narrative
- standardizing the placement of the text output for the "say" commands (currently, the word bubble is placed unpredictably in different parts of the screen)
- clarifying visually how to communicate in a "say" command, and
- altering the wording and placement of the "page" and "yell" commands.

For example, in one user-testing situation, Hughes and Moshell found that "students requested a means of private communication, even though this capability already exists" ("Shared"). I found similar responses among my graduate students who used the program at West Virginia University in March 1998. These responses suggest the need to alter the interface to foreground this information graphically whenever possible.

In addition, the process of loading characters, props, and scenery objects that one creates into a new world, and assigning these objects particular behaviors, needs to be made easier. This would allow new groups of students and teachers—who are Guests and Cast Members attempting to become World Builders—to be less dependent on a small core of expert developers. If it proves too difficult or costly to provide enhanced functionality on a world-building level, ExploreNet developers might consider adding graphical templates of standardized figures to speed up the process of developing world objects. For example, templates are offered by the Microsoft Chat 2.1 program (in comic-view mode) for background scenes and the body and facial expression of an avatar. At the same time, some of the existing objects in ExploreNet worlds are well designed for direct manipulation and feedback.[15]

Some especially nice features of the current ExploreNet interface, which are not present in MOOs, are its ability to provide the participant with a composite script of dialogue in all scenes within a world (accessed by selecting the Dialog button), and the History feature, which allows participants to replay an image of their avatars' physical movements and corresponding dialogue in a scene.

## EVALUATION

The existence of ExploreNet as a freeware, multiuser graphical, world-building program was itself a feat when it was first developed in the early 1990s. Few other freeware programs existed in the early to mid-1990s that offered the participant—using only a 486 PC—the tools to author a multiuser, graphical online world.

Empowering people to develop their own virtual worlds remains important on a theoretical, political, artistic, and practical level. The issue of how much control to give participants cuts across multiuser environments, multimedia, and hypertext. In a discussion of hypertext writing and the "tripartite agency of reader/writer/programmer," hypertext poet Jim Rosenberg foregrounds the role of the programmer and the need for readers to gain agency at this level. Rosenberg asks:

> Should extensibility be extended to the *reader*? If we are to give the reader the freedom to participate in constructing a hypertext, it is arbitrary and unreasonable to impose an artificial boundary prohibiting the reader from participating in constructing algorithms in a more general sense. ("Locus," 155)

As a programmer and artist, Rosenberg recognizes the need to gain access to the artist's tools. In a discussion of hypertext and digital art in general, he says: "If you're an artist and you want control of your materials, then if you're not programming, you're ceding that control to someone else" (Discussion). I respect that Moshell and Hughes are extending some measure of control to all users of ExploreNet; they are dealing head-on with the difficult process of combining democratic access to the artist's tools with practical needs for expertise in order to use them.

It is also noteworthy that Moshell and Hughes have attempted to keep schools from having to pay anything for ExploreNet beyond providing their equipment and Internet access. They are clearly concerned about the material circumstances of people who use their software, and they want to deliver a curricular tool "that does not have to be purchased" to "avoid contributing to the widening gap between 'haves' and 'have-nots'" (Moshell et al., "Building"). They also develop their software with "constant attention to sources of support" for teachers and school systems by providing groups of people to assist a teacher when using ExploreNet.

Moreover, the vision of ExploreNet is admirable for its community basis. Moshell and Hughes are attempting to move beyond the sole reliance on the teacher as the source of technical knowledge (Moshell et al., "Building"). To foster communities of learners and mentors, they train in-school students, hospitalized/homebound students, and university and community volunteers, including retirees and parents. Consequently, while ExploreNet's participatory "audience" or the community of participants who interact in the program could be identified as such based on their online attendance, they are simultaneously often part of a physical-space community that ExploreNet developers have worked with in developing a world, such as the community of K–12 students in the Orlando, Florida, area, or the third-grade students in an elementary school in Germany.

In addition, the objective of encouraging cooperation and embedding this in the narrative structure of worlds such as EggQuest is admirable. Although the cooperation has not been as readily observed in practice, developers have tried, for example, to make "stealing eggs from the hens . . . extremely difficult for one guest, but . . . relatively easy for two who are working together" (Hughes and Moshell, "Shared").

Finally, program designers aimed to enact a constructionist model of learning within ExploreNet. Yet they acknowledged from the outset that constructionist learning theory has been criticized for its idealism and reliance on "unique charismatic leaders and advocates for change." Nevertheless, they set out to "put super-teachers and their students in a role of catalysts for large bodies of other teachers and students" (Moshell, Hughes, and Kilby, "Virtual Academy: The Educational Model"). So their approach could also be criticized for the continued reliance on what in practice remains a small group of experts.

With an eye toward the future and a new version of ExploreNet that is being developed in Java, I remain cognizant that the program must improve in usability and graphical display to maintain people's motivation to participate and build in the environment. New incarnations of the program will do well to move away from the heavy reliance on the super-teacher and super-student who pre-script the scenarios, to a more flexible authoring environment that allows beginners a greater sense of agency.

To analyze ExploreNet sufficiently, one would want to examine not only constructed worlds but also the ExploreNet program itself as an authoring environment. The current version, 3.5–014, however, makes the process of authoring a world arduous.

Yet I still appreciate the option that ExploreNet offers for the participant to become a World Builder. It is empowering for the student/participant to be offered agency on the programming and development level, even if the bridge to reach this barely populated island is currently difficult to cross. It is particularly difficult for students and teachers at West Virginia University in Morgantown, West Virginia, and for others in remote sites, who would need the assistance of the small group of expert developers located in Orlando at the University of Central Florida. In the current version of ExploreNet, the learning curve is too steep, perhaps because of the limitations of the interface or the capabilities of the program or the dramatic or literary model underlying the conception of the program. Decreasing the learning curve should enhance the incentive for people to become agents to contribute to the making of the online environment.

Ultimately, the assessment of ExploreNet must be stratified according to which role one analyzes in the development process. For example, Moshell and Hughes describe the Cast Members' "control of story" when they write: "Cast members know the overall story line and collectively serve like 'Dungeon Masters' in a game of Dungeons and

Dragons. They have to improvise as necessary to move the Guests toward the goal" ("Virtual Academy: A Simulated Environment").

While the improvisation allowed to the Cast Members (who include the mentor figures) is admirable, their position of superior knowledge, which keeps the Guest guessing about the story line, may be disempowering to the Guest who is accustomed to a greater sense of control and input in a collaboratively developed story line in other multiuser environments.

If the developers improve the interface and program capabilities and adjust the dramatic model underlying ExploreNet worlds, they may be able to help participants feel a greater sense of agency and a greater stake in ExploreNet worlds. This goal remains frustrated by the current state of the program, though the vision and achievements of the ExploreNet developers remain inspiring.

## NOTES

1. In 1991 Myron W. Krueger described Allan Kaprow's Happenings of the 1960s as the artistic antecedents for artificial realities (computer-generated simulation environments for multiple or single users). According to Krueger: "A Happening was theater without an audience. Nothing was conceived with the passive spectator in mind. A loose series of possibilities was planned; the participants were the ones who actually gave the work its final form. . . . Artificial realities also require the artist to accept reduced control, to think in terms of a structure of possibilities that leaves the final realization of the piece in the hands of each participant" (Krueger, 7).

Others have similarly viewed theater as a precedent for designing online environments. Looking to Aristotelian theater to inform an understanding of software design, Brenda Laurel remarks that there are "at least two reasons to consider theatre as a promising foundation for thinking about and designing human-computer experiences. First, there is significant overlap in the fundamental objective of the two domains—that is, representing action with multiple agents. Second, theatre suggests the basis for a model of human-computer activity that is familiar, comprehensible, and evocative" (Laurel, 21).

2. I refer to a software environment for multiple users who interact in the environment synchronously or asynchronously as a "multiuser environment." The issue of how to conceptualize and name an online real-time interactive environment for multiple people is one that a number of literary and theater theorists have wrestled with. For example, Espen Aarseth conceptualizes text-

based MUDs (Multi-User Domains) as "cybertexts." Aarseth argues that this term allows a greater sense of dynamic change and interaction than the term "text" alone allows. I conceive of synchronous communication software programs such as MUDs and ExploreNet within a theatrical context as a type of orchestrated and/or improvised event and as a "multiuser environment" (see Warshauer). By articulating multiuser environment studies as an area of inquiry and "multiuser environments" as a term for these hybrid literary and theatrical environments, I offer an approach to studying these environments that gains from analytical insights from literary and theater theory.

So the MUD or multiuser graphical environment such as ExploreNet may be seen as a type of text and a type of theatrical event. Indeed, viewing a work of art as both performative and literary is intrinsic in the field of theater studies; a common split that is still embedded in the very division of academic disciplines in the university occurs in the study of plays—typically in English departments as dramatic literature or scripts written in words on a page—and in theater departments as performative events.

Yet what we have in the emergence of a range of multiuser environments online is in fact a tighter convergence of the real-time performance and the real-time script, which is collaboratively authored and remains as a remnant of the performance after the event is over. What we still have *before* the real-time event, however, is the programming—the pre-written set of procedures that allow particular actions to take place online. In this sense, there is still a pre-written script, one that is contained in a file with data and algorithms. This pre-written "script" or program manifests itself in the real-time experience or set of events. At the same time, the performance event may have a subsequent "script" or saved file with dialogue and graphical characters and movements replayed in the exact timed sequence (ExploreNet has an option to save such a performance record).

So in this instance, in contrast to a theatrical play with a singular pre-written script, at least two types of scripts exist—a script of the program that determines options for actions in a multiuser environment and the residual script that remains after the online experience takes place. The real-time event itself may be considered a third type of script, whether conveyed through the medium of written words, visual images, or audio. Moreover, with an expanded notion of text, one may read the real-time event as a type of cultural text.

3. I am using the term "community" to describe a group of people in online or physical-space environments or both environments at once; the group of people is present in some way in the same physical, online, or psychological space. So I use the concept of community in the sense of a group of people

being united by their common representation or presence within what is perceived as a unified environment or psychic space (at the very least, unified by the singular name of the software being used, the title of the virtual world, the Internet address(es) of the servers the world resides on, or the name that self-represents or is given to the community and that demarcates it in people's minds).

The idea of a virtual community draws from the concept of community that has been developed for physical-space environments. Linda McDowell offers a couple of definitions for community, one of which is "a small-scale and spatially bounded area within which it is assumed that the population, or part of it, has certain characteristics in common that ties [*sic*] it together" (McDowell, 40). She broadens this definition by considering community a "fluid network of social relations," a definition amenable to interpretations of virtual communities. She remarks: "Communities are context dependent, contingent, and defined by power relations; their boundaries are created by mechanisms of inclusion and exclusion" (100). The fluid, context-dependent, contingent quality that she describes is well suited to the notion of community in a multiuser environment where people may visit online once or consistently and the constitution of the group is perpetually shifting. McDowell's expanded definition is consistent with my understanding of online community.

Moreover, Kimberly Cordingly adds a psychological sense to the concept of community: "If we think about community as a social network that binds individuals together in some way, this concept is less tied to physical location than to how that sense of community is formed in the minds of those who claim to belong to it. A city is a physical/cultural location but can be comprised of numerous communities. . . . the African-American community, the feminist community, a neighborhood community watch, or a community of writers. The communities we belong to provide us with places where we can share common interests and concerns and feel a part of the group" (Cordingly).

Within my concept of community in an online environment, I do not assume that a group of people would possess common interests or concerns, though I would expect a high correlation with some type of common interest or common qualities among people in a group. I am defining as a community the group of people who visit ExploreNet or other multiuser environments, and in some sense I am basing this identification on people's technical connection and logging in to the environment—once they are there—and having visited it, they become part of what I identify as the community of ExploreNet or some other multiuser environment. This is admittedly a limited concept of community, and I could address additional nuances of it, including how an online community of visitor-participants is similar to or distinguished from the concept of audience or the group of programmers or participants who work ahead of time to develop the environment—but such a discussion would require more space than is available here.

4. Such a progressive political agenda is reminiscent of the community-organizing principles of U.S. activist Saul Alinsky and the "pedagogy of the oppressed" philosophy of Brazilian educator Paulo Freire. Alinsky and Freire aim to break the cycle of disempowering dependency that would otherwise situate citizens and learners in a passive role. Alinsky's philosophy encourages people in a community to gain the agency to proactively represent themselves in the political process in mass "People's Organizations"; community organizers would be the catalyst for this to occur, similar to the way that ExploreNet developers and those skilled in the program's use would serve as catalysts for empowering less-knowledgeable users to develop worlds (Alinsky, xxv–xxvi, 3). Likewise, Paulo Freire encourages an educational philosophy in which learners take an active part in the learning process rather than remaining passive recipients of the doctrine of others (see *Pedagogy of the Oppressed*). The similar opposition to being passive in an educational system and a political system is apparent in philosophies that encourage students or community residents to "talk back" in dialogue and gain the means to actively question establishment versions of knowledge and the political status quo.

Finally, Brazilian theater artist Augusto Boal was profoundly influenced by the educational philosophy of Freire's *Pedagogy of the Oppressed*. Steeped in the desire for dialogue as a humanizing force, Boal articulated participatory theater principles for an activist theater in the Theatre of the Oppressed. Boal's participatory theater principles, although not followed in the current instantiation of ExploreNet, could help inform future upgrades and developers of synchronous communication environments in general who aim to grant more agency to online participants.

5. Narratologists have offered numerous definitions of narrative. Marie-Laure Ryan, for instance, writes that "narrative can mean a discourse reporting a story, as well as the story itself" (683). She describes three types of narrative: sequential, causal, and dramatic. Her concept of sequential narrative comes closest to my broad conception of narrative in a multiuser environment. Ryan explains, "In an interactive system, a sequential narrative will be automatically created by the presence of a user spending a variable amount of time in the virtual world" (683).

6. The presence of the helper figure in the mentor/guide may also lead to cooperation with an existing online figure. At the same time, the mentor figure who is online in real time may encourage dependence on a more knowl-

edgeable source who intentionally limits the amount of information distributed at any one time, which may become frustrating to participants. Yet this helper/facilitator figure is present in other multiuser interactive systems as well, including virtual reality environments (3-D, immersive, navigable worlds) such as the Interval Research Corporation's Placeholder project (see Laurel and Strickland). Ryan writes that in Placeholder, the Goddess character, who is played by a live actor, "functions as online help, initiating users into the secrets of the virtual world" (697). To minimize the frustration that participants may experience from speaking with live participants who are cognizant of a whole set of narrative possibilities but who are instructed to give out only small amounts of information at one time, it would be helpful for developers of ExploreNet and other multiuser environments to consider using bots (short for "robots") or artificially intelligent agents to assist in providing help information. This would also keep interaction in the worlds from being as reliant on the real-time availability of human helper figures, although access to some human assistance can be refreshing when environments rely only on pre-scripted replies of artificially intelligent agents.

7. For instance, the authorial role becomes that of a facilitator's role in an environment such as Habitat. In the early days of Habitat, some of the participants wanted to kill each other while others strived to establish a community. Habitat organizers compromised by "creating a wilderness land in which violence was routine and a town where it was outlawed" (Murray, 266). Murray charts out the useful role that a "central author," or what I interpret as a facilitator, could play in this environment: "The role of a central author (or team of authors) in such an environment [Habitat] might be to negotiate such boundary issues . . . by insisting that the improvisational elements remain consistent with a general story line" (266).

8. Although narrative elements are pre-written and one discovers them, they may be as interesting to experience as any pre-written narrative that one would be accustomed to reading in a paper-based novel. For example, as one innovative narrative feature in Dinosaur world, the Zora character has an option in her action menu to "Start the Next Day." Upon selecting this, the participant watches the screen turn completely gray with only the words "Night is falling" written in the middle; next, the screen turns a darker shade of gray, and the line of text is replaced with the line "It's getting darker." Then a black screen replaces this one with the single line "The darkest hour is here" onscreen; finally, a lighter gray screen replaces that with the text "The dawn is coming," and the next image offers a view of the world one saw before the "Start the Next Day" option was selected. The sequence of events is pre-written and the viewer cannot change them fundamentally, but the satisfaction in

experiencing this pre-written narrative should be familiar to readers of paper-based linear stories.

9. Yet, as a Guest, if one accepts the objective of participating in a quest or a lesson plan to learn certain material to progress in the food chain, then discovering the narrative or taking the steps to learn the lesson may be sufficiently motivated. Some ExploreNet worlds are in fact useful in teaching specific subject matter. Autoland is especially helpful for teaching about U.S. geography, resources, and industry located in various cities, via the participant's quest to amass required resources to make steel and glass and other components for building a car.

10. In the case of ExploreNet, I am using the term "audience" to refer to a group of participants who are logged on to ExploreNet synchronously or asynchronously. Whether this group of people is actually a unified whole that should be referred to in one fell swoop as "the audience," however, is an issue. The cohesiveness of a unified, singular concept of audience could be questioned as much as the concept of community is. It is not clear whether the audience is in fact united by their common attendance in the same physical space at a performance (or online space in a multiuser environment such as ExploreNet), or even by culture, economic class, ethnicity, gender, sexual orientation, or political outlook. In fact, in the same way that gender has been viewed as a construct in Judith Butler's work, as the effect of the performance of particular acts, the notion of audience, and that of community, have also been considered types of constructs, the result of the interpretation of particular acts or signifiers that point to the signified concept of audience or community.

Theater theorist Herbert Blau, for instance, asserts: "If the audience is not altogether an absence, it is by no means a reliable presence," given the diverse characteristics of its constituents (Blau, 1). For the purposes of this study I have not problematized the concept of audience, or community, as much as I could have. Such discussion would deserve more space than is available here. In addition, I am sometimes merging the concept of community with the concept of audience for a performance (which could be equivalent to a set of people who show up online to interact in a multiuser software environment); from performance studies and anthropological perspectives, the people who are present at varying times in an ExploreNet world could be considered both a type of audience and a type of community.

11. This strategy of leaving one's own mark on a scene is used effectively in Brenda Laurel and Rachel Strickland's Placeholder project, an immersive virtual reality environment that people experience through head-mounted displays. In Placeholder, participants have the option to attach their speech in the form of audio files or "Voicemarks—bits of spoken narrative" to persistent

objects such as rocks and trees that remain in the visual environment (Laurel and Strickland).

12. I distinguish community theater from community-based theater. Community theater connotes local theater companies taking existing scripts and staging them in smaller productions than would be done by professional, mainstream theater companies such as those on Broadway in New York.

13. I am emphasizing community-based theater that utilizes participatory theater practices, but community-based theater and participatory theater methods do not always overlap. For instance, the Blue Man Group uses participatory theater methods but is not considered community-based theater.

14. In 1990, ExploreNet developers Charles Hughes and J. Michael Moshell found out about and were inspired by Habitat, a cartoon-like graphical multiuser environment. They write that they "immediately realized that this environment offered great opportunities for education, and embarked upon building an educational version" ("ExploreNet").

15. Since these objects, as well as the overall worlds, are products of collaborative development situations, all the student and adult participants who contributed ideas and programming expertise should be commended. Zworld has a small tree that, upon being clicked on, grows twice as large right before your eyes. A similar object, the bumper sticker with indiscernible type in Autoland, offers an action menu with the option to magnify the image. After selecting the textual words to do so, one sees it change size accordingly and present a larger, legible bumper sticker: "Spam is Cool!" This nice action could be even more direct if clicking on the indiscernible object would directly yield the bumper sticker's magnified words, while clicking on it again might cause it to diminish in size. Design elements involving direct manipulation and feedback should continue to be encouraged to embed the narrative in the visual language of the environment; at the same time, if the objective of the lesson involved learning vocabulary words such as "magnify," then the existing intermediary step of selecting textual actions would be appropriate.

## REFERENCES

Aarseth, Espen. *Cybertext: Perspectives on Ergodic Literature*. Baltimore: Johns Hopkins University Press, 1997.

Alinsky, Saul D. *Rules for Radicals: A Practical Primer for Realistic Radicals*. New York: Random House (Vintage), 1971.

Blau, Herbert. *The Audience*. Baltimore: Johns Hopkins University Press, 1990.

Boal, Augusto. *Games for Actors and Non-Actors*. Trans. Adrian Jackson. New York: Routledge, 1992.

——. *Theatre of the Oppressed*. Trans. Charles A. and Maria-Odilia Leal McBride. New York: Theatre Communications Group, 1985.

Carlson, Marvin. *Performance: A Critical Introduction*. New York: Routledge, 1996.

Cordingly, Kimberly. "Locating the Self in Cyber/space: A Consideration of the Spatial Geographies of V-Chat." Unpublished paper. West Virginia University, Morgantown, West Virginia. 4 June 1999. Available from author, kcording@wvu.edu.

ExploreNet™, version 3.5–014. Developed by Charles Hughes and J. Michael Moshell. Available online: http://www.cs.ucf.edu/~ExploreNet/ExploreNet.zip. University of Central Florida, Department of Computer Science. July 1997. Runs on Windows versions up to Windows 98; see the ExploreNet website for information on subsequent Windows versions.

Freire, Paulo. *Pedagogy of the Oppressed*. 20th rev. ed. Trans. Myra Bergman Ramos. New York: Continuum Publishing Group, 1993.

French, William W. *Maryat Lee's EcoTheater: A Theater for the Twenty-First Century*. Morgantown, W.Va.: West Virginia University Press, 1998.

Gingold, Chaim. "Multi-user Interface, Character, and Plot." Unpublished paper. West Virginia University, Morgantown, West Virginia. May 1998.

Hatch, James V., ed. *Black Theater U.S.A.: Forty-five Plays by Black Americans, 1847–1974*. New York: Free Press, 1974.

Hughes, Charles E., and J. Michael Moshell. "ExploreNet™." 2 July 1997. http://www.cs.ucf.edu/~ExploreNet/.

——. "ExploreNet User's Manual." 28 June 1995. http://www.cs.ucf.edu/~ExploreNet/manuals/Xnet.Refman.html.

——. "Shared Virtual Worlds for Education: The ExploreNet Experiment." 13 November 1995. http://www.cs.ucf.edu/~ExploreNet/papers/VA.Experiment1195.html. Also published in *ACM Multimedia* 5, no. 2 (March 1997): 145–154.

——. "Using ExploreNet: A Guide for Guests, Cast Members, and Level 1 World Builders." Orlando: University of Central Florida, 2 February 1997. http://www.cs.ucf.edu/~ExploreNet/manuals/Xnetman1.rtf.

Kaprow, Allan. *Essays on the Blurring of Art and Life*. Ed. Jeff Kelley. Berkeley: University of California Press, 1993.

——. "Excerpts from 'Assemblages, Environments, and Happenings." In Mariellen R. Sandford, ed., *Happenings and Other Acts*, 235–245. London: Routledge, 1995.

Krueger, Myron W. *Artificial Reality II*. Reading, Mass.: Addison-Wesley, 1991.

Laurel, Brenda. *Computers as Theatre*. Reading, Mass.: Addison-Wesley, 1993.

Laurel, Brenda, and Rachel Strickland. *Placeholder: Landscape and Narrative in a Virtual Environment.* Project documentation. Fifteen-minute video and paper insert. Palo Alto, Calif.: Interval Research Corporation, April 1994.

Lebkowsky, Jon, Paco Xander Nathan, and Allucquere Rosanne Stone. Allucquere Rosanne Stone Interview for Mondo 2000. 1993. http://sandystone.com/Mondo-interview.

Living Stage Theatre Company. "About the Living Stage Theatre Company." Publicity flyer. 1999.

McDowell, Linda. *Gender, Identity, and Place: Understanding Feminist Geographies.* Minneapolis: University of Minnesota Press, 1999.

Morningstar, Chip, and F. Randall Farmer. "The Lessons of Lucasfilm's Habitat." In Michael Benedikt, ed., *Cyberspace: First Steps*, 272–301. Cambridge, Mass.: MIT Press, 1993.

Moshell, J. Michael, and Charles E. Hughes. "The Virtual Academy: A Simulated Environment for Constructionist Learning." 29 September 1995. http://www.cs.ucf.edu/~ExploreNet/papers/VA. Explanation1095.html. Also published in *International Journal of Human-Computer Interaction* 8, no. 1 (1996): 95–110.

——. "The Virtual Communities Experiments at Hungerford Elementary School." 27 July 1995.
http://www.cs.ucf.edu/~ExploreNet/papers/ VA.Hungerford0795.html

Moshell, J. Michael, Charles E. Hughes, and Mark Kilby. "Virtual Academy: The Educational Model." 27 July 1995.
http://www.cs.ucf.edu/~ExploreNet/papers/VA.EdModel0795.html.

Moshell, J. Michael, Charles E. Hughes, Mark Kilby, and Joel Rosenthal. "Building ExploreNet Worlds: The 1995–96 Developmental Experiment." 10 December 1995.
http://www.cs.ucf.edu/~ExploreNet/tutorials/Xnet.Experiment.html.

Murray, Janet H. *Hamlet on the Holodeck: The Future of Narrative in Cyberspace.* New York: Free Press, 1997.

Rohd, Michael. Personal interview. 14 June 1999.

——. "A Summer Hope Is Vital Institute." Publicity flyer. June 1999.

——. *Theatre for Community, Conflict, and Dialogue: The Hope Is Vital Training Manual.* Portsmouth, N.H.: Heinemann, 1998.

Rosenberg, Jim. Discussion following his presentation at the Ninth ACM Conference on Hypertext and Hypermedia, Pittsburgh, 23 June 1998.

——. "Locus Looks at the Turing Play: Hypertextuality vs. Full Programmability." *Proceedings of the Ninth ACM Conference on Hypertext and Hypermedia*, 152–160. Pittsburgh, PA 20–24 June 1998. Available online at http://www.well.com/user/jer/LLTP_out.html.

Ryan, Marie-Laure. "Interactive Drama: Narrativity in a Highly Interactive Environment." *MFS Modern Fiction Studies* 43, no. 3 (Fall 1997): 677–707.

Warshauer, Susan. "Multi-User Environment Studies: Defining a Field of Study and Four Approaches to the Design of Multi-User Environments." *Literary and Linguistic Computing* 13, no. 4 (1998): 199–215.

Worthen, William B. *Modern Drama and the Rhetoric of Theater*. Berkeley: University of California Press, 1992.

# 12

# Communication, Community, Consumption: An Ethnographic Exploration of an Online City

DAVID SILVER

Roberta enters the space for her upper-division computer engineering class at Virginia Tech and notices that no other students are here at the moment.[1] She sifts through last week's lecture notes and this week's homework assignments and takes what she needs. Then she strolls over to the community center, checks which films are playing at the Lyric Theater, and notes their times. Finally, she makes her way to the Bamboo House, orders some cashew chicken and half a dozen potstickers, and requests a delivery.

Then she logs off.

Derek wakes up, gets dressed, logs on, reads his e-mail, and checks the newsgroups. He pays special attention to Bburg-L, where an interesting thread on the proposed smartroad is beginning to take shape. He reads the messages, saves one or two for future reference, and posts a query regarding a recent feasibility study. By the time he reaches work, a number of users have responded to his posting, offering statistics and related citations. During the same time, his initial query has supplied some fuel for a flame from Harry, the list's unappointed yet unquestionable gadfly. Once again, a flame war is on.

Like Derek, Mark begins his day with a quick online session. Working for Public Services Programs at Virginia Tech, he coordinates Internet endeavors for a number of Virginia's artists and artists' organizations. Upon responding to all his work-related e-mail, he uploads some new material to his online art gallery and updates the site he maintains for a local online theater show. Next, he makes his way toward Bburg-L. Finding Harry at it again, he switches to a more tame list, Ferrets Digest, and begins to read the messages. Finally, recalling that it is his turn to do the shopping, he surfs over to Wades, checks the weekly specials, and downloads a few coupons.

Welcome to Blacksburg. Or, to be more precise, welcome to the Blacksburg Electronic Village. The BEV is a community network, a collection of geographically based Web sites, mailing lists, newsgroups, and e-mail accounts established for and around a particular town, city, or region. As illustrated by our vignettes, however, community networks like the BEV are more than digital assortments of wires, software, and servers. They are spaces in which to learn, share information, download class lectures; they are places for cultural presentations, exhibitions, and interactions. They can be forums for social and political discussions, debates, and discourse; they are often sites of commerce, digital malls, sources of infinitely printable coupons. They are, in a phrase, online communities.

In an attempt to understand this online community better, I have spent the last six years studying it. I followed its initial inception as a university network, its early design and implementation, and its eventual escalation into what the *Philadelphia Inquirer* called "perhaps America's most wired municipality" (Farragher, D-1) and what the *Washington Post* labeled "without a doubt, the most computer-connected place, per capita, on the planet" (Chandrasekaran, A-1).[2] Later, I analyzed the utopian rhetoric surrounding the BEV, paying special attention to project administrators' promises for a rejuvenated community for its participants.[3] Next, I focused on the network's digital architecture and explored the ways in which the interface helped to influence, foster, and thwart particular kinds of participation that take place within the wires. Finally, I fused my interface analysis with an examination of the network's outreach programs to understand more about what kinds of participants were recruited and encouraged to "come online."[4]

While my online odyssey was fruitful, it proved lacking. For although I had come to a healthy understanding of the wires, workshops, power, and politics that made up the BEV, I had bypassed the voices that gave it life. This changed in 1998 when I enrolled in a graduate course in ethnography. The course, taught by anthropologist John Caughey, demanded a change in my own positionality, a shift from the perspective of a detached observer analyzing computer screens to that of an active participant traveling within the wires. Within a few weeks, I was hooked. As I listened to members' online conversations and followed their interactions, I better understood the need for time, patience, and acceptance in healthy community building. As I witnessed the online arguments, flames, and silences, I became more aware of the community's barriers, limitations, and hostilities.

This ethnography is an attempt to listen to, learn from, and make sense of the *human element* of the Blacksburg Electronic Village. In some ways, the goal is misleading, for all of the BEV—its inception, development, design, and outreach—is nothing if not a human construction. Therefore, perhaps a better articulation of my project's goal is to say that it aims to explore the ways in which users use the network and make meanings of their use, interactions, and contributions. In other words, while the developers of the BEV designed the network for particular and preferred modes of communication, the users accept, alter, or tweak those modes—or create new ones. Is the BEV, for example, a digital public sphere, a "place" where users congregate, debate, and discuss? Or, borrowing a page from media theorist James Carey, is it a sacred space for communion? Is the community network a forum where "no rules" is the only rule or are measures taken to establish and maintain peace? And finally, as one of the many so-called American public spheres, how is the BEV understood by its users as a place for point-and-click commercial consumption?

## CONTEXTS AND COMMUNITIES

Throughout the 1990s, academic and popular interest in cyberculture has exploded. This growing academic interest in the cultural, social, political, and economic considerations of cyberspace is apparent in countless panels at such diverse conferences as the American Studies Association (ASA), the American Historical Association (AHA), the Modern Languages Association (MLA), and the National Communications Association (NCA), and in a handful of degree- and certificate-granting programs like Georgetown's Program in Communication,

Culture, and Technology, MIT's Program in Comparative Media Studies, and Australia's Curtin University's Internet Studies Graduate Program. Recently, a number of newspapers have introduced regularly appearing sections and columns devoted to cyberspace, including the *New York Times*'s Circuits, the *San Jose Mercury News*'s Silicon Life, and the *Washington Post*'s Fast Forward. Moreover, feature articles on cyberspace regularly appear in such mainstream magazines as *Time*, *Newsweek*, and *Rolling Stone*.

Until recently, however, very little attention has been paid to community networks, one of the fastest-growing Internet applications. In the most simple terms, community networks incorporate Internet technologies to connect residents of a specific place—a town, a city, or a municipality, for instance—with one another and with local institutions, services, and businesses (Schuler, *New Community Networks*). For example, the Seattle Community Network attempts to wire the residents of Seattle, Washington, and the Boulder Community Network connects the residents, institutions, and businesses of another particular place, Boulder, Colorado. Thus, while virtual communities are constituted by members' shared interests, community networks are based on members' shared location. As Schuler notes:

> Community members and activists all over the world have developed and are developing community-oriented electronic bulletin boards of community networks with a local focus. These community networks, some with user populations in the tens of thousands, are intended to advance social goals such as building community awareness, encouraging involvement in local decision making, or developing economic opportunities in disadvantaged communities. They are intended to provide "one-stop shopping" using community-oriented discussions, question-and-answer forums, electronic access to government employees and information, access to social services, email, and in many cases, Internet access. . . . The most important aspect of their community networks, however, is their immense potential for participation.
>
> ("Community Networks," 39)

Harrison and Stephen offer a similar definition, one based on local, progressive participation. They note:

> Community networks are organized for a variety of purposes that range from bringing the resources of information technology to individuals who have not historically enjoyed access to the Internet to using technology to address traditional issues in community development, such as unemployment, economic stimulation, health and social welfare, environmental concerns, educational needs, and so on. In addition, an important objective for many developers has been to use community networks to stimulate interest and enhance participation in local government or in other forms for community decision making. (222)

Perhaps one of the most popular and certainly one of the most publicized community networks in the United States is the BEV. Developed in 1994, the BEV is a collaborative project between Virginia Tech, the town of Blacksburg, and Bell Atlantic of Virginia.[5] Rich and deep, the BEV includes literally hundreds of Web sites for local community, governmental, and commercial organizations, e-mail accounts for residents and students, and sixteen mailing lists and newsgroups devoted to topics germane to Blacksburg citizens.

In an attempt to explore the digital terrains of the BEV and the online travels of its users, I conducted what both George E. Marcus and Christine Hine call a "multi-sited ethnography." Accordingly, I assumed three positions. First, I became a participant-observer of Bburg-L, a BEV newsgroup devoted to "general talk about Blacksburg." I selected Bburg-L for two reasons. First, because it was a general list, rather than one devoted to a specific subject, it offered the most diverse range of discussion topics. Second, its archive of postings indicated that it is one of the most frequently used mailing lists. Next, as a result of a message I posted to Bburg-L, I conducted brief online interviews with eight members of the list, asking general questions regarding list members' use of the network, its Web site, and Bburg-L, as well as basic demographic questions. Finally, in an attempt to triangulate my findings, I met face-to-face with six of my informants and conducted in-depth ethnographic interviews in the town of Blacksburg in late October of 1998.

As noted previously, the field of cyberculture studies has undergone dramatic growth during the last ten years. Thus far, the majority of cyberculture scholarship has focused on the concept of virtual communities. Linda M. Harasim and Howard Rheingold are among the earliest cyberculturalists to articulate the characteristics of online communities. Harasim describes a number of social, workplace, and educational online communities in terms of what they lack. Unlike face-to-face and more traditional means of communication, communication among members of online communities takes place regardless of time and space, creating what Harasim calls atemporal and aspatial communication. More important, online communities, or what she refers to as "networlds," help to erase social status:

> Networlds can free people from the bonds of physical appearance and enable communication at a level of ideas. For example, in face-to-face situations physical and social cues extend authority and influence others. Cues such as dress, presentation, voice intonation, and seating arrangement denote power, leading to unequal communication between people. . . . Communication in the networld is "blind" to vertical hierarchy in social relations. (26)

In this manner, networlds, according to Harasim, are less about traditional sites of power—class, race, and gender, for example—and more about ideas, offering what some scholars have labeled the online public sphere model, a network of users who trade, exchange, debate, and discuss ideas and information.

The most popular and prolific proponent of this model is, of course, Rheingold. In "A Slice of Life in My Virtual Community," for example, he describes virtual communities as "cultural aggregations that emerge when enough people bump into each other often enough in cyberspace" (56). He continues:

> A virtual community is a group of people who may or may not meet one another face-to-face, and who exchange words and ideas through the mediation of computer bulletin boards and networks. In cyberspace, we chat and argue, engage in intellectual intercourse, perform acts of commerce, exchange knowledge, share emotional support, make plans, brainstorm, gossip, feud, fall in love, find friends and lose them, play games and metagames, flirt, create a little high art and a lot of idle talk. We do everything people do when people get together, but we do it

> with words on computer screens, leaving our bodies behind. Millions of us have already built communities where our identities commingle and interact electronically, independent of local time or location. (58)

Rheingold extends this definition in his book *The Virtual Community: Homesteading on the Electronic Frontier*. While notably more cautious toward the Internet-as-public-sphere model, the author continues to characterize online communities in Habermasian terms, adding temporal duration and "sufficient human feeling" to the mix: "Virtual communities are social aggregations that emerge from the Net when enough people carry on those public discussions long enough, with sufficient human feeling, to form webs of personal relationships in cyberspace" (5).

Writing four years after Rheingold, Nessim Watson argues that online communication does not in and of itself produce a thriving online community. Drawing upon the work of James Carey, Watson examines Phish.net, a particularly popular listserv devoted to the neo-hippie band Phish, and concludes:

> Communication creates, re-creates, and maintains community on Phish.net and other online discussion forums through the continued interaction of participating members. However, the technological ability to communicate does not in itself create the conditions of community. Community depends not only upon communication and shared interests, but also upon "communion." (104)

Thus, for Watson, the key characteristics of online communities are similar to those traditionally associated with acts of communion: sincerity, intimacy, and the creation of behavioral norms.

In addition to conceiving online communities as public spheres and places of communion, many cyberculture scholars, including Peter Kollock and Marc Smith, have begun to characterize them in terms of maintaining the peace. The sociologists note:

> One way of increasing the stability of a group is by actively restricting its membership. The overwhelming majority of news-

> groups in the Usenet are potentially open to anyone. . . . There is, however, a technical device already in place, known as a kill file or bozo filter, that an individual can use to create a kind of customized personal boundary. If someone's actions in the Usenet are considered objectionable, an individual can put this person in his or her kill file, which filters out any future posting by this person. In some ways a kill file reduces a member's reliance on the larger group's ability to define and defend a boundary. This offers both individuals and groups greater flexibility—the effects of some sorts of violations of the commons can be minimized without the costs of restraining the offending activity. (120)

Further, they note the need for established rules and regulations, as well as some form of institutional memory. For Kollock and Smith, such elements are usually found in the frequently-asked-questions (FAQ) file: "On the local level, and consistent with the principle that rules should be tailored to local conditions, many newsgroups have also established a body of information about the newsgroup, complete with prescriptions and proscriptions, that is known as a Frequently-Asked Questions file, or FAQ" (121).

Finally, let us turn to Lisa Napoli's aptly titled "The Latest Internet Buzzword: Community," a short online essay that appeared in the *New York Times*'s Cybertimes section. According to Napoli, high-profile Internet companies such as Yahoo! and Excite are busy building online communities for two reasons. First, "companies are realizing that what makes a viable business isn't a one-time surge in traffic. It's lots of people who come back to a particular Web site every day—or, better yet, several times a day." Second, there is a symbiotic relationship between the users who are attracted to such communities and advertisers who are attracted to such users. As Napoli notes, "Besides repeat visitors, these groups also offer ready-made target audiences for advertisers. A wine merchant can buy ads on a gourmet food network, while a financial services company can seek out an investment group. Or, advertisers can create special interest groups themselves."

To summarize, academics and journalists have employed a range of models to help them better understand online communities. These models include four dominant paradigms: the Net as public sphere, cybercommunion, peacekeeping, and portals for consumption. Yet how do the users view the communities to which they belong? More to the point, how do members of the BEV community conceive the online environments within and through which they travel, communicate, and congregate?

## FLAME WARS: WELCOME TO BBURG-L

We begin, alas, with a flame war. The flame war began, as so many do, with a particularly invective subject line: "ugly female in treasure's [*sic*] office." The poster, Harry, had just returned from a day of bureaucratic calisthenics, twisting and being twisted by the rules and regulations at the county treasurer's office. Having lost the receipt to his old vehicular decal, Harry was forced to spend twenty dollars to buy a new one. Adding to his aggravation was what Harry perceived to be the manager's dishonesty; according to him, the manager scammed him into paying an unnecessary and avoidable fee.

Upon his return home, he fired up his computer, logged on, and composed a message to Bburg-L. Summing up his account of the day's events, he noted: "I was halfway back to Blacksburg when I remembered an adage cruel but often true: 'never trust a fat person,' and I will add 'especially not one so layered in makeup.'" He continued: "I nominate the short fat bleached blonde red-dressed manager for BIg TwitCHing Ugly Female Person of the Day." He concluded by offering sympathy for the plight of "pink men," noting, "Maybe I'm just being sensitive by wondering again also if women and minorities are getting better treatment these days then pink men [*sic*]. Has anyone ever been scammed like this by a man?"

The response was immediate. Within twenty-four hours, numerous members of Bburg-L flooded the listserv with messages. They called Harry a "troll," "an asshole," and "a vitriolic village idiot." Further, in an action seldom witnessed within virtual communities, one user brought the online squabble into the physical world: "Well everyone should be happy to know that this note will be seen by the people in the treasurer office since I showed it to some people who have relatives who work there. . . . P.S. I hope all your [Harry's] taxes are paid up to date." Interestingly, no one called Harry sexist. Nor did anyone question his right to post. Perhaps interpreting such absences as an invitation to continue, Harry did just that:

> I have it from a seemingly reliable source that the ugly woman, Miss Piggy, has referred the matter of her fatness and ugliness to the Commonwealth's Attorney. Of course it goes w/o saying, that she has probably failed to render to him her account of how she lied. I would like to suggest to her, so my little communications-go-between can relay it to her again, that she go on a diet, get a face lift, and best of all quit being a bitch about her public duties. That will get her much more results than whimpering about someone's reaction to her perfidity [*sic*].

Following a stream of "Harry's a jackass" messages came a fork in the thread. One camp, led by Bill, a system administrator at Virginia Tech, argued that while Harry's complaint was germane to the list, its hostile wording violated the acceptable use policy of his Internet service provider (ISP). Bill pressed list members to take action against Harry on a contractual basis:

> Please, folks, drop a note to staff@usit.net and ask that the U.S. Internet Acceptable Use Policy (AUP) be invoked. You may get a response, but so far, that is doubtful. Go to http://www.usit.net/members/usepolicy.html where you will see that [Harry] has violated several of the prohibited actions in item #1 by "transmitting on or through any of U.S. Internet's services, any material that is, in U.S. Internet's sole discretion, unlawful, obscene, threatening, abusive, libelous, or hateful, or encourages conduct that would constitute a criminal offense, give rise to civil liability, or otherwise violate any local, state, national or international law."
>
> [Harry] may have had a valid complaint about the _actions_ of the employees of the Montgomery County Treasurer's office. He was perfectly within bounds to air that complaint in bburg.general/bburg-l (as many folks have done about various businesses and operations in the area). But he stepped over the line (again and again) with his unflattering physical descriptions of an employee whom he identified by position.

The post was signed "[Bill], annoyed electronic citizen of bburg.general/bburg-l."

A second camp, led by DJ, a professor at Virginia Tech, arose. Using the subject line "let's reflect on the 'censorship mob,'" DJ countered:

> [Bill], why don't you, and all the other self-appointed Gatekeepers of Public Speech (e.g., Ms. xxx) who have been trying so vigorously and self-righteously to "silence" [Harry] from participating in this public forum just take a little "quiet time" and reflect on things a bit?
>
> I was having a discussion with someone the other day: they were claiming that in THIS country it was not possible that we could ever have the kinds of attacks on civil liberties that occurred in the axis countries during WW2. I disagreed, and in my opinion the comments seen from you and the others in the "censorship mob" that has formed on this newsgroup/list over the past few weeks provide compelling evidence in support of my position.
>
> Obviously, your intent is to censor this admittedly unpopular individual, and indeed, prevent him from even having Internet access. Unfortunately for you—but fortunately for free-speech in general—you (apparently) don't have the power to turn your intent-to-censor into reality. However, the mere fact that you, Ms. xxx, and the rest are even TRYING so hard to censor [Harry] makes a very sorry statement with respect to where "free speech" rights stand in this country—and on the Internet in general—when self-righteous mobs and unpopular individuals clash.
>
> The comments made by another member of the "censor [Harry]" mob also offered strong evidence in support of my argument that it very well COULD happen here: you remember, the one that was whining about how awful it was that those darned liberals on the Supreme Court keep upholding the right to free speech, and that such decisions were just so morally WRONG, and that there ought to be something that good moral folk could DO to silence threats like [Harry] . . .
>
> You should all be ashamed of yourselves. I certainly don't agree with the comments that [Harry] made about the treasurer's office

> employee; however, unless they're libelous (which I doubt), then he's got all the right in the world to express them.
>
> In contrast, the mob-mentality and zealous desire to silence those whose opinions offend them that has been exhibited by the "censor [Harry]" mob should cause all citizens who believe in the right to free speech very serious concern.

With fuel for the fire, the camps continued to flame.

With few exceptions (Danet; Millard), most scholars of cyberculture take every effort to avoid flame wars, both in their online experiences and in their offline research. I find this strange, for flames, like face-to-face debates, arguments, and even fights, provide a privileged site from which to witness the negotiation of behavioral norms, cultural values, and group rules. While often the result of senseless immaturity, flame wars are more commonly the product of a user or users' attempt to challenge the often agreed-upon, often unstated customs of the group, the group's attempt to thwart and defend against the challenge, and the cultural negotiation that takes place within and in between the two camps. In other words, a flame war is a process by which community members negotiate and self-define their communities; it is cyberculture in its works-in-progress stage.

I am particularly drawn to this flame war because it contains four different conceptions of the BEV invoked and reinvoked repeatedly by my informants. In the discussion that follows, I wish to discuss these four themes—an online public sphere, a space for cybercommunion, a place defined by rules and regulations, and a site for commercial consumption—in terms of members' meanings of the BEV in general, and Bburg-L in particular.

## AN ONLINE PUBLIC SPHERE

According to its charter, the BEV was designed to serve as an online town hall. As noted in its June 1995 online Vision Statement, "The goal of the project is to enhance the quality of people's lives by electronically linking the residents of the community to one another." In many ways, this goal has been met; besides being linked to one another, BEV users are linked to Blacksburg institutions, such as the local government, community service groups, schools, the public library, and businesses. Yet interestingly, none of my informants conceived of the current manifestation of the BEV in similar terms. Many did, however, hint at such a model in relation to the network's initial intentions. When I asked Roberta to discuss BEV's original goals, she noted it was developed to be used for

> anything you would ask your neighbor about. You know? Like my neighbors moved in at the end of the summer and they were looking for some place to go for Mexican and so they went, "oh you live here. Where's good for that?" And so I told them about Udeles and Guadalupes. Or I need to get my knives sharpened. So, I tried asking that on the newsgroup and got [Harry] responding saying he would be happy to sharpen them and I said, "nooooo thank you." But I did get several people pointing me to a store that does knife sharpening. I think stuff like that. You know, "what's good for this, who do I talk to, I want to get a fence put in, what public official do I talk to?"

Significantly, when asked to list their most common uses of the BEV home page, all answers focus on one element of the traditional public sphere—information gathering—at the expense of others, namely discussion and debate. Indeed, the unanimous top two selections were checking local movie listings and downloading coupons for nearby businesses. As Roberta remarked, "Actually the movie homepage for the theaters is about the most useful thing on there. Because trying to call the theaters is impossible. This isn't an area where a whole lot of people get the local paper so that's pretty much the way you get movie listings, either to call or check their Web page. And the Web page is about a thousand times easier."

Why no discussion and debate? Most of my informants were quick to note the network's lack of critical mass. "There aren't many people on it," Roberta noted. "I have a feeling that there's a bunch of people who just lurk, like I do. But if you follow it, you know there are just a handful of people who spout off to no end and fight with each other and call each other names." For Derek, a lab administrator for the Department of Computer Science at Virginia Tech, the list's low level of participation prevents the network from achieving excellence: "I think the thing that makes it decent as opposed to really excellent would be just the typically, relatively low level of activity. I read bburg.general all the time but you don't get postings about local events."[6]

For Harry, the network gadfly, the lack of discussion stems from a lack of common interests. A longtime resident of Blacksburg and an independent motorcycle repairman, Harry notes, "No one talks. They don't have any common interests among themselves to make it float." When I ask him whether the creation of more diverse lists would result in more discussion, he laughs, gulps some coffee, and responds: "I don't see those topics coming up, so I don't think there would be much user interest. If the topic were to come up they would have come up in Bburg-L. Now, I haven't seen anyone else express an interest for a call . . . oh yes, come to think of it, some one suggested an alternative, 'I hate [Harry]' newsgroup."

"Would you subscribe to it?" I ask.

"Hell, yeah, I guess so!"

Most of my informants attributed the low activity to two interrelated elements: the structure of the network and the communication styles that such a structure makes possible and promotes. James, a graduate student and instructor in political science at Virginia Tech, believes the network's design *discourages* participation: "The structure it has doesn't require a lot of involvement. You can participate if you want but the BEV as a general structure doesn't require involvement . . . it's a Web page that you can visit on your own, it doesn't have to be your portal, it doesn't require participation of the community at large. And I think that's one of the things—requirement of participation—that's usually one of the defining aspects of a political community." Further, and more important for James and most of my informants, the network's lists are unmoderated:

> You need to have moderated lists. I think they are moderated to some extent but very little. If you start yelling swear words, you get canceled pretty quick. If you start yelling things about pornography, bburg cancels those out. But they aren't moderated to the extent that you need to build a consensus. For instance, for [Harry], when you would browse anything, you would have a kill line at the server. . . . It's easy enough to do but they don't do that here because it's probably one of the few life-giving things that keeps this going.

According to my informants, what follows is, at best, sparse discussions and, at worst, flame wars. As Mark, the independent artist and employee for the Public Service Programs at Virginia Tech, notes, "I think a lot of times it's just a grinch-fest, it's a place for people to whine and complain." Roberta concurs: "I follow the blacksburg.general newsgroup to try to kind of keep up with stuff in town, although it's mostly, if you have read it all, just flame wars." And while Derek is willing to acknowledge the potential of flame wars for community building he is quick to note the need to produce a higher understanding:

> I think community is not just a discussion but an understanding of the issues of concern and being able to discuss those issues in a useful manner. Like for Blacksburg, it would be talk about AEP [American Electric and Power], talk about the smartroad. For example in the CS [Computer Science] department, if you go to a faculty meeting when all the faculty are there, that's not a community. Now, if they're discussing relevant issues—talking about, "geez, what do we need to teach the undergrads next semester? how can we change the program?" and it's useful discussion—that builds community. But if they start saying, "well, geez, Dr. xxx is a bozo anyways, what do we care about what he says?" and Dr. xxx and Dr. yyy get together and they're like, "oh yeah? Well Dr. zzz is a nincompoop who just plays with multimedia stuff." I mean that's not a community. So even though they are a community of colleagues they are not a community because they are not achieving anything. They are just separate factions pushed together. And warring.

## CYBERCOMMUNION

In many ways, my informants' reluctance to equate communication with community articulates perfectly the difference between first- and second-generational understandings of virtual communities. While scholars like Harasim and Rheingold tend to equate online communications with online communities, later scholars such as Nancy Baym, Beth Kolko and Elizabeth Reid Steere, and Nessim Watson are wary of using the two terms interchangeably. Indeed, as we witness within Bburg-L, the ability to communicate online does not necessarily generate a warm and fuzzy community. Something more is needed.

For example, when asked whether flame wars play a crucial role in fostering discussion, which in turn helps to build community, James responds, "No. That isn't discussion, that's argument. That's not going to build community. That's going to create 'I participated in the bburg.general argument center.' You won't find me generally participating in such things—I don't think it's beneficial."

Echoing James is Derek. I mention to Derek that one definition of community is a collection of dialogues and discussions. Using that definition, I suggest that Harry's posts, however vitriolic, generate the most posts on Bburg-L, making him, by extension, the principal community builder. To which Derek replies:

> Maybe on a very literal interpretation of this definition, perhaps. Because his postings generate by far the most discussion but I think that I would probably disagree in that a community is not JUST discussion. I mean we could all get together and talk about the Super Bowl. Does that make us a community? No, that makes us a bunch of people talking about the Super Bowl. I mean, if you focus and generate discussion on worthwhile activities, that's one thing. But it's a complete waste of my time to be posting flames to Harry, except for the occasional entertainment value.

For Derek, therefore, community exists when knowledge is shared, when "worthwhile activities" take place. Community exists when members "bring higher levels of attention to topics important to the community." He continues:

> For example, his latest post . . . the smartroad thread which rapidly digressed into another bash [Harry] thread. Someone posted a comment on the smartroad being stupid—for a reason: the road cuts were on unstable ground. And so both Shirley and Brian [former members of the smartroad development team] sent informative posts like, "oh, well, when they were planning it, such and such knew about this, but they went about it anyway." And Shirley was talking about how a local engineering student ran a simula-

> tion of what the bridge would look like and what all the road cuts would do and he mentioned the fact that the soil was too unstable to do the road cuts and stuff. And I think those are very, very good posts because they do bring higher levels of attention to topics important to the community. I mean the physical community. Brian posted his comment at 10:30 on Friday. Then at 10-something in the evening, Harry's post was posted and it consisted of "Oh, you're posting on company time again, you just don't learn, do you?" And I'm like, well, okay: what does that have to do with the smartroad?

Similar to Derek, Mark was careful to distinguish between community and communication. According to him, Harry's flames are nothing short of poison: "I think he is more of a destructive force than anything. I think that what he has managed to do is to create two camps. One which has surrounded itself around his poison—and I really see it as poison—and then another that [is] expressing outrage. Now, people grouping together about something very negative does not make a community, I don't think." Instead, echoing Carey and Watson, Mark believes the BEV becomes a community when ideas are shared in a positive manner. "I think that for a community to really exist," he notes, "there has to be something positive, there has to be something nurturing. You know, the whole being able to get a cup of sugar from your neighbor. Something that has really, in a lot of ways, been lost in urban America."

My informants' comments reveal a naïveté found in much of the contemporary cyberculture scholarship. Too many scholars note the Internet's ability to foster communication, celebrate this ability in terms of new forms of communities, and stop there. Their celebrations resemble those of Al Gore, who believes the Net is nothing less than the seed of social and economic equity, and Ross Perot, who equates online voting with a new stage of democracy, as well as the commercials for Microsoft, which sell the Net as a breakdown of physical and national barriers and ask viewers, "Where do you want to go today?" Learning from the members of the BEV, cyberculture scholars must be wary of such simple equations and dig deeper into the *kinds* of communication that this new medium makes possible, fosters, and encourages.

## MAINTAINING THE PEACE

Interestingly, for many of my informants, the act of maintaining the peace, or, conversely, the act of disrupting the peace, stands in between a thriving or a hostile public sphere, a sacred sphere for communion or a battleground for flame wars. This act of maintaining the peace comes in many forms, including kill files, petitions for online exile, and calls for moderation. Ultimately, however, while users can maintain individually based online peace, network-wide peace is, as we shall see, almost impossible to achieve.

As discussed previously, flame wars, or, to use the phrase of many of my informants, *Harry's flames*, dominate many of the discussions of Bburg-L. These flame wars inform, in part, the participation of many of my informants. Indeed, they have led Roberta to lurk rather than post; for Derek, they have spelled the end of otherwise interesting threads on such relevant topics as the smartroads; for Mark, they are nothing short of "poison." Why do the flame wars take place? How do members avoid them? And how can the community as a whole work through them?

Although most of my informants explained flame wars as a by-product of the antisocial nature of their originator (Harry), one informant, Mark, attributes them in part to the anonymity that computer-mediated communication makes possible. "Sometimes I think Bburg-L is less successful than it could be just because I think people tend to be less polite when they're not talking to somebody face to face," he notes. "When they don't necessarily know the person in another context, there's a certain sort of anonymity that posting provides you."

Interestingly, however, it is this same sense of anonymity that allows Roberta to derive a detached sense of entertainment from Harry and his online shenanigans: "I'm not sure that anybody takes him seriously . . . well I guess people take him fairly seriously, I know that I can't change his mind and I don't really care to. I mean, you know, as far as I'm concerned he's a jerk, he's probably a sexist jerk, but it's not my problem. You know, it's not something I have to deal with on a daily basis." She continues: "He's sort of interesting in a bizarre kind of way. Sort of like a car crash—you can't help but look." Ultimately, however, the flames became too much and in Roberta's case she "finally put him in a kill file because it was boring me." A kill file is an option offered by most e-mail packages and newsreaders that allows users to block or filter postings originating from particular users or containing particular key words. While the "killed" users retain the ability to post to the list, their messages will not be read by those list members who have put them in a kill file.

Troubled by the kill files, I prod Derek, who spoke so eloquently on the topic of community building, to explain his decision to put Harry in one. "Aren't kill files," I ask, "killing community?" Derek responds at length:

> If the president came on TV and you changed the channel, is there something wrong with that? If someone publishes a newspaper, do you have to buy it? No. There's nothing that says, any valid philosophy that I know or American law, people have to listen when you talk. You can establish a readership based on the respect you've gained from what you have said. And I think that would be Harry's weakest point—that no one really respects what he said, because of what he said previously. In all honesty he has semi-decent points. Sometimes. But, if someone consistently posted semi-decent points, they would gain the respect of the community; when they posted, people would read them. And it may not be earth-shaking stuff, but people are going to read them and sometimes it would change stuff. But because of Harry's—how did someone phrase it?—reputation as a "goofball and tadler," it diminishes the respect of anything that he posts. If Harry had posted the Monica Lewinsky story twenty-four hours before it broke in the mainstream media, nobody would believe it because it came from Harry. But twenty-four hours later we hear Dan Rather say it and we say, "Oh, okay." Kill files are not an expression of repression against somebody; it is an expression of a way to manage your time. If I have to manually skip every post by Harry, well that wastes time for material that I value more.

He continues by describing kill files as online versions of offline communication practices. For Derek, a kill file is "just a technological implementation of what people have been doing for years."

> Think about meetings nowadays. For example, if Dianne Feinstein gets up in Congress, Dick Armey might as well be doing this [puts hands on ears]. He's probably not in the building. In our current organizations, we might not sit there and say "nannny nanny boo boo, I'm not listening," but people know who are talking and who's not. And even if you're sitting there acting attentive, you may be filtering everything they are saying out and thinking about your income taxes.

Thus, for many of my informants, kill files serve as useful elixirs for individual peace within a not-so-peaceful BEV. Yet what about extending this peace from the individual to the community? What actions can members collectively take to ensure healthy public discussion and peaceful interactions?

Members of Bburg-L did try to maintain community peace, however. Mark notes: "There has been some attempt by the citizens of Bburg-L to moderate it themselves. Most significantly is, I think, when [Harry] got booted off of his ISP. Now it didn't work for very long because, well, he got a new ISP."[7] In the early days of the BEV, such actions would have proved more effective, for all accounts were processed and approved through the BEV main office. Yet in 1996, two years after the community network's launch, network administrators opened up the BEV to commercial ISPs. Today, the worst punishment bestowed upon an individual user is to be booted off from his or her ISP. The result, however, is hardly banishment from the BEV; instead it translates into an hour or two of bureaucracy signing up for and configuring a new account.

Neither flames nor kill files trouble Harry. He knows he's hated, and he attributes this hate to his attitude: "They don't like my attitude. That's perfectly understandable. Hell, sometimes I don't like my attitude!" Yet besides the attitude and beyond the flame wars is a concept that Harry regards as more important than anything: his right to type whatever he wants. And this is what troubles him: "If there is one philosophical basis behind all of what I do it is a man should be able to speak his mind in America."

To protect his right, Harry has gone techno. Having been booted out of "around three or four" ISPs, he has found a new solution. "I went out and got a new account at a new server," he says. "A double account. I got an anonymous account that receives and forwards all of my mail to my other account so no one knows where I am." And with that he smiles, flexes his large biceps, and slugs down the rest of his coffee.

## CONSUMPTION

Returning briefly to Harry and the "Miss Piggy" flame war, it is interesting to note that the entire thread came from a physical, geographic encounter. Harry's initial tirade stemmed from an on-foot visit to the local treasurer's office; its hostility is born from a face-to-face encounter with the manager. Further, the subsequent response works on a local level: one user hand-delivers Harry's post to the treasurer's office; Bill presses list members to appeal to Harry's local Internet service provider. Finally, in his argument against what he calls the "censorship mob," DJ compares the actions of Bburg-L's "Gatekeepers of Public Speech" to a recent censorship debate at the neighboring university, Virginia Tech.

Such examples point toward a virtualization of real space and a realization of virtual space: offline encounters generate online interactions; online interactions fuel offline encounters. A less hostile example of this process comes from a number of professors at Virginia Tech who use the BEV as a tool to transmit course materials. As noted by Roberta, an undergraduate computer engineering major at Virginia Tech, "A lot of my classes, they don't even hand out papers any more, you know, assignments. You just go to the class Web site, download it, and print it." This phenomenon is also apparent within the rapidly disappearing borders between Blacksburg's physical workplaces, telecommuting, and the virtual office. Mark, an employee at Virginia Tech's Public Service Programs in charge of developing Internet content and curriculum for Virginian artists and artists' organizations, notes: "So, you know, in the morning I'll get up and I'll check my email pretty much every morning because my job really depends on it. I work with groups in Richmond, I work with groups in Washington and also various individuals on campus. So basically I'll get up, check my email, read the listservs, and reply to any email that I need to deal with that [has] to do with the university."

Although BEV developers wish to interpret the virtualization of real space as a form of digital community activism, the translation is problematic. To illustrate, one of the most commonly touted features of the BEV is its collection of minutes from the town council meetings. Significantly, however, none of my informants were aware that the minutes were online. When asked about them, Roberta remarked: "I had no idea they were available online. I mean, if somebody asked me, 'are they available online?' I would have said, 'oh, yeah, well, probably.'" With that in mind, perhaps a more accurate metaphor than the online town hall would be the online shopping mall. Indeed, according to my informants, by far the most popular use of the BEV Web site was for consumption.

I began my study of the BEV by reading its initial charter. As noted previously, its first goal is "to enhance the quality of people's lives by electronically linking the residents of the community to one another." Yet beneath the communitarian rhetoric is commercial realism. As mentioned in the Vision Statement, "in essence, the Blacksburg Electronic Village offers companies interested in 21st century information services an opportunity to test new products and delivery mechanisms in a real-life community laboratory prior to their large-scale introduction" (online document). As John Knapp Jr., a spokesperson for Bell Atlantic, notes, the "Blacksburg Electronic Village has proven to be and will continue to be a test bed of services that will be demanded by customers in the future" (Farragher, A-1).

Taking these twin goals into consideration, it is particularly interesting to hear my informants speak about their everyday use of the BEV. Mark reveals: "Yeah, I use the Web site mostly for checking movie listings, to be honest. . . . I've gotten coupons off it as well. Yeah, you can pick up grocery store coupons for Wades, for Kroger, so, if I know I'm going to be purchasing certain products, it's real convenient to be able to do that and not have to search through a newspaper or something like that." Roberta concurs: "I don't use the BEV homepages for much. I usually use that to replace the yellow pages. We [she and her husband] almost never use the phone book, we just look it up online. Blue Ridge Outdoors has coupons that you can print out—as if I could ever afford anything there or use it—but I did print out that."

Echoing this idea of the BEV as an online Yellow Pages, David remarks: "I access it some but mainly when I'm trying to find local businesses or something because on their Web site they have a big directory of all the people they know have a Web page locally." Significantly, however, David continues by suggesting that the BEV's commercial newsgroups can produce more interaction between the citizens of Blacksburg and Virginia Tech, thereby bringing together town and gown: "It does provide something for the students to interact with the local people in." Likewise, James credits the more commercial elements of the BEV for helping to foster greater expansion: "Business is always a good thing. What they did was targeted these groups and expanded. They targeted the businesses and soon you had not only business but local bands, things like that. When you target things it will generally expand."

James's repeated use of the word "targeted" is not accidental. Indeed, one of the key stages in developing the BEV was the deliberate attempt by the town of Blacksburg to recruit and wire local businesses. During the summer of 1995, the town offered grants of up to $500 to local businesses interested in establishing Web sites to be mounted on the BEV. Significantly, in order to qualify, both the business being advertised and the Web service provider/consultant had to be local, thereby promoting local, "in-house" Web development. Faced with more than seventy applications, the town of Blacksburg awarded forty-seven grants, totaling approximately $15,000 (Silver 1999). To date, no grants have been given to community groups or nonprofit organizations.

In some ways, the BEV's outreach strategy is a 180-degree twist on what appears to be the reigning business model for today's Internet companies. The BEV sought ways to bring the community to commercial products, or, stated differently, looked for ways to encourage the community to consume. The opposite is characteristic of many multimillion-dollar companies such as AOL and GeoCities. They begin with a commodity and create a community to consume it; in other words, they foster ways for consumers to build communities. These communities—online in the case of Amazon.com, online and offline in the case of BarnesandNoble.com—are built, of course, around their commodities.

Wired folks occupy wired environments. The majority of my face-to-face interviews took place in dark computer labs, sterile teaching quarters, or messy offices littered with swirling cables and discarded hardware. In one case, I was asked to wait outside for more than twenty minutes while my informant leisurely checked his e-mail. My meeting with Harry, however, was different. He suggested meeting at Lulu's, a crunchy, neo-hippie diner that reminded me of the ones I frequent back home in Santa Cruz. He welcomed me with a huge handshake and a bigger smile. As the hostess led us to our table, Harry said hello to a few locals. Upon sitting down, he offered brief histories of some of the photographs on the wall. Harry is fifty-three but looks forty-five. He is large, fit, and serious. In my weeklong stay in Blacksburg, he was without a doubt the warmest person I met.

Upon and through the screens of most Bburg-L members, Harry is a sexist pig. At one time or another, all of my informants (save Harry) had put him in a kill file. Significantly, however, all of them eventually took him out. As previously noted, Roberta admits, "He's sort of interesting in a bizarre kind of way. Sort of like a car crash—you can't help but look." And as James remarks, he is "probably one of the few life-giving things that keeps this going." In a community network that is designed largely for consumption, communication—however rowdy and offensive—becomes a precious element.

Harry serves a purpose. He gets things started, shakes things up. Although his means are abusive and at times abhorrent, his ends are less so. It is difficult to imagine Bburg-L without the "BEV gadfly." For as Harry is quick to point out, "Not to pat myself on the back, but unless they're jumping on my case, the only messages that come along are refrigerators or sofas for sale and now and then a motorcycle for sale."

In the mid-1990s, community activists (Beamish; Mitchell; Schuler) touted community networks like the Blacksburg Electronic Village as panaceas for America's crumbling infrastructures. Many community networks were developed to facilitate a direct route of communication between a city's institutions and its citizens, to foster dialogues within and between its diverse cultural groups, and to promote local awareness and activism. Although these goals have not been met, they have been better reached by more-progressive, user-built projects like the Seattle Community Network, a community network that offers free accounts to all Seattle residents, boasts a culturally diverse selection of mailing lists and discussion groups, and translates much of its online content into languages other than English.

Yet like so much of cyberspace in the late 1990s, community networks like the BEV have largely become online spheres of consumption. The most glaring piece of evidence revealing this development is the recent competition between CitySearch and Microsoft's Sidewalk.com. Competitors in the market for offering information about local entertainment, news, and shopping, CitySearch bought Sidewalk.com for a whopping $240 million in stock (Ard and Pelline; Tedeschi). Indeed, as both Harry and Bill Gates know, online communicators make perfect online consumers.

## NOTES

The author wishes to thank John Caughey and Beth Kolko for their helpful and sustaining questions and suggestions.

1. All names have been changed. The pseudonyms reflect informants' gender.
2. See Silver, "Parameters and Priorities."
3. See Silver, "Localizing the Global Village."
4. See Silver, "Margins in the Wires."
5. The BEV is located online at http://www.bev.net. For more on the history of the BEV, see the author's "Parameters and Priorities: The Formation of Community In the Blacksburg Electronic Village" and "Localizing the Global Village: Lessons from the Blacksburg Electronic Village," as well as the boosteresque yet interesting *Community Networks: Lessons from Blacksburg, Virginia*, edited by Andrew Michael Cohill and Andrea Lee Kavanaugh. For more on the design of the BEV, see Cortney V. Martin, "Managing Information in a Community Network," and John M. Carroll and Mary Beth Rosson, "Developing the Blacksburg Electronic Village."
6. Members of the BEV have the option of accessing discussion groups in two forms: as a mailing list, Bburg-L, or as a newsgroup, bburg.general. My informants use the two terms interchangeably.
7. ISP stands for "Internet service provider," a company, such as AOL or Prodigy, that offers access to the Internet.

## REFERENCES

Ard, Scott, and Jeff Pelline. "CitySearch Set to Acquire Microsoft's Sidewalk." *CNET News*, 18 July 1999. Online. Internet. http://www.news.com/.

Baym, Nancy. "The Emergence of Community in Computer-Mediated Communication." In Steven G. Jones, ed., *CyberSociety: Computer-Mediated Communication and Community*, 138–163. Thousand Oaks, Calif.: Sage, 1995.

Beamish, Anne. "Communities On-Line: Community-based Computer Networks." Master's thesis, Massachusetts Institute of Technology, 1995. Online. Internet. http://sap.mit.edu/anneb/cn-thesis/.

Blacksburg Electronic Village. "Vision Statement." June 1995. Online. Internet. http://www.bev.net/project/vision95/Goals.html.

Carroll, John M., and Mary Beth Rosson. "Developing the Blacksburg Electronic Village." *Communications of the ACM* 39, no. 12 (1996): 69–74.

Chandrasekaran, Rajiv. "In Virginia, a Virtual Community Tries Plugging Into Itself." *Washington Post*, 11 April 1995.

Cohill, Andrew Michael, and Andrea Lee Kavanaugh, eds. *Community Networks: Lessons from Blacksburg, Virginia*. Norwood, Mass.: Artech House, 1997.

Danet, Brenda. "Text as Mask: Gender, Play, and Performance on the Internet." In Steven Jones, ed., *Cybersociety 2.0: Revisiting Computer-Mediated Communication and Community*, 129–158. Thousand Oaks, Calif.: Sage, 1998.

Farragher, Thomas. "Electronic Village, U.S.A." *San Jose Mercury News*, 1 May 1995.

——. "In Blacksburg, Va., There's No Wired Place Like Home." *Philadelphia Inquirer*, 14 May 1995.

Harasim, Linda M. "Networlds: Networks as Social Space." In Linda M. Harasim, ed., *Global Networks: Computers and International Communication*, 15–34. Cambridge, Mass.: MIT Press, 1993.

Harrison, Teresa M., and Timothy Stephen. "Researching and Creating Community Networks." In Steven G. Jones, ed., *Doing Internet Research: Critical Issues and Methods for Examining the Net*, 221–241. Newbury Park, Calif.: Sage, 1999.

Hine, Christine. "Virtual Ethnography." Paper presented at the Internet Research and Information for Social Scientists International Conference, March 1998, Bristol, United Kingdom. Online. Internet. http://sosig.ac.uk/iriss/papers/paper16.htm.

Kolko, Beth, and Elizabeth Reid Steere. "Dissolution and Fragmentation: Problems in Online Communities." In Steven Jones, ed., *Cybersociety 2.0: Revisiting Computer-mediated Communication and Community*, 212–229. Thousand Oaks, Calif.: Sage, 1998.

Kollock, Peter, and Marc Smith. "Managing the Virtual Commons: Cooperation and Conflict in Computer Communities." In Susan C. Herring, ed., *Computer-Mediated Communications: Linguistic, Social, and Cross-Cultural Perspectives*, 109–128. Amsterdam: John Benjamins Publishing, 1996.

Marcus, George E. "Ethnography in/of the World System: The Emergence of Multi-Sited Ethnography." *Annual Review of Anthropology* 24 (1995): 95–117.

Martin, Cortney V. "Managing Information in a Community Network." In Andrew Michael Cohill and Andrea Lee Kavanaugh, eds., *Community Networks: Lessons from Blacksburg, Virginia*, 235–276. Norwood, Mass.: Artech House, 1997.

Millard, William B. "I Flamed Freud: A Case Study in Teletextual Incendiarism." In David Porter, ed., *Internet Culture*, 145–160. New York: Routledge, 1997.

Mitchell, William J. *City of Bits: Space, Place, and the Infobahn*. Cambridge, Mass.: MIT Press, 1995.

Napoli, Lisa. "The Latest Internet Buzzword: Community." *Cybertimes*, 6 December 1998. Online. Internet. http://www.nytimes.com.

Rheingold, Howard. "A Slice of Life in My Virtual Community." In Linda M. Harasim, ed., *Global Networks: Computers and International Communication*, 57–80. Cambridge, Mass.: MIT Press, 1993.

——. *The Virtual Community: Homesteading on the Electronic Frontier*. Reading, Mass.: Addison-Wesley, 1993.

Schuler, Doug. "Community Networks: Building a New Participatory Medium." *Communications of the ACM* 37, no. 1 (1994): 39–51.

——. *New Community Networks: Wired for Change*. New York: ACM Press, 1996.

Silver, David. "Localizing the Global Village: Lessons from the Blacksburg Electronic Village." In Ray B. Browne and Marshall W. Fishwick, eds., *The Global Village: Dead or Alive?*, 79–92. Bowling Green, O.: Popular Press, 1999.

——. "Margins in the Wires: Looking for Race, Gender, and Sexuality in the Blacksburg Electronic Village." In Beth E. Kolko, Lisa Nakamura, and Gilbert B. Rodman, eds., *Race in Cyberspace: Politics, Identity, and Cyberspace*, 133–150. New York: Routledge, 2000.

——. "Parameters and Priorities: The Formation of Community in the Blacksburg Electronic Village." Master's thesis, University of Maryland, 1996.

Tedeschi, Bob. "Microsoft to Sell City Guides to Rival." *Cybertimes*, 19 July 1999. Online. Internet. http://www.nytimes.com.

Watson, Nessim. "Why We Argue About Virtual Community: A Case Study of the Phish.net Fan Community." In Steven G. Jones, ed., *Virtual Culture: Identity and Communication in Cybersociety*, 102–132. London: Sage, 1997.

13

# Can Technology Transform? Experimenting with Wired Communities

MARK A. JONES

Technological visionaries believe that we are on the verge of a fundamental transformation of local communities, enabled by the proliferation of information and computer networking technologies. They predict that the widespread adoption of these technologies will lead to improvement in the quality of community life. Although it may be years before we can fully understand the impact of computer networks on communities, experiments in several locations shed light on aspects of this future. The organizations leading these initiatives seek to exploit technology by introducing new applications to support the needs of residents and community organizations. While the presence of networking technologies in communities has the potential to alter their character without interference by community planners, these initiatives attempt to accelerate change and influence its direction. Results from several initiatives indicate that communities can employ networking technologies to significantly improve how they function.

I refer to "community" as a geographic region in which the boundaries of a city or metropolitan area identify a distinct cluster of residents. This community is relevant to all its members because local governments and institutions provide services that directly affect the quality of life in the region. For example, residents rely on local hospitals for emergency health care, depend on the police for their safety, and choose homes based on the quality of schools. This geographic definition of community is distinct from social definitions that refer to groups of people with shared identities, norms, interests, or practices.

The initiatives discussed here all strive to improve the ways in which local communities function by exploiting networking technologies to provide easier access to information, increase service efficiency, and facilitate inter-organizational coordination. The following discussion is based on a case study of leading-edge initiatives in eight cities in North America and Europe. The primary form of data collection was through interviews with project managers, city representatives, technical support personnel, and end users. In addition, the study included the activities and progress of many other initiatives, to enrich the data set. While this sample is not exhaustive, it is representative of initiatives taking place worldwide that can inform us of the most developed thinking about the use of information and computing technologies to advance community agendas.

In this essay I adopt a framework for explaining the approach of pilot organizers and the impact of their efforts on their respective communities. The framework consists of three components: *visions* for community change, *organizations* involved in implementing change, and *users* of the new capabilities. An analysis of each initiative along these three dimensions reveals the interrelationships among the three elements. Collectively, these initiatives suggest that the successful introduction of new technologies into communities requires a delicate balance of grand visions, new organizational structures, and involvement by the intended user population.

## A LOOK AT ONE LOCATION

An examination of the use of computer-networking technologies in Blacksburg, Virginia, illustrates how visions, organizations, and users are represented in community initiatives. Blacksburg, which is one of the most extensive experiments in community networking, has one of the world's highest rates of resident access to the Internet, with approximately 85 percent of the population online. This connectivity rate has been sustained for several years, presenting a unique opportunity for researchers to assess the impact of the Internet on the residents of the community. A new community *organization*, the Blacksburg Electronic Village (BEV), was formed in 1993 to create and manage a community Web site that would collect and post information from community organizations and resident interest groups. The staff at BEV is explicitly interested in encouraging resident communication about local issues. The *vision* that grounds their research is the idea that community networks can serve as a forum to facilitate community interaction and over time can become a catalyst for increasing civic engagement. This hypothesis has not yet been confirmed, but the founders of BEV are not alone in their vision. In North America there are now hundreds, if not thousands, of community Web sites very much like the one in Blacksburg.

The vision for community networks is driven by the belief that access to shared community information and forums for discussing regional issues will empower residents so they can make informed decisions about local affairs. Proponents also tie the inclusive nature of these initiatives to notions of a new form of electronic democracy (Schuler, 2). At work here as well is an implicit hope that lowering the threshold for public participation in local issues will reverse the alleged long-term decline in civic involvement chronicled by social critics such as Robert Putnam (Putnam, 1). The staff at BEV hope that their research will confirm their community vision that community networks exert a positive influence on social engagement.

The residents of Blacksburg are the intended *users* of the system. Since the vision for social engagement requires residents to interact more frequently, the BEV organizers set up a series of discussion topics that would allow residents to voice their opinions on issues such as education or health care. To date, these discussion spaces have failed to become the center of community involvement as envisioned. Since such a high percentage of Blacksburg residents were connected to the Internet, they had the capacity to participate, but they chose not to. Specific explanations vary, but the BEV organizers say that the residents just did not understand what to say in the discussion spaces. The topics were quite broad, and few of them galvanized discussion. Most successful have been postings regarding car repair or items for sale in the "Blacksburg—General" section of the Web site. This response makes sense, for people in communities often turn to each other for advice about such needs. Similarly, the listings by residents seeking to sell items are a natural extension of the classified section in the local print newspaper.

In addition to the BEV, other local *organizations* have developed two applications that are popular with the community: online movie listings and coupons from local businesses. A grocery store and a couple of restaurants offer the coupons, and some residents report that they never go to those restaurants without first downloading and printing out an online coupon. The grocery store coupons provide evidence for the store management that investing in a Web presence is worthwhile, since residents who bring in coupons have clearly read the online promotional materials. Despite the popularity of these applications, however, it cannot be said that they are supporting BEV's goal of encouraging civic engagement.

## COMMUNITY TECHNOLOGY FRAMEWORK

The three elements (visions, organizations, and users) identified in Blacksburg are also present, whether or not they are recognized by the project leaders, in every community experimenting with information and computing technologies. In other communities too, there are often critical deficits in one or more of the three elements that result in a less than desirable outcome, frequently because of the limitations of the organization managing the initiative. Though a single initiative managed by a small team cannot ensure that the targeted residents are computer-savvy and interested in trying new applications, the success of the initiative is nevertheless dependent upon resident preparedness. This essay will refer to the framework to explain how each of these forces affects the patterns of technology adoption in communities, and why communities that have the resources to take action on all three levels can attempt the most ambitious change. While leaders can try to control the patterns of technology adoption within their communities, the complex, systemic relationship among visions, organizations, and users makes it difficult to predict the outcome of even a well-conceived plan. It will be helpful at this point to define more clearly what is meant by visions, organizations, and users.

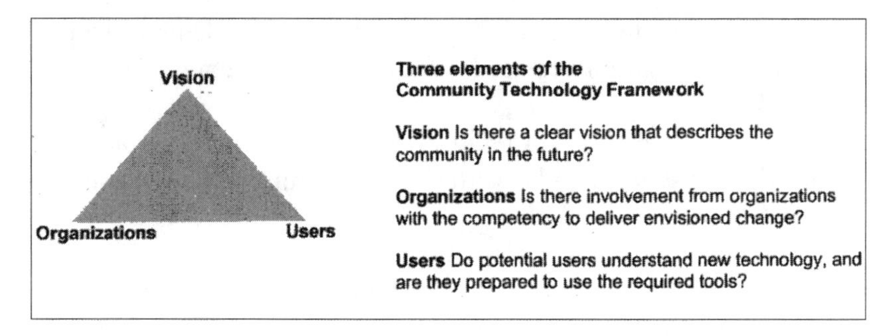


FIGURE 13.1. Three Elements of the Community Technology Framework

## VISIONS

Visions are stories of societal change championed by people who believe that there is a reason to actively promote, influence, and sometimes manage the introduction and use of new technologies. The nature of the underlying vision is a key factor in setting community agendas. Equally important is the level of awareness and support of the vision among members of the community. There are four distinct types of visions that address how technology will affect communities in the future: political visions, economic visions, social visions, and consumer visions.

### Political Visions: The Vision of the Information Society

The vision of the Information Society, which drives much public debate and policy in the European Union, is primarily a political vision for European competitiveness and quality of life in the next century. The drive to become an information society influences broad policies for education, business development, and information services. Backed by funding at the European, country, and municipal levels throughout Europe, it is a vision with enormous impact. The Information Society in Ireland writes:

> The vision for the future is one where Ireland is a unique community, rich in culture, learning and creativity, where the Information Society is embraced:

- to support the talents of our people;
- to create education, employment, wealth and vibrant inclusive communities;
- and where citizens can participate more actively in government, by availing of information technology.

The Commission will seek to ensure that Ireland puts itself in a position to take maximum advantage of the opportunities that this new environment offers. We will urge action where necessary to ensure that the necessary skills and infrastructure are available to place Ireland at the cutting edge of the Information Society. To achieve a successful transformation of our society with its resultant benefits we require the knowledge and preparation of every aspect of Irish society, the general public, the business sector and the Government. (www.isc.ie/cgi-local/index.igi)

**Economic Visions: Smart Communities**

The second vision is that of a Smart Community, which is primarily an economic vision embraced by business leaders in North America who seek to make their communities more efficient for business and, in turn, provide an environment for new service structures. This pragmatic vision galvanizes support for focused initiatives with a clear return of investment. The Panel on Smart Communities in Canada wrote in its 1998 report: "The richness of abundant services that will become possible with technological convergence will embrace every aspect of economic, social, educational, recreational and structural needs, from healthcare to lifelong learning, from basic governance to culture and the arts" (Panel on Smart Communities, 1). The former chairman of Hewlett Packard, Lew Platt, expressed the emphasis on business development: "In this community, citizens are fully empowered to be effective in the information age. Even the smallest organizations can instantly expand their services and transform their businesses by combining modular services in many ways for a single client or even a whole group of clients worldwide" (Platt). In this vision, technology expands the realm of market efficiency that has driven business and pushes it into every sector of society.

### Social Visions: Community Networking

The third vision is a social one of civic involvement. The community networking movement is primarily a vision for a more inclusive, democratic society. While the vision for the Information Society promotes improved well-being for its citizens, primarily through better services, this vision explicitly focuses on an engaged resident population.

> These community networks (sometimes called civic networks, Free-Nets, community computing-centers, or public access networks), some with user populations in the tens of thousands, are intended to advance social goals, such as building economic opportunities in disadvantaged communities. A community network accomplishes these goals by supporting smaller communities within the larger community and by facilitating the exchange of information between individuals and these smaller communities. Another community network objective is to provide electronic "one-stop shopping" for community information and communication, by using discussion forums; question and answer forums; electronic access for government employees; information and access to social services; electronic mail; and in many cases, Internet services, including access to the World Wide Web (WWW). These networks are also beginning to integrate services and information found on existing electronic bulletin board systems (BBSs) and on other computer systems. The most important aspect of community networks is their immense potential for increasing participation in community affairs, a potential far greater than that offered by traditional media such as newspapers, radio, or television. (www.scn.org/ip/commnet/info.html)

### Consumer Visions: Technological Efficiency and Convenience

The fourth vision is one of technological efficiency and convenience. A passage from Bill Gates illustrates the vision: "You'll watch a program when it's convenient for you instead of when a broadcaster chooses to air it. You'll shop, order food, contact friends, or publish information for other people to use when and as you want to. Your nightly newscast will start at a time you determine and last exactly as long as you want it to, and it will cover subjects selected by you or by a service that knows your interests" (Gates, 10). While most community leaders champion one of the first three visions, their vision is often not communicated to the members of their communities. Meanwhile, the notion of technological bliss is so well promoted through the media that it becomes the de facto vision of residents in many communities.

## ORGANIZATIONS

Organizational involvement is a critical factor in determining how new technologies are adopted in communities. Some initiatives (like Blacksburg) are less successful because they fail to garner support from other community organizations. Other initiatives accomplish more because they carefully involve many community organizations, bringing additional expertise and perspectives to the initiative. While the goals, size, and scope vary widely, organizations share one common characteristic: they are social entities with overlapping goals and typically exist to structure and coordinate activities (Daft, 11). Three general types of community organizations were encountered:

1. *Local community organizations* such as government agencies, nonprofits, and schools; often there are new local organizations explicitly designed to exploit technology, such as the group running the Blacksburg Electronic Village.
2. *Organizations external to the community* that are critical to implementing applications. These include technology providers such as telephone company, computer hardware manufacturer, or systems integrator.
3. *Community coalitions* with a shared interest in an issue such as health care improvement or industry change.

## USERS

The potential of new community networking technologies cannot be actualized unless the residents of the community embrace them. Most users typically adopt technologies only when they see a tangible value and possess the technical knowhow to use the technology. A common challenge in community initiatives is that while online services are intended to be used by everyone, the actual experience of residents and their comfort with technology varies widely within a typical population. Notions of fair access and equality, common to many communities, inhibit typical marketing segmentation tactics that would allow organizations to target only early adopters of technology. Many communities have responded to this reality by initiating general computer literacy programs.

Two primary issues contribute to the overall success of an application and its adoption by users: (1) users must be able to operate the necessary equipment effectively and must understand how to use the appropriate software, and (2) users must understand the affordance of the technology and how it fits into the larger patterns of their lives. In short, users will reject technology and applications if they cannot discern tangible value.

A quantifiable indication that an application is valued is that large numbers of people use it. In The Hague, The Netherlands, the city's housing authority allowed residents to register for public housing through a teletext system. The Hague has very high rates of cable television access, and most residents have used teletext, so knowledge of how to use the system was present before the application was developed. But the takeup of the application surprised even the authorities: soon after the system went online, 50,000 people registered for housing by teletext (out of a population of about 500,000). Residents could register and track their applications without having to go to a government office multiple times—a convenience that was evident to anyone who had been through the process before. This shows that people will use even arcane technologies like teletext if they perceive that using the technology will result in a net gain for their lives.

## ANALYSIS OF THE PILOTS

Enabling community-wide changes in use of technology requires orchestrating a delicate balance of vision, involving community organizations, and enabling users to adopt new technologies. Many initiatives have successfully addressed at most two of the three elements of the framework. For example, the leaders of an initiative might have a clear vision for how technology can be integrated into society, and their application fits well with that vision. They may also have appropriate organizational support and funding to implement the new application. But the success of any new technology ultimately depends on having users who value the application and are ready to adopt it; if it does not resonate with users, the initiative will fail to reach its goals. This mismatch between the vision, the influence of community organizations, and the users explains many problems regarding the adoption of technology in communities. Initiatives often encounter problems when one of these three elements is not aligned with the other two.

## INFLUENCE OF ORGANIZATIONAL STRUCTURE

Returning once more to Blacksburg, one can analyze the situation there in terms of the three elements. The implementers of BEV have a very specific vision of how they think computer networks can affect community. Blacksburg also has an almost unparalleled advantage over other locations because such a high percentage of its population is prepared to use new online applications. And since it is a university town, most residents are savvy about how computers operate, and most of them are familiar with e-mail and the Internet.

But the initiative lacks involvement from the community's organizations in the development of meaningful applications. Although the town government was a passive supporter of BEV (it funneled small amounts of money to the project), it was not an active participant in its

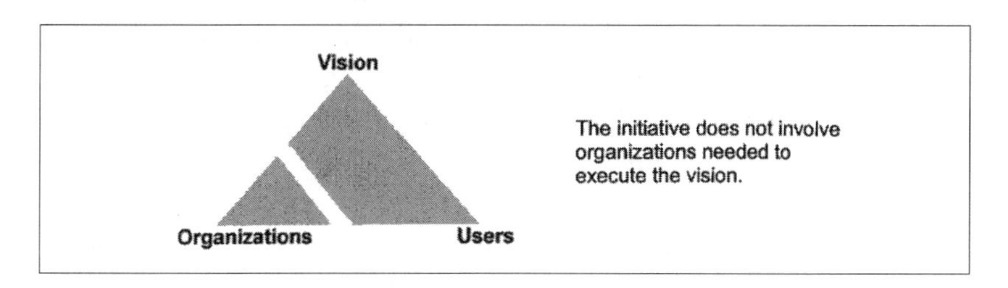


FIGURE 13.2. Influence of organizational structure.

development. The town government supported BEV because there was no reason not to; BEV was viewed as a potential marketing tool to attract investment to the area.

Realistically, however, the town government was in no position to do more. Like the governments in many other smaller cities and towns, Blacksburg's town offices were not computerized to any large degree, and BEV simply was not a fiscal priority. The government was not the only organization reluctant to embrace the community network in Blacksburg. The BEV staff tried to attract participation from local health care institutions to develop new community-centered health applications, but there was no interest from them.

One might make the case that BEV has tremendous organizational involvement, since its Web site is full of information provided by local organizations: descriptions of a wide variety of community entities, announcements for upcoming events, promotions for local services. But the impact of this aggregation is somewhat reduced because most of the information is already available through other channels. For example, many community organizations have their own Web sites, and the local newspapers are well-established vehicles for promoting local events. While it is useful to aggregate this information in one location, the lack of organizational involvement prevents BEV from creating entirely new or unique capabilities.

The success of online coupons on BEV shows that community entities will apply technology to their own ends, sometimes resulting in applications that residents do value. But these kinds of applications do not directly support the goals of the vision for civic involvement held by BEV. The coupons also highlight an important point: technology can be placed in a community with certain intentions, but local residents and institutions will act independently of those intentions, often in surprising ways that lead to unintended consequences. Cities and towns are extremely complex entities, and it is nearly impossible to control what residents and businesses do with technology once it is introduced. This problem appears to be endemic to community projects either offline or online.

Joel Getzendanner, a program director at the Joyce Foundation in Chicago, found that he was having difficulty in implementing projects in environmental policy, school reform, and inner-city economic development because they were designed with a top-down approach. The individual circumstances of the recipients went unaddressed, since the policies were intended to be implemented uniformly. Getzendanner now believes that the governing structure needs to be a framework for dialogue, deliberation, discussion, and ultimately coordination among partners in an egalitarian setting (Fast Company, 84). Forward-thinking city leaders agree. A consensus is emerging that old paradigms for city management are too inflexible for today's complex, fast-moving society, and that cities need to adopt a more inclusive management style.

Similarly, technology application developers should allow the local context to affect their designs, but application developers usually wait too long before seeking the participation of local organizations. An initiative in Canada illustrates how the lack of organizational involvement resulted in inferior services that were rejected by end users. "Netville" is a pseudonym for an experimental wired residential development of about one hundred homes located in suburban Toronto. The neighborhood was wired as an experiment by a consortium of public and private organizations and is one of the few locations in North America where all of the homes in a proximate area are wired for advanced communication services.

The initiative was sponsored by a consortium composed largely of technology companies; at one point the consortium had as many as seventy companies, including many of the leading telecommunications and high-tech companies. The group was held together by a vision of a world where advanced high-bandwidth services could be delivered to consumers in wired communities. The consortium had an interest in understanding the impact of new broadband online services on community residents, with an eye toward identifying lucrative markets in the future. They marketed the housing development heavily as a futuristic community that hosted advanced services such as fast Internet connectivity, online educational CD-ROMs, a music-on-demand jukebox, point-to-point video within the neighborhood (really a form of videoconferencing), and a community health care application (Hampton, 3). They also indicated that they would connect both students and parents to the local school system with a high-bandwidth network.

Because the initiative was based on the premise of having a completely wired neighborhood, the consortium wired all of the homes and arranged for any resident who did not already own a computer to purchase one at a steeply discounted price. The developers then conducted training sessions on basic computer literacy as well as the use of their custom applications and the Internet. Follow-up training sessions were conducted periodically in people's homes. They also established a twenty-four-hour help desk for the residents to help fix equipment or guide new users through the process of using unfamiliar applications such as the Internet.

The Netville initiative, even more than the BEV, failed to bring in the right kind of organizational support to develop meaningful content. The center of the consortium was composed almost entirely of technology providers, but creating the applications depended on content providers. Although the consortium developed several in-house applications, such as a music-on-demand system, it failed to connect residents to the local schools or deliver any locally relevant content. Even the music-on-demand application, which was initially well received by residents, ran into problems when music publishers limited the selection available for residents to use. The developers did lobby the town council to develop a local Web site, but the Netville neighborhood was quite small and the mayor of the town was unconvinced. The health care application ran into problems for similar reasons. No local health care organizations were involved in the initiative; the health care application consisted of links to information that was already on the Web and an already existing telephone health hot line. In the end every application that was developed by the consortium was hampered by a lack of organizational support.

The consortium apparently underestimated how difficult it would be to enlist the cooperation of organizations. Just as users need to understand the value of applications before they are willing to adopt a new technology, organizations that are considering whether to participate in an initiative need to have a clear reason to do so. Usually this entails involving them early in the development process as well as framing the project from their perspective.

After the initial excitement about the in-house applications died down, the residents soon found that the only application they continued to use was the Internet. But their comfort with e-mail brought about a change. Several months after people moved into the neighborhood, residents who had more experience with computers asked the consortium to release the e-mail addresses of the other community households. In July 1997 an e-mail list was created that included every household, and residents could either add additional addresses or remove their existing address. During most of the pilot, about seventy households remained on the list. Interestingly, residents reported that the e-mail list was the most important use of their computers, second only to general Internet connectivity.

The e-mail list worked as an effective community communication mechanism because the expectations for e-mail were modest and the content was limited to a familiar domain. For example, the residents shared information about problems that they were having with their new homes (such as driveways that were not finished properly). The fact that everyone in the neighborhood had a new home from the same builder raised the value of the mailing list. The subject that elicited the most discussion was the sudden and unexpected termination of the pilot program due to funding problems. Many residents had become accustomed to high-speed Internet connectivity at no cost, and they were angry that they were going to lose connectivity as well as twenty-four-hour technical support. In the end, the residents used the network installed by the consortium to become better organized in their opposition to the consortium.

Without organizational support, the initiative could not execute its vision, and the residents used the technology to organize and create their own value. Although postings on the e-mail list were sporadic and unevenly distributed, most residents credited the list as a key factor in helping them feel more connected to their neighbors. Residents reported that they interacted with other residents more frequently than they had in other neighborhoods and that their contacts were spread out across the neighborhood, instead of being concentrated on a few proximate houses, as is typical in suburban developments. Residents reported that they "knew who lived in their neighborhood" from the e-mail list before they actually met them, indicating that online forums may extend social networks.

In Blacksburg, the anecdotal evidence also shows that a high level of resident connectivity does affect how people coordinate ordinary daily activities and maintain social ties. Blacksburg seems to have reached the point where residents expect each other to be connected, and institutions and community groups are changing their behavior. Soccer chauffeurs are relying on the Internet to get last-minute updates on whether a game will be canceled, for example, and many local institutions such as churches are dropping expensive paper publications in favor of communicating with their members exclusively through the Internet.

Such changes are not without precedent. When the telephone was first introduced, it was nearly universally accepted as an important invention that would change people's lives. But there was no consensus on how it would be used. Phones were promoted as a way to extend people's world beyond their local communities, as a safety precaution, and as a method to broadcast news and information (Norman, 190). Claude Fischer, in an analysis of how the telephone affected social patterns in the early twentieth century, concludes that while the telephone did open up new communications channels outside people's immediate geographic communities, there is significant evidence that it increased local interaction as well.

But perhaps the most important finding is that communication increased mostly between existing relationships, whether personal or organizational:

> [The telephone] permitted people, especially women, to more intensely pursue organizational involvement. Although strictly speaking club and church work are public activities, they are usually restricted to the immediate social world. The home telephone allowed subscribers to maintain more frequent contact with kin and friends by chatting briefly perhaps a few times a week instead of at greater length once a week. There is little sign that telephone calling opened up new social contacts.
>
> (Fischer, 266)

Fischer further states: "Although, for example, Americans widely used the automobile to explore new worlds by auto touring, they used the telephone largely to reinforce their existing worlds" (Fischer, 269). One need only reflect on teen use of the telephone to see that an increase in local interaction is indeed one result of its introduction. But the promoters of the telephone could not have predicted that teenagers would embrace it as a way to maintain frequent contact with friends that they see every day.

In many ways, the Netville and Blacksburg cases are examples of what occurs in communities when technology is introduced without an actionable vision or organizational support: people tend to fit the technology into already existing patterns of their lives. The BEV had a vision for how community networks could affect resident engagement, but that vision was not communicated to the residents who had to participate in its execution. Visionaries hope that community populations will use the technology for new activities, but the evidence from Blacksburg and Netville shows that residents use new technology to help them do what they already were likely to do, albeit a little more efficiently. And in neither situation were the results close to the goals of the pilot. The introduction of technology takes on a life of its own, sometimes leading to unpredictable results.

The results observed in Blacksburg and Netville are typical of complex, adaptive systems like communities. Chaos theory suggests that groups cannot direct how such systems will function; they can only disturb them (Pascale, 85). Had different strategies been used, perhaps the leadership in Blacksburg and Netville could have exerted more influence over the events that took place in their respective communities. In the end, however, it is clear that the introduction of new technology has too many factors to predict exactly how it will affect communities over time. The best a leader can do is to provide a vision and set up the context for change (Pascale, 93).

## USERS ARE NOT PREPARED TO USE TECHNOLOGY

One problem with developing new services for the general public is a lack of a critical mass of residents equipped to use those services. (While Blacksburg has achieved a remarkably high connectivity rate, it

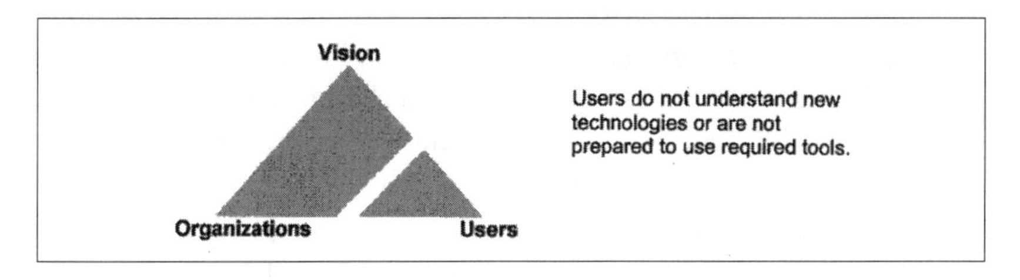


FIGURE 13.3. Users do not understand new technologies or are not prepared to use required tools.

is a somewhat unusual situation, since a marked majority of the population is affiliated with Virginia Tech.) In many locations, a lack of prepared users has prevented institutions such as governments from offering dramatically new services. Such moves are almost always costly and require major reengineering of internal processes. Until they feel that there are enough consumers for the new services, they will refrain from investing in new development.

But in some locations, particularly in Europe, governments are willing to fund experimental initiatives because they view them as an investment in the future. Most European governments have a long-term strategy tied in some way to the vision of the Information Society. There is widespread support for investment in new capabilities for government-citizen relationships, education, social equality, and small-business development. Many pan-European projects rely on European Union funds in addition to national funding, and in many locations, government funding supports such policies as achieving a target number of public access terminals. The result is the alignment of a vision for the future with the funding of community organizations to implement the vision.

Finland, for example, has funded a national agenda to become a leader in the Information Society. The Finnish government and major industry partners worked together to create a vision for their future that involves ubiquitous computer usage throughout all sectors of Finnish society. Equipping students with the knowledge to use computers is a key part of the long-term strategy. Finland also has very aggressive plans for a complete overhaul of its educational system, from both a technical and a pedagogical perspective. The country set goals for computer-to-student ratios and has required that teachers be retrained. Helsinki, as the capital and largest city, is taking the lead in this educational transformation.

The Helsinki Department of Education has installed a secure, high-bandwidth network linking 160 schools in the Helsinki metropolitan area. Centralized planning and control allow a remarkably lean technical support organization, with a staff of only twenty-three supporting the entire network. The department standardized equipment and limited computer applications to a select few, including the Microsoft Windows operating system. Custom applications are not encouraged. Helsinki has accomplished more than most education providers by at least solving the technical problems of integrating computers and education. One common problem that the department's plan has not overcome, however, is that users do not really know what to do with the technology.

What Helsinki has is a well-developed infrastructure with fewer users than the department hoped for. One of the most serious problems is getting the cooperation of the teachers in integrating computers into the curriculum. Even teachers who are excited about the potential of computers as a teaching aid have few well-developed methods for integrating them into the curriculum. Helsinki's answer is to invest heavily in training.

Teacher training takes place on computers, and teachers are encouraged to use online discussion forums to communicate with others in training. The goal is for teachers to become accustomed to communicating online and helping each other grapple with the problems of developing a new pedagogy. There is some evidence that a certain percentage of teachers do respond to this environment and, after training, want to pursue active integration of computers into the curriculum. But Helsinki acknowledges that it will be years before most teachers are using computers in meaningful ways. Without the core commitment from the highest levels of government, the patience required for such long-term change could not be sustained.

Another site, Barcelona, also has in place a regional strategy to prepare for the Information Society. But Barcelona has a training problem of a much larger scale, with an entire population that is unprepared to accept potentially useful applications because of their lack of experience with the Internet. Barcelona's Internet penetration is only approximately 8–9 percent of the population, even though the government is funding interesting and novel approaches for exploiting the potential of computer networking.

Infopime is a government-led initiative that aggregates statistical data from a number of government agencies into a searchable database with a common entry point. Designed as a research tool for small businesses and marketers, one feature of the database uses a geographic information system (GIS) over the Web to allow fast access to data for all of Barcelona, or for just a single neighborhood. The government's clear agenda and directives have enabled the city to enlist a large number of agencies to participate. While none of the data are new, placing the information in a centralized location provides a valuable service to the business community, saving time for businesses that already use the data. In addition, the site contains a listing of all 170,000 businesses in Barcelona, plus discussion forums, import and export opportunities, and monographs by industry specialists on current business issues.

While these functions seem useful for small businesses, the application developers were surprised at how few are prepared to take advantage of the services; most small businesses simply do not have the experience with computers or the Internet to understand the value of Infopime. The organizers have spent significant time promoting the application by holding informational sessions in community centers throughout the city. A typical session might draw twenty to forty people, but overall only a very small percentage of businesses even know what the Internet is. Even though many small businesses use computers to manage their operations internally, they have yet to use them to reach the outside world. With the help of government policy and funding, the organizers have an opportunity to address training issues. This assumes, of course, that the government policy is stable and that support will be ongoing, an assumption that the organizers are reluctant to make.

The City of Barcelona has sponsored another project that develops forward-thinking services without a prepared user population. Barcelona Activa is a small-business incubator located in the center of the city. Like other small-business incubators, its goal is to help new entrepreneurs establish themselves in a supportive environment, by providing, at reduced cost, strategic business consulting and marketing assistance. It also serves as a resource clearinghouse, directing businesses to people and resources that will provide them with the expertise they need to compete in their chosen markets.

At present, Barcelona Activa can house about eighty businesses in the physical incubator, and its staff can give cursory business advice to a few hundred more a year. Since the budget is controlled by the city and a fixed number of staff limits the number of businesses that can be served directly, Barcelona Activa decided to extend its reach by creating BarcelonaNetActiva, a virtual business incubator. BarcelonaNet Activa closely follows Barcelona Activa's well-established methods, and by virtualizing operations, the incubator can dramatically increase the number of businesses served and potentially improve the quality of the assistance, incorporating a larger network of business advisers than is possible in the real-world version. In addition, the organization hopes to maintain strong ties to entrepreneurs that have moved out of the incubator, enlarging and enriching a developing social network.

The core of the virtual incubator is a Web site with both public and private areas. All of the content in the public areas is produced by the BarcelonaNetActiva organization, including business directories, pointers to statistical information, course listings, and packaged business advice. While centralizing this information into one location is certainly a service to local businesses, it does not duplicate the qualities of a business incubator, which requires experts to advise and educate inexperienced business owners about how to succeed in their markets. But the private area of the Web site, open only to registered businesses (which must pass a preliminary evaluation by the BarcelonaNetActiva management), virtualizes the expertise that businesses need.

Currently, Barcelona's small businesses are unprepared to use the system. Some of the incubator's functionality, such as setting up knowledge-sharing forums, requires a balance of incentives and training that is complex for even the most developed organizations. But BarcelonaNetActiva is hoping to train users gradually by requiring them to use the online system to perform a few routine activities, such as communicating with a contact at BarcelonaNetActiva.

## NO COMMUNITY-WIDE VISION

Communities whose leadership promotes a single community-wide vision have a distinct advantage over those without a central vision. A

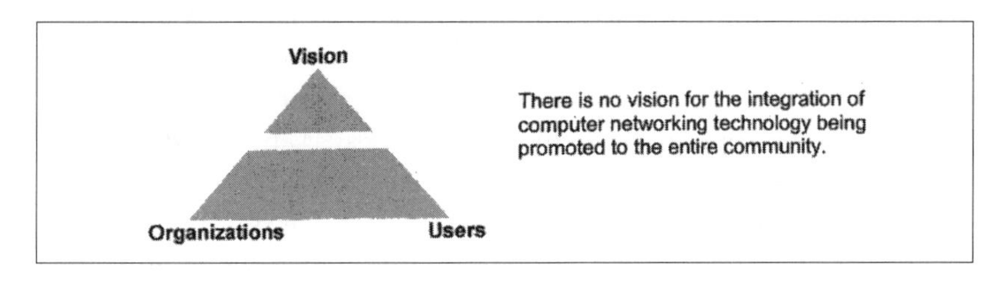


FIGURE 13.4. There is no vision for the integration of computer networking technology being promoted to the entire community.

vision serves to focus attention on a core set of projects and goals, and when promoted effectively, it draws support from large sectors of the community. Shared visions are particularly important when implementation of a project requires the participation of a large, diverse group of organizations and residents, as is the case for community Web sites. But many locations lack any sort of central vision, which is a necessity in order to coordinate efforts across the community.

Chicago, like many large cities, has several independent experiments in community communications. The *Chicago Tribune*, one of two major daily newspapers in the area, supports a well-developed set of community Web sites called Digital Cities for the city of Chicago and most of the suburbs. Each site includes community information, events, and links to local institutions' Web sites. Digital Cities also hosts Web pages for local nonprofit organizations in each community and sets up discussion rooms within which residents can interact.

At the same time, Pioneer Press, a regional newspaper organization with a network of more than thirty weekly community newspapers, has established its own set of community Web pages, with a mix of general community information, events, and links similar to that of the Digital Cities sites. To add to the stew, many local libraries and town governments in the suburbs have set up community Web sites that duplicate content yet again. Some local organizations respond to this confusion by posting links to their own Web site on all of the systems.

Some might argue that residents are benefiting from this race among local players to establish territory, but the result is a fractured community effort that wastes resources in its duplication of content. And none of the community Web sites can maintain the critical mass of consistent users necessary to make the information compelling. In addition, the lack of a central vision guiding the community initiatives has diffused efforts to enlist the involvement of local organizations. Most do no more than post information that is available in other places. The net result can in no way be considered a transforming change.

While broad initiatives such as community Web sites do require community-wide visions to be successful, locations without a vision can effectively employ networking technology to achieve some degree of change, such as improving a city service. Although a community-wide vision is not always present for these new technology initiatives, successful examples always have very clear goals, well-defined plans, and explicit value for end users. In addition, these initiatives can involve only a subset of the community, such as the health care or community safety sector. By limiting their scope and user population they can more easily account for organizational and user issues. One successful example is the City of Winston-Salem's Integrated Network Fire Operations (INFO) Project.

This initiative facilitates communication between fire stations in the city and provides critical information in graphical form to firefighters in emergency vehicles. ISDN technology provides the backbone for the network linking the fire stations, and geographic information system (GIS) software uses routing and location functionality to define the optimal route. Software links firefighters to documents containing critical information when it is needed, allowing them to view graphical information via a touch screen interface in each vehicle. This application gives them access to previously unavailable information as they perform routine tasks. It also augments their traditional work processes and creates new structures for decision making. The level of technological integration in this example is impressive, and one can guess that the faster response times enabled by the new technology will have a beneficial impact on communities; the clear value of the application elicits the cooperation of the end user, the firemen.

Community-wide visions are also unnecessary for pragmatic community coalitions seeking to focus efforts and coordinate activities within a narrow sector such as improved health care. The technology is just a supporting mechanism for already existing goals. Aiken, South Carolina, a city of about 30,000, is making remarkable progress in changing the way that health care is conceived and delivered in the local area. A nonprofit organization in the city has led the formation of a coalition consisting of more than thirty local organizations related to health care. Members include the local hospital, Planned Parenthood, a drug hot line, and the police. The organizations realized that many health problems are extremely complex and that problems being addressed by one organization may actually be related to other critical, and perhaps ignored, health issues.

The coalition based its efforts on guidelines promoted by the Healthy Communities movement, which adopts complex systems theory and applies it to health care in communities. Professionals familiar with complex community issues realized that health problems are far more interdependent than the institutional structure would suggest. Reducing teen pregnancy, for example, cannot be solved exclusively through sex education and the availability of birth control. Domestic violence and the prevalence of single-parent households also statistically affect teen pregnancy. Practitioners using this approach attempt to understand these complex relationships and take steps to rectify deficiencies.

While acknowledging that no effort will be able to control every community organization that touches health care, proponents of this approach believe that coalitions can serve to create a shared vision among a diverse group of organizations. This vision in turn can help community health care organizations to self-organize in more productive ways. Once a city conducts an assessment of local issues, these systemic relationships become more apparent, but the reality of bringing such a diverse group of organizations to the same table is an arduous and often frustrating experience for everyone involved. In Aiken, the unofficial leader of the coalition brought in networking technologies to improve the communication process, and a combination of determination and good humor cajoled the thirty organizations to begin the task of tackling health in a more integrated fashion. The group meets regularly and has established an e-mail discussion. The coalition leader knew that getting an online discussion started was critical to the success of the effort, but several organizations were infrequent users of e-mail. Eventually, after sustained effort, all of the coalition members were reliably online.

The coalition did not want merely to discuss health issues; it had set a specific goal, to take measurable action on them. Therefore, the coalition members agreed to begin tracking community health issues with a software application called the Outcomes Toolkit, a product developed by Health Forum, a nonprofit organization that focuses on community health issues. The application tracks a community's progress over time on a number of health issues designated by the coalition as vital to community health. The coalition members agree upon measurable indicators so that they can track the progress of community goals. The goals and indicators (and ultimately, organizational initiatives that are tied to improving the indicators) are structured in a database accessible to coalition members via a secure site on the Internet.

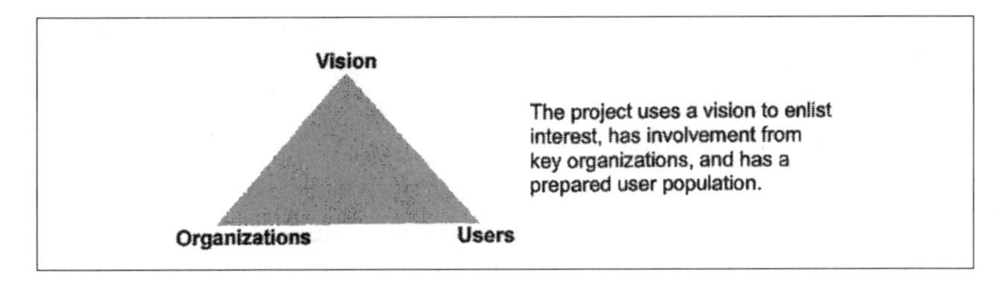


FIGURE 13.5. The project uses a vision to enlist interest, has involvement from key organizations, and has a prepared user population.

## ALIGNMENT OF THE THREE AREAS

Projects that attempt to develop applications that affect many parts of the community simultaneously take a comprehensive approach. These projects incorporate a strong community-wide vision, involve many organizations that have a stake in the outcome of the project, and account for how end users are prepared to adopt new technology. Smart Permits, a new way to deliver construction permits and manage construction projects, is the result of a four-year collaboration among public and private partners in Silicon Valley. Smart Valley, a network of individuals and organizations interested in the overall economic health of the region, spearheaded the project. Smart Permits is a direct result of *Blueprint for a Twenty-first Century Community*, a report issued in 1993 that is closely aligned with the Smart Communities vision. The report synthesized the input of more than a thousand people, collected in thirteen separate initiatives, all designed to understand emerging community needs for the future.

The Smart Valley coalition enlisted the involvement of all of the organizations that could potentially have been affected by changes in the permitting process. There were representatives from architecture, government, engineering and construction, as well as the delivery of public services. Over the next two years, the Smart Valley group developed prototypes, negotiated standards and systems requirements, and continued the discussion among the twenty jurisdictions that would be a part of the Smart Permit project. Eventually, the group committed to the development of a custom software package that would allow the management of permits across the various parties involved in the construction industry. By March 1998 the pilot software was installed in ten locations in the valley.

The result is a process that changes the way an entire industry does business. Early results from the initial test cities (Los Gatos and Sunnyvale, California) have shown significant economic benefit from the application. The time required to issue construction licensing has been cut in half in Los Gatos, from ten days to five days. In Sunnyvale, 95 percent of permits now get processed in one day. Businesses benefit because their work process is simpler and more streamlined, saving time and money. Residents benefit because their houses will be completed faster.

According to coalition members, the relationships that were built during the development process created an atmosphere of trust that made the project possible. Without such an atmosphere, the chances for success would have been severely compromised. The trusting relationships built up during this project are also a form of community capital. An atmosphere of trust, backed by a coalition process, will make the next community project easier to execute. But the project organizers caution that such cross-sector collaboration is challenging and not for the faint of heart. They credit the scale and ambition of the vision as an attraction that kept coalition members focused and interested in the project over the long development period. Members stated that a grand vision is essential to make the investment of the key partners seem worthwhile. (www.jointventure.org)

Large cities have an extremely hard time getting organizations to collaborate. In 1995 representatives from more than one hundred cities attended "Blueprint 2000; Communities for the 21st Century," in Washington, D.C. The conference centered on topics such as community revitalization, development, and cooperation. The most important need identified was community collaboration. Participants noted that "far too often, one hand doesn't know what the other one is doing, causing a duplication of services, lack of understanding, wasted time, and undue strife between local initiatives." Currently few models exist that illustrate how cities can encourage the right kind of collaboration.

But global businesses are offering new models for how cities may function in the future. An example of such an organization is VISA, which has tens of thousands of member organizations in two hundred countries, much like the large number of community organizations in any city. The company is not run in a hierarchical fashion from the top; rather, control is distributed across the organization, with many decisions being made at the local level. It is largely a self-organizing entity, much like an ecosystem. VISA's founder, Dee Hock, consciously designed an organization that pushed decision making down to the lowest level, all the while making the pieces add up to a synergistic whole through a strong vision of core principles. The result is an enabling organization that manages complexity effectively (Waldrop, 76).

Some community coalitions are trying to duplicate the combination of top-down vision and bottom-up participation seen at VISA. Next Generation Cities is a San Francisco–based public-private partnership seeking to develop an Internet-based infrastructure for enabling community-based electronic networks to function. It is a complex endeavor that will require the participation of many residents and community organizations. Next Generation Cities spent more than two years assembling a public/private partnership that includes the City of San Francisco Department of Public Works; CommerceNet, an industry e-commerce consortium; CB Ellis, a real estate group; the SOMA Foundation (South of Market Association Foundation); and other technology providers. The grand vision that Next Generation Cities established brought in these organizations, giving the effort validity within the local community, and through their time commitment these groups are invested in the outcome of the project. This buy-in is expected to benefit the coalition by having a diverse group of champions that represent groups of potential end users of the newly developed systems. Their involvement will also influence the outcome of the project, since they are decision-makers as well as end users. The staff at Next Generation Cities realize that they cannot successfully develop a solution with a completely top-down approach.

The goal of the initiative is the creation of a Digital Community Network, which consists of a series of electronic services that include the Trusted Public Databank, Intelligent Business Registries, and privacy filters for consumers. Together, these services function as a municipal operating system that both streamlines and stimulates interaction between governmental agencies, businesses, and citizens. If it is successful, this initiative will create a set of data protocols, standards, and processes for combining currently incompatible information. Initial applications are planned for the commercial real estate industry as well as services for small business in the South of Market area of San Francisco.

Many communities are embracing the vision that communications and computing technologies can precipitate positive transforming change for their residents. By developing new applications with the intention of altering resident behavior, local organizations are trying to influence how the uptake of these technologies occurs. Many communities are currently in the initial stages of forming task forces and coalitions whose mission is to craft strategies for leveraging communications networks. There is little doubt that communication and computing technologies will in time have a profound impact on community life everywhere they proliferate. But the changes wrought by the introduction of technologies will be influenced by the choices made by government, community organizations, businesses, and grassroots groups.

Communities must carefully evaluate their circumstances to determine an appropriate strategy for the development of successful applications. There needs to be proper alignment between visions for the future held by community members, whether they are actively promoted by community leadership or not, and the operational realities of organizational involvement and user value. Visions can serve as a powerful galvanizing force for large-scale change, and visions are essential for new systems that require buy-in from a large number of community entities, such as situations involving community-wide structural change, as in the Smart Permit initiative. In addition, new technological development must incorporate a mix of organizations that have the competency to deliver meaningful content to end users, a failing of many current initiatives. And most important, communities must understand the value for end users of new systems, how new applications will fit into their lives, and how to develop strategies to increase the likelihood that applications will be matched to real needs.

Community organizations that adopt comprehensive strategies will have a better chance of generating projects that will have positive impact. But these new systems will be only the beginning of a long change process that will not be controlled by those who introduce new technical infrastructures; such inherently powerful change agents as networked computers will undoubtedly lead to many unintended consequences. And every new initiative will add to the mix of community elements that will, in turn, form the foundation for new developments in the future. Communities that prosper will recognize this and become active facilitators and participants in an ongoing dialogue for long-term change.

## REFERENCES

Anderson, Robert H., et al. *Universal Access to E-Mail: Feasibility and Societal Implications*. MR-650-MF. Santa Monica: Rand Corporation, 1995.

Borsdorf, Del. "Charlotte's City Within a City: The Community Problem-Solving Approach." *National Civic Review* 5, no. 84 (Summer/Fall 1995). 6 pp. Online. WilsonSelect. 8 July 1999.

Couto, Richard A. "Community Coalitions and Grassroots Policies of Empowerment." *Administration and Society*, 1 November 1998. 20 pp. Online. New York: Dow Jones Publications Library. 25 June 1999.

Daft, Richard L. *Organization Theory and Design*. 6th ed. Cincinnati: South-Western College Publishing, 1998.

Davenport, Thomas H. *Process Innovation: Reengineering Work Through Information Technology*. Boston: Harvard Business School Press, 1993.

Dills, Jim. *Geographic Communities: Value System Strategies for Organization and Sustainability*. Report #98–33. 7 December 1998. 20 pp. Online. CommerceNet. 7 August 1999.

Drucker, Peter F. "The Age of Social Transformation." *Atlantic Monthly*, November 1994. 20 pp. Online. Internet. 7 August 1999.

Eger, John M. *Statement Before the Senate Committee on Energy Utilities and Communications*. 10 February 1998. Online. http://www.smartcommunities.org/cal/e_testimony.htm. 7 August 1999.

Fischer, Claude S. *America Calling: A Social History of the Telephone to 1940*. Berkeley: University of California Press, 1992.

Gamm, Larry D., and Keith J. Benson. "The Influence of Governmental Policy on Community Health Partnerships and Community Care Networks: An Analysis of Three Cases." *Journal of Health Politics, Policy, and Law* 23, no. 5 (1 October 1998). 21 pp. Online. Dow Jones Publications Library. 25 June 1999.

Gates, Bill. *The Road Ahead*. New York: Penguin, 1996.

Grantham, Charles E. *The Virtual Incubator: Managing Human Capital in the Software Industry*. Report #98–14. 8 July 1998. 12 pp. Online. CommerceNet. 7 August 1999.

Gurstein, Michael, and Bruce Dienes. "Community Enterprise Networks: Partnerships for Local Economic Development." Paper presented at Libraries as Leaders in Community Economic Development Conference, June 1998. 12 pp. Online. http://ccen.uccb.ns.ca/articles/CENs libraries.html. 1 December 1998.

Hampton, Keith N. "Netville: Globalization and Civic Society." Paper presented 17 July 1998.

Joint Venture Silicon Valley Network. "Smart Permit: Desktop Tools." Online. http://www.jointventure.org/initiatives/smartpermit/desktop.html. 25 June 1999.

——. "Smart Permit: History and Lessons Learned." Online. http://www.jointventure.org/initiatives/smartpermit/history.html. 25 June 1999.

Kasarda, John D., and Dennis A. Rondinelli. "Innovative Infrastructure for Agile Manufacturers." *Sloan Management Review*. 1 January 1998. 15 pp. Online. Dow Jones Publications Library. 25 June 1999.

Kavanaugh, Andrea L., and Scott J. Patterson. "The Impact of Computer Networking on Social Capital: A Test Case." Paper prepared for the National Communications Association, 21–24 November 1998.

Kraut, Robert, et al. "HomeNet: A Field Trial of Residential Internet Services." *Communications of the ACM* 39, no. 12 (December 1996): 55–63.

Next Generation Cities. "Next Generation Cities: Architecture, Technology, and Business Structure for the Development of a Next Generation City (NGC) in San Francisco, CA USA." Report #98–13. 12 June 1998. 13 pp. Online. CommerceNet. 7 August 1999.

Norman, Donald A. *Things That Make Us Smart*. Reading: Addison-Wesley, 1993.

Norris, Tyler, Gruffie Clough, and Darvin Ayre. "Creating and Sustaining Healthy Communities." *Trustee*. 1 March 1999. 7 pp. Online. Dow Jones Publications Library. 25 June 1999.

Panel on Smart Communities. *Report of the Panel on Smart Communities*. Ottawa: Industry Canada, 1998.

Parzen, Julia. *Innovations in Metropolitan Cooperation*. Center for Neighborhood Technology Report. 11 March 1997. 41 pp. Online. http://www.cnt._Hlt458824221o_Hlt458824221rg/mi/in_Hlt456416328o_Hlt456416328v ate.htm#VII. 7 August 1999.

Pascale, Richard T. "Surfing the Edge of Chaos." *Sloan Management Review* 40, no. 3 (Spring 1999).

Platt, Lew. "Cities of the Future." *Remarks to the Cities of the Future Conference*, 11 December 1998. Online. http://www.hp.co_Hlt456414232m_Hlt456414232/financials/textonly/personnel/ceo/cities.html. 17 February 1999.

Putnam, Robert D. "The Strange Disappearance of Civic America." *American Prospect* 24 (Winter 1996) 12 pp. Online. Electronic Policy Network, 7 August 1999.

Rochefort, David A., Michael Rosenberg, and Deena White. "Community as a Policy Instrument: A Comparative Analysis." *Policy Studies Journal*, 1 October 1998. 20 pp. Online. Dow Jones Publications Library. 25 June 1999.

Schuler, Doug. *New Community Networks: Wired for Change*. New York: Addison-Wesley, 1996.

Skrezeszewski, Stan, and Maureen Cubberley. *A New Vision of Community and Economic Development: A Multidimensional Convergence of Government, Business, and the Social Sectors of the Internet*. Online. http://www.twnic.net/inet96/b4/b4_4.htm. 7 August 1999.

Stewart, Thomas A. *Intellectual Capital: The New Wealth of Organizations*. New York: Doubleday, 1997.

Waldrop, Mitchell M. "The Trillion-Dollar Vision of Dee Hock." *Fast Company*. October 1996. 7 pp. Online. 7 August 1999.

Whiting, Randall C., et al. *Next Generation Cities: Building and Operating Internet Based Digital Community Networks (DCNi) for Cities of the Twenty-first Century*. San Francisco: Next Generation Cities, 1998.

Widmayer, Patricia, and Gary Greenberg. *Putting Our Minds Together: The Digital Network Infrastructure and Metropolitan Chicago*. Metropolitan Planning Council Report. Chicago: Northwestern University, 1998.

# INDEX

AARSETH, E., 292, 293, 317*n*2
ABC, 17
Access: architecture of digital environments, 255; to online banking, 94; children's, 119; computer, 204, 277; information technology, 196, 208, 209, 242–43, 248, 258–59; information, 28, 202; Internet, 28–29, 31–32, 36–37, 57, 186, 249, 258, 277, 315, 330–31, 337, 355, 356; mapping and, 104–5; network hierarchy, 31; portal site, 85, 186; public forum, 29; subsidized, 38; system administrator and, 100 ; through community networks, 330–31, 360; university, 272, 277; unwanted, control of, 147–52; to virtual cities, 116; virtual classroom, 93, 102–103; World Wide Web, 177, 179
ACTV, 185
Affect, 118–30; defined, 119–21
Africa, 33
Aga, S. M., 240
Alinsky, S. D., 320*n*4
Allen, J., 176, 185
Amazon.com, 154, 349
America Online (AOL), 186, 279, 349
American Bar Association Internet Jurisdiction Project, 60
American Historical Association, 329
American Studies Association, 1, 329
*America's Talking*, 179
Anderson, C., 45*n*33
Anonymity, online, 60, 144, 145, 150, 281, 344
Anti-virus software, 149
Applets (mini-applications), 148–51
Architecture of excess, 129
"Architectures of identification," 150
Ard, S., 351
Armey, Dick, 346
Aurigi, A., 116, 117

Bagdikian, B. H., 17, 28
Baier, A., 141, 153, 154
Balsamo, A., 5, 193, 194, 198
Banks, I., 45*n*31
Barber, B., 113
Barbie, Klaus, 69
Barcelona Activa, 372
BarcelonaNetActiva, 372–73
Barlow, J. P., 12, 15, 28, 79*n*42, 118
Barnes and Noble.com, 349
Barton, Mark, 18, 21, 22
Bascelli, D., 193
Baym, N., 341
Bburg-L, 327, 328, 331, 335, 338, 340, 342, 344, 346, 347, 350
Beamish, A., 241, 249, 350
Becker L., 141, 159
Beijing Conference, 196
*Being Digital* (Negroponte), 127
Bell Atlantic, 348
Benedikt, M., 246, 247, 255
Bergson, 123
Berk, R., 257

Berman, P. S., 3, 68
Biggens, Veronica, 197
Biklen, S. K., 242
Biometric identification, 151
Birkerts, S., 12, 15, 24, 28
Blacksburg Electronic Village (BEV), 328, 331, 335, 338–40, 343, 347–51, 356, 361, 363, 369; cybercommunion in, 341–43; health care application, 364, 366; local businesses, targeting of,349; maintaining the peace in, 344–47; online coupons, 364; as online public sphere, 338–41, 356–57; organizational involvement in, 363–69; as portal for consumption, 347–51; *see also* Bburg-L, Community networks
Blacksburg, Virginia, 355, 361, 367, 368; *see also* Blacksburg Electronic Village (BEV)
Blau, H., 322*n*10
Bloom, A., 274
*Blueprint for a Twenty-first Century Community*, 377
"Blueprint 2000; Communities for the 21st Century," 378
Boal, A., 287, 307, 310–12, 320*n*4
Boaz, D., 32, 34
Boddy, W., 176
Bogdan, R. C., 242
Boulder Community Network, 330
Bourdieu, P., 121
Braun, Neil, 175
Brecht, B., 311
Breslow, H., 13, 42*n*9, 275, 276, 280, 281
Bristol, England, 116
Broadcast television networks, 17, 18, 176
Brooke, C. G., 5
Brown, D. S., 97
Brown, J. S., 257
Brunvand, Jan Harold, 221
Bulletin Board Systems (BBS), 360
Burbules, N. C., 257

Calacanis, J., 175, 189*n*1
*Calder v. Jones*, 58
Caldwell, J., 189*n*4
Canada, 365
Capitalism, global, 67
Carey, J. W., 28, 126, 127, 195, 329, 333, 343
Carlson, M., 304
Carswell, L., 268
Castells, M., 246, 247, 257
Cato Institute, 32
Caughey, J., 329
CB Ellis, 379
CBS, 18
Certification Authorities, 151
Chandrasekaran, R., 328
Chaos theory, 124–25, 369; phase diagrams, 124; singularities, 124, 125;
Chartier, R., 271, 277, 278
*Chicago Tribune*, 374
Cialdini, 156
Cicognani, A., 4, 84, 95
*City of Bits* (Mitchell), 127
City of San Francisco Department of Public Works, 379
CitySearch, 351
Civille, R., 37
Civil society, 275, 276, 280, 281
Clinton/Lewinsky scandal, 18
*Closing of the American Mind, The* (Bloom), 274
CNN, 3, 29, 179, 181, 185
Cochran-Smith, M., 242
Cohen, S., 15, 16
Coleman, Elizabeth, 197
Columbine High School, 18 , 42*n*14, 119
CommerceNet, 379
Commercialism, 220
Communications Decency Act (CDA), 16, 17, 40*n*3
Communication technologies, 112, 113; and speed, 122
Communitarians, 12, 118, 120; *see also* Libertarians
Community, 113, 318–20*n*3, 354–55; capital, 378; coalitions, 375, 376, 379; educational, 267; of excess, 129; fluid,

117; health care, 375–76; idea of, 239, 240, 260; jurisdictional idea of, 53; life, 261; loss of, 112; moral, 114; normative, 115; organizations, types of, 361; perceptions of outsiders, 64–65; perceptions of topological and social space, 63–67; proximate, 115–16; web sites, 116, 374–75; wired, 365; *see also* Online communities; Virtual communities
Community access centers (CACs), 244
Community based software, *see* Software environments
Community computing movement, 241; *see also* Going to Class, Getting Online, and Giving Back to Community project
Community networks, 330, 331, 350, 356, 360, 379; one-stop shopping access, 330, 360; online coupons, 339, 357, 364; online movie listings, 339, 357; organizational involvement in, 361; organizational structure, influence of, 363–69; users of, 361–62; visions for, 36–61 356, 358–61, 364; 373–76; *see also* Blacksburg Electronic Village; Virtual cities; Virtual communities
Computers: access, 204, 240, 241, 244, 277; architecture, 90; games, 19, 20, 24, 25; literacy, 362, 366 ; obsolescence, 35, 36; prices, 34–36; security, 147–51, 152, 157, 158, 160, 161, 164*n*3; as teaching aids, 371; trailing edge technology, 34, 35
Condorcet, A., 270–74, 278
Constructionist learning theory, 289, 315, 316
Consumerism in higher education, logic of, 278, 279
Consumer protection laws, 70
Control society, 122, 128
"Cookies," 157
Cordingly, K., 319*n*3
Council on Women (Institute for Global Communication), 197
Cruz, N. I., 252, 257
Cryptography, 162; techniques, 149, 151
CULTSTUD-L, 30, 31
*Cultural Literacy* (Hirsch), 274
Cultural studies, 30, 188, 199
Cultural theory: feminist, 193, 206; of communication, 195; Gramscian, 200
Cybercommunion, 341
Cyberculture, 1, 15, 19, 329, 331; scholars of, 332, 333, 338, 343
Cyber-democracy, 31
Cyber-refuseniks, 28
Cyberspace, 136; commercialization of, 12, 178; geographical anonymity of, 60; public fears of, 14–28; territorialization of, 122, 123, 128, 129
Cyber-phobia and cyber-mania, 14
Cyberporn, 27
Cyber-utopians, versus cyber-skeptics, 12, 13, 28, 29, 38

Daft, R. L., 361
Danet, B., 338
Daniel, Sir John, 269
Day traders, 21, 22
De Landa, M., 124
Deleuze, G., 14, 121–23, 128–30
Democracy: and control, 30; electronic, 356; on the Internet, 28, 29, 31, 44*n*21; online voting, 343; and participation, 28, 32, 113; and radio, 185; and the university, 276–77; *see also* Online democracy
Democratic global village, 12
Democratic Republic of Congo, 33
Derber, C., 120
Derrida, J., 272
Dewey, John, 275
de Zengotita, T., 22–26
Diana, Princess, 180
Digital capitalism, 177, 188
Digital cities, 374
Digital community activism, 348
Digital Community Network, 379
"Digital Diploma mills" (Noble), 279
"Digital divide," 240, 244

Digital ownership, 100
Digital political activism, 192, 195
Digital public sphere, 329
Digital signatures, 151
Digital sublime, 127, 128
Displacement and ambiguity, 97, 100
Distance education, 265–69, 276–82, 283*n*1; access to, 277; advocates of, 269, 277, 279; anonymity of students in, 281; democratic ideal, and 282; fiscal implication of, 268; logic of consumerism in, 279, 280; networked classrooms, 281; opponents of, 268, 269; *see also* Virtual University
Distance learning, see Distance education
Doheny-Farina, S., 118
Doom and Myst, 25
Dougherty, Brian 187
DuBois, W. E. B., 306
Dungeons and Dragons (D&D), 19, 20, 316
Durkheim, E., 112

eBay, 59, 183
E*TRADE, 183
Eco Theater, 307–08
E-commerce, 90, 135, 150, 152, 153; and consumer trust, 159; Internet sales, 70, 80*n*48; and security
Education, *see* Distance education
Eichmann, Adolf, 71
Electric sublime, 127
Electronic Frontier Foundation, 118
Emotions, 120
English libel law, 52
Ethnography, multi-sited, 331
European Union, 61, 80*n*48, 358, 370
Excite, 334
ExploreNet, 286–89, 291–300, 302–5, 307, 309, 312–17; access to, 315; agency of participants, 291, 292; asynchronous narrative development, 297–300; asynchronous theater production, 304–5; dramatic model, 302–4; interactive drama, 296; interactivity and narrativity, balance of, 295, 296; interactivity levels of, 292, 304; interface, 313–14; narrative authority, 294, 296, 297; narrative structure, 293, 296, 315; narrative structure, emergent, 300–2; participation levels of 287, 293; worlds of, 293–94

*Family PC*, 175
FAQ file, 334
Faragher, T., 328, 348
Farmer, F. R., 298
FBI Web site, 229–31
Feenberg, A., 268
Feinstein, Dianne, 346
Felton, E., 163
Feminist Majority, 197
Feuer, J., 181, 182, 184
FIDNet (Federal Intrusion Detection Network), 168*n*52
Finland, 370
Firewalls, 148, 149
First Amendment protection, 16
Fischer, C. S., 368
Flame wars, 43*n*19, 327, 335, 338, 341, 342, 344, 346, 347; *see also* Kill files
Flynn, Mary Kathleen, 180
Foucault, M., 122
Fox news, 179, 181
Franco, R., 240
Freedom of speech, 118, 119, 162
Freire, P., 320*n*4
French, W., 308
Friedman, B., 163
Friedman, T. L., 27, 42*n*15
Fukuyama, F., 153

Gabler, N., 221, 223
Garner, James, 219, 223
Gates, B., 176, 351, 360, 361
Gehry, Frank, 86
Geist, M., 59, 60
Geller, M., 5
General Agreement on Trade and Tariffs (GATT), 61

GeoCities, 349
Geographic Information System (GIS), 371, 375
Georgia Institute of Technology, 193
Georgia Tech Telephoto Division, 194
Getzendanner, Joel, 365
Gibson, John, 180
Giles, D. E., Jr., 252, 257
Gingold, C., 298, 299
Giroux, H. A., 242
Gladieux, L. E., 269
Global village, 127, 188
"Go" network, 17
Going to Class, Getting Online, and Giving Back to Community project, 240–42, 245, 248, 261; *see also* Community computing movement; Kuhio Park Terrace and Kuhio Homes (KPT)
Gore, Al, 343
Goth subculture, 19, 20, 22, 23
Graham, S., 116, 117
Grossberg, L., 119, 121, 130
Grosz, E., 123, 124, 130
Guattari, F., 14, 121, 123, 129, 130
Gumpert, G., 224, 233

Habermas, J., 272, 274
Habitat, 298, 300, 303, 306
Hall, S., 16
*Hamlet on the Holodeck* (Murray), 295
Hampton, K. N., 365
Ham television operators, 186
Hanson, J., 89
Happenings, 287, 305–06, 317*n*1
Harasim, L. M., 332, 341
Hardin, R., 153, 154
*Harper's*, 22, 26
Harris, Eric, 18, 22, 23, 25, 26, 42*n*14
Harrison, T. M., 330
Hatch, J. V., 306
Hayles, N. K., 280
Health Forum, 376
Helsinki Department of Education, 370–71
Hesser, G., 252
Hewlett Packard, 359
Hierarchy; network architecture, 29, 31, 32; software developers and users, 292
Hillier, B., 89
Hine, C., 331
Hirsch Jr., E. D., 274
Hock, Dee, 379
Hocks, M. E., 5, 193, 194, 209, 210
Home Education Network, The (THEN), 279
Honnet, E. P., 259
Hope Is Vital, 309, 310
Hughes, C. E., 286, 288–90, 293, 296, 303, 304, 313, 315, 316
Humphrey, N., 68
Hurston, Zora Neale, 289
HyperCard, 292
Hypertext, 314

*Idea of a University, The* (Newman), 275
Infopime, 371, 372
*Information Age* (Castells), 246, 247
Information, haves & have-nots gap, 32–34, 37, 243, 248, 315
Information Society, 358–59, 360, 370, 371
Information Superhighway, 128
*Inset Systems, Inc. v. Instruction Set, Inc.*, 57, 58, 70
Integrated Network Fire Operations Project (INFO), 375
Intelligent Business Registries, 379
International Playback Theater Network, 308
International Radio and Television Society Industry Conference, 175, 186
*International Shoe Co. v. Washington*, 54, 56, 67, 74
Internet (Net): access to the, 28–29, 31–32, 36–37, 57, 186, 249, 258, 277, 315, 330–31, 337, 355, 356; Barcelona's residents use of the, 371–72; and civil society, 281;commercial nature of the, 177–78, 185; community networks, 330; control of

Internet (Net) *(continued)*
the, 27–28, 43*n*16, 61; educational value of the, 256; emotions and affect, structure of, 120, 122; feminist resources on the, 194; multiple media, 13; "Netville" residents use of the, 366–68; and online communities, 334, 349; political positions on the, 118; popularity of the, 14–15; proponents of the, 140; public discourse about the, 12–14; public sphere model of the, 333; public's fear of the, 14–16, 26–27; sales, 70, 80*n*48; and television, 175–78, 185–86; and traditional media, 17–18; urban myths and the, 221; and violence, 18–22; vulnerability of the, 135, 148–49, 151; *see also* Cyberspace; Internet jurisdiction; Online environments; World Wide Web

Internet jurisdiction: and community membership, 72; and cyberspace, 60; decentralist approach to, 61; emerging case law of, 56–61; and idea of the "Self," 74; internationalist view of, 61; internet sales, 70, 80*n*48; online interaction, 72–73; and the social construction of space, 63–64; traditional position on, 62

Internet Service Providers (ISPs), 34, 44*n*26

ISDN technology, 375

Izenour, S., 97

Jameson, F., 119

Java, 150, 316

Jefferson, Thomas, 277

Jenkins, H., 25, 26

Jensen, E., 180

Jones, M. A., 6

Joyce Foundation, 364

Jurisdiction: "additional conduct" test of 56; and animal trials, 68–69; background law of, 51–56; as community dominion, 68–70; as community membership, 70–72; "consent" theory of, 54; defined, 49; "effects" test of, 58, 59; "minimum contacts" test of, 54, 56, 77*n*15; over war criminals, 69, 71; personal test of, 52, 56, 57, 58, 59, 76*n*7; psychic burden of litigating in a different, 65–67; social meaning of, 62–63; "stream of commerce" test of, 55, 56; subject matter test of 52; targeting analysis of, 59–60; U.S. Supreme Court on, 50; *Zippo* test of, 59; *see also* Internet jurisdiction

Kahin, B., 37

Kang, J., 58

Kansas State University, 40*n*1

Kant, I., 269, 272, 273, 276

Kaprow, A., 305, 306

Keller, J., 37

Kelly, K., 118

Kennedy, John F., 183, 184

*Keywords* (Williams), 114

Khare, R., 148

Kilby, M., 289, 293, 304, 316

Kill files (or Bozo filter), 334, 344–46, 350; *see also* Flame wars

Klebold, Dylan, 18, 22, 23, 25, 26, 42*n*14

Knapp, John, Jr., 348

Kogan, T. S., 64, 66, 80*n*44

Kolb, 241

Kolko, B., 40, 341

Kollock, P., 333, 334

Komito, L., 114, 115, 117, 128, 129

Kramer, R., 156

Krigwas Players, 306

Krueger, M. W., 317*n*1

Kuhio Park Terrace and Kuhio Homes (KPT), 239–40, 244–45, 247, 249–55, 258–62, 262*n*1; *see also* Going to Class, Getting Online, and Giving Back to Community project; Parents and Children Together (PACT)

Kurland, P. B., 54

Lacan, J., 220

Landler, M., 180

Landow, G. P., 267, 268, 275
*Late Show with David Letterman* (television program), 223
"Latest Internet Buzzword: Community" (Napoli), 334
Laurel, B., 194, 317*n*1
Lebkowsky, J., 291
Lee, Maryat, 307
Legard, D., 58
Lessig, L., 150
Lewinsky, Monica, 345
Libertarians, 23, 118, 189*n*2; *see also* Communitarians
Lindahl, Charlie, 237*n*15
Lingus, A., 129
Lisman, C. D., 259, 260
Listservs, list owners control of, 30, 31
Living Stage Theater Company, 308, 309, 310
*Logomachia* (Derrida), 272
Luhmann, ,N., 138, 155, 162
Lytle, S., 242

McChesney, R., 17, 28
McClellan, F., 115
McDowell, L., 319*n*3
*MacLean's*, 278
McLuhan, M., 118, 127
McPherson, T., 4, 17
Maidenform Corporation, 197
Malware (malicious software), e-mail propagation of, 148, 149
Manson, M., 22
Marcus, G. E., 331
Markham, A., 42*n*15
Marvin, C., 26
Marx, L., 126
Mass media, 119
Massumi, B., 119–21, 124, 130
*Matrix, The* (film), 23–25
Mechanical sublime, 126, 127
Media monopoly, 17, 28
Mellon Foundation, 193
Melissa virus, 149, 152, 161
Meyrowitz, J., 105
Microsoft, 11, 201, 343; betatest program, 222; merger with NBC, 176, 179, 181, 185
Microsoft Chat 2.1, 303, 313
Microsoft Internet Explorer, 186
Microsoft Sidewalk.com, 351
Microsoft V-Chat, 303
Microsoft Windows, 289, 370
Microsoft Windows 95, 41*n*6
Millard, W. B., 338
Mitchell, W. J., 100, 127, 271, 275, 277, 350
Modern Languages Association, 329
Monaco, 33
Mongela, Gertrude, 194
Montaigne, M. de, 215
MOO (MUDs Object Oriented), 39, 113, 116, 281, 296, 298, 300, 303, 306, 314
Moral panic, 15, 16, 19, 20, 25, 42*n*10
Morningstar, C., 298
Morris Worm, 148
Mortal Kombat, 19
Moshell, J. M., 286, 288–90, 293, 296, 303, 304, 313, 315, 316
MSNBC (Web site), 17, 176, 177, 179–84, 187; illusion of liveness, 181–82, 186; "Kennedy Remembered" page, 183; "live votes" feature, 182, 187; News alert feature, 181; news anchor function, 184; Surround-Video feature of, 183, 184; volitional mobility, 183, 185, 188
MSNBC-TV, 179, 180
MUDD (Multi-User Domain or Dungeon), 39, 113, 116, 188, 298, 318*n*2
Multimedia, 204, 314
Multinational corporations, 72
Multiuser environments, 288, 298, 304–07, 313, 314, 317–18*n*2
Murray, J. H., 295–97

Napoli, L., 334
NASA, 27
NASDAQ, 14, 187
Nast, Condé, 119

Nathan, P. X., 291
National Communications Association, 329
*National Forum*, 281
National Information Superstructure (Information Superhighway), 128
NationsBank, 197
Nation Telecommunications and Information Administration (NTIA), 244, 247
*Natural Born Killers* (film), 23, 24
NBC, 17, 176, 179–81
Neal, E., 281
Negroponte, N., 32, 41*n*7, 113, 118, 127, 221
Neoliberalism, 177
Neoliberalist project, 189*n*2
Neo-Luddites, 12, 192
Netscape, 11, 41*n*5, 186
Netville, 365, 366–67, 368, 369
Network architecture, 29
Network control, 29
Networked information systems, 135
Networlds (online communities), 332
Newby, H., 115
*New Community Networks* (Schuler), 330
Newman, J. H., 275
*Newschat* (MSNBC-TV program), 180
*Newsweek* (magazine), 330
*New York Times*, 27, 29, 181, 330, 334
Next Generation Cities, 379
Nissenbaum, H., 4
Nixon, Richard, 217, 218
Noble, D. F., 279, 282
Nongovernmental Organization Forum, 193, 194–96, 198, 207–10
Norman, D. A., 368
Nua Internet Surveys, 32
Nye, D., 125

Oklahoma City Bombing, 22
Online banking, 89, 93–94
Online communities, 31, 67, 83, 106, 107, 112, 114, 129, 328, 332–34
Online democracy, 28, 29, 31, 32; and Lambda/MOO, 44*n*21; voting, 343; *see also* democracy
Online environments, 83, 84, 85, 88, 97; accessibility of, 100, 107; author and participants in, 295, 296; design of, 91; design, architects role in, 90; design, control over, 99, 100; design, replacement process in, 97 ; design, speed as aspect of, 99, 182; digital ownership of, 100; displacement and ambiguity in, 97, 100; mapping in, 104, 105; metaphorical coherence of, 96, 97, 106; physical space, 87–89, 95–100; protocols of, 96, 103, 104; sustainability of, 98, 106
Online forums, 30
Online gambling, 97
Online learning, 100–2; access and flexibility of, 101–3; format of information in, 102, 103; time and, 101, 102
Online pornography, 16
Open University (England), 269
Outcomes Toolkit (software), 376
OXFAM International, 193
Oxygen network, 178

Panel on Smart Communities in Canada, 359
Parents and Children Together (PACT), 243, 244, 249, 258–60
Pascale, R. T., 369
Pauley, Jane, 180
*PC Magazine*, 34
Pelline, J., 351
Pennoyer v. Neff, 53, 54, 56, 64, 65, 67, 73
Perot, Ross, 343
Pettit, P., 139, 142, 156
*Philadelphia Inquirer*, 328
Phish (rock band), 333
Pillar, C., 187
Pinochet, Augusto, 76*n*6
Pioneer Press, 374
Platt, L., 359
Pollitt, K., 20

Pope, K., 180
Posner, R., 154, 162
Post, D., 60
Postmodern society, 112
Poulsen, S. J., 259
Pred, A., 63
Presley, Elvis, 225
Principle of Indifference (of reality), 247, 255
Printing press, 270, 271, 276
Prodigy, 186
*Public Access to the Internet* (Kahin and Keller), 37
Public interest, 269, 272
Public sphere, 18, 29, 32; digital, 329; elements of, 338–39; online model of, 332; and the university, 267, 273, 274, 276, 278, 282
Purple Moon, 194, 211*n*2
Putnam, R. D., 139, 356

Quirk, J., 126, 127

Rand, Tamara, 224
Rather, Dan, 345
Readings, B., 269, 272, 273, 278
Reagan, Ronald, 121
Reality, 247 *see also* Principle of indifference
Regan, A., 5
Realism, theatrical, 303–4
Reingold, H., 13, 41*n*8, 114, 120, 127, 332, 333, 341
*Reno v. ACLU*, 16, 17, 40–41*n*3
Rifkin, A., 148
Robertson, Patsy, 194
*Rockford Files, The* (television program), 219, 220, 223; Rockford's answering machine, 219, 220
Rodman, G. B., 3
Rohd, M., 309, 310
*Rolling Stone* (magazine), 330
Rosenthal, J., 314
Ross, A., 128
R.U.OUT.THERE, 216, 228–32
Rushdie, Salman, 70, 71
Ryan, M., 295–97, 320*n*5

*St. Petersburg Times*, 21
Sandberg, J., 180
*San Jose Mercury News*, 330
Santiago, Irene, 194
Schiller, D., 177, 178
Schiller, H. I., 28
Schneier, B., 148
Schor, J. B., 34
Schuler, D., 330, 350, 356
Schwartz, J., 32
Sclove, R., 112, 113
Seattle Community Network, 330, 350
Security, *see* Computer security
Seiter, E., 178
Seligman, A., 141, 142, 153
Shalala, Donna, 197
Shapiro, A. L., 113, 114, 117
*Silicon Alley Reporter*, 175
Silver, D., 6, 349
Simpson, O. J., civil trial, 179
*Site, The* (MSNBC-TV program), 180, 185
*60 Minutes* (CBS program), 18
"Slice of Life in my Virtual Community" (Reingold), 332
Slotkin, R., 126
Slovik, P., 159
SmallTalk (programming language), 288
Smart Community, 359, 377
Smart Permits, 377, 380
Smart Valley, 377
Smith, Benjamin, 18–20, 22, 23
Smith, Beverly, 19
Smith, David, 152
Smith, M. R., 126, 333, 334
Social capital, 139, 158
Social cohesion, 112, 113
Software environments, 287, 288
SOMA (South of Market Association Foundation), 379, 380
"Spect-actor," 287
Spelman College, 193
Spolin, Viola, 309
Stahl, Lesley, 18

Stallard, S. F., 277
Stam, R., 183
Stanton, T. K., 252, 257
Starkweather, Charlie, 23
Steere, E. R., 341
Stephen, T., 330
Stokes, Lori, 180
Stoll, C., 36, 41*n*7, 45*n*31
Stone, A. R., 43*n*20, 291
Stonor, T., 89
Streeter, T., 176, 185, 189*n*2
Street Fighter, 19
*Structural Transformation of the Public Sphere, The* (Habermas), 272
SurroundVideo, 183, 184
Surveillance, 122, 127, 151, 152, 155, 156, 204; *see also* Web tracking
SysAdmin (systems administrators), 29, 31, 88, 100

Tamblin, C., 194
Technology: access to, 209, 210; articulation and rearticulation, 200, 203; as controlling, 127; critical philosophy of, 199; determinism, 192, 200; digital sublime, 127, 128; feminist theory of, 199, 201; gender, impact on, 196; infrastructure, 246; ISDN, 375; literacy, 242, 261; progress, idea of, 126; technological sublime, 125, 126; theory of, 198
Tedeschi, B., 351
Telecommunications Act of 1996, 16, 17
Telephone, effects on social patterns, 368
Teletext system, 362
Teletruth, 217, 218, 229
Television, 185, 186, 217; news, 183, 184; and the Internet, 17, 18, 175–78, 182, 187, 188, 189*n*5
Ten Commandments, 22
Tennessee Valley Authority, 127
TexChrisT, 226
Theater: activist, 306–7; community-based, 306–10; participatory, 287, 288; production, asynchronous, 304–5; *see also* ExploreNet
*Theater for Community, Conflict and Dialogue: The Hope is Vital Training Manual* (Rohd), 309
Theatre of the Oppressed, 287, 307, 309, 310–12
Third World Conference on Women, 196
Thompson, K., 115
*Time* (magazine), 330
*Time and Again* (MSNBC-TV program), 180
Tönnies, F., 112
Trust, 36, 153; conditions of, 140–44; confidence and, 137; functions of, 137–40; and identity, 144–45, 150–51; "insurance," 144; motive based, 159; mutuality and reciprocity, 143; online, 134, 135; and roles, 143, 146; and setting, 143; as social capital, 139, 158; and surveillance, 151, 152, 155, 156; value for individuals, 138; and vulnerability, 154–55, 157; *see also* Computers, security
Trusted Public Databank, 379
Trust management systems, 151
Truth, concept of, 215, 216; teletruth, 217, 218, 229
Truth and Reconciliation Commission, 71
Turoff, M., 283*n*3
Tyler, T., 159
Tyner, K., 246

UCLA, 279
United Nations Conference on Environment and Development (Earth Summit), 194
United Nations Conference on Population and Development, 194
United Nations Fourth World Congress on Women, 192, 193
United States Congress, 16, 26
United States Department of Justice, 40–41*n*3
United States House of Representatives, 22

United States Internet Acceptable Use Policy (AUP), 336
United States Supreme Court, 16, 17, 50, 53, 54, 55–57
Universal Studios, 29
University: access to, 271, 272, 277; common language in, 271, 278; consumerism in, 278, 279; Kantian, 269, 273; as model of civil society, 276, 280; and the public sphere, 276, 282; spatiality of, 275; virtual, 265–67, 280, 282; *see also* Distance education
*University in Ruins, The* (Readings), 278
University of California at Berkeley, 279
University of Central Florida, 286, 288, 316
University of Colorado System and Real Education, Inc., 279
University of Hawaii system , 240, 243
University of Illinois, 20
Urban myths, 221–25
*USA Today*, 175
Usenet, 13, 334
*U.S. News and World Report* (magazine), 278

Venturi, R., 97
Video games, *see* Computer games
Violence, 18–26
Virginia Tech, 327, 331, 336, 339–41, 349, 370
Virtual: defined, 123; versus online, 83, 84
Virtual Academy, 289–91
*Virtual Academy, The* (Hughes and Moshell), 290
Virtual cities, 116
Virtual classroom, 91–93
Virtual communities, 116–18, 128, 241, 246, 248, 249, 258, 259, 262, 289, 319*n*3, 330–32, 335, 341; of excess, 129
*Virtual Community, The* (Rheingold), 115, 127, 333
Virtual public, 130, 178, 195
*Virtual Publics* (Kolko), 124
Virtual reality, 23, 24, 280, 296
Virtual selves, 150
Virtual space, 241, 247, 255
Virtual university, 265–67, 280, 282, *see also* Distance Education
Virtual worlds, 314
VISA, 378–79
Visions for community networks, political, 358–59; civic involvement, 364; community-wide, 373–76; consumer, 360–61; economic, 359–60; *see also* Community networks
Vitra Design Museum, 86
VRML, 107, 229

Waldrop, M. M., 379
*Wall Street Journal*, 181
Walpole, Horace, 25
Warshauer, S. C., 6
*Washington Post*, 32, 328, 330
Watson, N., 333, 341, 343
Web sites: "active" versus "passive," 57, 58, 78*n*28; commercial, 114; community, 116, 374–75; corporate architectures of, 178; evil," 148; hierarchy, 85, 87; interactive, 202; liveness, 183, 186; Seaworld, 180; and urban myths, 221–23; volition and mobility, 182, 183, 187; *see also* Online environments
Web tracking, 157, 159, 160
WELL (Whole Earth 'Lectronic Link), 13, 41*n*8, 115, 128
West Virginia University, 313, 316
Wiebe, R., 65
Williams, Brian, 181
Williams, M., 189*n*5
Williams, R., 28, 114, 179
Wink Communications, 187
*Wired* (magazine), 33, 118, 119, 128, 175, 181
Wired communities, 365; *see also* Netville
Wired School, 118
Wired World Atlas, 33

Wise, J. M., 4
Women in Development, 193
Women of the World Talk Back project, 192–95, 198, 210; design of, 204–09; "Video dialogues," 206, 212*n*6
World Intellectual Property Organization, 61, 79*n*38
World Trade Organization, 61
*World-Wide Volkswagen Corporation v. Woodson*, 55, 56
World Wide Web, 11, 98, 113, 128, 136, 177, 179, 194, 201, 244, 360; *see also* Web sites
Worthen, W. B., 303
Wresch, W., 33
Wulf, W. A., 279, 280

*X-Files* (television program), 225, 227

Yahoo!, 70, 334

Zettl, H., 219
Zippergate, 182
*Zippo Manufacturing Co. v. Zippo Dot Com, Inc.*, 57–59
Zuern, J., 5